THE DISPOSSESSED

THE
DISPOSSESSED

America's Underclasses
from the
Civil War to the Present

JACQUELINE JONES

BasicBooks
A Division of HarperCollins*Publishers*

Library of Congress Cataloging-in-Publication Data

Jones, Jacqueline, 1948–
   The dispossessed : America's underclass from the Civil War to
the Present / Jacqueline Jones.
      p.   cm.
   Includes biographical references and index.
   ISBN 0–465–00127–0
   1. Afro-Americans—Economic conditions. 2. Rural poor—
Southern States—History. 3. Southern States—Rural conditions.
I. Title
E185.8.J77   1992
305.5'69'0973—dc20   91–37289
                                                                               CIP

To Kitty

Contents

CONTENTS

Preface

This book represents the culmination of an intellectual odyssey that I began several years ago while writing a history of black working women in America. Certain parallels in the household organization and daily work routine of black and white sharecroppers seemed to contradict conventional wisdom that race constituted a great divide of sorts within Southern, and indeed all of American, history. From this initial observation I developed a larger concern for the history of poverty in America and, more particularly, for the places where poor people lived and worked. In significant respects, this study advances an argument made in my two previously published books—that in their commitment to formal education, to family, and to hard work, African-Americans have adhered to values shared by other Americans regardless of race, class, or regional identification. At the same time, by emphasizing patterns of resourcefulness common to blacks and whites of a similarly low material condition, this book departs from my earlier exclusive focus on black history and seeks to illuminate the historic forces of marginalization that engulfed the poor of both races.

I started and finished this book while teaching at Wellesley College, and I am grateful to the college for a sabbatical leave that allowed me to devote full time to research. I received excellent assistance from the staff of Clapp Library, particularly the reference librarians, Sally Linden, Claire Loranz, and Joan Stockard; the interlibrary loan librarian, Karen Jensen; and the circulation desk staff, especially Jeannette Augustin, Rosemary Janson, Susan Hand, and Peggy Cronin. In classic Wellesley fashion, the administrative staff of the history department, Helen Atkins and Thelma Pellagrini, ministered unto me from day to day. Nina Tumarkin and Paul Cohen proved loyal friends, though I went without seeing either one of them for months at a time. During my sabbatical year (1986–87) I benefited from a research associateship at the W. E. B. DuBois Institute for Afro-American Research at Harvard University, where the late Nathan I. Huggins offered helpful suggestions and crucial support during the earliest stages of the project. Through the generosity of the Henry Luce Foundation, I served as Clare Boothe Luce Visiting Professor at Brown University from 1988 to 1990; a reduced teaching load enabled me to make considerable research progress and at the same time enjoy the chance to share ideas over lunch with Naomi Lamoreaux, Howard Chudacoff, Mari Jo Buhle, Jim Patterson, Gordon Wood, and Tony Molho. The good graces of Karen Mota, Karla Cinquanta, Cherrie Guerzon, and Charlene Blake made my time there particularly pleasant. In 1990 a research grant from the Social Science Research Council provided me with the resources to adapt some of the material here for an essay in a volume on the historical origins of the Northern underclass. In the process I benefited from the valuable insights and editorial advice offered by Michael Katz, the editor of the volume, and by other members of the research group. I also appreciated the opportunity to give several formal presentations related to this material to various groups of undergraduates, graduate students, and faculty members at Brandeis University. My new colleagues, especially David Hackett Fischer, Mickey Keller, and Jim Kloppenberg, were especially encouraging about the project.

In various ways people close to me reminded me that stories of individual hardship and resourcefulness are not characteristics of a distinct subculture of poverty exclusively, but rather embedded in the histories of many ordinary middle-class households. My extended family provided a great deal of information, some of it firsthand and quite unexpected, about the themes explored in the book. My parents, Sylvia and Albert Jones, kept me informed, through newspaper clippings and specialized publications, about the persistently grim plight of agricultural migrant laborers all along the eastern seaboard. I benefited from the scholarship of my economist brother, Kent Jones, on the subject of displaced Midwestern steel workers. My husband's parents, Rose and Albert Abramson, sent me news stories from the Philadelphia area and offered their recollections of the Eastern European immigrant women and children who, in the early years of the twentieth century, abandoned Philadelphia for the summer in order to work on New Jersey truck farms. Len and Helen Price, parents of my sister-in-law, Tonya Price, graciously consented to be interviewed on the subject of Appalachian migration to southern Ohio. It also gives me great pleasure to acknowledge the help of two gentlemen who early took an interest in this project and offered their personal accounts of life in the rural South around the time of World War I. Daniel D. Ewing, Jr., my next-door neighbor, spoke to me freely about labor relations on a large plantation in Mounds, Louisiana, where his father worked as a gun-toting accountant. Dr. Thomas B. Davis of Bridgeport, Connecticut, wrote the equivalent of his own book-length manuscript in response to my questions about his experiences as a cotton field hand, and a keen observer of black-white interaction, in the vicinity of Wichita Falls, Texas.

In addition to acknowledging the efficient work of the staffs of the National Archives Reading Room and Still Picture Branch (especially the timely help of Holly Reed) and the Reading Room of the Manuscript Division of the Library of Congress, I would also like to single out the assistance I received from Debra Newman-Ham, specialist in Afro-American History and Culture, Manuscript Division of the Library of Congress; Joan Morris, curator of the Photographic Collection of the Florida State Archives; and the photographers Joseph Sorrentino, Alan Dorow, and Kit Luce.

Tom Sugrue passed along valuable citations and reference material on Appalachian whites in Detroit and offered suggestions on the chapters dealing with Southern migration to the North. I appreciated his willingness to tolerate these distractions while he was busy finishing his dissertation. Two of my students, Colette Blount, an undergraduate at Wellesley, and Melani McAlister, a graduate student at Brown, kindly permitted me to quote from their interviews with sharecropping female kin. Lyde Cullen Sizer and Ruth Feldstein helped to compile and check data, and Gary Murphy of Basic Books expedited the use of several photographs.

Several scholars indulged my impatient requests to see their as-yet-unpublished works; Crandall Shifflett, William Cohen, Kathryn Edin, and Rhoda Halperin sent all or portions of their studies in manuscript or galley form. On the aspirations of African-Americans as citizens, family members, and workers, I learned much from the published work and public presentations of Ira Berlin and from the work of the other editors of the Freedmen and Southern Society Project at the University of Maryland.

The historians who consented to read the manuscript at various stages, and especially those unwieldy working papers I foolishly called chapters, deserve special thanks. Jim Patterson, Harold Woodman, and Pete Daniel saw some material early on and helped me to clarify the arguments and tighten the organization. A longtime admirer of Gavin Wright's work, I was grateful to benefit from his comments on my own; he read a complete draft of the manuscript, and his suggestions proved particularly helpful during the last stages of revision.

Ellen Fitzpatrick belongs in a category—or at least a paragraph—all by herself. Friend, colleague, and counselor in times of panic, she has in abundance that rarest of qualities, good common sense. Just as she was contemplating a summer respite from her hectic teaching, research, and committee responsibilities at Harvard, she received an untimely request to read a long manuscript; this she cheerfully agreed to do, and provided me with careful and detailed criticisms, well over and above all collegial duty. I appreciate the myriad kinds of encouragement she has offered me over the years and express special gratitude for her suggestions dealing with this study.

My editor, Steve Fraser, long ago urged me to transform a rather narrow study of Southern labor mobility into a bolder and more sweeping interpretation of the history of American poverty. When mired in the minutiae of details, I could count on him to remind me of larger issues. More generally, he patiently read innumerable drafts of the manuscript, providing extensive comments—and providing, as well, reassurance that someday the chapters would indeed say what I wanted them to say, in a coherent way. Whatever this book contributes to our understanding of American social history is due in large measure to his skill and dedication as an editor and to his insights as a historian.

My friends and neighbors gave me a great deal of emotional support during the seven years I worked on this project. Sigrid Bergenstein, Karin Lifter, and Sally Merry shared with me their wisdom, their laughter, and their children, especially during those difficult, cranky hours of the late afternoon. And Ingrid Kondos has blessed our family with her love for our children, and all children, over a ten-year period; without her patience and dedication I would have written nothing at all.

In the midst of studying the painful choices made by people who could not afford to stay in one place for very long, I became more appreciative of my own family's blissfully sedentary existence. My husband, Jeffrey Abramson, is my sternest critic; and now, in hindsight, I can admit that he was right on every—or rather almost every—point. Our discussions on topics ranging from the Civil War to this morning's lead story in the newspaper enabled me to develop and refine my views on a wide variety of issues. He brought to those discussions a scholar's insistence that I get things right and a political theorist's clarity of thought. I am fortunate to share with him, among other things, my ideas about what is wrong and right with the world today. Throughout my work on this project, my daughters, Sarah and Anna, remained understandably ambivalent about it; if pressed, Sarah would no doubt say that she wished I could have been her Brownie troop leader instead of writing a book. I hope in a few years she will appreciate the decisions I made. During the last hectic months of writing and revising, both Sarah and Anna honored my request and managed, through sheer force of will, to avoid contracting the chicken pox, though provided with ample opportunity to do so. For this, and much more, I am grateful to them.

This book is dedicated to Kathryn T. Preyer, professor emerita of history at Wellesley College. For many years I have admired her devotion to her students; her knowledge of American history, profound in its depth and breadth; her generosity toward her colleagues; and, together with her husband, Bob, her active involvement in the struggle for civil rights, in the Boston area and around the country. My own scholarship has been enriched by her ideas and by her passion for the study of history. As a result of the inspiring example of her life's good work, I have come to believe that the story of our nation's past is an integral part of any effort to advance the cause of freedom and justice for all dispossessed peoples. This dedication is in modest repayment of the enormous intellectual and personal debt I owe her.

THE DISPOSSESSED

Introduction

Poverty abides no line drawn by color or culture. In late twentieth-century America jobless coal miners in Appalachia, displaced Midwestern factory workers, Haitian and Cambodian immigrant migrant laborers, and the chronically unemployed in Northern inner-city ghettos all bore the brunt of a transformed, postindustrial economy. Isolated in communities dying from the lack of good jobs, men and women belonging to a wide variety of social groups foraged, looked to neighborly cooperation, and sought out piecemeal wage work in an effort to keep their families together. And yet as these pockets of poverty grew and spread, from the agricultural migrants' "home base" of Belle Glade, Florida, to the faltering working-class neighborhoods of Waterloo, Iowa; from the *barrios* of El Paso to the public housing projects of Detroit, middle-class Americans in general and public policymakers in particular persisted in defining the nature of social distress in purely racial terms.

1

Aiding and abetting this misguided endeavor was the pervasive use of the term "underclass." News media sensationalized a violent black youth street culture and then imputed its self-destructive characteristics to all African-Americans; social scientists focused their attention on "concentrated" poverty, thus ignoring the majority of the poor, people who lived outside the black ghetto; and the two major political parties became mired in a debate over the nature of race, a debate that obscured the economic forces which were dragging readily identifiable groups of whites as well as blacks into an abyss of hopelessness and despair.

Poverty has a history. Out of the devastation of the Civil War emerged a class of landless Southern families that picked the cotton that fueled the South's economic recovery. The fathers and sons from these families, men of both races, worked elbow to elbow in the steaming phosphate pits and side by side in swampland lumber camps and turpentine stills throughout the rural South. From the late nineteenth century onward, forces of the global market economy intruded into the countryside, dispossessed large numbers of Southerners of their homes and the living they wrung from the soil, and pushed them into nearby towns and, after 1916, up north or out west. Deep South black migrants joined with Appalachian white migrants in an effort to establish a foothold in Northern industry; but the declining demand for unskilled labor relegated some of the whites, and most of the blacks, to the margins of modern society. In the 1960s and 1970s automation at home and competition from abroad rendered more and more manual workers entirely superfluous within a reordered world economy. At the same time an influx of refugees from Latin America and Southeast Asia provided cheap labor for the sweatshop owners of New York City and the truck-farm employers up and down the East Coast. This process of displacement and dispersal represented a variation of larger, worldwide migrations that had affected rural folk through the centuries. By the 1990s America's internal colonial economy had grown to the point that observers likened conditions in the South Bronx, and in the hills and hollows of Appalachia, to those in the Third World.

Throughout this period the federal government and national news organizations continued to manipulate the statistics that measured poverty and, in the process, created the false impression that all black people were poor and that all white people were middle class; the category "Hispanic" conflated data related to race, culture, and national origin, further confusing the issue. Dramatically, race came to permeate public discussion of a wide variety of issues,[1] for many whites assumed that African-Americans constituted a group apart from "mainstream" America. Some observers went so far as to charge that ghetto life in general represented a distinct subculture "with a different language, economy, educational system and social ethic" compared to "white" society.[2] This view suggested, wrongly, that the majority of black people in the ghetto did not share with whites of all classes the desire for safe streets and good schools and jobs. Ultimately, the ethnic, regional, and cultural diversity of the poor population became lost in an exclusive focus—more rhetorical than substantive—on black people in the urban North. Americans in a postemancipation society thus continued to view poverty through a lens ground and polished in the days of slavery.[3]

The historical processes that created impoverished groups represented political as much as economic forces. The growth of various "stranded communities" over the generations reflected decisions made by a variety of people—Southern cotton planters and Northern factory owners, city council members and senators and presidents. Even if we understand poverty as an inevitable concomitant of America's peculiar political economy, we need not ignore the role of the state in abandoning the poor to fend for themselves within a rapidly changing society. Historically, federal and state governments first advanced the interests of private employers who were driven by the need for profits and "efficiency," and then failed to reintegrate into the labor market men and women thrown out of work as a result of those interests. In the first three years after the Civil War, the federal government through the Freedmen's Bureau imposed an annual labor contract arrangement on a seasonal form of production (cotton cultivation) and thereby helped to create the exploitative sharecropping system. Throughout the South, from the postbellum period through the twentieth century, state governments parceled out tax breaks to rural nonagricultural industries such as coal mining and lumbering, industries that were notorious for hazardous working conditions and low wages. The social welfare legislation implemented during the 1930s pointedly excluded a number of already vulnerable groups from the benefits that more fortunate Americans would soon take for granted. Domestic servants, agricultural workers, and part-time employees of all kinds thus had little hope of accumulating the resources that would gain them access to such federally supported "entitlement" programs as Social Security, unemployment compensation, and the minimum wage. And finally, public programs to aid the poor reflected a view of household and gender relations that ultimately proved destructive to family life— specifically, the view that, as American citizens, neither men nor women

3

were deserving of decent jobs, and that support to poor families should go only to a (presumably unemployed) mother, thus opening the way for the moral stigmatizing of people already victimized by the state's policies toward private enterprise.[4]

By the 1990s poverty had become both the most visible and an invisible part of the American political agenda—visible because each day brought fresh new horror stories about drug dealing, random violence, urban blight, and homelessness; invisible because people of privilege gradually became inured to these stories, occupying as they did a permanent place in newspapers and on the nightly news. Among politicians, the values of good jobs and fair wages, affordable housing, and universal quality health care constituted a bored, tired lament, a mantra, backed by neither passion nor purpose. War and revolutionary upheaval abroad fired the American public imagination, while the plight of the poor in the Northern inner city, the rural South, and the nation's heartland inspired only cynicism and moral condemnation.[5]

Central to the issue of poverty over the years was the nature and meaning of productive labor as a moral virtue. Among Americans marginalized within a prosperous nation, the household economy had always demanded resourcefulness and hard work. A lack of steady employment meant that fathers and sons and mothers and daughters would have to make a living when and where they could find it. Nevertheless, employers and public officials who expected from workers time-oriented discipline argued that hunting, fishing, scavenging, and bartering did not constitute "work" at all; only wage earning under the watchful eye of a plantation overseer, white housewife, shop foreman, or fast-food restaurant supervisor qualified as morally redeemable behavior. Recently freed from slavery, black people near Mt. Pleasant, South Carolina, showed considerable ingenuity in providing for themselves at a time of year when there was no cotton to tend; in the words of a federal official, these "idle, vicious vagrants, whose sole idea consists in loafing without working" were subsisting on green corn, pond lily beans, and alligator meat, and also appropriating from the estates of their former masters what they believed to be their due in these desperate times: "Lead pipes taken from wells and cisterns, Harness from stables, cotton from the fields and even the iron from the cotton gins and engines."[6] Whatever their other shortcomings, Christ Church Parish blacks were hardly "idle." Clearly "scuffling" for food and cash could shade off into criminal activity; Appalachian farmers produced great pots of moonshine in the 1920s and worked as "wildcatters" mining coal illegally in the "mailbox economy" of the early

1990s, when "Everybody gets [welfare and pension] checks."[7] Much
more pervasive over the generations though than either poaching on the
postbellum plantation or dealing drugs on city sidewalks in South Side
Chicago were everyday forms of mutual assistance that bound together
networks of kin and neighbors. After the 1930s, when single mothers
qualified for meager amounts of public assistance, they took "under the
table" or "off the [welfare case worker's] books" the hard-earned money
they made from cooking, sewing, and babysitting for friends, and then
endured the opprobrium heaped upon them by public officials who saw
only helplessness and dependency.

Place is a major theme in the history of poverty. Over the generations
a large proportion of poor people have lived in places where they lacked
access to the employment opportunities and educational resources that
would enable them to improve their lot in life. Former slaves as well as
Appalachian farming folk held dear the notion of home place, defined
as their own piece of land in proximity to kin and friends; but thwarted
in their efforts to achieve stability, they remained restless in their quest
for a better way of life. White middle-class people boasted that their
own freedom of movement was proof of a distinctive "American dream"
of upward mobility, while they simultaneously condemned the
"wandering" poor for their apparent irresponsibility, their apparent
attempt to avoid productive labor. At the same time, all over the country
communities have relied on the residential stability of households; and
the poorest families, propertyless and with high rates of job and
residential turnover, often lacked the resources to maintain community
ties.[8] Local and regional labor markets produced patterns of mobility,
and patterns of stability, that spoke eloquently to the forces that
constricted the movements of the poor of both races and either
confined them to, or expelled them from, a particular place. Though the
poor might not always prosper in pursuit of better jobs, their migrations
were often purposeful and revealing of the arduous labor that claimed
their energies; in the 1980s a black sugarcane cutter in Florida, a native
of Mississippi, wondered aloud, "Would you call a man lazy that travels
this far from home to find work?"[9]

This study focuses on the poorest Americans of both races, and at the
same time stresses African-Americans' persistent vulnerability to racial
prejudice within the workplace and the body politic. Beginning in the
period immediately after the Civil War, the major economic transformations that affected black Southerners affected plain white folk in
similar ways. Moreover, the black and white people who shared so much
in terms of household organization and a lowly material condition

5

produced some of the most impressive, if for the most part short-lived, biracial organizations in American history. The Populist party of the 1890s, the Southern Tenant Farmers Union of the 1930s, and the Congress of Industrial Organizations (particularly in the 1930s) drew their support from the laboring classes of both races. In the 1980s the demise of labor unions, coupled with the increasing preoccupation of both Democrats and Republicans with a single black "underclass," signaled the decline of class-based activism and the revival of race-based politics. In the 1860s poor whites throughout the South feared that progress in the area of black civil rights would jeopardize their own life chances, just as some white voters in the 1990s interpreted Affirmative Action guidelines as a threat to their own well-being as breadwinners.[10]

From the time of slavery onward, white farmers and nonagricultural workers maintained historic advantages over black people, no matter how outwardly similar the situations of the two races. When whites benefited from the explicit preferences of their employers and labored as tenants instead of sharecroppers, as semiskilled instead of unskilled factory workers, and as "outside" instead of "inside" men in the coal mines, they retained modest but not insignificant advantages over the black people who toiled near them. From 1865 until the mid-1960s in the rural South, white men regardless of class held political sway over all blacks, men and women who refrained from voting for fear of violent reprisal. Moreover, as the residents of beleaguered communities, blacks in Northern ghettos remained isolated from good jobs, schools, medical care, and police and fire protection. The ability of white Appalachian migrants in the Midwest to move around within their host communities at will, to seize job and housing opportunities wherever they existed, contrasted mightily with the confinement of all black people to ghettos. In the 1970s, with the dismantling of the machinery that had perpetuated the legal status of blacks as second-class citizens, the ghettos decayed even further when middle-class black families moved out to pursue newly opened opportunities in the suburbs. The problem of racist hiring practices became almost moot when few jobs paid a living wage to people lacking formal educational credentials. In contrast to the slaves and sharecroppers who had played a necessary part in the Southern staple-crop economy, blacks in the late-twentieth-century ghetto found themselves unable to rise above the poverty line with service-sector wages. Thus over time vanished the reserve-army status that had allowed black manufacturing workers to enjoy at least temporary well-being in times of war and other periods of intense labor demand. In this fate they were joined by, among other groups, blue–collar workers in Midwestern cities, some of whom by the 1970s understood that their own initial foothold in heavy industry was but a fleeting form of success.

The current convergence in the plight of inner-city blacks, displaced steel and auto workers, and East Coast migrant laborers of myriad cultural backgrounds is revealed most clearly in their similar patterns of household disorganization, substance abuse, and adherence to an "underground economy" of money-making. Yet this convergence should not mask certain continuities in the structure of racial prejudice, continuities linking the postbellum South with the postindustrial North. The analogy between Southern plantation and Northern ghetto springs not from theoretical constructions or statistical models but from the deeply felt pronouncements of men and women who had experienced both worlds. Interviewed in the late 1960s and early 1970s, for example, a group of Southern-born black Northeasterners portrayed Northern society as an extension, or reflection, of the South. Conspicuous in their absence from this set of interviews are references to those themes that implied that migration had involved a radical departure from a caste-bound past—the ability of blacks to vote and participate in party politics, and the transition from sharecropping to industrial wage work. According to anthropologist John Langston Gwaltney's informants, "the business of the white man is to rule": "During all our history here [in the United States] we have been right and they have been wrong and the only man who cannot see that is a fool or a liar." In the end, despite a change of scenery for the grandchildren of slaves, "It just has not changed all that much."[11]

No matter where or when they lived, most black folks could say "I work. I work hard—you can ask anybody out here—but I don' seem to get nowhere." Though forced to perform the heaviest, hottest jobs— "that plantation thing"—blacks had received from whites only contempt in return: "These lazy Negroes are the ones who dig ditches and build roads and lift heavy pots and things." Ultimately, a black person's class status was irrelevant: "the one fact that we were the children of slaves and that the word 'nigger' meant the same things to [all of] us is very important." In the eyes of whites, blacks remained outside the boundaries of a consumer society that supposedly conferred materialistic aspirations on people in an equal-opportunity way: "See, they do everything to keep us down, and still we got things they think we ain' got no business with!"—the sharecropper with a Model T Ford, the welfare recipient with a color TV. A rude cabin in the middle of a cotton field, a tiny apartment in a concrete housing project—"it is *how* you live that's important," and "people need space and they were never meant to be jammed on top of each other." Overcrowded and underfunded schools made a mockery of the ideal of public education, whether in Jim Crow Alabama or the South Bronx. Despite variations over time and within regions, for slaves as well as for mothers receiving Aid to Families with Dependent Children, enforced dependency seemed designed to maximize the humiliation of black people: "I done had all that whitefolks' help I can use!" And always, the code of racial etiquette rewarded deference and dissembling: "My father used to say, 'Laugh with your friends, but smile with strangers.'"[12]

Despite deep structural similarities in race relations North and South, these similarities were not fixed, static, or ahistorical. Blacks would not have moved north in such large numbers during the twentieth century had their aggressive quest for higher wages and greater political power not been successful to at least some extent. However, by the late twentieth century, several generations of underemployment among black men had eroded the economic underpinnings of the nuclear family. As a starving body begins to feed upon its own vital organs, the black community began to turn inward and feed upon itself. The streets were "the North's lynch mobs," wrote novelist Ann Petry in 1946.[13] Nevertheless, the AIDS epidemic, crack cocaine addiction, and the casual use of semiautomatic weapons in the 1980s had no literal precedents in the nineteenth-century rural South.

The broad parameters of Southern history, including the social and political consequences of emancipation, the descent of formerly self-sufficient white yeoman farmers into tenancy, and the texture of race relations on the countryside, fit squarely within a context of worldwide dispossession in rural areas as well as cities. For example, like postbellum Southern planters, Cuban elites cited the "vicious, vagrant habits" of former slaves and debated the necessity of placing legal restrictions on the mobility of landless agricultural laborers. Both groups of landowners soon discovered the inherent paradox in immobilizing workers within an economy that depended on seasonal migration; Cuban officials abandoned the idea of legislation, while their American counterparts passed more than their share of vagrancy laws and then obeyed or ignored them just as they pleased.[14] The process by which yeoman farmers in the Piedmont of the American South lost control over their own productive energies to some extent paralleled the English Enclosure Movement, which also transformed the web of local community relations and disrupted patterns of mutual assistance among households.[15] Recent research on the history of rural South Africa suggests that there, as in the southern United States, even a legal system of racial segregation could prove to be unexpectedly fluid and flexible when viewed from the perspective of more private relations within homes and out in the fields. Although contact between members of the two races could lead to personal accommodation on an everyday basis, such contact could also provoke status anxieties among whites, now "shreiking for 'Seggregation.'" [16] And finally, in the late twentieth century the global assembly line and the permeability of national boundaries brought new job competition to bear on poor people in every area of the United States, when Latin American and Southeast Asian immigrants took jobs in Florida sugarcane fields or on Pennsylvania mushroom farms, and when the collapse, or departure, of heavy industry deprived towns in the American heartland of an economic base, leaving them to strangle slowly.

Through the centuries, all over the world, elites have expressed outrage over the moral implications of poverty but less concern for its economic causes. By the 1980s or so middle-class white Americans had identified a supposedly postmodern phenomenon, a Northern urban black "underclass" located with an otherwise "classless" (or exclusively "middle-class") society.[17] "Underclass" was but one more term used to label and objectify people believed to be morally dissolute and criminally inclined; other, historic terms also stressed the otherness, or separateness, of such people, especially urban dwellers who seemed to inhabit the subterranean reaches of society; these were the denizens of the underworld, the *lumpenproletariat,* the lower orders and the dangerous classes. A perceived congenital *wanderlust* formed the essential, and common, characteristic among all these groups, in America and Europe, in the sixteenth century or in the twentieth. While American employers were condemning "restless" freedpeople and "roving" poor whites, the respectable classes in Europe likewise fretted over a veritable "melange of transients," a perennial "parade of itinerants" composed of seasonal agricultural and construction workers as well as skilled artisans.[18] Thus every generation, here and abroad, felt the need to "discover" the unique, and uniquely degrading, qualities of their "own" poor. In the 1980s in the United States, a small number of streetwise ghetto youths took to their logical conclusion all the mainstream vices glorified by presidents, Wall Street bankers, and Hollywood producers—the rapacious pursuit of wealth, the exploitation of women, consumption that was conspicuous for its arrogance, and a savage drive for self-aggrandizement that mocked the notion of community. The result was a public and media fascination with a few young black men whose actions represented a particular and by no means typical manifestation of poverty. Largely ignored in public debates over poverty were other distressed populations within and outside the ghetto—groups more mundane in their survival strategies, especially the hardworking people whose main shortcoming seemed to be their inability to satisfy American preoccupations with sex, violence, and a mass-consumption professional sports complex best represented by expensive high-top sneakers.

The attempt to restore America's dispossessed to a central place in the country's history amounts to more than an intellectual exercise in recovering the past. Today, in a nation polarized by class and splintered into diverse cultural groups, myriad sources of social fragmentation threaten to rend the civil fabric and reduce political discourse to the level of bitter, mutual recrimination, or even physical strife. Among the very poorest citizens the family—that bulwark against social dissolution, traditionally so resilient—is in mortal danger of becoming overwhelmed by the combined plagues of physical want, drug addiction, disease, murder, and mayhem. Meanwhile, more well-to-do persons turn away with scornful indifference. It is therefore a timely, if not urgent, enterprise to recall that, ever since the Civil War, the desire among men and women for a stable job and a settled home place has transcended class, cultural, and racial lines; the white middle class has had no monopoly on the virtues of hard work, love of family, and commitment to schooling for their children. Moreover, the same spirit of enterprise that has yielded a cornucopia of plenty for many also helps to account for the dispiriting conditions in, among other places, Tunica, Mississippi, in 1990 the poorest county in a nation of unequals. To recapture the history of people who worked to share in that plenty but failed, we need not romanticize their poverty or sentimentalize their struggle; but we must place their story where it belongs—at the center of a drama that was less Southern than American, and less American than universal.

PART I

THE SOUTHERN "LABOR QUESTION" IN BLACK AND WHITE DURING THE CIVIL WAR ERA, 1860 TO 1870

1

At the Crossroads of Freedom: Black Field Workers

In October 1865 a committee "in behalf of the people," the former slaves of Edisto Island, South Carolina, protested a recent decision by the federal government to deprive them of legal title to parcels of land abandoned by their former masters. Writing to General O. O. Howard, the head of the Bureau of Refugees, Freedmen, and Abandoned Lands, members of the committee argued that, as a landless people seeking to make a living in an agrarian society, they would remain vulnerable to the whims and wishes of the men and women who had enslaved them: "We are at the mercy of those who are combined to prevent us from getting land enough to lay our Fathers' bones upon. . . . we can only do one of these things[:] Step Into the public *road or Sea* or remain . . . working as In former time and subject to their will as then. We can not resist It In any way without being driven out Homeless upon the road." In the eyes of the freedpeople of Edisto Island, such "choices"—either to revert to a neoslave status, as an agri-

cultural proletariat, or to embrace a perpetual form of rootlessness—
mocked the very notion of freedom. The rich cotton and rice fields of
the Sea Islands had been nourished with the tears and blood of generations of slaves; such was their title to property once forfeited and now
reclaimed by traitors to the Union.[1]

In a separate letter also dated October 1865, this one addressed to
President Andrew Johnson, the petitioners sought to stress their rights,
and aspirations, as American citizens. They stood ready and eager to
acquire the modest land parcels that would, they hope, guarantee them
the economic and political independence of yeoman farmers, an ideal
valued not only by Thomas Jefferson but also by ordinary men and
women throughout American history: "Land monopoly is injurious to
the advancement of the course of freedom, and if Government Does not
make some provision by which we as Freedmen can obtain A
Homestead, we have Not bettered our condition." In their belief that,
without property, they would continue to "be subject To the will of these
Large Landowners," the Edisto committee proved prophetic.[2]

Determined to resist a slavish dependence on whites, black people
throughout the South demanded land; in this regard the Edisto letters of
1865 expressed a widely shared sentiment, though they gave particularly
eloquent expression to it. One freedman in Virginia joined with many
others in claiming a form of sweat equity *in extremis:* "We has a right to
the land where we are located. For why? I tell you. Our wives, our children, our husbands, has been sold over and over again to purchase the
lands we now locates upon; for that reason we have a divine right to the
land. . . ." And yet it soon became clear that the federal government
would not initiate any meaningful land distribution policies; to the contrary, Presidential Reconstruction guaranteed that almost all Southern
land in federal possession at the end of the war, land either confiscated
from Confederates or abandoned by them (850,000 acres by 1865),
would be restored to its former owners. Without material resources or
landed kin, the former slaves and their descendants would remain at a
permanent disadvantage in their efforts to acquire property and accumulate cash; such was the bitter irony of their "equality" within the postbellum Southern marketplace.[3]

If one theme characterizes the story of black freedom after the Civil
War, it is the former slaves' quest for autonomy, a life independent of
power brokers in any guise. The goal of landownership served as the
heart of this quest; but the former slaves also seized the initiative to
build their own schools and found their own churches and to exercise
their rights as citizens by voting and speaking their minds. In these pri-

orities they resembled other groups of Americans at the time—Western homesteaders and Northern workers, foreign immigrants now settled in the Midwest, and Appalachian farmers. Nevertheless, throughout the Civil War and postbellum period, white politicians and ideologues, whether vanquished Confederates or triumphant Northerners, tried to reinforce the view that blacks, whether formerly free or slave, existed as a people apart from other Americans.

Specifically, Southern white landowners did their best to distinguish all blacks from all whites, no matter how poor, in the turbulent era of war and Reconstruction. In the process these elites focused on what they perceived as an irrational "restlessness" on the part of freedpeople who, in a seemingly endless search for true freedom, deserted the plantation for the city, or suddenly abandoned one plantation in favor of another one nearby. Among black people dependent on white landowners for both wages and shelter, labor and residential mobility were inextricably linked. Freedom of movement was a right supposedly enjoyed by all American citizens, and the former slaves quickly claimed it. At the same time, persistently high rates of plantation turnover testified to the exploitative nature of the postwar Southern labor system; confined within this system, black people would find no settled home place that would reward their strenuous efforts in the fields. Refusing to accommodate themselves to the demands of their employers, landless black families would remain, to a great extent, "Homeless upon the road."

"Negroes rove from place to place," declared a Texas cotton planter in 1868. "They love change, and a month's work at a place, and are reluctant to make a year engagement." Landowners throughout the former Confederate states seemed to agree that the slave as "fixed capital" had quickly degenerated into the wartime runaway, and then to the freedman, with his family's confounding habits of "anxious locomotion." The Texas white man continued: "White people love home, take interest in making it pleasant, comfortable—as the spot from which issue all their money and comforts."[4] In his view, then, the slave South had yielded to a new South in which black households would continue to wander, forever "taking a mind to move," oblivious to the benefits of steady toil, while whites regardless of class would prosper through capital accumulation, the fruits of devotion to place.

Northern Republicans, including politicians, military officials, and Freedmen's Bureau agents, saw blacks in general as uniquely unschooled in the work ethic, people who needed to be taught that a day's honest work would yield its own reward. Yet these men concurred with secessionists that unsettled workers would undermine all hopes for a reconstructed staple-crop economy. Presumably a householder's attachment to a specific piece of land represented the steadiness of character that would make him a worthy credit risk to bankers and a reliable provider for his family. Not long after the war, federal officials began to rank the abandonment of "migratory habits" with adherence to the traditional Yankee virtues of education, industry, and respect for marriage vows as ingredients essential to the personal and collective well-being of Southern blacks.[5]

The issue of labor mobility forms the crux of the freedpeople's struggle for political and economic self-determination, a struggle that remained centered on the plantation. The subduing of the former slaves, turning a "wandering" and "strolling" people into sedentary agricultural laborers—or rather, returning them to a more sedentary condition akin to slavery—constituted a major priority for both white Southerners and Northerners after the Civil War. Rebels and Yankees differed on the chief end of their joint endeavor—whether to secure for the rural South a large parcel of neoslaves or a new class of yeoman farmers, and on the means necessary to achieve that end—physical compulsion or labor-market incentives. Neverthless, blacks resisted all efforts to keep them literally "in their place" working for white employers. The ensuing battle was waged in courtrooms and legislative halls, at the ballot box and at the point of the gun, all over the South; but everyday conflicts between employers and employees over who should labor in the fields, where and for how long, constituted the primary force shaping patterns of Southern rural labor mobility. This is not to ignore the significance of the political gains achieved so fiercely, and tenuously, by blacks and their Republican allies at the state and local levels, nor to minimize the legal machinations of Southern whites to restrict black movement through vagrancy legislation, both before and after Radical, or Congressional, Reconstruction (beginning in 1867). Rather, it is to suggest that the source of these highly charged, violent conflicts stemmed from a single, central problem of labor management faced by all staple-crop employers in the immediate postwar period—how to maintain a labor force that would prove reliable at certain times of the year but not burdensome on a year-round basis.

The annual contract system, initiated during the war by federal military officials and implemented throughout the postbellum South by the Freedmen's Bureau, served to ensure planters a year-long labor force, men and women held to their place of work and residence by the force of law and the promise of payment on December 31. By attempting to organize seasonal agricultural production on a twelve-month basis, federal authorities, with the implicit (and long-term) approval of Southern employers, instituted a process by which black people in the rural South would remain integral to Southern staple-crop production but economically marginalized through a system based on chronic underemployment. The "annual" nature of labor contracts masked the fact that black labor was needed on cotton, rice, or sugar plantations for only a part of any year, and employers felt little obligation to feed and clothe people during the slack season. For their part, black families sought to provide for themselves by foraging, gardening, fishing, and seeking wage work off the plantation, thereby lessening their dependence on a single employer. December reckoning time enabled whites to evict or "run off" unsatisfactory workers, but it also provided many black men and women with an opportunity to leave one employer and go elsewhere. Consequently, a sufficiently secure and tractable agricultural work force would continue to elude Southern planters as long as the sharecropping system remained in existence—until the 1930s, when mechanization and crop-reduction programs led landowners to replace large numbers of resident workers with day hands.

Because of the repressive nature of the Southern labor-management system, freedpeople and their sharecropping children and grandchildren never conformed to the Northern ideal of "free laborers"; and yet in their ability to move around within the rural economy and (at times) to leave one employer for another at the end of the year, most were better off than peons. As individuals and community members, they retained a faith in formal education and a commitment to formal political activity that distinguished them from peasants mired in fatalism.[6] If we must categorize black labor after the Civil War, it is possible to suggest simply that, like other groups of rural folk at the time, they worked together as farm family members, as fishers and foragers, gardeners and wage earners. Therefore, in their efforts to establish for themselves a modicum of self-reliance within the parameters of the annual plantation routine and to share in the rights of citizenship already accorded to white people, the former slaves embraced an idea of freedom long familiar to, and cherished by, other groups of Americans.

PATHWAYS CUT BY SLAVERY, WAR, AND FREEDOM

Before, during, and after the Civil War, there existed in the South an enormous labor flux, and the white landowners and black workers who produced it acted out of radically different self-interests. Throughout the nineteenth century, the Southern staple-crop economy depended on the fluidity of labor. Slaveowners and, later, employers of sharecroppers were constantly in the process of deciding which workers to get rid of and which to retain. In this regard they were not much different from other kinds of labor lords in other parts of the country. And like other kinds of workers, Southern slaves and, later, wage hands, tenants, and sharecroppers sought to control their own movements as much as possible; at times they wanted to remain on an estate, at other times to leave. Not until the onset of military conflict in 1861 did Southern black people have any meaningful opportunity to decide when they would labor and where they would live. Yet their varied experiences as slaves, and as actors in Confederate and Union war mobilization strategies, help to explain how a people whose moves were so closely monitored before the war might prove so bold in ferreting out kin and jobs after emancipation.

As a system of social control, slavery flourished to the extent that a few whites could oversee the tasks performed by many blacks within a geographically confined area. Nevertheless, one of the great benefits (to slaveholders) of human chattel as a form of personal property was its movability, in discrete pieces (that is, individuals as opposed to a whole labor force) and on short notice. Masters might adjust the size and composition of their slave holdings in response to immediate financial considerations or disciplinary problems presented by an unruly few. Whites speculated in slaves, bequeathed them to kin, and bestowed them as gifts. The evolution of a diversified economy in late-eighteenth-century Virginia encouraged masters to hire out black men as craftsmen and as laborers on railroads, docks, and steamboats and in mines, factories, and lumberyards. Black husbands and sons saw a small world of towns, blacksmith shops, gristmills, and tanneries that contrasted with the narrow lives of their plantation-bound womenfolk. Likewise, the mountains of North Carolina provided ample opportunities for large slaveowners to profit from nonagricultural enterprises such as mining, rock quarrying, and road and railroad construction, and from farm-related ventures, including the herding of cattle and sheep, that required the absence of black men from home for extended periods of time. In the interests of the great Mississippi Delta sugar and cotton planters, Louisiana parishes provided for the regular maintenance and repair of levees so essential to flood control; local slaveowners periodically contributed able-bodied men to these public works efforts. Clearly, hiring-out patterns reflected the commercial value placed on black men in contrast to women's more sedentary tasks of domestic service, field work, and childbearing. Exceptional were the South Carolina low-country planters who encouraged their bondswomen skilled in West African trading practices to bargain and exchange goods (albeit briefly, for no more than a few days at a time) in Charleston's lively marketplace.[7]

These modest manipulations of the local black labor supply differed in degree, but not in purpose, from the massive, forced migrations of slaves from the Upper to the Lower South and from the eastern seaboard to the old Southwest. During the six decades before the Civil War, the South retained all the restlessness of a frontier society, dotted with caravans of slaves, some on their way from Virginia to Georgia, but others pushing on to Texas after five years' worth of disappointment in Alabama. Interviewed by a Federal Writers Project worker in the 1930s, one black man, Berry Smith, recalled a familiar sight when he described slave women and children atop wooden wagons, husbands and older children walking alongside, as his family journeyed from Alabama to Mississippi, traveling one hundred miles in five days and nights. On the whole, freedpeople actually moved long distances less frequently than slaves, a fact that contrasts, perhaps, the economic opportunism of the slave master with the freed family's loyalty to kin and community. Ironically, as a group, free blacks in the antebellum South were apparently also less mobile than slaves; a variety of pass and curfew laws inhibited their movement, and few could hope to find more favorable conditions outside their home state. Thus slaves were not necessarily immobile, but their mobility was (or at least was intended to be) a carefully controlled phenomenon.[8]

Despite such constraints, black people did leave the plantation in ways that reflected their own impulses and deepest desires. This side of the equation also emphasizes the greater mobility of men, compared to their womenfolk, on both a short- and long-term basis. Slave women and men of all ages looked forward to an occasional Saturday afternoon or holiday excursion to nearby towns—a concession granted only grudgingly by owners. Husbands in "abroad" marriages more frequently visited their wives than vice versa, at times furtively and under the cover of darkness. Runaways, of course, posed a most serious threat to plantation stability, whether they hid out in a nearby swamp or headed for a distant freedom by light of the North Star. As several historians have shown, women were not entirely absent from newspaper advertisements for fugitives, but their grown brothers and sons greatly outnumbered them.[9]

The Civil War wrought havoc on the fragile ties that bound slave families together; at the same time, the conflict revealed to freedpeople a new view of their physical surroundings and future possibilities as wage earners. These horizons beckoned to many blacks, a consequence of

travel; new kinds of work; and acquisition of skills, both forced and voluntary, during the war years. Confederate mobilization policies routinely
separated black men from their parents, wives, and children, and at the
same time introduced many to rail travel for the first time. (A Columbus,
Georgia, master broke with precedent when he managed to persuade
local Confederate officials to accept responsibility for the wives of his
male slaves, newly hired out. The women were put "to work with the
shovel or spade at grading land" alongside their husbands.) Escaped
slaves who fled to coastal Union outposts at times made their way back
up intricate waterways in search of loved ones left behind. All over the
South, in an effort to lessen chances that their slaves might be seized by
soldiers of either army or tempted into running away, owners criss-
crossed the region, their most valuable chattel in tow, from Georgia to
Louisiana, from Louisiana to Texas, from Virginia to the Deep South,
from the eastern seaboard to the Piedmont. Those black men "druv up
the country by de Rebels" realized they might never see their homes
again. Together with impressment policies, these movements, called
refugeeing, left whole plantations deprived of men. Indeed, on some
holdings, such as the expansive Hurricane estate near Vicksburg, only
women and children remained by the end of the war.[10]

Black people in general proved to be a subversive force within the
Confederacy; the would-be nation, built on a fragile consensus of white
Southerners, faced persistent difficulty in sustaining the requisite men
and morale to prosecute a successful military effort. Blacks of both sexes
and all ages deprived the rebel cause of their labor when they responded
eagerly to the incursion of Union forces within their vicinity. Some
blacks, as individuals or family members, fled behind federal lines,
where they expected to find safety, employment, and even customers for
any cattle, chickens, eggs, and vegetables they managed to spirit away
with them. Thousands of slaves enlisted in the Northern war effort to
serve as soldiers (after 1862) and in capacities similar to those mandated
by Confererate policies—as construction workers, woodcutters, cooks,
teamsters, skilled craftsmen, and personal servants. (A total of almost
200,000 black men fought in the Union Army.) On the other hand,
Northern conscription practices could be as rapacious as those of the
Confederates, and in the end, the effects were the same—"the able-
bodied young men [on a plantation near Barnwell, South Carolina] . . .
carried off by the Yankees"; left behind were family members vulnerable
to abuse from vengeful slaveowners or from labor-hungry lessees of gov-
ernment-owned plantations. In their efforts to establish some semblance
of economic stability in the Union-occupied areas of Louisiana, federal

military officials arranged for local planters to hire as workers the black people who had fled to Yankee camps for safety, and set about putting people to work in the rural districts without thought to their family attachments. At greatest risk for their lives were elderly, ill, and handicapped blacks who had neither the physical resources to escape nor the productive capacity valued by whites.[11]

During the war, when Louisiana sugar workers were impressed to labor in sawmills or Georgia cotton pickers to toil at turpentine extraction, when refugeed slaves en route to Texas traversed hundreds of miles of unfamiliar terrain, and when Virginia female field hands worked as laundresses and chambermaids in the Union hospital at Hampton, they learned much about survival away from home. Meanwhile, these black women and men took stock of times and places that were fast slipping from their masters' control. The war years thus opened some of the hazardous highways that freedpeople would travel during Reconstruction and beyond.[12]

Given the eagerness with which slaves embraced freedom, it was not surprising that, as Southern territory fell to the Union army, many men, women, and children deserted their masters and mistresses; but it is doubtful that most left just for the sake of leaving. For a large proportion, a nearby town or city provided the first destination of choice, where they might "seek refuge from humiliated and incensed masters." Moreover, military maneuvers had severely disrupted the 1865 growing season, and only a few freedpeople could hope to find steady employment in the fields until the following year, an inducement for the rest to migrate to urban areas and eke out an existence doing odd jobs. Yet if the city exuded a "magnetic attraction" for many rural folk, others simply used it as a way station in their search for work or missing kin. When eighteen-year-old Mary Armstrong fled her native St. Louis determined to locate her mother, her odyssey took her down the Mississippi River, through New Orleans, and then on to Galveston, Houston, and Austin before a long-awaited reunion in the small Texas town of Wharton.[13]

Though statistics are lacking, turnover among the rural black labor force was sufficiently high immediately after the war to cause great consternation among whites, who feared social chaos and economic ruin. Writing from Charleston in June 1865, one planter, Joseph Daniel Pope, observed freedpeople "running all over the country vagabondizing from city to city and idling from one place in the country to another." Stock figures in postbellum Southern mythology were those loyal blacks who cast their lot permanently with their former owners. In fact, many freedpeople who remained on their former owners' plantation through 1865 apparently moved away eventually, responding to changes in the composition of their households and to evidence related to the good faith (or lack of it) of their former owners and current employers. Turner Jacobs's parents kept him and their other children on a Mississippi plantation "after freedom," but when his father died, his mother "jest grieve herself to death soon after." In their sorrow, Turner's kin "cided to leave and try somewheres else." At times, a lack of attractive alternatives could prove paralyzing, especially for single mothers. Seventeen years old at the time, W. L. Bost recalled that, "after the war was over we was afraid to move. Jes like tarpins or turtles after 'mancipation. Jes stick our heads out to see how the land lay." With six children to worry about, Bost's mother stayed with her former master for a year, until "ole Solomon Hall made her an offer," and then she moved them to a nearby farm. The freedpeople on a Pike County, Mississippi, plantation soon found their mistress's kind blandishments overshadowed by an abusive overseer: "Dey all sed dey wus gwine to stay wid Mistress but dat overseer wud still whup dem an drive dem 'round like dey wus slaves an' most uf dem left." Indeed, the bitter disappointment that accompanied "settling time" after the meager 1865 harvest impelled many black households throughout the Cotton Belt to move in search of better prospects for the coming year.[14]

Later the former slaves would associate their travels with a search for gainful employment, in contrast to their white contemporaries who accused them of an aimless "drifting," movement perverse in its sheer purposelessness. Mary Anderson remembered her clan "wondering around for a year from place to place," but they were all "working most of the time at some other slave owner's plantation." Levi Ashley recalled, "We had a hard time an' went frum place to place—git work fer a while an' den go on ag'in." Henry Bobbitt was a teenager when he left his master and walked all the way to Raleigh to make certain he was really free: "[D]e first year I slept in folkses woodhouses an' barns an' in de woods or any whar else I could find. I wucked here an' dar, but de folkses jist give me sompin' ter eat an' my clothes wuz in strings 'fore de spring o' de year."[15]

Blacks who managed, or even just attempted, to quit their slave homes represented the emergence of a new social order, if not the death knell of bondage. At the same time, some planters hastily abandoned all show of paternalism and sought to "set adrift," "run off," or "kick out from home" all the "useless ones"—black men, women, and children who afforded prospective employers only mouths to feed and bodies to clothe. In their new roles as employers, white men and women now began to calculate the potential profit value not only of prime hands but also of "people who had grown old and feeble while slaves and who are now unable to do steady labor in the fields." If workers were to be singled out and paid as individuals, then a parcel of blind, lame, and infant dependents would serve only to drain the landowner's resources (food more often than cash), not to mention whatever residue of goodwill remained after emancipation. These financial considerations wrought great hardship on black families. A woman might be young and healthy, an excellent cotton picker, but her offspring would put her at a competitive disadvantage compared to her childless sister, since planters resisted supplying "nonworkers"; "no person will pay a woman with six children as much as one with one or two, although both women would be good 2nd class hands," noted a Helena, Arkansas, Freedmen's Bureau agent in June 1865. For the time being, at least, the prized "breeder" was now an economic liability to men who had once valued her reproductive capacity. The expulsion of blacks from holdings where they had lived and worked as slaves provoked outrage and suffering among those forced to leave a community of kin behind; those with nowhere else to go; and those with plans to leave in their own good time, now driven off with "nothing but their two hands to start out with."[16]

During the postbellum years most geographical mobility among rural blacks was short range—within a county, a staple-crop economy, or to a nearby town and then back to the countryside again. Yet some freed families traveled great distances, if not always willingly. For example, many blacks sought to return to the area they had been forced to leave under slavery or had chosen to abandon in the heat of conflict. A Freedmen's Bureau report issued during the middle of the war from a Cairo, Illinois, refugee camp noted that the Southern blacks there "all have a repulsive idea of going back into slavery, but would prefer going back to their old places, if they could be free there." A Bureau agent in Georgetown, South Carolina, testified to the determination of two hundred people, probably refugeed during the war and currently in his district, who "made an arrangement with a sloop to take them to a plantation on Wando River, Christ Church Parish," near Charleston, "where some of them formerly were domiciled as slaves." A group of former rice plantation slaves took the first opportunity (in December 1865) to flee their wartime residence in the up-country, where forced labor in the cornfields had killed many of their original number: "No shoe, no cloes, an' den de fros' git up into deir body, tell when de sun come down so hot, dey dies too fas.'" In the same state, "Highland darkeys who had drifted down to the seashore" after emancipation now besieged relatives and government officials for railroad tickets so they could be "fotched home again." Although many war refugees and former refugeed slaves "seemed very glad at the thought of returning . . . to their former place of residence," they did not always intend to return to the estate of their former owner. A little girl named Louisa Adams and her brothers and sisters scrambled to keep up with their parents as they fled a North Carolina plantation in the direction of Fayetteville, clambering over fences; she and her siblings were "broke down children, feet sore." Exhausted and famished a few days later, "we come back home. Not to Marster's, but to a white 'oman named Peggy McClinton, on her plantation." "Home" was a region characterized by a particular climate, topography, crop economy, and an extensive network of kin, rather than the very same slave cabins they had once inhabited.[17]

In the Southwest, Northern planters at times relied on enterprising Union soldiers, with their wide range of contacts and official demeanor, to locate potential workers. The Freedmen's Bureau, eager to impose order on a bewildering postwar labor situation, arranged transportation for nearly thirty thousand blacks all over the South, mainly in an effort to drain overcrowded areas of refugees and accommodate the needs of planters in remote districts. These priorities help to account for the Bureau's attempts "to limit [the blacks'] noxious liberty" by moving them out of cities, where they generated "within themselves and around them a state of things productive only of trouble and misery," and by encouraging them to contract with any planter, including their old master, and then to remain on his plantation for at least a year. So active was the Bureau in this regard that one Georgia newspaper decried it as a "gigantic negro-trading enterprise," its agents overwhelmed by requests from destitute blacks for travel funds and from landowners quick to offer lavish promises about wages and the annual crop division.[18]

In opposition to these forces stimulating migration were the legal restrictions placed on the movement of blacks in all the former Confederate states. An apprenticeship system that emerged after the war allowed whites to retain the services of black youngsters with the full weight of the law behind them. Antebellum pass regulations, enforced by citizen patrollers, found renewed expression during the war years as Confederates reacted with alarm to the threat of slave insurrections and as Union military officials (provost marshals) forced black travelers to present signed notes from their white employers or risk imprisonment. After 1865 vagrancy laws, the cornerstone of Black Codes passed by unrepentant Southern legislators, provided for the prosecution of all freedpeople who could not show proof they were gainfully employed by a white man or woman; these laws gave sheriffs and planters the authority to exert strict control over the goings and comings of local black workers. Deputized citizen patrols subjected freedpeople out on the roads after dark to the "savagest treatment" (in the words of one Freedmen's Bureau agent). Near Demopolis, Alabama, "vagrant" laborers could be deprived of their wages even though they had been "run off" a plantation by the owner. A Texas statute passed in 1867 condemned unemployed blacks to jail or to forced labor on the state's public highways. Freedpeople who left their jobs for whatever reason, including physical abuse, were forbidden to find work elsewhere, with prospective employers subject to a "ruinous fine." Thus the demise of slavery brought a concomitant rise in the power of civil authorities over blacks, and the immediate postwar years yielded countless instances of local officials who prosecuted blacks for crimes that covered a broad spectrum of personal behavior in an effort to retain control over labor mobility. (A Freedmen's Bureau agent in Greenville, Alabama, reported in 1868 that the county sheriff repeatedly flouted the law "with impunity," but "any offense of a colored person is speedily and valorously noticed and prosecuted.") The overcrowding of tax-supported jails, and the consequent loss of available laborers, eventually helped to popularize and justify chain gangs. These work crews often consisted of black men plucked from back roads, convicted on frivolous charges, and now made to toil on the South's primitive transportation network.[19]

Extralegal violent measures buttressed the intentions of diehard rebels who could not always count on controlling juries and sheriffs once black men were enfranchised under the provisions of Radical Reconstruction (beginning in 1867). Vigilante groups appeared all over the South either to rid local areas of blacks or to force them to remain against their wishes. In fact, planters and poor whites could work at violent cross purposes, and it is difficult to sort out the class composition of lynch mobs, Ku Klux Klan Klaverns, beat companies, Young Men's Democratic Clubs, patrollers, bulldozers, and jayhawkers without reference to regional labor conflict. For example, in late 1866 planters with "blackened faces and disguised" banded into a Black Horse Cavalry in Franklin Parish, Louisiana, "for the purpose of whipping Freedmen and preventing their leaving the Parish." Well-to-do whites attempted to control the economic options not only of blacks but also of poor whites when, in Greenville, South Carolina, they "organized titled beat companies with Captains, Lieutenants, &c. to go about and whip and drive back freedmen employed away from their former owner, especially if the present employer was not formerly a slaveowner." On the other hand, large landowners in areas of Arkansas were "in terror of . . . outlaws," poor white men resentful of freedpeople who found work as croppers and tenants. These landlords appealed to local authorities and sought legal protection to safeguard their labor forces. In regions only sparsely populated by blacks, white farmers attempted to drive all freedpeople from their midst, provoking a reign of terror in the hill country of Alabama and North Carolina, in northwestern Arkansas, and in the Shenandoah Valley of Virginia.[20]

Regardless of their source, the hazards faced by blacks in groups and singly on the road undermined the guiding principle of "free labor" espoused by Northern Republicans. If workers were not free to move about and pursue economic opportunities more attractive, or at least less unattractive, compared to their current situation, planters would have no incentive to compete for them. The "bad roads and broken state of the Country," combined with the belief among Confederate diehards that public thoroughfares were off limits to blacks, made travel exceedingly dangerous. Near Sherman, Texas, black men were forced "to take off their hats and throw them down before their horse" upon meeting a white person. A freedman named Fed was "overtaken on the road in this county by a man unknown, who asked him where he was going. Fed answered him by saying[,] about my business[,] for this reply was immediately shot but lingered a couple of days."[21] Under these conditions, to move one's family to a nearby plantation, let alone hundreds of miles back home, was no mean feat. Whites sought to use the roads, just as they sought to control the workplace, for their own purposes.

The efforts of freed men, women, and children to move around within a regional economy, or within the South at large, corresponded to the striking residential and job turnover among white factory hands and mechanics in the North; these propertyless white men seemed constantly on the move in search of more favorable working conditions.[22] However, while the Northern free labor market required unfettered worker movement, the labor market of the South relied on certain kinds of restraints on the mobility of the poorest workers, those men, women, and children who would not voluntarily return to neoslavery. From this perspective, the story of the freedpeople marks a distinctive chapter in the history of the nineteenth-century American working class, a history of "restlessness" borne of hope for a better life in a place of one's own choosing.

CONTRACTS AT ODDS WITH BLACKS' "LICENTIOUS IDEAS OF FREEDOM"[23]

Landowning whites in the South would have regarded as absurd the suggestion that slavery and sharecropping spawned a debilitating "culture of dependency" among the former slaves. Although proslavery ideologues had advanced the notion that blacks were a childlike people unable to care for themselves, after 1865 that view was replaced by a more realistic, if ominous, critique among the planter elite—a view that stressed the freedpeople's determination to provide for their families without relying on Southern whites for food or wages—or on the favor of Yankees, for that matter. At the heart of the issue lay the definition of "work," which planters and Northern officials perceived narrowly, as any productive activity that directly benefited landlords and creditors or furnishing merchants. In August 1867 a Mississippi Freedmen's Bureau agent noted that "inexcusably idle and slothful" freedpeople managed "to exist by hunting, fishing, etc.," echoing the view of planters that only regimented toil in the fields qualified as labor.[24]

The efforts of freedpeople to exploit the rhythm of the cotton cultivation cycle to their own advantage reveal the politicized nature of an emergent annual labor contract system in the postwar South. In the Cotton Belt, where three-fifths of all Southern blacks resided in 1870, conflicts over the meaning of work came into explicit focus in the slack-season heat of middle and late summer and in the bleakness of midwinter, when all parties confronted the deficiencies of the annual share-wage system. Under this system, able-bodied hands contracted as individuals for a full calendar year, and planters agreed to pay their workers (whom they organized in the field in gangs) a share of the crop. This arrangement implied that first, employers had a responsibility to "furnish" (supply) and house their workers on a year-round basis and that, second, workers had an obligation to remain in residence on the plantation regardless of whether there was planting, chopping, or harvesting to be done. Thus Northern interests—to hold employer and employee accountable to each other—and Southern interests—to prevent blacks from absconding before picking time—dovetailed neatly in the form of the annual contract. Ultimately, the labor contract (and not the Black Code vagrancy and enticement laws passed by most Southern states in 1865 and 1866) served as the cornerstone of the planters' efforts to regulate the geographical movement of workers.[25]

Immediately after the Civil War it became apparent that many black people, never fully reconciled to selling their services to former slave-owners, would choose to "interrupt" their field labor in ways unpredictable to their employers. Ever on the lookout for a chance to adjust work and family relations more to their own liking, they came and went in defiance of seasonal labor demands. Cotton growers especially were aware of the dangers inherent in "overcropping" (that is, planting more than the available hands could cultivate and harvest). As early as June 1865 a Sea Island planter anticipated a major struggle that would come to characterize relations between white landowners distraught over the *"irregularity and uncertainty of the system of labor"* and freedpeople who "work when they please and do just as much as they please . . . and rely largely upon hunting and fishing to make up for what they lose in the field." A bountiful labor force during spring planting season produced only a thin fall harvest if any hands deserted the plantation sometime in between. The planter issued this warning: "Labor must be commanded completely or the production of the cotton crop must be abandoned."[26]

The widespread practice of docking workers for lost time was dramatic proof that postbellum planters waged a war against black people who, though residing on a plantation, resisted devoting their full time and energy to field work. For hands likely to see no cash at all at settlement (or any other) time, the standard fine of 50 cents to $1.00 per day for "time lost" was a logical absurdity, though a practical means to increase their indebtedness. It was not uncommon for planters to cite the "faithful labor" clause in contracts to justify withholding all compensation from laborers who absented themselves from the fields for more than two or three days at peak season. One contract signed in the Laurens District of South Carolina in 1868 included the provision that "should any of them [the three men and two women who signed] depart from the farm or from any services at any time without our approval they shall forfeit one dollar per day, for the first time and for the second time without good cause they shall forfeit all of their interest in their crop to me the enjured person." William Hughes, a planter near Hamburg, Arkansas, took this remedy to extremes when he charged a black family $1.25 for each lost day (presumably to cover housing as well as labor costs), though he was paying them less than 56 cents per day.[27]

Large landowners throughout the South experimented with various methods of securing, and then retaining, a work force sufficient for their needs during peak seasons of the year. The twelve-month contract seemed calculated to resolve this dilemma, but only if the form of payment could be manipulated to discourage laborers from seeking work elsewhere before harvesttime. Cotton planters who could afford, and were inclined, to pay monthly wages ran the risk of wholesale desertions in mid-July when there was little work to do. This fact of Reconstruction life prompted many whites to defer paying their workers until the crop was picked, ginned, pressed, and sold. The furnishing system (whereby a planter or merchant advanced credit and supplies at the beginning of the year) meant that workers had to reckon with their employer in December; contracts enforcing this system were "labor tying" on an annual basis. For their part, many freedpeople equated signing a year-long contract with "'signing them back to their masters,' as they express it." The many details these "agreements" covered—from the sexual division of labor in black families to provisions for visiting friends on nearby estates—were overshadowed by the larger, implicit demand that a worker be held accountable for any offense deemed obnoxious by an employer (the ubiquitous "improper behavior or negligence" clause).[28]

The Northern labor contract, as advocated by the Bureau, yielded unanticipated mutations when transplanted to Southern soil. In the South contract violations became criminal (not civil) matters, and the agreements themselves were at once more comprehensive and vague than those signed by Midwestern tenants and farm owners. The Southern planter sought to control the comings and goings of his workers around the clock, a fact that accounts for the precise stipulations in regard to off-plantation visits and personal decorum. Moreover, the furnishing system provided planter-merchants with, in the words of historian Harold Woodman, "a degree of control over their work force far beyond that available to employers elsewhere in the nation." These white men not only parceled out the supplies necessary to grow a crop and keep a worker's family alive; they also decided how, when, to whom, and for what price the crop would be marketed. Whether hired as individual share wage-earners, or later, as family sharecroppers, blacks existed as a rural proletariat without control over either the land or the fruits of their own labor. By the 1880s contracts existed in the rural South to verify the interests of planters only.[29]

Landowners' attempts to keep certain freedpeople bound to the plantation while ridding themselves of others revealed the complexities surrounding labor and residential mobility. On a basic level, planters understood that to permit blacks freedom of movement off the plantation was to grant them greater access to, and involvement in, an emerging political order and the legal process that sustained it. Whites had good reason to fear the larger consequences when black people left the plantation unsupervised—the ballots they would cast, the fellow workers inspired to do the same. And in fact, political activity represented a powerful lure for freedmen and women into towns and makeshift meeting places for local Union Leagues (grassroots organizations and the unofficial arm of the Republican party in the South). Thus at crucial times of the year when political passions were fiercest (usually in March or April, during planting, and in November, during harvest), Democratic cotton planters tried to reconcile their economic interests with their role as employers of Republicans by making an example of workers who engaged in election-eering. During the slack season, a time of low labor demand, planters faced the overwhlming temptation to brutalize their political antago-nists. In June of 1867 Bureau agent Samuel Gardner wrote from Greenville, South Carolina, of mounting tensions in anticipation of upcoming elections: "Several instances have occurred where employ-ment has been taken from capable and worthy Freedmen, on account of attending Republican meetings. . . . One planter declares to his friends, that he intends after laying by the crop to discharge, unpaid, every labor-er who will not pledge his vote as he dictates." One month later freed-men under contract to a Brooksville, Florida, planter lost their jobs and a year's compensation after participating in a Fourth of July celebration that featured the American flag. Four black men who registered to vote in Unionville, South Carolina, during August of the same year found themselves "turned off" a plantation. Later in the growing year, during harvesttime, such vengeful tactics posed a direct threat to the welfare of the cotton crop. A North Carolina Bureau agent testified to the planters' discomfort near Lincolnton on the eve of the 1868 elections; some whites threatened to fire all their black voters who refused to vote for the Democratic ticket, "but as the Freedmen are the hardworking & Laboring class, and the only class to depend upon for work in this Sub district, their labor can not well be dispensed with where Labor is necessary."[30]

In a different time and place, the routine use of fraud, violence, and intimidation on the part of employers would perhaps have led to increased litigation over contract disputes. Scattered throughout the South during the years of Radical Reconstruction were Freedmen's Bureau agents as well as black sheriffs and black grand- and petit-jury members ready and willing to grant freedpeople a fair hearing in the courts. Moreover, Republican-controlled state legislatures made some progress in protecting the legal rights of resident workers (those bound by annual contracts) to control the profits from the crops they grew. Yet workers found it difficult if not impossible to seek out justice centered in the towns. Plaintiffs faced overwhelming legal and practical problems once they decided to press their case—the wrath of their employer

("Dont you dispute my word or I will shoot you, I dont allow a nigger to dispute my word"); long distances to travel to the nearest authorities; the high price of bond demanded by civil courts; the fear of blacklisting and losing a share of the crop regardless of the outcome of the case. If a legitimate contract by definition presumes the ability of both parties to bargain freely and seek legal redress of their grievances, then very few freedpeople ever worked with the benefit of a contract at all.[31]

Neither employer nor worker regarded as sacred the twelve-month provision of labor contracts. In addition, the agricultural cycle itself mitigated against the confinement of black workers on a year-round basis. Soon after the war the problematic nature of annual contracts imposed on a seasonal system of production became abundantly clear. Under slavery, planters counted on the complementarity of staple crops and foodstuffs to occupy their laborers throughout the year. Stretching work out over the winter months inhibited technological innovation but at the same time kept the labor force resident on the plantation, and eliminated the financial need to hire out slaves, especially in the staple-crop economies of the Lower South. Presumably, the free labor system would inaugurate more flexible arrangements in terms of both crop mix and labor availability, but this was not the case. Indeed, the Freedmen's Bureau-sponsored contract, together with the share wages that compensated individual workers at the end of the year, put pressure on freedpeople to commit themselves to planters on a twelve-month basis, despite variations in seasonal work loads.[32]

When a planter stipulated that his hands should "labor faithfully . . . six days during the week, in a manner customary on a plantation," he intentionally left vague his plans for the cotton lay-by time and for the first weeks of the new calendar year. A Mississippi agent testified to a common occurrence when he reported that planters in the vicinity of Lauderdale forced blacks to "do all manner of work for weeks and months not specified in the contracts, and in the end, the Freedman is no better off pecuniarily, than he was when he commenced work." These demands grew out of "general maintenance" clauses in which planters intended the word "plantation" to imply not only protection of this year's crop but preparation for future ones as well. On the other hand, in the words of one Bureau agent, "The necessities of the freedmen induce some of them to employ the immediate time in working for themselves elsewhere instead of remaining on the plantation and at work clearing land and doing other work which is in no way connected with the growing crop and which carries with it no reward." Thus in their efforts to "extort [from blacks] unrenumerative labor which was never contemplated by the freedmen when making the contract," planters sought to preserve antebellum plantation management techniques in the face of postbellum political realities.[33]

Black people had no difficulty filling slack days and nights with work performed out of sight of their employers. Nancy Johnson, a slave on a Georgia plantation, was "served mighty mean" by her master and mistress during the war; forced to spin cloth and weave uniforms for Confederate soldiers, she never received "so much as a bonnet" in return. So when freedom came, she left, despite the entreaties of her former owner. Eventually, however, Nancy Johnson returned to the plantation, but not to do the bidding of her "old missus"; the white woman "asked me if I came back to behave myself & do her work & I told her no that I came to do my own work." Like Nancy Johnson, the large number of freedpeople who insisted on working "so many days for the planter, & so many for themselves" made a crucial distinction between wage labor that benefited an employer and subsistence activities that benefited themselves.[34]

When planters made a habit of cutting off or reducing food supplies to their workers during the slack season, they virtually assured that family members of all ages would divert their efforts from plantation maintenance and concentrate on their own vegetable gardens instead. In May, "when vegetables are growing in profusion wherever they have been planted," blacks found themselves distracted from keeping the grass out of the "general crops." A Virginia Bureau official reported from Amelia and Powhatan counties in January of 1867 that "as a general thing," black employees had "the privilege of raising one or two Hogs and a few chickens on the premises, and having a garden spot and *truck patch* (as they call it) furnished them." On the other hand, some Virginia planters, such as the ones near Lynchburg, forbade their workers to keep gardens.[35]

Tending a garden was not the only means by which black family members sought to keep themselves fed during these turbulent times. Although some freedpeople spirited rice from baskets and cotton from bins (to be disposed of on local black markets), most stalked livestock or raided smokehouses to stave off starvation. Indeed, blacks often perceived their ill-gotten gain as "a supposed right" not only in response to a system that exploited their labor in a most calculated way, but also in response to individual planters who reneged on their agreement, expressed or implied, to furnish freed families throughout the year. When Eutaw, Alabama, planters curtailed advances to their workers, "Shoats and Poultry seem to be mainly in quest and they are disappearing beyond precedent. . . . [Blacks must] Supply their families as best they can, this compels them to divide their Scanty rations with their families or resort to Stealing as the only alternative." In September of 1865 a Mississippi Bureau agent detected a direct relation between the labor disruption of the slack season and the number of thefts in an area, a complaint echoed by a South Carolina official exactly two years later. Stealing defined a "moral economy" practiced by freedpeople "claiming the privilege of living independently in the community."[36]

Predictably, employers complained bitterly about the efforts of blacks to provide for themselves; the authorities in Marksville, Louisiana, went so far as to arrest a black woman and three of her kinfolk for venturing "into a field and picking from the ground a few walnuts." The privileges or "customary rights" accorded some antebellum slaves evolved into prerogatives that freedpeople jealously guarded at their own peril. Women took time from the fields to sew for their friends and families, to dry fruit, and tend pigs and chickens. Husbands and sons made furniture and baskets to use at home or sell in the marketplace; chopped wood, always in demand by riverboats and mills; and trapped animals and fished in order to supplement the household's diet. As a matter of law, foraging permitted by slaveowners became unacceptable to postwar employers. Under South Carolina's Black Codes, for example, blacks who hunted and fished could be prosecuted as trespassers or vagrants. During the 1860s and 1870s throughout the Black Belt, planters pressed for new legislation that would restrict access of blacks (and landless whites) to forests and streams and thus curtail opportunities for foodstuff self-sufficiency.[37]

Under such conditions, the guns owned by freedmen served as a potent symbol of the new order. To husbands and sons who shouldered rifles en route to the fields—to furnish the family larder with game—firearms represented an impulse for autonomy and self-protection; but to whites they posed the threat of bloody insurrection. States, local authorities, and individual planters imposed criminal penalties on armed black men who ventured more than half a mile off a plantation; levied prohibitive taxes on guns and hunting dogs; required of a freedman the written consent of his employer, or a probate judge, to carry firearms; and in some cases outlawed weapon possession among blacks altogether. The result was additional hardship for families with a "big bunch of chillun cryin' for bread."[38]

If freedpeople pressed employers for formal recognition of the "customary rights" they had won as slaves, they also eschewed the most obnoxious features of plantation work now that they were no longer slaves. However, they risked eviction from their homes in the process.

Reporting from Demopolis, Alabama, in October 1868, a Bureau agent noted, "Men who are free will not clear land under the broiling sun of midsummer, while plantation work is slack, as was the case in times of slavery. . . ." As the need for plantation labor during the off-season increased during the early years of Reconstruction—needs provoked in some areas of the South by flooding and in others by the devastation caused by years of wartime neglect—the man-hours provided by black workers declined dramatically. As long as share wage earners failed to comply with the slack-season demands of their employers, late summer and early fall produced a chorus of complaints from blacks all over the rural South that they had been unfairly discharged. Bureau agents testified to the recurrent nature of the problem. In September 1865 planters near Tuskegee, Alabama, "are willing to break their contract, and turn off their hired hands, now that the summer's work is done, and the *crop* made." In Hillsboro, North Carolina, a Bureau official's report for the month of July 1868 included the observation, "a disposition to drive off the Freedmen, on frivolous pretexts, from the Plantations where they have been working is, I regret to say daily becoming more manifest on the part of many whites."[39]

More generally, the seasonal decline in labor demand encouraged planters to dispense with workers whom they considered politically offensive or economically burdensome. A Bureau report from Hamburg, Arkansas, for July through September 1866 revealed that planters were "driving off" workers who had served in the war as Union soldiers. In the vicinity of Elizabeth City, North Carolina, employers took advantage of the slack season to send on their way former soldiers as well as less productive widows and children. Drought, floods, and an invasion of army worms, all natural disasters that severely damaged crops ripe for harvest, could prompt whites to discharge workers "on the slightest provocation . . . on the pretended ground of idleness, insolence, or something fully as trivial." One Bureau agent in Alabama likened the planters' tactics to "terrorism," now that the "severe labor in the crop is over and pretexts are evidently sought upon which to get rid of the laborers."[40]

For many freedpeople, more than lost share wages were at stake when they faced forcible ejection from their homes, no matter how temporary. A Bureau agent in Jefferson County, Mississippi, acknowledged that the large numbers of blacks in his district who were "driven from their homes for one trivial or fancied offense" in September 1865 mourned not only their pay for a year's labor (their promised share of the crop) but also the opportunity "to reap the benefits of their own industry in raising for themselves small crops of corn, potatoes, peas, etc."

Workers who lived near the Mississippi River collected the moss that hung "in long festoons" from live oak trees, processed it, and then took it to market in New Orleans; they also sold vegetables, dairy products, and pigs to the peddlers who plied the Mississippi. If hounded off the plantation, these freedpeople lost a means of livelihood. Additionally, employers routinely confiscated the "humble wardrobe or stock of housekeeping articles" of workers forced to flee.[41]

Planters who offered daily or weekly (instead of deferred, end-of-year) cash wages found themselves at a competitive advantage in attracting new workers—even blacks under contract nearby—during the slack season. For these employers, an early cotton crop was a special blessing, yielding a bountiful supply of pickers from far and wide. Near Jacksonport, Arkansas, freedpeople disregarded agreements with their employers during the summer doldrums "because at this season of the year cotton opening sufficiently to pick they can obtain better wages at one dollar a day and board (that being the wages offered to cotton pickers) than they derive from their contracts." In this case, the original employer presumably would have to offer at least the same, but perhaps higher, wages to lure back his workers. Some planters anticipated these problems and, on the first of January, took on more workers than they would need for picking, under the assumption that they would lose a portion of their work force one way or the other in the first nine months of the year. The unpredictability of labor in the critical harvest season continued to plague planters after the war; some cotton regions (such as the bottomlands of Georgia) suffered from a chronic shortage of workers, while others had to compete with extractive industries for hands.[42]

Local economies and regional variations in labor supply shaped the opportunies of freedpeople to find off-plantation wage work during the slack season. A high demand for laborers in a particular region produced black "masters of the situation" on the one hand, even as it impelled cotton planters to desperate measures to hold onto their workers. Jefferson County, Mississippi, employers who mistreated or prematurely discharged their workers ran the risk of filling them "with such a distrust for the white man that they prefer any situation, any employment, to returning to, and giving faithful hard labor on plantations, where such labor must be secured in order to insure any degree of success." In certain areas, the availability of alternative kinds of work served to discourage blacks from making or adhering to contracts altogether; "a negro won't plough at ten dollars per month, where he can get twenty on a railroad. . . . there is a strong tendency to seek other employment in preference to the more laborious task of cotton planting. . . . [the] most tedious of all crops." At times freedpeople found that a local labor shortage meant they could force planters to raise share wages and offer more favorable working conditions. Reported instances of physical violence against individual laborers declined every year in December and January, as planters vied with one another to attract a labor force large enough to plant, and eventually harvest, a good crop.[43]

Faced with a regular crisis every autumn peak season, planters responded in one of two ways, or a combination of the two. The first response relied on the willingness of persons not under contract but resident on the plantation—mostly women and children—to go to the fields at this time of year. A second, more expensive, option involved attracting workers from the neighborhood or luring errant ones home by paying cash to pickers. Black workers of both sexes and all ages from nearby towns had the advantage of not requiring lodging, although there were numerous men from all over, especially the young and unattached, available for temporary work.[44] These factors help to account for the origins of the system of family sharecropping, which provided planters with extra workers during busy times of the year but without the added cost of hiring and maintaining wage workers.

Freedpeople resented the work-gang system of labor organization prevalent on plantations after the war; it smacked of slavery. Under sharecropping, the family (either nuclear or extended) constituted the unit of agricultural production. It was a flexible unit, with the number of members deployed in the fields expanding during the peak seasons of planting, chopping, and picking, and contracting during the late-summer slack season. The prevalent "fifty-fifty" arrangement divided proceeds of the crop sale evenly between family and landlord; then the landlord claimed payment for and interest on furnishings supplied through the year. The transition from (individual) share wages to (family) sharecropping occurred unevenly, with some employers preferring various combinations of kin-based "squads" of workers, renters, tenants, croppers, and wage hands. Still, contemporaries noted that sharecropping lessened the planters' anxieties and reduced their costs around harvesttime and simultaneously eased the vulnerability of black women and children dependent on the food and furnishings earned by a family's breadwinners. With an entire household, rather than specific individuals, now under contract, children became less of an economic liability and more of an asset to their parents. Sharecropping also helped large planters to compete against small family farms; under gang labor, employers who needed twenty field hands had to support twenty-five or thirty additional blacks "in idleness [that is, as nonwage laborers] as the freedmen will not permit their wives and children to work in the field."[45]

The sharecropping system and, indeed, kin-based tenancies of any kind were the product of seemingly contradictory forces. On the one hand, families sought to stay together and translate affective ties into a viable basis of economic production; this impulse placed a high priority on the cohabitation of kin, either within nuclear households or within kin clusters scattered throughout the countryside. On the other hand, seasonal variations in the demand for labor on the cotton plantation encouraged some family members to depart, on either a regular or a sporadic basis, to make up in personal initiative what employers had denied to the household as a collective over the course of the year. More often than not, it was the fathers and older sons who went out from these households, a reflection of the gender-based structure of the rural nonagricultural workforce and of the fact that men in general had experienced greater labor mobility as slaves and as wartime workers. Behind the superficial simplicity of the annual labor contract lay an intense power struggle between planter and field hand, a struggle that went to the heart of power relations in the rural South, and one that could not be contained in the course of any one calendar year.

CASH, KIN, AND BLACK
LABOR MOBILITY AFTER THE WAR

Their hopes for economic autonomy thwarted, black people chose to minimize reliance on individual planters by combining farm work with nonagricultural wage work. Postbellum black households organized themselves in ways that conformed to the stereotype of neither "isolated" sharecropping family members nor purely economic actors, "rational" individuals who sought only to maximize their earning potential. In the rural South nonagricultural wage work was inherently unstable and temporary, affording few possibilities for long-range advancement. Forced to sell their services within an economy characterized by high labor supply and low wages, black day laborers existed under a new set of compulsions that surpassed slavery but fell short of freedom.[46]

Whatever stability or permanence freedmen and women did achieve in their lives came from their kin relations rather than from a sense of rootedness to a particular piece of land or commitment to wage earning as an end in itself. (Sea Island blacks, with their unusually high rates of landownership and their "almost religious attachment . . . to their homes," were the exception that proved the rule.[47]) Consequently, when deciding whether to relocate at the end of a year, families considered the proximity and welfare of kin, including prospects for their children's education, affective ties were at the center of those decisions. The resourcefulness of people in taking care of themselves (whether through foraging or making money) reminds us that they demonstrated a form of economic "ambition" equal to the times.

The desire of Southern blacks for wages—for proof of their free-labor status—manifested itself during the war, when fugitives fled to Union army camps and sought out work as domestic servants and military laborers. Cash could afford a relative kind of freedom that deferred payment could not. In the cities odd jobs yielded only a precarious existence, one more easily endured by single men and women than by household heads who needed steady employment. These urban in-migrants encountered the opprobrium of Bureau agents and planters alike; although "the irregular employment and small, bartering ways of the city and village" might bring a little cash, at the same time these opportunities appealed most to those persons least suited for a life of "responsibility" and hard work, as defined by Northerners in authority: "They [wage earners] are unruly, insolent, and disobedient, and will not 'stick'" (that is, remain at a job for any length of time). However, most black people, like the Morganton, North Carolina, railroad hands who complained that their employers had broken agreements with them, and the freedman Coleman of Sherman, Texas, who, along with his sons, made six thousand rails for a white employer but never received the horse due them in return, had few illusions about wage work as an inherently less exploitative labor system compared to share wages or sharecropping.[48]

Wartime mobilization placed severe strains on black family life, but so too did the postwar economy, which often forced black parents and children to make a living by working apart from each other. In contrast to the planters' ideal of all members of a black household toiling in the fields together, side by side, it was not unusual to see a freed father head for town with a load of firewood to sell, while "his little cotton farm was rapidly going to grass . . . His wife was housekeeping and his four children had gone fishing." Responding to a federal interviewer in the late 1930s, Mary Anne Gibson pictured her mother sitting at the door of a brush arbor in the wilderness northwest of Austin, armed with an ax and on the lookout for Indians, while her father went to the city to sell charcoal. In some instances a father might take along one of the children and leave home for an extended period of time, as did the Virginia black man accompanied by a teenage son on his journey to Danville to sell tobacco. At other times the woman of the house might have to let her family fend for themselves while she went out to peddle apple cider or "a right good snack," consisting of "corn-bread with the leg of a fowl" or "tied together into a compact package a piece of bread, three fried eggs, and a slice of ham." Depending on the location of markets (a nearby rail station or distant city) and the perishability of goods offered for sale (brass ornaments and beads as opposed to fried pies), these trips might last for a day or for several weeks; in any case such separations made it difficult for freedpeople to work a piece of land together as families.[49]

Jobs in the rural nonagricultural sector followed seasonal rhythms and offered daily wages, making them attractive sources of alternative employment for plantation laborers. Some of these jobs, such as work in sawmills and on railroads and waterways, were accessible to rural populations in many areas of the South, while others, especially in extractive industries such as turpentine and phosphate, characterized unique regional economies that were well developed even before the South's modest industrial revolution began in the mid-1870s. Refugees from the cotton slack season could find jobs clearing war debris; working on docks; or hawking home crafts, baked goods, and fresh produce. Some rural folk took up temporary residence in or near a town, while others made the trek in on a regular basis. Aaron Nunn's father produced at home and then sold split-cottonwood shuck mattresses, charcoal, and ladies' sewing baskets in the public square of nearby Brenham, Texas, during the late 1860s. At times whole families migrated to cities for short periods of time. In December 1865 the Freedmen's Bureau provided free transportation to Charleston for almost four hundred Orangeburg blacks, so that they could seek work after the cotton harvest and before the New Year's negotiations. Likewise, the seasonality of certain forms of urban employment, including the tobacco industry, affected the decisions of rural households that sought to divide their energies between field work and the city.[50]

Railroads and water transportation offered a variety of jobs, all of which paid cash wages. Local railroad booms could even affect compensation provided by planters. For example, in Virginia during the late 1860s, the relatively high pay for railhands, $1.75 to $2.00 per day, drained the countryside of farm laborers and bolstered the bargaining position of those who remained at work in the fields. Black men hauled wood and laid railroad ties as the South's transportation system was repaired and expanded after the war. Some men rode the rails and fed wood to engines, while others could be seen, according to disapproving whites, forever "lounging about the railroad stations, who are willing to work 'by the day,' but are not desirous of contracting by the season," waiting for the next load of passengers who might want to buy meat pies or pay someone to carry their baggage. Similarly, black men found work as cooks and servants aboard boats that plied the Mississippi River and hundreds of inland waterways, and they waited hopefully at docks for cargoes to unload and travelers to serve. Edward King, who visited the South in the early 1870s, described a night of feverish activity during which forty black men loaded a Mississippi River steamboat with sixty cords of wood in two-and-a-half hours.[51]

Employers at times found themselves squeezed between antebellum precedents and a new but unformed social order. Near Georgetown, South Carolina, a sawmill proprietor whose enterprise antedated the war offered $25.00 per month, plus rations, to his black workers. Two of them insisted on taking an hour off in the morning for breakfast and an hour for noon at dinner. In response to a Bureau agent's admonition (in the fall of 1865) that Northern workers routinely toiled without a morning break, the freedmen replied, "We want to work just as we have always worked," referring to the hours demanded of them as slaves. On the other hand, a Northern man trying to run a mill "a few miles out of town" near Tuscaloosa, Alabama, met with resistance not from his workers but from local whites. Apparently they resented this Yankee interloper, with his offers of gainful employment to local blacks. The employer was ordered to fire his workers if he did not want poor whites in the area to take matters into their own hands and "clean them out." In another instance, work that slaveowners had grudgingly tolerated when performed by their bondsmen now became a source of friction between freedpeople and their employers; such was the case among blacks in the Chesapeake Bay region who preferred to tong for oysters (to eat and sell) in the winter, forcing white farmers in the area to "go abroad for laborers" until the end of the season (around the first of April).[52]

The work history of John Belcher, born in 1849 in Valdosta, Georgia, illustrates how black men could shape their job priorities according to their roles as family members. After freedom, he remained with his parents and siblings as they loaded their belongings in a two-wheel cart pulled by "a old mule that wuz crippled and no count" and left the home of their former master. A new employer forced them to secure a pass from him before leaving their own house at night or going to church on Sunday ("dey 'specked the niggars to be runnin away"). Eventually Belcher left his parents' household and went to work for a lumber company in Waynesboro, Mississippi, where he toiled "from sun up to sun down" cutting fifty cross-ties a day. He and other men lived in tents near the sawmill, reflecting the nomadic nature of the enterprise. While working for this company Belcher also helped to dig a narrow trench fifty miles long used to transport lumber to Mobile, Alabama. He next found a job in a turpentine factory near Waynesboro. By this time the young man had a family and divided his time between gainful employment and fishing; this latter activity enabled him to put food on the table, make some money, and supply his neighbors once in a while as well.[53]

The freed family represented a blend of individual initiative and kin cooperation that extended outside the boundaries of nuclear cohabitation. A Bureau agent in Greenville, South Carolina, noted the opposition of black men to "binding out" their children, and he therefore believed these fathers "have an ambition to live in a patriarchal manner by getting as many of the children of their kinsmen around them as possible; evidently with the intention of being supported by their labour." In fact, the determination of freed families to reconstitute themselves after the war testified to the strong affective ties that bound them together, ties that survived slavery. The strenuous efforts of black men and women alike to recover long-lost kin, rescue children from white-initiated apprenticeships, and divide "their little with their more needy brethren" ultimately served as ligaments of a freed black community. At the local level that community consisted of overlapping kin clusters which helped determine patterns of end-of-year mobility. A planter in Barbour County, Alabama, wrote of the drive for cooperative self-sufficiency among the freedpeople, one of the greatest threats to white hegemony in the postwar period: "The freedman is satisfied so he can *set up for himself,* as his wants are 'few and far between,' and those wants he can supply himself and his half dozen other nonproducers with, if they are within five miles of his hut—with no conscience as to right of property." "Nonproducers"— that is, blacks of all ages who foraged, hunted, fished, gardened, and stole—offered tangible contributions to the family welfare.[54]

When freed families moved on at the end of the year, they tended to stay within the same county. Only rarely did they venture long distances or into a crop economy different from their own. Antebellum kin ties produced postwar "clannishness," solidified by patterns of local migratory movements. The powerful effect of of kin relations on working and living arrangements among blacks suggested that feelings of mutual obligation and dependence, as much or more so than just economic motives, determined whether a family wanted to stay on a plantation or leave, and how far family members were willing to travel in December or January.[55]

Determined to escape from a world of enforced ignorance, freedpeople blended a "modern" commitment to formal education with "traditional" concerns for kin and place. Planters tried to turn these priorities to their own advantage when they established schools on their land both to attract new workers and to prevent high turnover rates; no doubt whites had in mind the Louisiana black man who told a Northern reporter, "That was one of his reasons for wanting to move away, so he could put the children [his wife's grandchildren] to school." These were the "plantation schools" mentioned in contemporary accounts during Reconstruction. The old adage that a little learning would unsuit blacks for agricultural labor was challenged by at least some planters who "found that the freedmen worked better when their children had the advantages of education, and were very glad to have schools established." (Whether the young people's appreciation for schooling would eventually translate into loyalty to a particular white landowner was a different issue.) Rare indeed was the Arkansas planter who put his daughter to work teaching a school for freed children; but he did exist, and he represented no more a curiosity than the Texas employers who asked a Bureau agent to find them teachers—employers "who are learning that whatever contents and dignifies their labor, is a reciprocal benefit to themselves." Of course, plantation schools had no life apart from the needs of the crop; some whites made it a condition of employment that teachers toil in the fields at peak season, or allowed schools to operate only during the winter and late-summer months. Most planters agreed, however, that schools were too high a price to pay for a reliable work force, especially since "reliability" was measured not in terms of contentment but rather subordination.[56]

Evidence that black men and women had some leverage in negotiating with employers—through the threat of seeking work off the plantation during the calendar year or moving elsewhere for schooling—should not be construed as evidence of a free labor market in the postbellum South. Indeed, within most regions and locales, unfair labor practices prevailed so generally that few white landowners had an economic incentive to break with community norms; as one Alabama Freedmen's Bureau official described the situation after reckoning time, "[even the most vicious] Employers think that there will be plenty of freedmen in the same condition as they have left their own and that in the general confusion that will then exist" these employers will find an abundance of poor souls "willing to try the experiment again." In essence, workers who were evicted or who refused to contract with an employer would once again be at the mercy of individual employers who abided by a general, universal standard of plantation management. From Princess Anne County, Virginia, came the report in January 1867 that despite a great demand for workers, whites refused "to encourage and protect their labor," instead doing "everything to discourage them[;] they employ them in a great many instances and turn them off without compensation for their services, then lodge them in jail for the slightest offense." This example suggests that the more planters depended on a limited source of black labor, the more havoc they wrought in the lives of their employees. Desperation begat not concessions but rage and more forcible methods of worker control.[57]

Members of the Monroe County (Alabama) Agricultural Association and the Duck Creek (Mississippi) Planters Association made no secret of their efforts to set wages at low levels and to enforce an oppressive labor code on freedpeople. Yet in certain communities, informal collusion among planters, enforced by vigilante attacks on those who offered blacks more favorable prospects, served the cause of white hegemony just as well as either an oversupply of labor or formal agreements among landowners; standardized contracts produced "localized labor" that was for all intents and purposes bound to stay within a constricted geographical area. The Bureau's assumption that black workers would avoid cheaters, liars, and gun toters held no relevance in a county where all planters adhered to such behavior as a matter of principle, and politics. A manager in the Natchez District of Mississippi observed that the blacks stayed on the plantation they had worked as slaves "partly to be at home and principally because they don't trust our neighbors." Such were the tangible benefits of an exploitative labor ideology held in common by Southern planters.[58]

In 1865, when three-and-a-half-million American slaves won their freedom, they found no willing allies among other laboring groups in the cities or on the countryside. The racial prejudice that pervaded all segments of white society during this period offers only a partial explanation for the estrangement between Southern black people and other men and women beholden to people of privilege for use of the machines and land that produced their livelihood. In fact, white workers and farmers of modest means might have divined in the plight of the former slaves the seeds of their own uncertain future, and so disdained embracing blacks as fellow laborers with, if not a common history, then a common destiny. The Northern white "working classes," clinging to the shreds of a free-labor ideology rendered increasingly obsolete by the casualization

43

of labor, recoiled from recognizing that they were in the process of being reduced to "wage slavery"; some of their leaders argued that such was their fate, already sealed by the new industrial order. On the plains and prairies of the Midwest, aided and abetted by new forms of agricultural technology, family farmers prided themselves on their independence of spirit and seemed to have little in common with Southern blacks, with their reliance on primitive plows and hoes; and yet these whites all too soon found themselves ensnared by the trappings of commercial pro-duction that resulted in their subjection to creditors and railroads. And finally, in the years after the Civil War, Southern white yeoman farmers, now caught up in a staple-crop market economy, came to understand that their antebellum world of republican self-sufficiency had disap-peared forever. An emerging rural white proletariat, accustomed to defining the social landscape in stark black-and-white terms, readily believed that the "elevation of the blacks" necessitated their own "degra-dation." Ironically, then, in their efforts to distance themselves from the fate of the Southern freedpeople, white laborers throughout the country inadvertently affirmed the common elements that bound all of them, North and South, black and white, together.[59]

For Southern white plain folk struggling to make a living for their own families, those common elements would soon become readily apparent, though few seemed willing to discuss the situation in public. Before the Civil War, freedom had been the great equalizer, the great leveler (or rather, great bolsterer) among Southern whites; all whites occupied a higher legal status than all blacks. After the dismantling of the legal machinery of slavery, international market forces—combined with the peculiar racial ideology of white elites—rushed into the breach to create a new system of class relations in the rural South. Until 1865 poor whites were as free as their social superiors, but after emancipation they became as vulnerable as the former slaves to the worldwide demand for cotton—a demand that had no respect for skin color or former condition of servitude or freedom. And so postwar planters and ideologues quickly set about the task of domesticating another group of people who sought freedom from landlords and labor contracts—the poor whites whom they had once succored as political allies, and now contemplated subordinating to the needs of a resurrected, and grasping, King Cotton. The ensuing intersec-tion of the histories of poor whites and former slaves would represent an assault on the "Southern way of life" no less traumatic than bloodshed and defeat on the battlefield.

2

The Pride of Race and Its Limits: White Field Workers

In January 1868 a South Carolina planter named John D. Williams summoned his employees for the coming year and set before them a contract stipulating work arrangements. To the people who signed it, the contract granted one-third of the crop of cotton as well as corn, oats, wheat, and sweet potatoes, and outlined in great detail the routine of White Plains Plantation, which was located in the state's Lower Piedmont county of Laurens. Laborers were expected to maintain and repair all fences on White Plains, and their employer intended "at all times to command theire Services until Jan 1st, 1869." Williams's share wage earners would labor under compulsions familiar to most freedpeople throughout the South; for each day's absence they forfeited a dollar, and they were forbidden to keep firearms or indulge in alcohol. Workers also faced dismissal "for all wilful Disobedience of any lawful orders from me or my Agent[—] drunkenness moral or legal misconduct want of respects or civility to me or my Agent or to my Family or any elce," a warning sufficiently broad to cover any form of speech or behavior that Williams and members of his household might conceivably find objectionable. In its format and provisions, this contract was unremarkable, save for one fact: Williams appended to the main document (signed by three men and two women) another statement that read, in its entirety:

> We the white labores now employed by John D. Williams on his white plains plantation have lisened and heard read the foregoing Contract on this Sheet of paper assign equal for the black laborers employed by him on said place and we are perfectly Satisfied with it and heare by bind our selves to abide & be Governed & controwed by it.

The names of seven white men, including one George Washington Pollard, follow.[1]

This "separate but equal" contractual arrangement evokes an image of two groups of workers standing apart from each other and, while listening to the same words, comprehending two different political and historical realities. Based on their surnames, the five black workers represented at most three kin groups (Nathan, Chappal, and Williams), as did the seven whites (Wyatt, Hughes, Pollard). All of the freedpeople and two of the whites made their mark on the contract. Therefore we might speculate about similarities in the strength of kin ties and in literacy rates between members of the two groups. Indeed, this contract raises more questions than the historical record can easily answer, questions concerning the past and present circumstances of a man like George Washington Pollard, now at least implicity agreeing to terms demanded by white employers of former slaves. John D. Williams might have enforced contract provisions differently for black and white workers and might have taken pains to keep them apart in the field so that they would never toil side by side. Certainly the freedpeople were accustomed to restrictions on their movement as stated in the contract, but it is doubtful that Pollard and his co-workers had previously capitulated to this kind of regimen, whether they had been yeoman farmers, tenants, or field laborers before the war.

The postwar, evolving system of class relations among Southern whites grew out of patterns of antebellum politics, wartime military mobilization, and the South's human geography. Diehard Confederates understood the political hazards of exploiting the labor of white men who had sacrificed so much for, and had so little to gain from, the secessionists' cause. Nevertheless, the twin evils of wartime dissent and military desertion paled in comparison to the threat to Southern society posed by the Yankee victory and the occupation of Union forces. Even Southern white men with qualms about the Confederacy could rally around the bloodstained banner of white supremacy after Appomattox. If the prewar consensus held out the hope that all white men could one day be slaveowners, then the postwar view promised native whites that their declining status would never approach the lowly condition of freed-people.[2] In the Laurens District of South Carolina, for example, Democratic vigilante groups (the Ku Klux Klan in 1870–71, "rifle clubs" in 1877–78) terrorized Republicans of both races and suppressed a fledgling biracial political movement based on the shared grievances of freedpeople and poor whites against their landed betters. George Washington Pollard and the freedman Mack Williams signed the same labor contract in 1868, but by the 1870s, at least, they probably pledged allegiance to radically opposed political parties.[3]

The Civil War claimed the lives of 260,000 Confederate soldiers, and the ensuing dislocation of Southern society—devastation wrought by famine, the loss of fathers and sons, the migration of refugees and starv-ing families—disrupted the social networks that had knit together ante-bellum communities. In some areas neighborly connections between rich and poor whites changed to employer-employee relations after the war; in other areas planters encountered poor whites for the first time. A Piedmont landowner such as John D. Williams, wealthy before and after the war, might now pay wages to whites who had always lived nearby, men and women whom he knew previously as small farmers and fellow church congregants.[4] On the other hand, when a Black Belt landowner initiated contract negotiations with a group of white employees in 1865, he probably could not fall back on social expectations established before 1861; if he did not recognize the faces of these men and their families, they, like the freedpeople, became workers to be exploited rather than kin or community members to be patronized according to Old South tradition.

Poor-white native-born laborers violated the cultural and political sensibilities dictated by a caste-bound society. Indeed, as more and more whites faced a future of debt and dependency, Southern elites seemed to conspire among themselves, within the public realm at least, to ignore—or conceal—that fact. As a result, white tenants and sharecroppers were conspicuous in their absence from the postbellum debate on the Southern "labor question." In contrast to this form of self-censorship, white politicians, journalists, and public-spirited planters expended much time and energy concocting schemes to import foreign immigrants. Presumably the newcomers would share with the former slaves a capacity for hard work, but without clamoring for "equality," political, social, or otherwise. But in fact, newspaper editorials and political pronouncements on this subject have about them an air of unreality; despite all the furious sound about the need for immigrant labor, most efforts yielded little in terms of long-range gains, and native-born white women and men provided the South with an ever-increasing proportion of agricultural labor. Within a decade of the war's end, white hands picked fully two-fifths of the South's cotton crop; in Texas and Arkansas the figure was about three-fifths. In contrast, before the war, slaves had produced about nine out of ten bales.[5]

Few white political leaders chose to speculate openly about the relative cost of black and white labor, calculated in both financial and political terms, and about the integrity of white family life now that white women and children were reduced to steady, backbreaking toil in the fields. In the long run these issues would be resolved not by Southern ideologues or Northern officials but by ordinary white households and by the employers who sought to turn the hardship of these households to their own advantage.

THE POOR-WHITE LABOR QUESTION

Despite the energetic debate over the postwar "labor question" in Southern newspapers, legislative halls, and county courthouses, neither planters nor politicians evinced much interest in assigning to poor whites a formally acknowledged role as agricultural workers. In the summer of 1867 a writer for *Debow's Review* suggested "measures of relief" to combat the baneful consequences of a diminished black labor force caused by the urban in-migration of freedpeople; the withdrawal of black women from the fields; and "the fearful effects, both moral and physical, of the license which, in their ignorance [blacks] look upon as their liberty." The writer advocated the importation of foreign workers as well as workers from the Northern states and the use of "Improved Labor-Saving Implements and Machinery." But he devoted no attention at all to the possibility that native white labor might be used (and indeed, was being used) on the South's great staple-crop plantations.[6]

Regardless of the shape of their individual longings for the past, propertied Southerners could not reconcile the emergence of a large class of white agricultural labor with their vision of the future. A few gave lip service to "dignity of labor" sentiments long held by the hated Yankees, and after the war Southern periodicals published their share of poems and articles dedicated to the novel proposition that hard work was more a duty than a disgrace. In 1867 a former Confederate general from South Carolina, Daniel H. Hill, composed an essay entitled "Work," in which he called upon the Southern white man to "rebuke 'womanish effeminancy'" and embrace toil, so that he might free "Himself from sluggish sloth and ease." Yet this idea never found wide favor among elites, though it might have served as a calculated means of exhorting white sharecroppers to double their efforts to further enrich their employers. When postbellum Southern writers praised the virtues of farm life, they did so with planters and yeomen in mind; when they extolled the productive abilities of whites of the "lower classes," they did so with cotton mill workers in mind. These views anticipated a new society, one in which technological advances reduced some of the "drudgery" associated with crop cultivation, and mill operations provided gainful employment for poor whites of both sexes and all ages.[7]

For their part, Freedmen's Bureau agents and other Northerners remained mired in antebellum stereotypes that portrayed nonelite whites as vagabonds and miscreants. Looking back on his days as a Freedmen's Bureau agent in Greenville, South Carolina, John DeForest never tired of remarking on the lack of "industry and forethought" among the white people under his charge; "what they got by begging, they spent for clothing, provisions, and tobacco, and then lay down in their 'rotten laziness' until routed out of it by hunger. No exertion was welcome to them except that of gossiping from cabin to cabin, or visiting some village to stare at the shops and learn the news." DeForest considered these particular men and women—the "low down people" prone to "rovin' round"—even more contemptible than freedpeople, but he maintained an anthropologist's sense of detachment in searching for the roots of their deviant behavior: "The Celtic race seems to possess a special alacrity at sinking; and Irish families left on the track of Southern railroads became vagrant poor-whites in a single generation."[8]

Northerners believed that, whatever their other failings, freedpeople had a history of hard field labor, and their comings and goings, though as frequent as they were lamentable, could be monitored and to some extent controlled by law enforcement officials. Writing from Atlanta in February of 1868, Colonel C. C. Sibley of the Bureau noted coolly, "With the whites destitution prevails in a much greater degree [than among blacks]; though there is as yet little severe suffering, and it is deemed best for the present to leave them dependent upon the charities of their neighbors, and the civil authorities, as nothing but extreme want and suffering will force many of them to labor. . . ." The same charges were leveled against the mass of Southern whites who "loved the wild free life of the hunter and detested the plow," a vague amalgamation of squatters, herders, and drifters. These folk included "the dull, unlettered, hopeless English farm laborer grown wild, indolent, and nomadic on new land and under the discouraging competition of slavery," and the ubiquitous migrant drawn irresistibly to train stations so that he might "lounge around" them.[9]

In fact, Bureau agents, clustered in towns, rarely had the opportunity to witness firsthand the community life and culture of plain white folk. Noted one agent near Gainestown, Alabama, in October 1866: "Destitute persons are not here to be found about towns, for there are really no towns in the county, nor are they to be met with on the public roads[;] deep in the pine solitudes the poor white Vanishes and hides his wretchedness." Too often when Northerners did encounter such people, they focused on outward evidence of degradation, or curious personal habits; hence, in contrast to the rich descriptions of black women as wives and workers contained in the Freedmen's Bureau records, we have from Northern journalists and foreign visitors a static portrait of poor white women, one which inevitably and exclusively highlights their love of pipe smoking, snuff dipping, and expectorating.[10]

When planters called for the importation of workers to compensate for the "roving" freedpeople in any particular area, they rarely suggested recruiting either black or poor-white workers from other regions of the South; instead, they focused their efforts on ambitious but short-lived schemes to exploit foreign laborers, usually single men. In certain areas of the South, the exigencies of war had led to a recent and unfortunate reliance on immigrant laborers. For example, toward the end of the conflict J. W. Lapsley, a Confederate railroad director based in Selma, reported on the progress of rail construction in the beleaguered Lower South. Lapsley admitted that the production of precious pig iron was endangered by a critical lack of both menial and skilled labor. White workers in the iron mills hailed from Europe, or from Europe via New England, and they composed an extremely unstable, unpredictable work force: "These men do not feel identified in any great degree with the South, and are not imbued with sentiments and feelings calculated to impress them so strongly in favor of our cause, as to induce them to make any great sacrifices of interest or feeling in its behalf." Lapsley feared that it was only a matter of time before large numbers of these men defected to the Northern side ("by avoiding the public routes, and places where our scouts and cavalry are stationed") in order to escape military service and seek even higher pay. Devoid of loyalty to the Confederate cause, free of family encumbrances that would tie them to the South, and suffering from war-induced food shortages, they would "be induced to leave this country" (that is, the Confederate States of America).[11]

Lapsley's difficulties with the Selma ironworkers foreshadowed enthusiastic but ultimately unsuccessful experiments with foreign labor on Southern plantations a few years later. Members of most white ethnic groups resisted the subordination that rural landowners expected of them. Officials of Southern immigration companies heralded the arrival of small groups of sponsored Europeans, including Czechs, Scandinavians, Portuguese, Poles, Germans, Irish, and Italians, during the five or ten years after the war. These people were hailed as the progeny of hardy peasant stock, men who tilled the ground in the tradition of their forefathers and would continue to do so contentedly for Southern landowners. Yet a group of Germans brought over to toil in the Louisiana swamps after the war quickly slipped away from their employers; they had agreed to the arrangement only to take advantage of free passage to America. Thirty Swedes who arrived in Alabama in 1866 also deserted at the first opportunity, declaring "they were not slaves." South Carolina planters soon discovered that their modest colonies of Germans and Italians were "not willing to settle down and live on bacon and corn bread"; they too fled to Southern towns and then (perhaps) up north. The unwillingness of freedpeople to tolerate the hard work necessary for ditching rice fields in the Georgia and South Carolina low country prompted short-lived experiments with Italian and Irish laborers. Likewise, the arduousness of rice cultivation failed to appeal to Portuguese ditchers hired in the mid-1870s on the Corrine Plantation south of New Orleans: "Hoe hands left the field, because they said the task was too large," read a March 1876 entry in one foreman's diary.[12]

If white immigrants failed to satisfy because they were white—and hence filled with expectations (no matter how unrealistic) about the privileges of free white men in America, and at the same time able to escape the legal liabilities black workers faced—then Chinese coolies initially seemed particularly well suited for servile labor (as indicated, perhaps, by the fate of their countrymen worked to death building railroads in the Far West). But attempts to secure Chinese from Cuba and then bind them to long-term contracts (on Louisiana sugar plantations, for example) encountered unanticipated, external problems. International agreements converged with American foreign policy to curb the "coolie trade" in the Western Hemisphere, and Chinese "voluntary emigrants" residing in California proved unresponsive to calls for workers in the steamy sugarcane fields. The tiny numbers imported directly from Cuba to Mississippi and Arkansas produced little cotton but much interest among curiosity seekers.[13]

For the purposes of large Southern landowners, then, the Chinese were inaccessible and the Europeans were too ambitious. What were the characteristics of native poor whites that disqualified them for inclusion in the great labor debates that raged in the postbellum South? Perhaps mindful of the fizzled attempts to recruit foreign laborers over the last few years, one Southern planter issued a sweeping indictment of white agricultural labor: "The attempt to introduce hired white men from any quarter to carry out the exclusive cotton system is, from various causes, preposterous. In the southern climate, with the habits of the people and the wages they can afford to pay, no laborer can be a substitute for the negro."[14] It is clear from these comments that at least some employers continued to hold the time-honored belief that whites could not withstand the heat of a cotton field in midsummer and that their inexperience with a forced pace of labor "unsuited" them for work on large plantations. The scraggly, on-again, off-again crops tended by up-country farmers before the war grew to fruition without intensive cultivation; hence, postbellum planters considered their poorer (white) cousins hopelessly undisciplined and ill trained in comparison to the former slaves; or, to put it another way, landowning whites feared that "crackers" and "clodhoppers" would be either unable or unwilling to submit, day in and day out, to close supervision in the fields.

Nowhere is the delicacy of the whites-for-hire issue so evident as in the studied refusal of Southern elites to call for poor white women to take to the fields as employees. Certainly the antebellum period furnished countless examples of poor white wives, the sun reddening their necks, picking cotton and worming tobacco plants, in the up-country, and at times in the company of slaves. During the war Confederate officials could readily acknowledge that, back on the home front, "indeed it is a common thing to see the women and children industriously engaged on their farms, and . . . the people as a general thing are doing all they can to supply themselves. . . . " Distress on the countryside flowed not from the laziness of soldiers' families but from a fact of farm life—that is, menfolk were necessary to cut wheat and pick cotton if the household was to produce enough to survive. After the war poor whites of both sexes laboring in the fields in remote areas outside the Black Belt excited few comments among outsiders; many households had for generations grown corn and a little cotton, requiring that all family members work outside together for at least part of the year.[15]

In fact, after the war, landed white Southerners' persistent (rhetorical) abhorrence of the idea of white "wage slavery" was disingenuous at best. Although the white poor had coexisted in the same society as slaves for generations without eliciting much interest, in the postbellum period the growth of this class of unfortunates became ominous. If the similarities in the material condition of black and white sharecroppers represented the promise of a new, biracial coalition of the dispossessed, and hence the promise of Reconstruction for American society, those similarities also challenged all that whites—all whites—had held dear throughout Southern history.

CLASS AND LABOR RELATIONS IN THE LATE ANTEBELLUM SOUTH

The Browns, a white family residing in the cotton district of northern Alabama during the mid-1850s, seemed incapable of earning much of anything besides the scorn of their more well-to-do neighbors. The father, John, maintained an aversion to field labor regardless of the wages offered. When approached by one farmer who wanted help "at his harvesting," Brown "said he didn't feel well, and he reckoned he couldn't work." A promise of a dollar and a half a day prompted a more vehement reaction on Brown's part; he "spoke out plainly and said, 'he'd be d—d if he was going to work anyhow." Brown later presented his neighbor with a peace offering of venison, but this act of conciliation hardly raised his status in the community. According to local gossips, John Brown "pretended to plant a corn patch, but he never worked it and didn't make any corn . . . , [living] pretty much on what corn and hogs he could steal, and on game." Once in a while Brown's wife, the mother of "his half-starved little wretches," received some corn for picking cotton nearby. One industrious farmer lamented the fact that local authorities failed to enforce existing legislation "by which [men like John Brown] might be taken up (if it could be proved that they have no 'visible means of support') and made to work to provide for their families"; such "vagabonds" who lived by hunting, stealing, and scavenging scorned the steady work habits of respectable (white) folk. With his dislike of wage work and his efforts to eke out a living apart from cotton planters, John Brown had little to offer potential employers; no landlord could expect to exact much field labor from him. Moreover, since John Brown was a white man, his neighbors lacked the legal leverage (and, presumably, the inclination) to harness the labor of his household to their own interests. Yet other whites in the neighborhood could hardly conceal their disdain for Brown, who let his wife "go in [to the cotton fields] with the niggers and pick."[16]

Convinced of the deleterious effects of the slave system on both blacks and whites, Northern journalist Frederick Law Olmsted was more than happy to highlight John Brown's makeshift existence; but in the process, Olmsted also gave voice to Brown's indigenous critics. These were men who possessed the semblance of a work ethic and felt superior to their neighbor, although they appreciated his attempt to compensate for his contrariness with a voluntary gift of game. After the war these distinctions between groups of whites—the proud, hardwork-ing yeoman on the one hand and the "no-account" hunter and forager on the other—became conflated in the minds of white elites, once it became clear that both groups would resist the enforced field labor demanded by crop-lien merchants and creditors. Moreover, as the most vocal opponents of secession and, later, of Confederate draft and taxation policies, nonslaveowners of all descriptions had proved wor-thy political antagonists of the planter class, a legacy that continued to pose a threat—however briefly—to Southern Democrats immediately after the war.

No matter how effective in combatting the Yankee presence during Reconstruction, exhortations on behalf of white unity could hardly hide the divergent class interests among Southerners, rebellious and other-wise. Even before the war, popular terminology for poor whites indicat-ed that this group, or rather, these groups, were perceived as different from, and inferior to, well-to-do folk: "poor white folksy", "poor white trash," "mean" and "shiftless" whites, "wool hats," "hillbillies," "back-woods farmers", South Carolina "sandhillers," Georgia "clayeaters" and "crackers," Alabama "clodhoppers," and North Carolina "beechers." Some lived in the Black Belt or rice and sugar regions, but most were concentrated outside the staple-crop districts in the up-country, the mountains, the wiregrass region, or the coastal pine barrens, as various derogatory labels indicated. Depending on the locale, as many as 20 to 33 percent of Southern whites in 1860 possessed neither slaves nor land; about one-fifth of all white households owned at least one slave (with 1 percent of that number qualifying as "planter-aristocrats"), and about half of the total white population were yeoman farmers.[17]

During much of the antebellum period, up-country farmers managed to avoid the trappings of a commercial economy so integral to the marketing of staple crops. These yeomen aimed for household self-sufficiency, and their production of more corn than cotton testified to their desire to remain free from credit and consumer relations represented by banks, railroads, and towns. Women in yeoman families engaged in forms of household industry similar to those practiced by housewives in colonial New England; they grew, processed, and preserved food and materials necessary to their families' welfare, and sold or bartered modest surpluses of eggs, butter, and cheese to friends and neighbors. The type and amount of labor required to grow corn and practice household industry was significantly less intensive, and considered less personally degrading, than that associated with large-scale cotton, rice, sugar, and tobacco cultivation. On the other hand, the rude exterior of a yeoman's cabin might at times serve as a façade hiding the feverish activity that went on within its walls, helping to account for travelers' reports that compared the Southern white family farmer to his New England counterpart and found him lacking in thrift and energy.[18]

Not all up-country whites worked their own land. In the Upper Piedmont of Georgia, for example, tenancy reached levels as high as 40 percent among all farm operators in the 1850s, and the region also included poor "hardscrabble farmers" and miners who owned no real property. However, antebellum tenants apparently enjoyed some control over decisions related to crop mix (corn assured a measure of foodstuff self-sufficiency, in contrast to a staple crop such as cotton) as well as the use of farm implements and the labor of individual household members. Accordingly, antebellum tenancy more nearly resembled the postwar system of renting. Moreover, for young men related to landowners, this form of tenure status represented a step on the agricultural ladder that a significant proportion of them could aspire to climb.[19]

In the piney woods region of the Southern coastal plain, white communities remained both physically and culturally isolated from the great cotton plantations. The wiregrass regions of Georgia, Florida, and Alabama were home to a large percentage of small landowners as well as stock farmers and employees of such rural nonagricultural enterprises as sawmills and turpentine camps. In these and other areas of the South, herders lived a more productive existence than the oft-repeated epithets "squatters" and "nomads" would suggest. Though constantly on the move, these families managed to accumulate property, and they were jealous of their open-range privileges that well-to-do landlords sought to curtail with fence laws passed and enforced during the years of Reconstruction.[20]

Some yeomen lived near large planters in the Black Belt, but they could hardly boast of the political and economic independence so prized by small farmers in the up-country, because they planted so much more cotton and less corn. As the price of slaves increased and large plantation owners prospered during the late antebellum period, modest landowners left the Black Belt in droves. For example, between 1850 and 1860, 66 percent of adult white males migrated out of the wealthy plantation county of Dallas, Alabama. Primarily young and single, they either sold what little property they owned to land-hungry neighbors and then sought fresh lands to the west, or hoped to avoid the stigma of wage labor (mandated by an increasing concentration of wealth) in favor of more attractive tenancy arrangements elsewhere. Similarly, the white population in Greene County, Georgia, declined during these years, as poor whites moved to the northern reaches of the state or pushed on to Mississippi or Texas in search of land and opportunity.[21]

Existing on the margins of antebellum Southern society was an amorphous group of white men who had sporadic contact with slaves in the course of making a living. Infrequently, whites and blacks would labor together openly, as when they laid railroad ties through the mountains of North Carolina, but interracial work forces in fields and factories were rare. (Owners of small numbers of slaves—"honest Southern yeomen . . . .the industrious poor whites"—could be seen outside at work with their bondsmen, plowing, picking cotton, or even toiling together in the naval stores industry deep in the forest; but in their closeness men of the two races maintained a master-slave relationship.) Much more subversive to the Southern social order were instances of collusion between slaves and poor whites for the purpose of appropriating livestock and chickens from their owners, distilling liquor, and "fencing" pilfered goods of all kinds, from piping stripped from sugar works to plows and harnesses. In the Delta, boats manned by white "chicken thieves" (a generic term) plied the Mississippi River, picking up booty gathered by slaves and departing at night to sell the ill-gotten gain in New Orleans. Black-white cooperation of this sort, no matter how tentative and opportunistic, convinced well-to-do whites of the inherent shiftlessness of their social inferiors, even as it raised the specter of a more formal, or violent, political alliance between the poor of both races.[22]

For all their devotion to skin color, antebellum Southern elites could not help but identify certain temperamental and cultural characteristics shared by slaves and "no account" white folk. Both groups were landless; hence in a society that measured personal value in terms of property and slaveownership, such whites were deemed "honorless." Blacks as well as poor white "tackeys," preferring a life "half agricultural, half piscatorial," seemed outside the pale of culture and civilization. Illiterate, they clung to superstitious beliefs in ghosts, witches, and spirits; elderly women of both races, gray-haired "crones" all, specialized in "palm-reading, card-cutting or the revelations of coffee-grounds left in the bottom of the cup after the fluid has been drained off." Alone or in each other's wretched company (according to planters, yeomen, and Northern observers), these people loved to indulge in "busthead" or "rot-gut" after a hard day spent avoiding productive labor of any kind. By nature sexually promiscuous, their women mocked the enforced chastity of plantation belles and mistresses and of righteous and devout middle-class wives, or so the landed gentry believed.[23]

Chronicling his own modest origins, one white man in Tennessee later recalled, "The poor class of peopl was al moust slaves them selves . . . had to work and live hard." However, the "ligaments of community" that bound whites of all classes in the antebellum South made racial caste distinctions real, even if material differences between slaves and poor whites were at times muted. Within remote neighborhoods, white families, rich and poor, could share kin loyalties, seasonal household routines mandated by crop growing, standards of social behavior, religious ties as well as, of course, their legal superiority to all blacks, slave or free. Ambitious young white men, together with their destitute elders, often found themselves obligated to large landowners for credit, food, jobs, and loans of slaves. Certainly class relations varied according to regions of the South; the Virginia farmer who had to reckon with white field hands probably felt less sentimental about notions of brotherhood among white men than the Black Belt planter who had no need for white unskilled labor. In addition, religious denominational affiliation, political loyalties, and temperance agitation could divide the individual white communities in a way that class interests could not.[24]

Even before the war, though, planters put yeomen on notice that the spread of commercial market relations would eventually eliminate regional boundaries that separated large-scale cotton producers from households of modest proportions. Although Black Belt slaveowners had no compelling political interest in subordinating the up-country, beginning in the 1850s they sponsored the extension of local improvements and financial institutions into areas where the white residents steadfastly tried to resist such intrusions. As a result, yeomen feared "bondage" to planter-merchants, land speculators, and bankers. The war only intensified this process of economic development and exacerbated these anxieties; the Yankees attracted political heat away from large landowners after 1861, but the conquering army sealed the fate of poorer people, a fate predetermined by the planters themselves in the late antebellum period.[25]

Most scholars view the late antebellum South as an increasingly stratified society; nevertheless, the society remained fluid in significant ways. In the 1850s nonlandowners could still hope to accumulate both property and slaves. Moreover, migration patterns suggest that a certain optimism, if not raw ambition, continued to fuel even segments of the society deemed "lazy." The young white man who abandoned the Alabama Black Belt and moved to Mississippi might not have prospered once he got there, and he might have felt compelled to try his luck in Texas, but at least he experienced the freedom to start over again in a new place. In numerical terms, at least, the large-scale movement of wealthy planters from the eastern seaboard to the Southwest was overshadowed by a parallel migration of plain folk, not only small slaveholders and "men on the make" but also impoverished families, some of them forced to move from land they did not own: "When the lands temporarily occupied by them, finally come into market, the Squatters once more hitch up their little one-horse carts, pile in all their worldly store, and [reach] . . . only beyond the limits of civilization, when they 'squat' as before, raise their little 'craps' of corn and garden truck, shoot bears, deer, and Indians, and vegetate generally like all other nomadic races." The notion of a (south) western safety valve had some basis in fact for nonslaveholders in the East.[26]

WHITE DESERTERS AND "HIRELINGS" DURING THE WAR

The Civil War accelerated the pace of population movement. Among white men, almost all travel produced political or military consequences, no matter how modest. Waves of recruits and conscripts were constantly making their way to army posts and then (for the fortunate ones) back home again. Refugees fled the hostilities in search of safety. Bands of armed men roamed the countryside; some were dissenters who staged guerrilla raids against Confederate army units, while others were highwaymen and thieves ready to prey on hapless individuals and family caravans. Finally, the high rates of desertion from rebel ranks (about one-third were absent without leave at any one time) meant that at a given moment during the war, several thousand men were in the process of abandoning their posts or avoiding capture by their former comrades-in-arms.[27] If, by 1865, ordinary soldiers showed reluctance to shed blood (their own as well as others') to preserve the Confederacy, to elites their actions seemed to indicate more general flaws of character, flaws perceived as personal "unreliability," a sense of individualism run rampant. Ultimately these perceptions would be superimposed on the postwar labor crisis.

The war rubbed raw the lesions of antebellum class conflict—lesions so carefully, but ultimately ineffectually, bandaged during state secession campaigns and conventions, and finally left exposed and bleeding by the plight of poor white conscripts and their families. In contrast, large planters, as the beneficiaries of the twenty-slave law (which exempted overseers and plantation owners from military service) garnered life-saving privileges by virtue of their wealth and standing in the Confederate community. Significantly, wartime expressions of general disaffection and formal Unionist sentiment (for example, in the Alabama hill country and the North Carolina "Quaker Belt") spilled over into postwar support for the Republican party. Thus the link between traitorous elements of 1863 and coalitions of blacks and poor whites in 1867 demonstrated a continuity in political opposition to the planters' interests.[28]

Wartime manpower mobilization policies, through their sheer inconsistency, compressed a number of volatile issues regarding the use of white menial laborers, whether or not they toiled alongside black men. John M. Gregory, former governor of Virginia, made clear during the earliest stages of conflict that he "deprecated the use of negro slaves in our army for any purpose whatever" on the grounds that blacks in rebel camps would become a subversive force, and he warned that slave labor was more desperately needed on the plantations in any case. From the outset of hostilities, however, his warnings were ignored, and black men and women became an integral part of the Confederate war effort on the front lines. Yet hired and impressed slaves were never sufficient to meet the demand for workers needed to erect fortifications and to serve as "teamsters, company-cooks, and hospital nurses." The result was that "one fourth of the men in the army . . . *wait* on the others, in attending upon wagons, and other things necessary for the movements of the main body."[29]

White men waiting on other white men presented a novel situation for Southern army officers who were not quite certain where their class and racial sensibilities should end and their military acumen begin. The commander of an Alabama regiment deplored the fact that his troops were forced to unload ships, diverting them from their "legitimate duties of a Volunteer Soldier"; "I think there are Negros & hirelings enough to do the menial labor of unloading transports," he wrote to one of his counterparts stationed in Yorktown in June of 1861. The latter officer noted difficulties in securing enough black workers in his area of Virginia, and reported, "My own Regiment has done two thirds of the unloading at this point without a murmur though a very large portion of the men had never labored a day in their lives," reflecting, perhaps, the initial enthusiasm for military combat among wealthy Southerners. He continued, "Under such circumstances, the wants of the service ought not to be embarrassed by points of etiquette."[30]

Difficulties in Confederate mobilization led white elites to doubt the ability of their countrymen to serve as steady, tractable laborers. The ill-fated attempts of Confederate officials to exploit the labor of small numbers of native white Unionists yielded little of tangible value to the war effort, but much trouble, political and otherwise. When members of the dissenting "Heroes of America" (a political association in North Carolina) were forced to toil in the Wilmington salt mines, they either urged or enabled their slave co-workers to escape; this episode revealed the radical potential of white and black men working together in close quarters. Men of modest means, even Confederate enthusiasts, might hire runaway slaves and thus profit from losses suffered by their planter-neighbors. This form of opportunism contrasted with the antebellum slave patrols, volunteer groups that often represented a cross-section of whites while serving the immediate interests of slaveholders. Moreover, the biracial "underground economy" fueled by moonshiners and black marketeers in evidence before secession became ever more visible during the war years. A South Carolina farmer complained in 1865, "there is a class of white folks . . . , meaner than the Negroes, who have been made more lawless by the war, who never would work, and they now encourage the Negroes to come about them. . . . It is these people who demoralize the Negroes." And finally, antebellum complaints about the unreliability and ruthlessness of slave overseers echoed among the cannon of war, suggesting that military necessity alone could not transform these particular poor white men into a highly disciplined work force. In Mobile the chief engineer of the Confederate Department of the Gulf charged that "the overseers sent by planters from the several counties with their negroes are but seldom efficient and reliable men . . . ; the strictest vigilance is not sufficient to make these men do fully their duty. . . ." In the context of war, labor turnover took on a new and particularly sinister meaning.[31]

It is worthwhile to speculate about the impact of desertions from the Confederate army on the postwar "labor question" as it related to plain white folk. Certainly the analogy between soldier and field hand leaves much to be desired; to state the obvious, soldiers faced mortal danger in a way that cotton choppers and sugarcane cutters did not. Nevertheless, the similarities between the regimen of army life and that of plantation life offer some intriguing parallels which might have contributed to postwar ideologues' tendency to dismiss whites as potential agricultural laborers. For instance, both Confederate soldiers and postbellum field workers were closely supervised by their social betters. The mark of a good sharecropper, like the mark of a good infantryman, was his ability to follow orders precisely without presuming to make decisions for himself or his co-workers—or, we might add, for his family. When Johnny Reb absconded from camp and (more often than not) headed for the hills, he not only defied a general system of military discipline, he also fled from a particular commanding officer and weakened the Confederate cause in the process. As the war raged throughout the South, deserters became a highly mobile and dangerous lot. In the course of the conflict, they gradually shed their image as moral reprobates and assumed the mantle of folk heroes within many backwoods neighborhoods. By March 1865 "So common is the crime [desertion], it has in popular estimation lost the stigma which justly pertains to it, and therefore the criminals are everywhere shielded by their families and by the sympathies of many communities." In the hills and swamps of the Confederacy, some outlaw bands of deserters numbered as many as four hundred persons; these men were armed and ready to wreak vengeance on military authorities and common soldiers.[32]

Harnessed to the cause of dissent and desertion among poor whites, new meanings of womanhood and family life challenged the sanctimonious platitudes of antebellum elites. The "corn women" and female bread rioters who roamed the countryside and looted bakery stores for food to feed their families brought to the fore the potential of nonelite women as political activists in their own right. In Alabama's Black Belt one white man recounted the temerity of poor women who insisted on their due from more fortunate citizens of the Confederacy: "They soon became perfect nuisances. When you objected to giving they abused you. . . ." It was women like these who implored their menfolk to hasten home regardless of their formal status as combatants. Many husbands, brothers, and sons deserted from the army during springtime planting or autumn harvest, often in response to letters like the one Edward Cooper received from his wife Mary: "Last night, I was aroused by little Eddie's crying. I called and said 'What is the matter Eddie?' and he said, 'O mamma! I am so hungry.' And Lucy, Edward, your darling Lucy; she never complains, but she is growing thinner and thinner every day. And before God, Edward, unless you come home, we must die." Edward Cooper's desire to return home meant that he intended to place his family's immediate interests over and above the Confederate cause. After the war, when blacks and whites tried to scratch out a living for themselves in the forests, and out of the reach of planters, they too were condemned for their errant ways.[33]

The physical destruction wrought by military conflict, combined with the incursion of the cotton economy into the up-country and south into the pine barrens, produced new forms of population mobility that transformed social relations. Stripped of their land and livestock by marauders on both sides, by new forms of property taxes and by indebtedness borne of bad crops in the first years after the war, small white landowners were forced to plant cotton, often at the expense of corn and other food crops. Between 1860 and 1880 South Carolina and Georgia together showed a 24 percent drop in corn production but an increase of similar proportions in cotton bales. The spread of railroads and banks facilitated this process of crop specialization, and the availability of commercial fertilizers gave a new sense of urgency to each farmer's race down the long cotton rows of autumn. The Depression of 1873, combined with insidious crop-lien laws (which in turn spawned more and more merchant-creditors), only accelerated foreclosures and the sale of family homesteads. In the Georgia up-country, landowner-ship among whites declined from 90 percent on the eve of the Civil War to 60 to 80 percent (depending on the county) twenty years later. Under these conditions of loss and deterioration, more and more yeomen took to the road as transient farm laborers. Up-country folk helped to replenish the Black Belt work force to some extent after 1865, when they migrated south in modest but noticeable numbers throughout the Tennessee Valley. In the heartland of Tennessee, black urban in-migration stimulated an exodus of whites out of the cities and into the countryside, where they sought work as field hands. In Alabama poor whites left their homes to labor on the railroads and in coal mining and steel. Whenever poor whites migrated, they severed their ties to elites in one area; consequently, new employer-employee relations lacked the intimacy and long history of shared common values that characterized relations among whites in formerly relatively stable neighborhoods.[34]

In fact, planters with an available supply of black and white labor in their immediate neighborhood faced novel choices in selecting a postbellum work force. Despite loud lamentations and anxious hand-wringing over a shortage of black labor, and the "unreliability" of whatever supply existed, some planters who had an opportunity to hire whites shunned them in favor of freedpeople. When pressed to explain their choice for black workers, white employers usually cited one or some combination of three factors: the freedpeople's ability to "get by" on the the most meager compensation; their "willingness" to perform almost any kind of labor for very low pay; and finally, their acquiescence in contractual arrangements that recapitulated the master-slave relationship. A Freedmen's Bureau official in Fort Smith, Arkansas, reported in March 1866, "I see no lack of energy among the Freedmen in preparing their lands for cultivation and though the white citizens contend that the Freedmen will not work yet almost invariably they employ them in preference to white labor." Black men and women remained more vulnerable, and hence more easily exploitable, compared to landless whites. Planters believed black families were "satisfied with their daily bread, and . . . willing for the morrow literally to take care of itself" because the former slaves seemed to survive on remarkably little in the way of cash, credit, or merchant advances. Whites rarely assessed in any systematic way the alternatives available to these workers, preferring instead to argue that blacks by virtue of their congenital inferiority to whites simply "needed" fewer material resources to keep body and soul together.[35]

No matter how desperate their situation, white men and women showed a decided reluctance to stoop to the position of cotton picker if the workers in the next row were former slaves. The large number of black people in the rural South tended to depress wages, and mute contract promises, for persons of both races. At the same time, freedpeople were forced to accept employment at rates of compensation that many whites not only found demeaning but also avoidable by taking their families elsewhere. From Princess Anne County, Virginia, came a report in 1866 that "the introduction of White laborers proving more expensive and difficult than they had been led to believe, [employers] are anxious to make engagement with Freedmen." Landlords such as the ones near Lexington, Virginia, in the winter of 1866–67 hired white laborers only as a last resort; "Some gentlemen, who would prefer them [blacks], but cannot secure colored laborers for the year are either hiring white hands, or curtailing the size of their prospective crops."[36]

By the end of the postwar decade, a number of white planters had ceased complaining about blacks and had begun to extol their virtues as tractable workers. According to the firsthand observations of an Arkansas farmer, blacks surpassed whites "because they are easier to get on with, and less apt to grumble and find fault than native whites. . . ." It was all a matter of workers' past experience and their expectations for the future. In Louisiana a rice planter agreed that "he would rather have negroes than whites for tenants because they paid [their rents or debts] more promptly."[37] Again, we can only speculate about the divergent penalties that might await white and black households lax in their compliance with contract terms. Behind these paeans to black "manageability," of course, were the realities of the Southern legal system, which offered little if any protection to black victims of fraud, intimidation, and violence. We lack evidence on the question of whether white sharecroppers could more easily, or were more likely to, bring suit against an employer, or pressure him in some other way to give fair treatment. But certainly poor white laborers were not the objects of terrorist attacks during Reconstruction; to the contrary, they were more often the perpetrators of such attacks upon their black competitors. And finally, white households presumably kept a lookout for chances to buy land, opportunities that presented themselves to blacks far less frequently. With enough good weather and some fertile soil, a small homestead could presumably take all family members out of the plantation wage economy at least temporarily, or for certain seasons of the year, affording them greater control over their own destinies relative to sharecroppers and tenants.

To listen to the pronouncements offered by diehard Confederates and even staunch Unionists after the Civil War, one would think that the broad outlines of antebellum social structure had survived the war intact; black people were still destined to pick the cotton grown on land owned by whites, and whites, for the most part regardless of class (except for a few scalawags), were still arrayed defiantly against the Yankees. Nevertheless, everyday realities in the Piedmont, the mountains, and the Black Belt belied this view, as some white tenants and sharecroppers began to confront, at the ballot box and in the fields, the larger meaning of their new dependency.

TAKING SIDES: PLAIN FOLK AFTER THE WAR

In 1867, as they contemplated a political alliance with the freedpeople, white Alabama hill-country Republicans pondered the question "Shall we have him [the black man] for our ally or the rebel for our master?"[38] For poor whites, such seemed to be the choice between two evils during a brief moment in the early years of Radical Reconstruction. Yet tentative coalitions between voters of the two races faltered all over the

South, as planters and their allies engaged in a concerted campaign of race-baiting and violent intimidation. The well-timed murder of a political foe, or the harassment of Republican plantation workers, sent a clear and forceful message to all landless men and women. Moreover, the demographic disaster of war—a disaster that culminated in new patterns of labor mobility in the rural South—produced unsettling encounters, in unanticipated places, between the poor of both races. Without a firm political framework in which to interpret these encounters, poor whites clung to an old historical consciousness of racial superiority, even as they met the freedpeople on a new and common ground.

In ways not unlike those felt by blacks, poor whites, especially those who had been less than halfhearted about the "cause" to begin, felt the ravages of war and the wrath of vanquished Confederates. Adding economic injury to class insult, poor-white families in the Southern upcountry bore the brunt of military hostilities as the Union army swept down the Mississippi Valley and pushed its way through the Tennessee mountains and on to Georgia and the sea. Fighting men caught up in a rich man's war returned home in the late spring and early summer of 1865, too late to plant crops for the year. Accounts of white families foraging for food in desolate regions of the South duplicate descriptions of freedpeople engaged in the same grim struggle for survival. These included white parents and children who tried to make do with scanty reserves of corn, who were "living in the woods, with no shelter but pine boughs, and this in the mid-winter," at times emerging to beg "for bread from door to door." The plight of "lone wimmen"—the widows and daughters of slain soldiers, or menfolk who departed for the war, never to return—had a special poignancy. To Freedmen's Bureau agents, single white women might appear "improvident" and "idle," but the fact was that they, like their black counterparts, exhibited great resourcefulness in keeping their children alive and in some cases applying to the Bureau for aid—all activities that required energy and persistence, though not necessarily considered "productive" labor by mid-nineteenth-century (or present-day) standards.[39]

If their commitment to the rebel cause had been less than steadfast, returning soldiers might find themselves persecuted as Unionists and denied employment by their unforgiving neighbors. In the North Carolina Piedmont, the Ku Klux Klan sent an all-purpose note of warning, which members were glad to make good on, to Republicans of both races: "Let a word of warning suffice. Your life is in danger. Brave men live. Thousands have sworn *traiters* death. Beware lest *you* are included, and ere long fill an unknown grave. To prevent—change and too, quickly." For the white men who were targets of these threats, the decision to cast their lot with the Democratic party offered the hope of salvaging not only their reputations but also their livelihoods and their lives.[40]

All over the South blacks and whites came together in ways that had no antebellum precedents. Testifying before the Southern Claims Commission in 1873, a Georgia freedwoman recalled meeting whites from different social classes as a result of post-1861 disruptions. She and her husband, "a good Union man," harbored a Yankee prisoner for a day and then helped him make his escape. For this act of defiance their "old master" sent "one of his own grandsons" to threaten the couple in the hope of extracting information from them. The black woman and man had also taken in a group of deserters from the rebel army; "They were opposed to the war & didn't own slaves & said they would rather die than fight. Those who were poor white people, who didn't own slaves were some of them Union people. I befriended them because they were on our side."[41]

This freedwoman's opinion of whites depended on the kind of politics they professed, and certainly some contact between the races was elevated to the high ground of principle in response to wartime exigencies. The Southern black and white men who met each other on grand juries, in Union League meetings, political conventions, or state legislatures, debated with one another as equals for the first time in American history. Yet in most cases blacks and poor whites found themselves in close proximity because they were too destitute to have much choice; few people who sought refuge from the war, and shelter from the elements, could afford to be particular about their cohabitors. Poor colonies sponsored by the Freedmen's Bureau were often interracial, though we can only wonder about the relations among, for example, the sixteen whites (ten children, five women, and a man) and seventy-two blacks (forty children, twenty-five women, and seven men) in residence at the Montgomery, Alabama, "home colony" in 1866. A deserted hotel in Greenville, South Carolina, served as home for some "low down whites and a set of equally low down Negroes"; they included "poor-whites [who] wandered up and down on the earth, rarely staying many years in one neighborhood."[42]

When black and white cotton pickers signed annual contracts on the same postbellum plantation, they forced their employers to formulate new techniques of labor management. Accounts of biracial work forces on individual plantations fail to indicate how integrated these work forces really were. In parts of Mississippi white tenants balked at working in the fields next to freedpeople, but they agreed to family tenancy arrangements that preserved a modicum of racial separation and precluded daily contact between blacks and whites. In Alabama and Louisiana the scattering of sharecroppers' cabins seemed to facilitate the hiring of workers of both races (the old slave cabins offered unacceptably close quarters), and as early as 1867 some planters were willing to give less stringent tenancy contracts to white workers in order to attract more of them. Finally, like the South Carolina farmer who employed "four white men to run the ploughs, at twelve dollars a month and board and washing," some employers chose to solve the problem of "race mixing" by instituting an explicit racial division of labor where none had existed before.[43]

For the most part, poor whites responded to these changes in work and race relations by fearing for their relatively privileged place in Southern society. In the mountain counties of Alabama, they initiated a terrorist campaign against blacks, who were forced to seek refuge in Black Belt counties to the South. In some regions free blacks and whites vied directly with one another for employment on plantations, a life-or-death competition among hungry and desperate people. Near Little Rock, Arkansas, in 1867, poor whites were "not disposed to tolerate the preference shown by the planters for freedmen as tenants and laborers"; consequently, "bands of disguised men" patrolled the region and attacked field hands, "determined to drive them from the country." Along the coast of South Carolina black families squatted on small parcels of land owned by poor whites; again, this type of racial conflict was new to the postwar period. Near Charleston the "lower orders of the white population" made no attempt to hide their displeasure toward blacks, especially those "who show a disposition to be industrious and provide for themselves." In Drummondtown, Virginia, blacks could expect justice from no segment of the white population; the civil authorities remained steadfastly unsympathetic to them as did the poor whites, "whose hatred arise[s] from the fear that the Freedman will outstrip them in bettering their condition, whose doctrine is that the 'niggar' has not even the right to live, and whose prejudices are only equalled by their ignorance and bad morals" (in the words of a Bureau agent).[44]

Access to formal education was indicative of the life prospects of members of both races, or so whites of all classes believed. Therefore, the appearance of schoolhouses for the exclusive use of blacks during the Reconstruction era cast in bold relief the deprivation of their poor white neighbors, whose children had no formal education although they were "in as much need for some body else beside their parents to provide for their education as the colored ones." In Dewitt County, Texas, white parents evinced less interest than blacks in sending their offspring to school; they "seem to be satisfied to teach their children to hunt crows etc." Black education in the rural South was problematic at best—a few small, scattered buildings hardly sufficed for the entire population. Those schools with teachers sponsored by the Freedmen's Bureau, Northern benevolent societies, or black parents themselves were not integrated racially, due to both their sponsors' inclination and the whites' disdain for "race mixing." Nevertheless, at least some of the deep resentment felt by whites toward black schooling stemmed as much from envy as from racist impulses.[45]

Changes wrought in household routine and organization by the increase in postbellum tenancy varied according to specific groups of whites. Men and women who before the war roamed the backwoods, herding cattle and squatting on someone else's land, found intensive crop cultivation a severe break with the past indeed; it is difficult to know what percentage of this group became agricultural laborers during Reconstruction, but certainly their traditional "habits of restlessness" might help to account for high rates of labor turnover among white employees on postbellum plantations. Now reduced to the status of dependent workers, men who were formerly sturdy yeomen also experienced a radically new kind of life; as tenants and sharecroppers they now labored for landlords who watched their every move in the fields and stripped them of power to make all but the most modest decisions affecting the work and welfare of their families. These men were obligated to put their wives and children to work chopping cotton and worming tobacco plants and to forgo any kind of household industry that would have rendered their families less beholden to local storekeepers. The reduction in household foodstuff production—the ears of corn replaced by cotton bolls, the vegetable patches disallowed by annual contracts, the hogs and cattle denied an open range for grazing—amounted to the most compelling symbol and potent cause of rural Southerners' abject poverty throughout the late nineteenth century. If in the prewar period this class of whites adhered to a "leisurely" way of life (due to their practice of extensive agriculture), then their postbellum "laziness" gave evidence of widespread, chronic anemia produced by protein-deficient diets.[46]

The Civil War and its immediate aftermath unleashed great intraregional movement among black and white people now cut loose from their moorings. Therefore, it is not surprising that few whites had the prescience to understand—let alone accommodate themselves to—a still unformed social order of class and race relations. White elites, relieved that most former slaves had little choice but to head back to the cotton plantation by 1867 or so, failed to incorporate native-born white field hands into a new political economy that seemed to recapitulate the old order in significant ways. For their part, poor whites remained hopeful that their new dependency was only a temporary condition, a postwar aberration, and that their status would eventually improve with the help of more fortunate Democrats. With their expectations based on the racial caste system and their emergent grievances born of economic exploitation, white tenants and sharecroppers were truly caught between the pride of color and the power of class. Hence their reluctance to cast their lot permanently with people who represented the degradation of slavery incarnate; the former yeomen and their children looked to racial, not class, consciousness as their salvation.

Upheavals in the configuration of Southern politics represented by the Freedmen's Bureau, Radical Reconstruction, and the rise of an indigenous Republican party amounted to brief though potent challenges to white supremacy rather than large-scale social transformations. With its sprawling jurisdiction and its skimpy resources, the Bureau sponsored labor contracts that its agents could neither oversee nor purge of fraud and abuse, contracts that the planters appropriated for their own use. The enfranchisement of black men and election of six hundred of them to state legislatures organized under the provisions of Radical Reconstruction yielded a genuine revolution, and the uneasy coalition that formed under the banner of the Republican party openly supported civil rights for blacks (at least within the former Confederacy) and progressive legislation on behalf of all farm laborers. Nevertheless, it is questionable whether the brief tenure of egalitarian-minded state and local officials affected in any meaningful way the everyday lives of the mass of rural workers, black or white. Maintained by employers' threats and bookkeepers' machinations, plantation discipline seemed impervious to changes in lien laws or even the novel appearance of a black sheriff periodically, here and there, between 1867 and the end of Reconstruction in the various states (in 1877).

The federal government, through the Republican party, was not necessarily intentionally—or murderously—complicitous with Southern planters; at the same time, during the war era federal policies contributed to the marginalization of poor Southerners. As a group, Republicans rejected land redistribution proposals and instituted an annual labor contract system that condemned field workers to chronic underemployment. Though never fully implemented in a region bound to labor management techniques born of a slave past, the Yankee free-labor ideology held little promise for the long-term welfare of landless whites and blacks; until the Great Depression, Northern Republicans and Democrats alike agreed to let market forces run their course in the South. Consequently, the losses suffered by whites sinking into tenancy accompanied the gains won by blacks rising to freedom. Sharecropping and other forms of family tenancy quickly took root in the Southern soil, but their seeds were sown by Union officials together with cotton planters, and their most repressive aspects were nourished by Northern neglect and indifference for years to come.

PART II

THE EMERGENCE OF A RURAL PROLETARIAT IN THE SOUTH, 1870 TO 1990

3

The Family Economy of Rural Southerners, 1870 to 1930

Antebellum slaveholders liked to boast that cotton was the perfect crop because it could not be eaten by the people who grew it. But the "New South" of the 1870s offered up a different lesson to William Holtzclaw, the son of black sharecroppers in Alabama. Later in life Holtzclaw recalled his bewilderment each December when his parents were told by their employer that they had already "eaten" their share of the cotton and so would receive none of the proceeds from its sale. Yet the white man routinely cut off their "furnishings" between July and September; "All the rest of the time we had to find something to do away from the plantation in order to keep supplied with bread and clothes, which were scanty enough." Holtzclaw's mother "cooked for the 'white folks,'" a job that at times kept her away from her own home overnight. Together the children spent hours in the nearby swamps and marshes, "wading in the slush" above their knees in search of the tasty hog potato, which, together with the persimmons, nuts, and muscadines they managed to scrounge up, kept "body and soul together during those dark days." His father had to engage in "continuous effort . . . to keep the wolf from the door." Together with white co-workers from the area, the older man hauled logs at a nearby sawmill for 60 cents a day until the mill moved out of the neighborhood in search of fresh timber. Then he left the family behind for a year and found a job working on a railroad fifty miles from home, returning every three months (a journey that took two weeks) to deliver the proceeds of his labor, $40 to $50, to their landlord; every penny went to pay for the advances consumed by the household in his absence. No letters united the family; "we only knew that the three months were up, and that it was time for him to come to us." As a ten-year-old, William split two thousand rails one fall to pay for his own clothes. That same year he hired out to work for a white man but "became morose, disheartened" by the abrupt termination of his schooling.[1]

In 1880 Holtzclaw's father realized the family would never advance by farming on shares and decided to rent a forty-acre farm. "He bought a mule, a horse, and a yoke of oxen, and so we started out for ourselves." The children were ecstatic; "we were so happy at the prospects of owning a wagon and a pair of mules and having only our father for boss that we shouted and leaped for joy." But misfortune came in many guises—a mule, suffering from a "peculiar" ailment that kept it from getting up on its feet in the morning; an ox, its neck broken from a farm accident; and a horse, "so poor and thin that he could not plow." Holtzclaw's father suffered a crippling accident when he stepped on a stub of cane in the field one day, and then their "splendid" crop of corn, gathered by the other family members and carefully piled in heaps, washed away after a storm. It was this last blow "from which we were never wholly able to recover." His father, by this time able to walk, took a job off the farm. But after four years all this effort yielded only a monstrous debt that prompted the family's creditors to "clean them out"—"they came and took our corn and finally, the vegetables from our little garden as well as the chickens and the pig." At the end of the year the Holtzclaws "applied to a white man for a home on his place—a home under the old system," and the father was never able again to lift himself out of the status of sharecropper.[2]

Years later William Holtzclaw would record the observation of a Mississippi farmer that, for poor folk, "times don't never get no different." That generalization held a certain truth for landless Southerners as a group in the six-and-a-half decades after the Civil War. Compared to other American workers, Southern sharecroppers and tenants experienced remarkably little improvement in their standard of living during these years. Burdened by high interest rates and mortgages (liens) on their crops, rural households of cotton pickers and choppers followed essentially the same daily and seasonal rhythms as the newly freed slaves. They organized the productive energies of their families and kept alive the dream of landownership in a way that defied the passage of time. Black and white, they sustained folkish ways at work and in church, ways that employers in 1930 as well as in 1870 decried as evidence of their inherent ignorance and "irresponsibility." Their rude cabins cluttered with large numbers of children, they in fact constituted an agricultural proletariat, farmers who owned no farms, tillers of the soil perennially "rootless" themselves. Like the Holtzclaws, rural families were subjected to a Southern form of progressive underdevelopment; and yet individual families did indeed have histories of their own, histories characterized by both hard work and hard luck. Though separated from each other by a racial caste system, black and white families through the years demonstrated patterns of striving and struggling that belied the fatalism often attributed to the poor across time and cultures.

The rural South constituted a "low-wage" economy of staple-crop agriculture and extractive industries, its labor market isolated from the more dynamic markets of the North and Midwest; nevertheless, no matter how stunted its development, the South existed as part of a world and national commercial economy. On the Southern countryside, many meager family fortunes dwindled over the generations, as the price of cotton on the world market gradually declined during the latter part of the nineteenth century and then bottomed out in the 1930s. In addition, the options of Southern households were shaped at least partially by the decisions of Northern businessmen. For example, in their hunger for unskilled factory hands, Northeastern and Midwestern manufacturers favored Eastern European immigrants over poor whites or blacks from the rural South. In some areas of the South, Northern industrial interests dominated rural nonagricultural enterprises—beginning in the 1880s, when lumber and mining companies made their initial forays into Appalachia, for example—and imposed their own hiring practices and preferences on local labor markets. The limited job opportunities of poor Southerners regionwide reflected to some extent the "agglomeration effects" that had already accrued to Northern and Midwestern cities, leaving Southern businesses at a perpetual disadvantage in terms of marketing their products and attracting high-wage industries. Finally, the depressions of 1877, 1893, and the 1930s produced downturns in economic activity throughout the nation and affected agricultural as well as industrial workers, prompting new forms of political and labor-union agitation in the rural and urban South and North.[3]

In fact, dependent rural Southerners lived lives in many ways akin to those of urban wage earners. In the Upper South, a majority of blacks were not family farmers at all but wage laborers, and during the latter part of the nineteenth century, all of the former Confederate states took steps to reduce the ability of sharecroppers and tenants to control the marketing of their own crop. Yet even more generally as a group, and in more specific ways related to work patterns, poor whites and blacks in the rural South were caught up in a national (and ultimately international) process that rendered workers of all kinds more vulnerable to the whims of a commercial economy and to the idiosyncratic demands of employers. Many unskilled nonagricultural workers all over the country lacked real property and relied on the efforts of all household members, including wives and children, to produce a "living wage." Like Georgia croppers, Massachusetts shoemakers and Ohio steel workers had to contend with slack seasons and enforced underemployment. They moved often, usually within a circumscribed area, prompting employers to harangue them about the virtues of "faithful" labor. In the face of a host of employment insecurities and their reliance on employers for tools or land, many workers regardless of race aspired to independence—for Northern workers, as self-employed businessmen; for rural Southerners, as landowners.[4]

This is not to minimize the differences between the Northern and Southern economies, or between whites and blacks within the South. Southern tenants and croppers arranged themselves into productive units as families and signed annual labor contracts, in contrast to more individualistic and free-floating northern factory hands. In the wake of war's devastation, landless white Southerners probably were forced to relinquish household autonomy more quickly than artisan groups in the North;[5] and black Southerners had never enjoyed that form of independence which constituted such a powerful part of the collective memory of white laborers in general. New England shoemakers as well as small-to-middling farmers in the South could look to the past, and to their tradition as proud republican householders, for confirmation of their worth as workers; in contrast, black people could look only to the future—that is, to the possibility of landownership—at a time when precious few families were able to achieve redemption from the commercial economy in those terms.

The Jim Crow South produced some of the starkest images of poverty and oppression in all of American history. This was a "stagnant" region devoid of capital, an impoverished people "mired" and "ensnared" in state-sanctioned neoslavery, their political power substantially reduced (and in the case of the black vote virtually eliminated) after 1910. The Southern countryside blazed with the crosses of Klu Kluxers and the torches of White Caps, the air filled with the stench of burning flesh, the writhing victims of lynch mobs. By 1900, as a result of both steadily declining cotton prices and the specialization in cotton imposed by the crop lien system, tenancy had spread through the up-country and into the Appalachian Mountains, bringing with it hookworm, pellegra, and malnutrition to whites as well as blacks. An "industrial counter-revolution" (marked by the breakup of large plantations) was checked somewhat by the revival of highly centralized units of agricultural production, farm factories with rigidly supervised labor forces. Beginning in the late nineteenth century, the boll weevil made its way up from Texas and east to Georgia, devouring large portions of the Southern cotton crop through the 1920s.[6]

To counterbalance these forces of dispossession, poor families made efforts to resist injustice, no matter how brief or disorganized that resistance. Wrote a Mississippi black man to officials of the National Association for the Advancement of Colored People in the 1920s, "We want only one thing, primarily. That is the ballot. Ballot everywhere. My people cannot vote down here. . . . We want the damnable curse of disfranchisement in primary elections [re]moved in every form of state government." Throughout the South, black communities assumed the task of educating themselves, reducing their illiteracy rate a remarkable degree, from 80 percent in 1870 to 16.4 percent in 1930—and this, of course, over the strenuous objections of whites of all classes. Sporadic strikes in the cotton and rice fields, lumber camps, and phosphate mines, coupled with intra- and interregional migration, kept alive a spirit of defiance that is more accurately gauged by patterns in the withdrawal of labor than by the ballots cast in any single election. Southern statutes designed to limit labor mobility proved surprisingly ineffective in stemming high rates of annual plantation turnover, revealing an ongoing tug-of-war between employees and employers. The refusal of families to acquiesce completely in an exploitative labor system accounts for the trickle of urban in-migration from the surrounding countryside throughout the late nineteenth century, and the torrent of northward migration beginning in 1916.[7]

The life experiences of poor white rural households overlapped in significant ways with those of their black counterparts during this period and constitute a vital, if relatively neglected, part of the history of the Jim Crow South. The agricultural "tenure ladder" in fact exerted a gravitylike pull downward on small farmers of both races, gradually eroding whole communities of white yeoman farmers and making the climb upward into the ranks of small landowner a feat of heroic proportions among the sons and grandsons of former slaves. The lien laws that reduced sharecroppers to wage laborers applied equally to workers of both races, as did fence laws, vagrancy and contract enforcement legislation, and high personal property taxes. Between 1890 and 1903 white landowners' efforts to limit political opposition to the Democratic party—efforts achieved through constitutional restrictions on voting by way of the literacy clause and poll tax, for example—reduced white voting strength by an average of 25 percent (and black strength by 62 percent) throughout the South. The trends toward proletarianization as well as the good government movement that spurred disfranchisement of "unworthy citizens" were then ultimately national developments with regional variations. During these years, in the South an emergent class of working families faced an increasingly precarious existence yet remained split along lines of culture and consciousness.[8]

LADDER RUNGS AND RAILROAD TIES: FARM TENURE AND RACE

In the eyes of a young black man named Ed Brown, the road to success for a Georgia cotton farmer in the 1920s consisted of specific steps, precise increments of personal well-being: "every time you come up in the world you got a better mattress." According to Brown, a wage laborer had to make do with a mattress "made of wheat straw or oak straw or crab grass." A sharecropper might "keep back or steal, you might call it, some of the cotton he was supposed to take to the gin," though a bed of unginned cotton, lumpy from the seeds, needed a "tickin . . . mighty thick." In contrast, a family that farmed on standing rent owned whatever cotton they could pick and slept on mattresses stuffed with soft ginned cotton: "That's what my wife wanted." And during his early years as a wage laborer, newly married, so did Ed Brown, for the comfort of a mattress provided a measure of both his own independence as a farmer and his worth as a husband and father. In the decade before the Great Depression, Brown's quest for a mattress of his liking took him to six different plantations, six different white employers. From some places he moved willingly, even eagerly, to search out better prospects down the road. But in other instances, hounded by debt, fraud, and violent threats, he likened himself to a rabbit: "Zigzag, zigzag, dodgin one hunter then the next." In time the elusive mattress of ginned cotton would become a fitting symbol of Brown's own bone-tiredness in the struggle to make a living.[9]

Though illiterate, Brown considered himself "pretty schemy." His earliest years had provided bitter lessons in resourcefulness. Born around the turn of the century to a white father and black mother in Wilcox County, he would later say of his black stepfather, "a farmer and a turpentine man was what he call hisself but he was mainly a possum hunter." Within the Brown household, each person contributed to the family welfare in ways not readily predictable from their status as share-croppers on a cotton plantation. His stepfather alternated among work-ing for wages on a nearby turpentine farm, selling wood, hunting, and cultivating a cotton crop. Brown's mother cooked for their employer and then, "along about August, . . . would stop cookin and go to pickin cotton because there was more money in it," taking her five-year-old son with her to a neighbor's farm. Worked hard by their stepfather, the children hunted for possums and rabbits, stole peanuts and chickens for the fami-ly larder, and dusted the family crop with arsenic in a futile attempt to check an invasion of boll weevils. At age twelve Ed Brown left home to work for "ten dollars a month wages at Mr. Joe Lynn's store" ("Then I didn't know any colored man that work for straight cash wages"). While he was "coming up," Brown's parents tried unsuccessfully to move to new employers who might offer them a better house; in one cabin, the chimney amounted to little more than "clay dirt between sticks," pro-ducing "smoked smutty" tight quarters. Looking back years later, Brown faulted his stepfather for failing to reap a just reward; "after bein an awful hard worker he wouldn't put his money in the right thing, such as a home."[10]

Soon after he married in 1920, Ed Brown realized that he was not going to make any money working for his current employer Joe Lynn: "You could make a good crop and still be lef in a hole. A lot depend, Mr. Lynn said, on what he got out of it." Brown's sister-in-law and her hus-band persuaded him and his bride, Willie Mae, to move near them; the young couple left Joe Lynn's place late one night; "We was running away." Their new employer, Jim McHenry, offered them wages and pro-visions, but Brown resented the work he was forced to do after the cot-ton crop was laid by in the summer: "cuttin logs at the sawmill, doin road work, and cuttin ditches, . . . shuckin corn or haulin black manure or compost, or cleanin out fence corners." When, after a couple of years,

McHenry acted "slippery" with Brown and reneged on a promise to let him farm on shares, Ed and Willie Mae moved again, this time to work for a white man with the same name as Ed Brown: "he was nice. But he just didn't have nothin. He was poor." After a disastrous year of rain and boll weevils, the white Ed Brown announced, "Well Ed, you don't owe me nothin and I don't owe you nothin." Ed and Willie Mae then decided to sign on with Emory Oakes, the landlord of the young man's parents.[11]

The next year, 1925, was a good one for cotton, and Ed Brown made his "first real money" by working a "good little farm on shares . . . with no bossman on the place. . . . " Then a poor white man began to harass the Brown family (he "would lay down on my porch drunk"), and they decided to leave Oakes's place rather than risk a confrontation. New employers, Mr. and Mrs. Addison, seemed to be fair people—"you could put your foot on anythin any of them said and stand firm"—but they cut off Brown's credit in July for the duration of the summer slack season, and he was forced to take a series of extra jobs, working in a sawmill, helping to run a peanut picker on a nearby farm, and (with white co-workers) baling hay. On the Addison estate, Brown resisted the threats of yet another menacing white neighbor and determined to stay, though he realized (in 1928) that he "didn't have one dollar." The next year Addison bought a tractor and reduced his work force from fifteen to four hands. The Browns subsequently embarked on a "turrible year" with Leslie Prince.[12]

Initially Ed Brown had high hopes for this arrangement because Prince's tenant houses had glass windows, and Willie Mae said he seemed like "a nice man." Her hunch proved to be wrong, for at the end of the year Prince confiscated all seven of the cotton bales that the couple produced, and also seized their store of velvet beans and sweet potatoes. Willie Mae managed to hide the family milk cow before Prince could take it to cover the remaining $24 they owed him. Ed Brown regretted that he had not followed the lead of other tenants who had left Prince in July of that year. In the late fall the white man sabotaged Brown's efforts to move once again, informing a prospective employer (he told Brown later) that the black man was "mean and your wife is sick and your little girl too small to do anythin." One day in 1930, sitting under "a black gum tree which was still scarred up from a lynchin that took place when I was a boy," Ed Brown looked around and saw "all our work—mine and the other tenants'—piled up around" Leslie Prince. At reckoning time Prince failed to abide by his promise to pay Brown for some extra work he had done, and Ed and Willie Mae left for good.[13]

Despite their failure to find a place of their own, or to accumulate

A. Rural Southerners at Work

Between the Civil War and World War II, the rural Southern labor force consisted of men, women, and children of various races and ethnic groups, bound and free, organized as individuals and as family members. Work in the extractive sector, especially in the naval stores industry, was so arduous, dangerous, and ill-paid that industrialists often resorted to (mostly male) convicts and peons, who remained isolated in remote work camps deep in swamps and forests (1). The staple-crop economy relied on sharecropping and tenant families; black and white women and children were integral to plantation agriculture (2, 3). However, these families often fragmented in the course of the year as husbands and older sons sought out wage work in the the rural nonagricultural sector during the winter and late summer slack seasons (4). Beginning in the 1920s, the collapse or contraction of rural industries such as coal and phosphate mining, turpentining, and lumbering, forced whole families to abandon plantation work and follow truck crops "on the season" up and down the East Coast in an effort to eke out a living (5, 6). The eagerness of rural employers to recruit foreign-born laborers resulted in depressed wages and poor working conditions for all employees in the rural South. In both agricultural and mining communities, older people remained most vulnerable to periodic contractions in the economy (7, 8) and dependent on assistance provided by kin, neighbors, and, after the 1930s, the federal government.

A1. Convict chain gang turpentine crew, Escambia County, Florida, ca. 1910. Florida State Archives.

A2. Family of cotton pickers, 1941. Photo by Paul Wilkerson. National Archives.

A3. Spanish-peanut picker, North Carolina, 1942. Photo by J. T. Mitchell. National Archives.

A4. Worker at hydraulic oil press, Dawson, Georgia, Cotton Oil Co., 1943.
Photo by Pace. National Archives.

A5. Migrant fruit picker, Polk County, Florida, 1937. Photo by Arthur Rothstein. Florida State Archives.

A6. Migrant vegetable pickers waiting to be paid, Homestead, Florida, 1939. Photo by Marion Post Wolcott. Florida State Archives.

A7. Romanian coal miner, "Too old to find employment," Scott's Run, West Virginia, ca. 1936. Photo by Lewis Hine. National Archives.

A8. Woman caning chairs on a rural rehabilitation farm near Zebulon, North Carolina, ca. 1934. National Archives.

much in the way of worldly goods, Ed and Willie Mae Brown could hardly be faulted for their lack of initiative or even cunning. In late 1925 Oakes had pronounced Brown free of debt and entitled to $3 in cash; a few days later Brown produced two extra cotton bales that he had held back from the initial reckoning settlement and received $150 for them. While the couple worked for Jim McHenry, Willie Mae did the white family's laundry, in the process earning a little cash and adorning her own spare cabin; she regularly used Mrs. McHenry's table linens to entertain her own guests. Brown admired his wife's attempt to "beautify a place" beyond their means—her ability to take "a shell of a house not sealed in any way" and hang curtains made of flour sacks "with the writin bleached off"; to make a home out of a cast-iron stove, some bedding, a dresser, chairs, a few cooking utensils, "and a crippled white hen."[14]

In his peripatetic search for the right combination of soil, landlord, and contract, Brown traveled often within a limited geographical area, though it is difficult to characterize these moves in all cases as voluntary. Throughout the 1920s his link with the national consumer economy remained tenuous at best; in 1929 the family bought an old Model T Ford, but found it too expensive to operate and soon swapped it for a cow and a butter churn and dasher. Although the price of cotton helped to determine the return he received for his field work, so too did the whims and calculations of individual white employers. In the interest of his family, first as a youth and then as a husband and father, Brown was forced to take jobs away from home, though these jobs paid but little, and then only on a temporary, seasonal basis. His wife, Willie Mae, tended the children, picked cotton as a cropper and wage earner, took in laundry, and kept "things . . . lookin very pretty" besides. Despite their thwarted ambitions, the Browns maintained an expansive outlook on life and its possibilities.

The "better mattress" defined Ed Brown's notion of upward mobility on the agricultural "tenure ladder," but rural sociologists and officials of the United States Department of Agriculture (USDA) had equally specific, if more detailed, measurements of farm tenure status in the post-Reconstruction South. The various rungs on the so-called ladder were fairly distinct from one another (at the bottom were farm wage laborers, followed by sharecroppers, tenants, share renters, cash renters, and owners), and a myriad of social-welfare indices were correlated with tenure status. For family members, moving up the ladder usually signified greater year-to-year residential stability; higher literacy and school attendance rates; more real and personal estate; a greater number of magazine subscriptions; diets with fewer carbohydrates and more protein; and larger, better-insulated houses with more windows, furniture, and rooms. Tenants, who usually owned their own mule(s) and at least some farm equipment, retained significant advantages over croppers, who owned little if anything and relied on "furnishings" of everything from cotton seed to clothing for the children. In the fields croppers and short-term wage hands were usually closely supervised; in contrast, renters paid the landowner a stipulated amount of cash rent each year regardless of the size of the crop. Hence the most significant benefits related to upward social mobility—the increasing independence of farmers as workers and as household heads—of course defy quantification. Conversely, the seemingly small matter of a vegetable garden denied by a new landlord to a former landowning family, now reduced to tenancy, could serve as a powerful symbol of a dreaded new dependency: "This was a blow to our freedom and pride. . . . It drove home the fact that we were not on our own."[15]

Around the turn of the century, rates of tenancy (a term referring to both tenants and croppers) increased in all areas of the United States. But the rise was most dramatic in the Southern states, where by 1910 fully half of all farmers were tenants (compared to less than one-tenth in New England and less than a third in the Midwest). Moreover, in the Midwest, tenancy lacked the moral stigma that it carried in the South; commercial farmers west of the Ohio River saw mortgages and credit as a way into a form of agriculture that required expensive machinery and large parcels of land. And, in the Midwestern states tenancy declined dramatically among older men, a pattern that held for the years 1890 to 1930, indicating that landlessness was a necessary precondition for sons and newlyweds who hoped someday to own their own farm. In the South matters were not so simple. Although data on the age of farming heads suggest a positive relationship between age and tenure status, in fact, many of the poorest tenants would often "fail and leave the farm" without advancing at all; once displaced by employers who sought young men with growing families, these older husbands became wage laborers or unemployed dependents living with kin. Also, beginning in the 1880s, a significant proportion of white men and women chose to renounce agricultural dependence in favor of a new life in the textile mills scattered along the fall line in the southern Piedmont; they too abandoned the tenure ladder to neighbors endowed with kin connections and other advantages. Despite this siphoning of poor whites off the countryside and into mill towns, tenancy among the black and white populations continued to climb. Between 1900 and 1930 the number of white-operated farms grew from 1.9 million to 2.3 million, reflecting the high fertility rates among rural white women; but the number of white farm owners remained virtually the same, at 1 million. In 1930, sixty-five years after emancipation, fully 80 percent of Southern black farmers worked land owned by someone else.[16]

As a conceptual tool, the idea of an agricultural tenure ladder—a vertical means of ascent for all farmers who had the skill and determination to climb it—has severe limitations for the study of the rural South after the Civil War. As USDA investigators pointed out in a 1923 study on farm ownership and tenancy, "the various successive stages may not always represent progress. . . . Moreover, progress in independence does not always mean progress in well-being." Here they were referring to the lowly material condition of all poor folk and to the extreme sacrifices that Southern owners might have to make, especially in terms of their children's education. In addition, as Ed Brown suggested, a family's aspirations developed incrementally, and opportunistically, over its lifetime. A host of dreams lay submerged beneath the outer trappings of poverty; a family might hope to own a few chickens or a pig to gain a measure of self-sufficiency. Women field hands took advantage of temporary labor shortages, and consequent increases in wages, to toil fewer hours outside under the sun; their goal was not cash accumulation but the ability to spend more time on household chores. Similarly, a father might replace his hoe-wielding spouse with older children, now able to do their share of the chopping and picking; the number of people in the household labor force remained constant though the mother was freed from field work. Within a family, practical considerations blended with idealistic goals; unable to purchase land, some families practiced a modest consumerism, proud of their purchases of clocks, pianos, or sewing machines. The daughter of a white Arkansas sharecropper recalled that, if her father realized a profit at the end of the year, he would splurge on store-bought food; "That was Mama's favorite thing in the world was sardines, and that was the treat if he had enough money to pay the bill. But if he didn't, we didn't get the crackers and sardines."[17]

Others invested their money in nontangibles—the education of a son or daughter, reported as "visiting kin" in a nearby town or city for months at a time, if an employer made an untimely inquiry. On her way back to Ferguson Academy in Abbeville, South Carolina, after her summer vacation in 1896, Jane Edna Harris found herself at the Pendleton train station without enough money to buy her ticket. Friends and neighbors who had come to see her off took up a hasty collection among themselves, paid for the ticket, and gave her an extra 50 cents as well. Individual welfare was an imprecise standard, and difficult to separate from surrounding kin and community; after his best year ever, Ed Brown used the first $500 he made to pay for his mother-in-law's funeral. These expenditures, often invisible to outsiders in any case, had little relevance to the agricultural tenure ladder, traditionally defined.[18]

The demographic and economic realities of Southern society mitigated against a widening prosperity for rural folk. Though encouraged by the sharecropping system, large families were in the long run counterproductive; the land could not withstand a high rate of population growth combined with falling crop prices within such a specialized economy. The weight of these combined forces pulled a farmer downward unless he began the fight fortified with substantial amounts of land and capital. Landowners, and especially the wealthiest planters, often received legacies from their kin; one need hardly have endured an arduous climb up the tenure ladder in order to perch securely on its uppermost rungs. The Census of 1920 indicated that 44 percent of Georgia farm owners, and 56 percent of those in North Carolina, had never worked as either wage hands or tenants. The difficulties associated with accumulating enough money to buy a homestead were expressed in various ways. For a tenant in late-nineteenth-century Tennessee, the prospect of saving 10 percent of his net annual income for eighteen years in a row (the amount needed to purchase a homestead) was remote indeed. The Federal Bureau of Agricultural Economics (BAE) estimated that, in 1916, the chances for a South Carolina tenant to become a landlord "other than by inheritance" were less than one in one hundred. In 1919 a USDA survey of the Black Prairie region of Texas found that the average share tenant had to work for twenty-eight years before he could afford to pay for the land he tilled. As part of a 1926 study of black farmers in Southampton County, Virginia, six out of every ten tenants interviewed reported that they had managed to accumulate less than $50 per year "since they began their earning life."[19]

Black tenants and croppers remained clustered on the lowest rungs of the tenant ladder, and differences in their tenure status were less meaningful among themselves than among their white counterparts. In 1920 black tenants as a group were about the same age as black owners, while white tenants were younger than white owners, indicating lingering opportunities for some young white men. A 1933 enumeration of cotton plantations showed that black wage hands, renters, tenants, and croppers had occupied their respective statuses for a longer period than whites in similar circumstances, suggesting that black farmers' chances for upward mobility were relatively limited. Studies of the South Carolina Piedmont in 1925 and 1930 detailed average land and building values for farmers of the two races. The range of accumulation for blacks was narrow; croppers and owners possessed similar amounts of personal property, a fact particularly striking in light of the gulf that separated whites at the bottom from whites at the top of the ladder. In fact, black owners were worth much less than white renters, and black renters had the same standard of living as white sharecroppers. The fact that a black family could not aspire to a more comfortable house once they became owners has prompted one scholar to observe that "black sharecroppers may not have had many purely economic incentives for climbing the agricultural ladder."[20]

Just because a family maintained similar contractual arrangements with landlords for several consecutive years did not necessarily imply that its members had settled into an inertia born of despair or indifference. For example, bad luck necessitated a great deal of running in place. Misfortune might grow gradually, tenaciously, in the course of a season, or spring up overnight, after the death of a mule or a fire in the barn. A father would adjust the work assignments of family members accordingly, and perhaps put added emphasis on foraging and fishing to see them through hard times. A poor market for cotton, combined with the machinations of individual landlords, could force households to double their efforts in the cotton fields just to maintain a meager status quo. In 1907 a young Alabama couple struggled mightily to produce six bales of cotton (four times more than in the previous year) and still owed every ounce to their employer; in the words of the husband, "In the place of prosperin I was on a standstill." Clearly, then, failure to advance from sharecropper to tenant, or from tenant to owner, could derive from causes other than inefficient farming methods, a lack of effort, or any of the other factors often associated with long-term, intra- and intergenerational landlessness.[21]

Ultimately, the options of people who remained on the countryside, regardless of race, were shaped more by landlords' priorities and prejudices, economic changes, and local demography than by their families' initiative in wringing a living from the soil. Planters throughout the South expressed strong convictions about the appropriate tenure arrangements for their particular holdings. They based labor-force assessments on the seasonal demands of their crops and on the age, race, and marital status of their workers. Conventional wisdom about such matters varied according to region and changed in response to patterns of local labor supply and demand. Arthur F. Raper, in his classic study of the Georgia Black Belt, *Preface to Peasantry*, noted: "The most dependent rural dwellers, almost always on the largest and most closely supervised plantations, have little choice but to occupy the tenure status the planters want them to. One year they will be wage hands—'Mr. George is doin' wages.' Another year they will be croppers—'Mr. George is halvin' 'em.'" In 1884 the Census Bureau documented numerous varieties of tenure-mix arrangements on plantations. For example, in North Carolina planters who favored the wage system reported that, as a result, "Laborers receive cash monthly; are better clothed and fed; cultivate with better judgment and have fewer failures in crops, and crops are not neglected. ..." In contrast, other employers in the same state held that the sharecropping system was particularly desirable because their workers were "provided for during winter months; they spend wages as fast as obtained. They can make more with proper work; gives a living at home and children can be made useful; take better care of the crop and are less wasteful." On the eve of World War I, more than half of all croppers and tenants lived on plantations employing ten or more families; many employers, then, had some flexibility in determining the proportion of wage hands, sharecroppers, tenants, and renters hired.[22]

Clearly, planters' racial prejudices, combined with the relatively more favorable bargaining position of white workers (considering their recourse to the law and to other kinds of work outside the cotton economy), helped to shape the nature of tenure arrangements. Few landlords showed the same equanimity toward white and black workers as the cotton planter in Polk County, Georgia, who approved of the performance of previously self-sufficient yeomen now reduced to tenancy; "as producers of cotton whites can be just as efficient in this part of the country" if subjected to close supervision, he suggested. Echoing their Reconstruction-era forbears, most employers cited (once again) blacks' lesser "needs" ("Hog and hominy, blackberries and plums"); their ability to withstand, "it seems, a great deal of discomfort"; and their reluctance (or inability) to voice demands for better working and living conditions. Black families had accommodated themselves "to the primeval curse" in a way their white counterparts had not, or so the argument went. Moreover, black fathers showed a greater willingness to send their wives and children to the fields, a fact that probably reflected not some sort of cultural proclivity, but rather the desperate need to farm every acre intensively; in general, black croppers and tenants were allocated smaller parcels of land than whites. On some plantations black people worked as sharecroppers, while cash renting was reserved exclusively for whites. Around the turn of the century the president of the Georgia State Agricultural Society testified before a federal commission that whites often refused to work in the fields with blacks; the tendency to group croppers near the owner's or overseer's quarters and to rent out more remote parcels provided for close supervision of blacks and at the same time kept the races segregated. In the North Carolina Piedmont, white women tobacco workers refrained from joining in the songs sung by black people toiling next to them in the fields—apparently in an attempt to preserve a small sphere of racial separation within a biracial work setting.[23]

Despite a general preference for black workers, planters had to contend with population movements that deprived them of their desired tenure mix. When, beginning in 1916, black migration depleted local labor supplies, landowners had to hire whites, or more whites, or abandon farming altogether. Yet even in areas with plentiful workers of both races, planters showed a decided determination to adhere to a strict racial division of labor. For example, the opinion that "the class of white men that offer [themselves] for hire . . . as a rule are a very sorry class of men" served as a rationale for placing and keeping blacks in the lowest tenure statuses and favoring "the better class" of laboring whites as renters. The few white hands employed received the same low pay as blacks, but there were proportionately far fewer of them. Consequently, levels of compensation for members of the two races hired by the same planter at the same time were not strictly comparable; the assertion that "equal wage payment [for blacks and whites] was the prevaling rule" ignores the social and racial structure of the South's agricultural work force.[24]

The tenure status of farm families also reflected a plantation's size, crop mix, and proximity to cities. By the 1920s, large holdings in the Mississippi Delta, many of them owned by corporations, were characterized by complex tenure systems. The Mississippi Delta Planting Company, for example, grew cotton with sharecroppers but grain and forage crops with wage hands; on other places, families might work as share tenants for cotton and as cash tenants for corn. Croppers, share renters, and cash renters labored for wages "on plantation improvements, and when such work does not interfere with the production and gathering of their own crops." The situation was further complicated by its fluidity, with families changing from one status to another from year to year. In general, the larger an estate, the greater its reliance on croppers and managers to supervise them; smaller farms near towns could depend on a "floating" population of wage laborers for cotton harvesting and routine plantation maintenance.[25]

Time and necessity wrought transformations in the most dearly held principles of plantation organization. Most whites probably agreed that "the negro renter's foot is poison to the soil," but the disastrous drop in cotton prices during the 1890s convinced more and more planters that their own economic salvation required the shifting of a larger proportion of risk onto their workers, and the prevalence of cash renting increased for both blacks and whites. In Georgia's middle counties, the boll weevil plague had the opposite effect, as planters came to rely less on renters; the pest promoted diversified farming, which planters thought called for more croppers and wage hands. In any case, perhaps as a result of increases in cotton prices during World War I, by 1920 the proportion of cash renters had dropped for farmers of both races (from 10.4 to 7.5 percent for whites, and from 32 to 20 percent for blacks, from the decade before), suggesting that landless farmers of both races were affected in the same direction, though to different degrees, by the same economic forces.[26]

Human geography served as the ultimate determinant of the racial makeup of any plantation's work force. The landless classes of the Mississippi-Yazoo Delta, for example, included few whites. In contrast, by the 1930s sharecropping was a predominantly white institution in Florida, Texas, and parts of Virginia and North Carolina. South Carolina's Piedmont actually consisted of two regions—an upper piedmont where, in 1900, one-half of all tenants were white, and a lower piedmont, where black tenants outnumbered whites three to one. Still, in most areas of the South, like this one, individual planters had some leeway in choosing members of a particular race for certain tenure classifications. This tension born of race and contract status shaped employer-employee relations throughout the rural South. In the early twentieth century, for example, south Georgia planters profited from a migration of poor whites out of the northern part of the state and into traditionally black areas; in the words of one Thomas County landlord, "I told my [black] renters that unless they did better, I would be obliged to sell and they would have nowhere to go. Many planters are dispensing with negroes and putting in white people. Some of the sensible darkies are seeing that they are going to be pushed out."[27]

Trends in post–Civil War Southern agriculture suggest not the inexorable upward mobility implied by the agricultural tenure ladder so much as a railroad track running flat or, more likely, descending gradually over the generations. Farmers might advance to the next tie on the track, but chances were good that their material condition would not register much in the way of "progress" in any case. In vast areas of the Cotton South, like the Mississippi Delta, the ladder was in practical terms irrelevant, so pervasive was poverty and dependency among all landless families regardless of tenure status. Black farmers remained stalled at the beginning of the tracks, the unfortunate beneficiaries of planters' "preferences" for unskilled labor. Whites were ever in danger of falling behind, consumed by the needs of their large families and a voracious credit system that demanded they produce more and more cotton to sell at cheaper and cheaper rates. During those few years when the price of cotton was exceptionally high—as much as 85 cents per pound during World War I—planters foisted more supplies and small luxuries on their employees, and then presented them with proportionately larger bills at the end of December.[28] To make ends meet, then, families came to rely increasingly on jobs unrelated to crop cultivation, jobs that filled the slack seasons and demanded more hard work of farm folk of both races.

NONFARM WORKERS AND FORAGERS IN A PLANTATION ECONOMY

In industrializing America, all large commercial farmers had to devise ways to deploy labor forces of different sizes at different times of the year. The Southern solution to this problem depended on the availability of nearby, off-plantation work for members of landless families. In effect, the plantation and rural nonagricultural economies stood in symbiotic relationship to one other, with employers in each sector subsidizing the seasonal, low-wage labor in the other. To ensure a full complement of hands at harvesttime, planters retained an ostensibly resident work force; in effect, women and children served as a form of social insurance that guaranteed the return of their menfolk for planting or picking time. Therefore, employers of croppers and sawmill hands did not need to compete with each other for workers as much as they needed to keep wages low and prevent workers of both races from accumulating cash and land. In contrast, Midwestern farmers, such as large wheat and sugar-beet growers, rejected full-time work forces as too expensive, preferring at first to hire wage laborers at peak times. The social and financial costs incurred by such a system, which involved the regular influx into otherwise stable communities of mostly young, unmarried men (menacingly called "tramps" and "hoboes"), proved prohibitive in the long run, spurring mechanization. While Southern planters fretted over holding their workers from month to month, then, their Midwestern counterparts devised ways to phase out as much unskilled agricultural labor as possible.[29]

Irregular employment was the fate of most late-nineteenth-century American workers, whether or not they partook of the economic revolution that propelled the nation into full-blown industrialization. Cyclical upswings and downturns in the demand for consumer products and the availability of raw materials; natural disasters such as fires and floods, which temporarily or permanently halted activity at certain work sites; the agricultural slack season, an inevitable accompaniment of all staple-crop economies; lulls and spurts in the construction industry—all of these facts of economic life made stable, year-round jobs the exception and not the rule in the North and South. Various groups of workers sought to resolve this problem of chronic underemployment according to the means at their disposal. In early-twentieth-century Chicago shop-floor committees of cattle butchers incorporated demands for regular workdays and full-time, evenly paced work years into union contract negotiations with meatpacking employers. In the Northeast building tradesmen routinely moved around within their hometowns to locate jobs that were in turn predictably temporary. New England farm families accepted "outwork" from garment, shoe, and hat manufacturers, work that filled long winter days and nights. In Massachusetts cranberry pickers on Cape Cod instituted an annual trek to New Bedford once work in the bogs was finished. A similar trend pertained in the rural South, where lines between agricultural and industrial wage work blurred. There black and white farmers sought nonagricultural jobs after the midsummer lay-by time and during the winter, after reckoning time. Lacking the political power to regularize their employment either on or off the farm, these workers were forced to accommodate themselves to the demands of employers in both sectors.[30]

Around the turn of the century, some cotton plantations still operated on the principles followed by slaveowners in their efforts to extract as much labor as possible from a year-round, resident work force more bound than free. The sprawling estate called Smithsonia, owned by Colonel James M. Smith of Oglethorpe, Georgia, employed many hundreds of workers, including tenants and convict laborers (housed in five hundred cabins) who together annually produced three thousand bales of cotton and a wide variety of other crops (corn, wheat, oats, cowpeas, sweet potatoes, turnips, and hay). Smith's diverse agricultural and industrial enterprise, combined with a large number of workers that remained constant throughout the year, freed him from the worries of smaller planters who had to pay for any labor not directly related to cotton cultivation. Smith pointed out to an admiring reporter in 1904 that "to keep his laborers on hand for picking time," he "must keep them busy" in the meantime. Therefore his estate included "corn mills, grist mills, a cottonseed mill, a syrup mill, a woodworking shop, a buggy-repair shop, a system of waterworks" as well as a blacksmith shop, cottonseed oil mill, and fertilizer plant. This sort of enforced, year-round work schedule for tenants and convicts alike apparently failed to appeal to men under contract to Smith, sixteen of whom attempted to abscond (at the behest of labor agents) to the Southwest in early 1900; the police managed to arrest them as they were waiting to board a train for Atlanta.[31]

To operate small businesses other planters had to appeal to residents of their own plantations, and others. Millwood Plantation in Abbeville, South Carolina, included a small gold mine and a gristmill and sawmill. The two mills each provided employment for two men who were paid in cash by the day, working full time six months of the year in the sawmill and two months annually in the gristmill. Planters usually contracted separately with their resident workers if they wanted trees felled, lumber cut, or ties split. Cash wages, paid over and above any share of the crop, served to hold labor to a particular plantation and ensure sufficient hands at harvest time. A USDA investigator reported in 1924 that, since small plantation enterprises provided tenants with spending money, "factory or shop work on a small scale for women and children during idle seasons would have an influence in stabilizing the labor supply on the farm."[32]

The plantation and rural nonagricultural economies, linked by a depressed wage level and dependent on complementary forms of seasonal labor, remained distinct from manufacturing jobs that were clustered in cities and mill towns and reserved exclusively for whites. Referring to blacks' tendency to take jobs off the plantation during the contract year, a Georgia planter named W. L. Peek observed in 1900, "Under our farming system the negroes catch at every little thing. . . . The wage system is constant work, constant employment, his time belonging to the other man. Under the tenant system he takes a good deal of time and has liberty to go and come as he pleases." Together, the rural poor of both races caught at "every little thing" that a local economy might have to offer in terms of ready-cash making. An agricultural statistician reported from Florida in 1923 that nonagricultural wages were on a par with farm wages, facilitating movement between the two kinds of work. The higher pay offered to cotton pickers during harvest served to lure back laborers who had left the farm during the slack season, and attracted additional pickers from the towns. Depending on the season, regional opportunities, and the prospects for a good harvest, the proportion of men seeking off-plantation employment varied from year to year. Almost two-thirds of Georgia landlords surveyed in the early 1920s reported that at least some of their black employees had left the farm at some time or another during the last few years to work in local sawmills, which offered wages of $1.50 a day, usually after lay-by time (between July and September) and during the winter months, after harvest. Few studies document the effects of such employment on resident plantation work forces with statistical precision, but it is clear that the practice was common throughout the South.[33]

Local economies determined the nature and range of off-plantation (often called "public") work during the year. The Mississippi-Yazoo Delta region, though characterized by a general lack of industry, offered jobs to blacks in cotton gins as crewmen and engineers (for $1.00 to $1.50 per day) and on levees (at the same wage rates). A public works project in the area might draw workers from a four-mile radius seeking the daily paydays that lasted until a levee was repaired or a road built. In 1923 an official with the BAE reported that "the main cause of labor shortage [in the Delta] is that the increase in lumber prices has caused a great number of small saw mills to start operating." The availability of work in various extractive industries might inflate agricultural wages within a limited area; for example, the lumbering and oil industries helped to ensure relatively higher compensation for workers in the rice belt of Lousisiana compared to cotton croppers elsewhere in the South. A particularly poor crop in northern Alabama drove dependent farm laborers and their sons to the iron mines or the railroads, again during the slack season in both the summer and winter months. In the North Carolina Piedmont white tobacco farmers routinely earned cash off their own farms, by cutting lumber, repairing farm equipment for their neighbors, and working for the railroad.[34]

In Virginia small farmers cultivated their patches and supplemented home-grown vegetables in the summer with tonging for oysters during cold weather (along the tidewater) or working in the diverse industries that dotted the landscape of predominantly agricultural counties inland. In the early 1920s, for example, silk and woolen mills, lumber operations, quarries, and flour mills offered seasonal work to Albemarle County residents. Until a disastrous hurricane demolished the industry along the South Carolina coast in 1893, Sea Island blacks depended on wage work in the phosphate mines as well as meager returns from tiny landholdings; thereafter, Georgia and Florida turpentine camps and dock work in Savannah offered hope to breadwinners who "had to keep the family up during the cold months." Lumbering and turpentining remained mainstays for blacks in lower Georgia throughout the late nineteenth and on into the early twentieth centuries. Such work was considered temporary; for example, the young men who left the farms for the Birmingham mineral district "always come back. They go there and work a few months and generally drift back to the plantations." Although some young people used wage work off the plantation as a stepping-stone north, fathers often felt a strong obligation to return to the family fold, and the duty of farming, for planting and picking time.[35]

Thus rural-based enterprises, often modest and somewhat ephemeral, depended heavily, if not exclusively, on plantation-based labor; "situated in places remote from towns and railroads, . . . they are managed in a very quiet and unambitious style, working but a small force of hands as compared with the great mills." In turn, sawmills, turpentine farms, ginning mills, and grist mills, and even whiskey distilleries as well as various construction projects provided the extra measure of annual cash income that croppers and tenants came to expect as their due and to rely on as part of their livelihood. In some communities the prevalence of convict labor had a direct impact on the well-being of dependent farmers who normally would have taken advantage of wage-work opportunities. In late-nineteenth-century Georgia, for example, the use of convict labor on farms, on roads and waterways, and in turpentine camps "takes the bread and butter out of [the] mouths of farm laborers."[36]

The heavy work associated with the construction, extractive, and processing industries favored the employment of able-bodied men. Nevertheless, other family members found ways to add to the household income in the course of the year. Wives earned "patch" money by marketing small surpluses of vegetables and dairy products. Black women took in laundry, served as midwives, and laborered as domestic servants, at times for their poor white neighbors as well as for their landlords. White women helped to make the whiskey that provided families with their only source of cash income. Children of all ages went with their fathers to cut firewood to sell, and hired themselves out as cotton pickers on nearby farms once they had fulfilled harvesttime duties at home. Local truck farms employed women and children to pick berries and vegetables during the cotton slack season. Country folk all over the South congregated on cotton plantations at the end of the year to earn some cash (usually between 75 cents and $1.50 a day). In Florence, South Carolina, a community with both tobacco and cotton farming, tobacco tenants could gather their own crop and then move down the road and find a job "while there is any cotton left to pick, sometimes even until Christmas." Planters in Leflore County, Mississippi, annually paid white labor agents to bring "hill negroes" down to the Delta, where "Labor for picking is very hard to get indeed."[37]

Foraging, including fishing and hunting, represented for many plantation workers a subeconomy that might yield small amounts of cash and rescue families from complete dependence on merchants' stores and planters' advances. These households depended on the ability of "women and children [to pick up] a precarious living out of the assets of the community—fruit, fowls, game and fish." Well-to-do whites (and some blacks, like Booker T. Washington) condemned fishing and hunting as leisurely pursuits, more akin to recreation than productive labor; but for the black women of the Sand Hills District in Sumter County, South Carolina, "muddying" for eels or mullet and fishing in nearby creeks and rivers afforded a major source of livelihood. (In contrast, their menfolk "went to nearby mills or into the forest to cut crossties for the railroad.") The skills and physical exertion expended on such pursuits indicated that they were more substantial activities than the term "sport" implied. The Sand Hills women who "muddied" the Pee Dee River "would hike their dresses up and wade in, taking up the fish in baskets or nets"—certainly not a simple task for the uninitiated. The young boys who, bleary-eyed, stumbled their way through thickets on moonlit possum hunts with their fathers, would have disputed their employers' contention that hunting appealed to the lazy instincts of men of both races. And finally, a good day's catch rarely came easily. It depended instead on a store of experience, patience, and intensity of concentration characterized by few truly "leisurely" pursuits. Interviewed in the late 1930s, John Belcher of the Delta, a seasoned deer trapper, seemed most proud of his fishing techniques, which supplied fresh food for his family, kin, and neighboring customers as well:

> Fer catchin' Buffalo now I uses flour dough an a little corn meal, mixed wid a little cotton worked in it, fer bait. Durin de time I'm not fishin I puts two or three "Draws" out in different places on de river. To make dese "Draws" I put chops, corn meal, or bread, in a crocker sack makin a roll bout 12 inches long by 10 inches wide. I attach a wire to dis and anchor de wire to a stob long de river bank. I leaves dis here fer bout 8 days to toll de fish to dis spot. When I gits ready to fish dere I partly draws dis wire in den drap in my line and I really catches dem buffaloes.

Belcher's elaborate preparations contradict the image of the indifferent, slumbering fisherman slouched over a riverbank on a lazy summer day.[38]

The sharecropping family economy demonstrated striking patterns of continuity between 1870 and the onset of the Great Depression. For example, Ned Cobb's early years echoed those of William Holtzclaw, and presaged those of Ed Brown a generation later. As children, Cobb and his sister cut cord wood for their father to sell in winter. "When he weren't sawin wood," the older man cut cross ties, a "nasty [thing] for a man to do—with a broad ax and a club ax and a cross-cut saw"—for 15 or 20 cents each. Beginning at age eighteen, Ned had a series of jobs that took him away from home for stretches at a time—working at a water gin and a sawmill, plowing for one white man, hauling cotton seed and guano for another. As a young married man starting out as a sharecropper on his own, Cobb "scuffled" (by making baskets and cutting wood to sell) and saved enough cash to buy a buggy. Cobb's children were still too small "to hand you a glass of water," and he refused to allow his wife to wash clothes for money—"My wife didn't wait on white folks for their dirty laundry," he declared proudly. Yet for all his ingenuity with a double-mule plow, Cobb recalled later that he was able to support his family only with the extra money he made hauling lumber for a nearby company after lay-by time: "what little I did get I had to work like the devil to get it. It didn't profit me nothin."[39]

Foraging and wage work off the plantation earned households small amounts of cash that benefited both them and their communities. The significance of this fact becomes most apparent in the case of black sharecroppers, who, though occupying a lowly position on the agricultural tenure ladder, managed to create and sustain their own churches, schools, burial societies, and benevolent associations throughout the South, from the end of the Civil War until well into the twentieth century. Croppers saw precious little cash at reckoning time in December, or on payday at the nearby sawmill, but a large portion of what they managed to accumulate must have gone to the upkeep of community institutions. Because planters in the Black Belt had little incentive to sell off parcels of their property to their employees, the outlet for small amounts of capital was necessarily limited within the black community. In effect, the nonagricultural wage work of individual farmers and their families served as the financial underpinnings of black associational life.

THE PRICE OF SMALL-FARM OWNERSHIP

The fathers of Ed Brown, William Holtzclaw, and Ned Cobb never owned their own farms; but if they had, they would have found that their struggles were far from over. Farmers with fifty acres or less faced stark trade-offs, for the status of landowner carried a hefty price tag for those who relied exclusively on the muscle power of their own households. Their "independence" from landlords actually came at the price of dependence on creditors and outside wage work. Still, owners lived a more settled existence than their landless neighbors, and those who managed to pass on tiny homesteads through the years left their descendants a legacy that seemed more precious with each succeeding generation.[40]

The story of the South's small farm owners in the late nineteenth century represents the intersection of the freedpeople's climb out of slavery and the poor whites' descent into tenancy. In 1920 black owners were concentrated in "areas of cheap land"—eastern Virginia, the South Carolina Sea Islands, and northeastern Texas, their modest gains nevertheless hard-won over the last half century. White owners were more numerous in the Appalachian Mountains and the Upper Piedmont; the Black Belt had the highest proportion of tenants and croppers. The rise of black-owned banks in the early twentieth century helps to account for the 180,000 full black owners in the South in 1920 (a figure that declined by 40,000 during the following decade). The number of white owners increased from 1,080,000 in 1900 to 1,230,000 ten years later (primarily due to an increase in the general population); however, the 1920s were also a disastrous period for whites, claiming 175,000 owners.[41]

Compared to their black counterparts, white landowners remained privileged in terms of access to formal education for their children and to home demonstration agents and regionwide farmers' institutes, all means to secure information about modern farming techniques. Black men with aspirations were forced to rely on the goodwill of whites under a patronage system that mandated specific qualifications for landownership; "In most cases where an individual [black] had bought the land he operated, the purchase was made possible only with the aid of a white person." Sam McCall, "the celebrated Negro farmer of Wilcox County, Alabama," was described by an approving government official as "an old-time darky, one of a type loved by every true Southerner but which, unfortunately, is rapidly passing." Twenty-nine years old in 1865, McCall remained, now as a tenant, on the plantation of his former owner after emancipation; this act of devotion earned him the "trust" of his white benefactors and the opportunity to buy 160 acres, though the land was "thin." Black homesteads were small (usually only twenty to forty acres) and located in out-of-the way places, in swamps and pine barrens. Virginia landowners, for example, subsisted on tiny "patches" that hardly qualified as "farms" in the traditional sense.[42]

Even modest landowners demonstrated a self-conscious pride in their well-deserved reputations as strivers and scufflers. For example, W. L. Bost and his new wife, Mamie, bought a "little piece of ground" for $125 near Newton, North Carolina, in 1895. By buying lumber "a little at a time," they built a house for their family of three children. Forty-two years later the Bosts still occupied the land and could note with some satisfaction, "It's been a good home for us and the children." Homeownership encouraged permanent improvements of cabins, outbuildings, and land, in contrast to croppers' makeshift efforts in the direction of "homelikeness." Sara Brooks's mother could afford to lavish her time and energy on flowering perennials—"a yard *fulla* flowers" that her family appreciated both for their beauty and their medicinal qualities (the headache leaf "had big leaves and . . . pretty blooms on it"). Throughout the South, farm owners could boast a more diversified crop mix and more varied diets than those of workers dependent on a landlord. A family like the Brookses might harvest their cotton in the late fall and turn next to pulling up the peanuts; "By the time the peanuts would be put away, it'd be time then to dig the potatoes." The gathering of red and yellow plums, peaches and pears signaled canning season for the mother of the household. Family crops also included corn, peas, and sugarcane. Descriptions of this household's bounty—the fruits and vegetables, fish, pork, beef, and chickens—present a striking contrast to the monotonous fare consumed by landless people throughout the Cotton Belt.[43]

Mamie Garvin Fields too remembered the luscious variety of fruit grown on her grandfather's farm in South Carolina; and he "never bought food, except maybe some flour." But perhaps the most dramatic proof of his stature as a farmer came every fall, when he hauled his cotton back from the local gin so he could "set it in his front yard. He always said, 'I won't sell until I get my price. . . .'" This sort of ostentatious crop display was highly unusual, however, because most small owners found the margin between effort and gain exceedingly slim; they had to sell quickly in December, when crop prices were low and creditors were menacing. For these families, backbreaking labor was a year-round, and not just a seasonal, imperative. In 1922 two rural sociologists described the plight of small farmers of both races in North Carolina as "purgatory"; "if the farm is ever paid for, it must be paid for in pinching self-denial, in the field work of [the farmer's] wife and children, and in the lack of school advantages, newspapers, magazines, and noble books." The son of one white farm owner confirmed this view, later recalling of his father's 150-acre homestead, "unless you's a big rich farmer, unless he had good equipment and everything, he couldn't make a living. We had plenty of food to eat, but our clothes wasn't too much. We got by, but it wasn't like people ought to have."[44]

Small family-owned farms were distinguished both from large plantations and from tenant holdings by their reliance on their own labor; in order to "get by," they had an incentive to limit their production of cotton so they could avoid any added expense at harvesttime. The ability of a farmer-father to retain his own land depended on his children's ages and their ability to help out in the fields. A newlywed couple working together might "lay up something every year," but when the babies started to arrive, "'it is just about tight and toody' to get through to the end of the year, and then they have to work at all seasons, from the chopping of the cotton to the harvesting." A 1917 survey of school attendance in rural Alabama revealed that, in general, owners' children attended school more regularly than tenants', but that daughters of the two groups were kept at home to do "housework" in the same proportions—a little more than a quarter of the time they should have been in school. The autobiographies of owners' children provide no indication that they were exempt from the most arduous labor, in or outside the house.[45]

The dream of total self-sufficiency eluded most small owners, who felt the same need as their landless neighbors to seek wage work away from home. During the late nineteenth century along the coast of South Carolina, black owners did "much to make the two ends meet" during the slack season by leaving their wives and children "to hoe and look after the crops, while they earn wages by diving for and cleaning the phosphates" at nearby dredging operations. In Wake County, North Carolina, 25 percent of white farm owners worked for other farmers and earned an average of $728 per year for their labor. In Alabama during the winter, Sara Brooks's father cut and rolled logs "at a place called Pineland," returning home only on weekends. He also made some extra money by digging and cleaning wells and by working on the railroad— "now he did that most often than anything else." The children hoed and picked cotton for a neighboring white man (for 50 cents a day). An older son never finished high school; he "went to workin out" in Springfield, where he would saw logs during the week and bring home his earnings to his father on weekends. Later, Sara Brooks described her parents' considerable efforts to keep the farm going and enable the children to get some schooling too:

When time come to plant the crops, we'd have to stay home some days to plant the crops, we'd have to stay home some days in order to help get things in line. See, it was four of us—my brother and Molly, Rhoda and me—plus Sally and them, too. They was small but they worked. My father would keep us out of school a half day—maybe two of us today or three today, and maybe two or three the next day. We'd work in the mornin and then go to school at noontime. Or sometime two'd work all day or three'd work all day and then go to school the next day. He wouldn't keep us out day after day—we'd rotate. Then we'd go to school until we finished school, and that was in May.

This family, like many others, faced painful trade-offs between sending the children to school and holding onto their land. The usual correlation between educational attainment and ownership did not pertain in all cases.[46]

And finally, most farmers regardless of tenure status had to live on credit during the year unless they could earn enough in wages or from the sale of chickens and eggs to support their families. Personal and real property taxes enforced a type of subordination that was as financially costly as it was personally demeaning; even the most industrious farmer could count on a creditor to "ride out and see if it's promisin enough to let you keep on takin up." After he inherited a piece of land from his father, one black farmer in Macon County, Alabama, found himself liable for $45 to $65 annually in taxes on the place. In the mid-1920s all his cows had been seized by the Macon County Bank to pay off part of his $900 debt, and "ever' year hit increases." The taxes were, he said bitterly, "Jest 'nough to kill folks." White farmers were not exempt from postbellum regressive tax policies. Fred Yoder's father was "maybe the most prosperous man in the immediate neighborhood" in Catawba County, North Carolina; but with no ready cash and a tax bill to pay, the white man "sacked up some wheat, and he sacked up some corn, and he sacked up some potatoes and maybe loaded a ham or two—half a dozen products—and went to the town of Newton" in a futile attempt to meet his financial obligations.[47]

Even when country life would not reward the "big eyes and high hopes" of hardworking men and women, loyalty to kin—the satisfaction of being "at home anywhere I went amongst my mother's and daddy's folks"—a love of the land, and pride in one's farming abilities kept many people of exceptional abilities on the farm, in lowly circumstances. Nevertheless, in the words of W. E. B. DuBois, "If [the farmer] is ambitious, he moves to town or tries other kinds of labor. . . . " The sociologist Charles S. Johnson agreed that "the more alert and ambitious of the men" left their rural homes for Southern or Northern cities.[48]

Still, a town dweller might mourn the loss of a modest, rural-based independence, or even the dream of it. The death of a male household head often brought to a bitter end a family's search for a settled home in the country. Interviewed in the late 1930s by Federal Writers Project workers, two elderly black women expressed their deep regrets that the strenuous efforts of their farming fathers and husbands had amounted to so little. Laura Montgomery, age eighty-seven, of McComb, Mississippi, enjoyed a twenty-seven-year-long marriage to her husband, Silas, and bore him nine children. He labored in the cotton fields and at "public work," and so they "managed to git us a little home"; but after his death and the departure of her children she was unable to hold onto it, "an moved in town an wuk for somethin' to eat in kitchens." Mary Anne Gibson felt similarly displaced in the city at the end of her life. She had grown up in east Texas, where her father sold charcoal, farmed on halves, and presided over frequent moves to new plantations. Her mother cooked for whites while her sister served as a nurse for their children, and Mary Anne worked in the fields. She described her father as a "noble man" who died at age thirty-eight, while he was in the process of "trying to build a house" for his family. Mary Anne's three marriages kept her on the farm (or rather, a farm), but at the age of seventy-six she found herself living in Austin: "I was bawn in de country, and lived in de country. I lak de country, and always did. I wouldn't be in town now, if I had a way to live on the farm." Just a couple of generations removed from slavery, the Montgomery and Gibson households lived a seminomadic existence until they could own their own home. The menfolk had to leave their families, this time not at the behest of slaveowners who hired them out, but according to their own calculations about the way wage work could best meet the needs of their families.[49]

White households pushed out of the mountains and off the Piedmont and into a city or mill village could also leave behind a trail of regrets. Ernest Hickum's father wrested a living from his farm in the mountains of North Carolina; the family raised tobacco, corn, and wheat, and never lacked for food from their garden. However, in the 1920s, a significant portion of the household's income was eliminated when trucks were introduced by local lumber concerns and Hickum could no longer make money hauling logs with his wagon; his son remembered the time: "Now it wasn't but a year or two that they got to bringing them other kinds of trucks in there and just cut the poor farmers plumb out of the sawmill, hauling lumber." The family sold their home and moved to Woodside Mill, to find work; but the father "just studied and grieved about selling everything he had and coming down here. He got around that machinery and he never seen nothing like it. You know what a racket machinery makes. I think the machinery scared him too much to try to run a job. . . . He couldn't work in no cotton mill, so he went back to the mountains."[50]

Mill work was an appealing option for white husbands and fathers who wanted to keep their families together at all costs, men who resisted taking "public work" while their wives and children remained back on the farm. Black sharecroppers, tenants, and small owners lacked this option; for them, life in the towns and cities meant not a harmony between work and family and home but fragmented households—wives and daughters in the white folks' kitchens; sons and husbands dependent on low-wage, temporary unskilled work that kept them constantly on the move. All of these families regardless of race aimed to make a home for themselves on the land. But if the eventual fate of their children is any indication, they failed. For aspiring tenants and sharecroppers, the rural South operated on the basis of a strange system of incentives and rewards, with hard work enforced and ambition scorned.

The history of the Populist party in the 1890s serves as a lesson in the persistence, and pitfalls, of racial politics in the South. The Populists sought to unite two strains of agrarian protest—the (white) Farmers Alliance and the Colored Farmers Alliance—and forge a program that would speak to the needs of all farm folk, from wage laborers to small owners. Thrown together by the contempt of white elites—"So disfranchise the negro and white man that hasn't any land and let us have a fair election," declared one Georgia landowner—the dispossessed of both races could agree upon the value of pro-cropper legislation, restrictions on the convict-lease system, and the redemptive value of the subtreasury (a plan that would allow farmers to sell their crops at the highest, off-season price). If this coalition represented a "democratic moment" of unprecedented biracial cooperation, it also owed its ultimate failure to the stubbornness of regional and racial loyalties that militated against a party with national appeal. The Populists failed to bridge fissures between North and South, and between rural and urban, agricultural and industrial workers. In the South the Populists exemplified a political principle revealed clearly by the racial division of labor in rural areas; even poor whites benefited from the color of their skin, both in terms of their tenure status and their opportunities to leave the countryside altogether.[51]

The vast majority of white Populists simply could not free themselves from the dictates of a caste-bound Southern past. A Georgia man expressed his fellow loyalists' ambivalence toward blacks in general when he noted in 1892, "Now as to lynching I am opposed to it except in extreme cases." White party members in the various states (clustered in the Piedmont and Wiregrass regions) played out their own brand of opportunism toward black voters (most of whom lived in the Black Belt) in response to local political considerations. In Texas even the most progressive leaders were unsuccessful in their attempt to win over more traditional-minded members on the value of biracial activism. Desperate to find congenial candidates tied to either major political party, Populists throughout the South inevitably encountered, on the one hand, the steadfast allegiance of blacks to the party of the Great Emancipator (making fusion with the national Democrats problematic), and, on the other, the feeling among many Southern whites that the Republicans were "tainted" by black followers (making fusion with the local Republicans, except in certain white areas of North Carolina, a recurring ordeal). By brutalizing and intimidating their black opponents, the Georgia Populists "after dark" borrowed liberally from the tactics of Ku Kluxers, Red Shirts, White Caps, and other terrorist groups. Awed by the power and viciousness of Democrats each election day, or perhaps simply exasperated by the whole racial issue, some Populist leaders eventually capitulated to the virulent racism of the Democratic establishment. Most whites regardless of class seemed to agree that their own fortunes would depend on the elimination of blacks from the body politic.[52]

While poor whites recoiled from the prospect of a public alliance with the former slaves and their children, blacks responded in kind with a deep distrust of the men and women who figured prominently among the minions of Judge Lynch in the turn-of-the-century South. Indeed, most black people, landed or landless, male or female, preferred to have as little as possible to do with whites of all kinds, in town on Saturday afternoon or in the fields all week long. When it came to white people, according to Ed Brown, "My motto was . . . Don't Meet Nobody." Recalled a black midwife in Alabama, "They avoided the whites period. They be afraid to meet em. If a white person comin, they'll go way around." Racial segregation amounted to a political humiliation but a practical necessity. Ollie Smith, a North Carolina sharecropper near Mocksville for many years, remembered an uneasy, superficial harmony based on institutional separation in churches and schools. Blacks and whites, she recalled, "tended to their own business. Just quiet—nothin but work. You never hear of no fussin or fightin." Ed Brown's mother,

Martha, testified to the enduring power of history when she told her son around the time of World War I, "If the white people would forget my color and I would forget slavery we could all be Christians together." Yet Martha Brown's vision of a world of color-blind souls united in religious faith would find no place in the Jim Crow Southern countryside.[53]

4

Shifting and "Shiftlessness": Annual Plantation Turnover, 1870 to 1930

Because they lived in an essentially rural and kin-oriented society, Southerners black and white, rich and poor, held sacred the notion of home, defined not only as the affective relations that bound a particular family (wherever it might reside) but also as a particular place. Harry Crews, the son of white Georgia croppers and a contemporary of Ed Brown's, recalled that his people believed "the *home place* is as vital and necessary as the beating of your own heart." Ideally, the place was "that single house where you were born, where you lived out your childhood, where you grew into young manhood . . . your anchor in the world." Crews acknowledged that the yearning for such a home was probably universal, "important to everybody everywhere," but he also suggested that the feeling was particularly intense in Bacon County, Georgia, because there "the people understand that if you do not have a home place, very little will ever be yours, really *belong* to you in the world." Crews's evocation of home derived from the fact that he never had one: "because we were driven from pillar to post when I was a child, there is nowhere I can think of as the home place." Only landownership conferred stability, a way of life and a source of memories for the rich but not the poor.[1]

Throughout the United States between 1870 and 1930, the workers with the highest rates of labor turnover and residential mobility were the poorest people; some found themselves "driven from pillar to post" (that is, fired) by employers who needed their labor for only part of the year, while others chose to leave of their own accord (that is, they quit), out of anger or in the hope of finding something better. In the mid-Atlantic region landless "flitting families" seemed ever on the move in search of more favorable tenancy contracts. In small towns and big cities black domestics made a full-time occupation of exasperating the white women who hired them. Lacking a sense of "moral obligation" that would tie them to an employer for more than a few months at a time, black cooks and maids would, in the words of one housewife, "leave when they knew that invitations were out for a dining in the house; they would just leave without any particular reason at all, but simply from some foolish desire for a change." Factory owners complained constantly about "uncommitted" workers, from immigrant "greenhorns" in Northern steel mills to Tennessee "hillbillies" in Piedmont textile mills; these same employers, however, rarely divined the connection between high rates of labor turnover on the one hand and poor working conditions and irregular employment on the other.[2]

In the rural South tenant households often "shifted," "hit the grit" or "lit the shuck" at the end of a contract year; they were more mobile than their counterparts in New England, the Midwest, and the Far West. The problem of dependent farm laborers who moved from one plantation to another annually had long been a source of misery to Southern employers, but the term "shifting tenant" (to denote a sociological phenomenon) came into use only in the early twentieth century, when United States Department of Agriculture (USDA) and Census Bureau officials began to view end-of-year plantation turnover as a distinct problem in rural life. Characterized by short-range geographical movement, shifting was defined as a change in residence with little or no change in formal tenure status, in contrast to upward or downward social mobility. Shifting plantation workers tended to stay within their immediate neighborhood; "their one outstanding means of asserting freedom is this mobility, although within an extremely narrow range." Hence they did not qualify as migrants. This type of mobility seemed somewhat circular; the workers of a subregion remained the same over time, while they changed their workplaces frequently. Thus "planters can never tell which of their tenants will be with them the following year, but of one thing they can be fairly certain—that they [the workers] will not leave the count . . . "3

Around the turn of the century rare indeed was the planter, journalist, agricultural agent, or scholar who had one kind word to say about the practice of shifting. In addition to throwing the long-range plans of landlords into disarray, shifting, according to contemporaries, ensured that "there is no sympathetic tie between [croppers] and their employers," a veiled reference to the demise of (supposed) antebellum-style Southern paternalism. Workers who moved frequently provided critics with evidence of the moral defects of an entire class of people—their "aimlessness and "irresponsibility." Government officials and scholars who saw a connection between stability and "creditworthiness" argued that the shifting population, in its shortsighted search for "better things," engaged in self-defeating behavior by failing to stay in one place long enough to obtain personal references and hence loans from banks and other sources of credit. Some white observers, Northerners and USDA men, chose to ignore the fact that planters did their best to prevent their workers from accumulating much of anything; these white observers went so far as to condemn shifting as the root of "all social and religious problems" that plagued the rural poor, the main reason that people were unable to rise out of dependency by committing themselves to a single piece of land and to the single-minded use of family labor that ownership required.4

In the minds of Southern planters, shifting was intimately related to croppers' "shiftlessness," an all-purpose term used to refer to indolence and moral laxity. Yet poor families of both races prided themselves on their ability and willingness to work hard. Indeed, they were hardly strangers to backbreaking labor because cotton could be grown no other way. Sharecroppers forced to rise at daybreak and hoe or pick cotton until dusk, their every move monitored by an owner or plantation manager, were by definition hard workers. Boys and girls were reared with the reality of a forced pace of field work in mind. Of her own apprenticeship as a sharecropper's daughter, Ollie Smith recalled, "I was raised to work." One rural sociologist noted that, in the households of white North Carolina tenant farmers, "Children are born to work not play. In listing for us the children's games in the various homes, one tenant housewife said with spirit, 'I wants you to understand that we works hereabouts, we ain't no sportin' neighborhood.'" Needless to say, some youngsters accepted these strictures with more equanimity than did others. And of course, for mothers with large numbers of children, and responsible for all the daily housework that huge families required, "laziness" was hardly an option.[5]

Though prominent in the Jim Crow pantheon of repressive laws, criminal statutes designed to limit the mobility of agricultural laborers proved remarkably ineffective. The system of debt peonage existed in the rural South until well into the twentieth century (perhaps as many as one-third of all croppers in Alabama, Mississippi, and Georgia were being held against their will in 1900), and vestiges of the system remained a stubborn component of East Coast migratory labor. Still, the prevalence of shifting revealed that a great deal of movement took place within the Southern plantation economy. Initially intended to restrict the freedom of movement among freedpeople (in the form of Black Codes), this type of legislation was eventually resurrected in the post-Reconstruction period by all the former Confederate states, now couched in race-neutral language. Laws designed to discourage vagrancy, labor "enticement," breach of contract, and the work of emigrant agents all provided employers with the legal wherewithal to hold workers against their will and to bring suit against other employers who sought to "seduce" workers away. This body of legislation was part and parcel of a general attempt to limit the rights of black people in the late nineteenth century; contract "false pretenses" laws as well as the racial segregation of transportation and public facilities and restrictions on black suffrage were all achieved without much in the way of interference from Northerners.[6]

Compared to other draconian measures of the Jim Crow South, however, efforts to bind employees to their employers proved problematic because the beneficiaries of these laws—the planters themselves—desired a certain flexibility in adjusting the size and character of their work forces each year; these white men therefore wanted to leave the way open should they wish either to pare down their number of employees or to enter the ranks of the ubiquitous "tenant stealers" at any particular time. In a study of plantation organization in 1924, a USDA investigator acknowledged that, given an abundant labor supply (true for most subregions of the South, at least before the Great Migration of 1916), "local restlessness [among workers] had never been a cause for anxiety or alarm to plantation operators . . . because the shifting labor was replaced by other shifting labor and no particular inconvenience was experienced." In times of acute labor shortage, such as World War I, employers could dredge up contract-enforcement and antivagrancy statutes with a vengeance; but otherwise planters reserved for themselves the chance to lure particularly promising tenants from a neighboring fold or to expel tenants at will during the slack season or in December, regardless of stipulated contractural arrangements. Just as planters could "expend a large amount of time, money, and emotion in preventing the criminals they employ from receiving their legal deserts," so those same whites could choose either to ignore or conform to labor mobility legislation as their immediate interests dictated.[7]

Ultimately, shifting resulted from the configuration of power relations on the plantation. In contrast to planters' and government officials' view that shifting was primarily a moral problem, a sign of weak character among the poor, modern economic historians prefer to view the practice in more neutral terms, the result of decisions of economically "rational" people responding to market conditions by "taking a mind" to move. Yet black and white families failed to respond in predictable ways either to the exhortations of their employers or to so-called financial incentives (which were in short supply in the rural South in any case).[8] Leaving a plantation at the end of the year, or making a special effort to stay, constituted a form of defiance toward the powers-that-be, and shifters reckoned their own best interests according to the needs of household and kin, or the seemingly counterproductive impulse to challenge a hated landlord. As a rural folk, then, workers of both races shared certain priorities in shifting, although for poor whites the textile mills offered a way out of the plantation economy, a way that was blocked to blacks. The complexity of the matrix of motives that produced annual plantation turnover—those of landlord and black and white tenant—ultimately reflected a struggle over issues that lay at the heart of the postbellum South's system of repression and domination.

THE RACIAL AND CLASS POLITICS OF SHIFTING

From the end of the Civil War to the beginning of the Great Depression, planters, government officials, and visitors to the South lamented the failure of black sharecroppers and tenants to remain rooted in one place for very long. In 1874 journalist Edwin DeLeon described the freedman as "restless and roving, . . . getting poorer and shabbier and sulkier at each remove instead of bettering his condition. . . . " The latter-day children of the Old Testament's Reuben, blacks were "'made like unto a wheel,' ever rolling, never resting, and never accumulating either money or realty." A native South Carolinian concurred: "The negro rarely possesses any home attachments. He is continually on the wing. . . . " A quarter of a century later a federal commission on agricultural labor heard testimony from several Southern whites who described the "restless disposition" of blacks, leading one panel member to cite the "natural shiftlessness of the negro . . . his carelessness, and his transient condition, travelling from one spot to another, losing time and opportunities." Nevertheless, by the end of the century such complaints had become more generalized to take into account the growing numbers of whites reduced to perpetual tenantry, "losing time and opportunities" after their own fashion. In 1930 black sharecroppers outnumbered their white counterparts, and blacks as a group predominated in the lowest tenure categories of cropper and wage hand, but landless whites accounted for more people in absolute numbers (1.4 million families compared to 1.1 million black families). In the 1920s investigators for the USDA saw no need to specify the race of the offenders when they warned of the "evil consequences . . . partly social and partly economic" that arose from the annual shifting of tenants.[9]

In the South between 1880 and 1930, an average of three or four of every ten sharecropping families resident on a plantation in any given year had arrived the previous January. Because residential stability increased with social status, a breakdown of the data according to race yields a somewhat unexpected conclusion; white croppers and tenants tended to move more often than blacks of similar status. As we have seen, within tenure categories blacks fared less well than whites; thus we might expect a black cropper to move more frequently than his white counterpart. Figures from the 1910 census, however, indicate the opposite quite clearly; 42.1 percent of white tenants and 28.8 percent of black tenants had resided on their present farm less than one year (cash tenants were more stable than share tenants, with the discrepancy according to race intact). A 1920 survey of ninety-three selected plantation counties included information on 164,389 black and white croppers, tenants (share, share cash), and renters (standing and cash). Here again the relationships held constant, though the fact that the census was taken on January 1 (and not April 1, as usual) served to underestimate the turnover rate; not all families planning to leave their home for the 1920 calendar year had done so by New Year's Day. Nevertheless, 28.4 percent of white croppers and 19.7 percent of the blacks had lived for less than a year on their present plantation. These percentages declined, in corresponding proportions according to race, with an increase in tenure status; cash renters were twice as stable as sharecroppers.[10]

Several possible explanations account for racial differentials in annual plantation turnover. The authors of a 1910 USDA study concluded that "tenantry amongst the white farmers in the South is increasing more rapidly than anywhere else in the country." Added to the households of newlyweds that each year entered the various tenure classes then were white families of higher status slipping into tenancy. Aggregate turnover data—expressed as "average number of years on present farm"—suggest another interpretation; proportionately more whites had more opportunities to improve their tenure status compared to blacks, and experienced modest, incremental, upward mobility. Moreover, for white families, social and geographical mobility was enhanced by certain kinds of wage work denied to blacks on a local and regional basis. An individual establishment, such as a Columbus, Georgia, iron foundry, might set its own racial policies in hiring, while entire industries, such as textiles, effectively denied employment to all black people. Between 1880 and 1930 the exodus of young, large white families off the farm and into textile mills, combined with disillusioned workers' periodic returns to the countryside, helps to explain at least some of the residential instability of white families in the Piedmont South. One North Carolina mill worker later recalled, "A lot of people leaned toward farming. But when they'd harvest their crops—say, their cotton in the fall—they had plenty of time during the winter, so they'd go to the mill and see if they could get them a job and work during the winter, and then they'd move back, as tenant farmers [to a different place?] to the farms in the springtime and plant another crop."[11]

Thus the rallying cry of "free, white, and twenty-one" had real meaning in the South, where many positions for laborers, in cities and mill towns, remained reserved for whites. Around the turn of the century, the black people who migrated to nearby towns and cities often did so to seek protection from white terrorists or education for their children, not necessarily to take better jobs. In 1901 an Augusta, Georgia, landowner noted that, while white workers were gravitating toward the cities, black labor remained "confined locally to the farm" because of the exclusionary policies of employers in the town's industrial establishments. Even the modest migrations of blacks to the labor-hungry Delta and to Texas and Arkansas in the late nineteenth century met with violent resistance on the part of employers back home in Georgia and Alabama. Not surprisingly, then, a number of surveys conducted by the Bureau of Agricultural Economics (BAE) in 1923 indicated that local, incremental movement was more significant than long-range migration either to other parts of the South or northward. For example, in 1923 a BAE statistician in Florida speculated on the destination of the blacks who had moved from their place of residence recently; he believed that 2 percent of the total black population had gone north, 1 percent had moved to other cotton states, and 6 percent, to other parts of (northern) Florida. After 1916 the Great Migration revealed that, as in previous years, a lack of demand for black labor in the industrial Northeast and Midwest—and not some universal (if vague) preference among blacks for Southern climate or "comforts"—accounted for the lack of movement out of the region.[12]

In 1898 a white man named Alfred H. Stone launched a five-year experiment to achieve an "assured tenantry" on Dunlieth, his expansive Mississippi-Yazoo Delta cotton plantation. This self-proclaimed expert on race relations and agricultural reform had long battled against the whims of his workers, with their "characteristic unreliability." He wrote in 1905, "The desire to move from place to place, the absence of local attachment, seems to be a governing trait in the Negro character, and a most unfortunate one for the race." Stone aimed to overcome the instability of his resident work force (produced by the "great . . . annual competition among planters for Negro labor") by offering "the best terms and most advantageous tenant relation" to carefully selected families. These terms included fixed cash rental of land; the lease of stock and equipment "upon exceptionally favourable terms"; close supervision over crop production; marketing of the crop by Stone and his managers; and a written contract to seal the agreement between tenant and landlord. In December of 1898 Stone added thirty new families to the twenty-eight who remained on his plantation from the previous year. Twelve months later almost half of the total fifty-eight households left Dunlieth, and Stone brought in twenty-seven more families to replace them. Turnover rates for succeeding years ranged from 22 percent in 1899 to 41 percent in 1902.[13]

Stone later acknowledged that his experiment was unsuccessful because he was unable "to create a satisfied and satisfactory force of reasonably permanent tenants." Indeed, he noted, the more prosperous his tenants (in terms of their ability to buy equipment and realize a profit at the end of the year), the more likely they were to abandon him and go elsewhere; the workers who remained on Dunlieth were the least efficient farmers, the ones he hoped to dismiss eventually. He concluded halfway through the five-year period that "even the most practical appeal we could make to radically improved material welfare would be generally overcome by an apparently instinctive desire to 'move.'" For his part, Stone was not interested in putting poverty-stricken blacks "on their feet" so that his competitors might take advantage of them; "converting shiftless and empty-handed Negroes into desirable and well-equipped tenants" amounted to nothing less than an "altruistic enterprise" that benefited other planters at his expense, and he would have none of it.[14]

Stone faced a planter's dilemma that the practical application of economic principles just could not solve: The best tenants were bound to leave, while the worst stayed behind. An employer might expel the lazy ones, in hopes of attracting the "better kind" of tenant, but this annual turnover necessarily undermined continuity of plantation operations. To Stone blacks appeared to shift for irrational reasons—"a migratory instinct . . . a characteristic easy-going indolence"—and even "material betterment" would fail to hold them to one place from one year to the next. Stone himself waxed eloquent in his denunciation of these field workers: "like one lost in a forest, they move but in a narrow circle, yet always in the same vain, aimless quest." He managed to follow the fortunes of former tenants from several years past, indicating that they had not "wandered" very far from Dunlieth; yet he saw no appreciable gain in their material condition as a result. In the end, their lack of a "love of home," their failure "to form local attachments or to develop anything akin to such a sentiment" would continue to ensure an "ever present reality" of "local drift and restless movement."[15]

Stone saw shifting as a baffling phenomenon, seemingly unrelated to the set of rational choices that any self-respecting worker would make; but in fact, both black and white shifting families sought to resist the close supervision that was the sharecropper's lot in life. The former slaves embraced a freedom that would set them apart from their forbears in bondage. Together, in family groups, they institutionalized the annual practice of running away, though they could deprive only one particular white man (a current employer) of their labor, and not planters in general. White families too feared enforced dependency, a fate that would seem to link their fortunes with those of black men, women, and children. In the words of historian and former Texas field worker Thomas B. Davis, "The specific percentages and details of the contract vary with the men involved, but always the percentage is so high that the cropper remains poor. It involves an owner-servant relationship that the whites inwardly resist and they tend to move on, even when they must sign up with another man for equivalent terms: hope for better luck, somehow." At the same time, the initiative for shifting often lay with an employer, and not with the people who actually engaged in the practice. O. B. Stevens, the agricultural commissioner of Georgia, put the balance of interests in perspective: "Sometimes you have a tenant on the place, and he finds he can do a little better somewhere else, and he

B. A Wavering "Color Line" in the Rural South

Transformations in the post–Civil War Southern economy affected plain black and white folk in similar ways. As members of an agricultural proletariat, they remained landless and, in many instances, ever on the move. For example, sharecroppers "shifted" to a nearby plantation every two or three years or so; some households were seeking more favorable contractual arrangements, while others were evicted by employers determined to retain only tractable, "efficient" workers. During the Great Depression and World War II, federal crop reduction policies and public works projects led to the displacement and dispersal of large numbers of families (1, 2). Male wage earners at times found themselves at work with members of another race; such was the case in rural industries such as phosphate mining, lumbering (3), and coal mining (4). In the southern West Virginia coal fields, black men took advantage of relatively egalitarian hiring practices, and men of the two races came together to advance their common interests through the United Mine Workers and other labor and political organizations (5). In other places, in particularly desperate times, the rigid color line that kept workers segregated by task and place crumbled, and white workers were forced to take jobs usually dominated by black men and women (6). As recipients of federal aid in the 1930s, rural Southerners were not always able to adhere to a traditional social division of labor that had kept blacks and whites, and men and women, apart from one another in certain work settings (7). During World War II, the defense industry and federal construction boom opened up job opportunities for unskilled workers in areas of the rural South; employers favored whites first and foremost for these positions (8). However, most construction jobs were highly temporary, and uprooted families, blacks and whites together, migrated out of the South in search of more stable employment.

B1. Farmer moving off a government reservation, Coosa Valley, Alabama, 1941. Photo by Irving Rusinow. National Archives.

B2. Farmer and sons moving to a new settlement, E. Carroll Parish, Louisiana, 1940. Photo by Mason. National Archives.

B3. Sawmill workers, Childs, Florida, 1937. Photo by Marion Post Wolcott. Florida State Archives.

B4. Logan, West Virginia, coal miners, 1944. National Archives.

B5. Unemployed miners, members of Scott's Run, West Virginia, Workers Alliance Council, ca. 1936. Photo by Lewis Hine. National Archives.

B6. Women workers at Dania, Florida, canning plant, 1937. Photo by
Arthur Rothstein. Library of Congress.

B7. Federal Emergency Relief Administration indoor canning project, Crystal City, Mississippi, ca. 1935. National Archives.

B8. Local construction workers at ordnance works, Coosa Valley, Alabama, 1941. Photo by Irving Rusinow. National Archives.

moves off and goes to the next place. Sometimes the landlord finds that he can get a better tenant than the one he has. He lets this fellow go and gets the other fellow. They are continually moving around from place to place." Thus at times workers were forced off a plantation by an employer eager to import hands more to his liking; but in other cases the separate histories of blacks and whites converged (that is, their common desire to distance themselves from a recent slave past); the result was turnover that did in some respects conform to critics' charge that it represented movement "for its own sake," without apparent "rational" rhyme or reason.[16]

Labor-enticement statutes discouraged interstate migration, and "oily tongued" solicitors throughout the South faced fines, beatings, and imprisonment. Nevertheless, at the county and community level, law enforcement agents played a much less prominent role in shaping the labor supply. Often located many miles away, the "closest law" usually deferred to planters who more often than not took matters into their own hands and forced an uppity family off the plantation simply by refusing to pay them for the last year, or furnish them for the next. The largest landowners had their own well-armed "managers" who could quickly put an end to untoward behavior. The experiences of Annie Mae Hunt's mother and stepfather reveal the fine line between voluntary and involuntary plantation turnover as a product of violence and intimidation. As an elderly woman, Hunt described to an interviewer an incident in Grimes County, Texas, in the early 1920s. After a few months' residence on the Navosta Plantation, her stepfather "said something out of line that wasn't for black people to say at that time." Threatened with a whipping, he hid near a creek, and then fled across the Brazos River after spotting "two cars drive up with five mens" to his house. The men, said Annie Mae Hunt, "pushed my mama around, pushed her up against the wall; told her she better get that nigger back, and course we were standing there trembling, me and my brother and sister, just like little leaves on the trees when the wind's going through it." That ordeal was enough to convince Hunt's mother that "she couldn't stay there, she was leavin." Informed of the family's imminent departure, the landlord confronted Hunt's mother; "He grabbed her and pushed her out the door and off the porch and she stumbled. And he pushed her out an old gate and when she got to the car, old man Moray hauled off and slapped her three or four times and throwed her in the front seat of the car." The beating that followed left her unable to walk for three months. Annie Mae suffered a broken arm, and her sister a broken nose, in the fight that ensued. It is unclear how long this fragmented family was forced to remain on the plantation. Annie Mae, at age fifteen, married soon after "the little tragedy in Navosta," as she called it. In any case, when they did leave eventually, the members of the family joined the statistical ranks of croppers who "turned over" each year; their decision to leave, born of fear and desperation, was apparently "voluntary" in the face of their employer's coercive efforts to make them stay. Yet certainly a sense of self-preservation drove them off the plantation in a manner inconsistent with the choices dictated by a free-labor market.[17]

Gunfire punctuating late-night darkness in the Delta sounded an ominous warning to tenants who attempted clandestine getaways at the beckoning of a neighboring planter; "You don't mess with a man's labor" was the code of honor within the rural South. Nevertheless, "oppressive tactics" were such an integral part of the rural labor system that violent confrontations were probably relatively rare. The lack of permanent, year-round alternative wage opportunities for blacks (in Southern cities or up north) produced a localized labor market that planters felt relatively free to manipulate without fear of losing large numbers of workers from year to year. In 1912 agricultural economist Lewis Gray noted that the plantation system of worker subordination relied on both more and less than a whip or pistol; "the present methods of coercion are more subtle and more difficult of conviction." For blacks in debt to their employer and "so densely ignorant that they know little of their rights under the law. . . . It is easy to impose . . . a practically coerced service. The mere moral prestige of the white and the fear of physical violence, rarely employed, but always a potentiality, are often sufficient." For Ned Cobb, "a practically coerced service" came in the form of signing a "note" with an employer; for others, an unpaid lien that advanced to the next year; and still others, a merchant's refusal to accept a debt payment at all, with the disclaimer that "he did not care whether his good customers paid [up] or not, just so they kept on paying." Despite the formal end to debt peonage in 1911 (as a result of the Supreme Court's Alonzo Bailey decision), black and white croppers throughout the South continued to believe that they risked bodily harm to themselves if they left a place over the objections of its owner; and they were right.[18]

DON'T DANCE WITH THE DEVIL: SHIFTING FAMILIES

The seemingly straightforward act of picking up one's family and furniture represented the common lot of all poor folk even as it exacerbated their hardship. A study of shifters in Mississippi concluded in an offhand way that "as the share tenant was supplied not only with a house but with most of his furniture, farm implements, and stock, moving was a relatively simple operation, in many cases consisting of loading all his household goods and family into a one-horse wagon and moving over to another farm without losing any time from work." A white North Carolina cropper expressed the process in slightly more colorful terms: "Ain't no trouble fer me to move. I ain't got nothing much but er soup gourd and er string of red-peppers. All I got to do is ter call up Tige [his dog], spit in the fireplace, and start down ther road." Accordingly, observers frequently correlated turnover with a lack of possessions: "The stability of the white renters is best indicated by the ownership of milk cows." And yet even short moves exacted considerable costs from families. For example, illness and childbirth often coincided with the annual end-of-year departure. In 1921, a social worker in Mississippi reported that:

> Emergencies similar to the following were not unknown: A mother confined in January said that during the latter part of her pregnancy her husband was taken ill, and the family was obliged to move to make room for other tenants. The mother had to assume the whole burden of moving and settling in the new home. She cut enough wood to last throughout the period of her confinement, and when labor pains began she was building a hogpen.

Moreover, croppers by definition lacked mules and horses, and the abandoned landlord was usually in no mood to lend an animal of any kind to transport shifting tenants' belongings. A nearby renter or small owner might pick up a few extra dollars around reckoning time in return for lending a family his wagon and horse or for transporting the household himself. Fortunate workers could rely on their more well-to-do neighbors or kinfolk to help them out in this way free of charge.[19]

The notorious "close outs" and "clean ups" that stripped families of all their worldly goods served not only as a mandate for acquiescence among all tenants but also as a way of appropriating every bit of the proceeds from a family's year-long labor before sending them on their way. Planters in states with so-called pony homestead laws might abide by the law and exempt from seizure a farmer's horse, his household goods, and a certain amount of provisions; on the other hand, they might not. In the mid-1920s Georgia tenants bought their way out of a "paper loss" by ceding to their landlord farm tools and other possessions when they left at the end of the year. Ollie Smith remembered that indebted croppers on the North Carolina plantation where she worked were "free" to leave at the end of the year, but "if you left, they took everything. They didn't have no mercy on you at all if you was a sorry worker." After a close-out that cost them all their corn and cotton as well as mule and buggy, one household demanded to see the reckoning statement that allegedly showed a remaining debt of $53. "The owner refused to send this but instead became angry," prompting the tenant to remark, "When you working on a white man's place you have to do what he says, or treat, trade, or travel." Many families traveled.[20]

Close-outs reveal that indebtedness was not necessarily incompatible with high rates of "shifting"; a family's fate depended largely on the self-interest of a planter who wanted them either to go or stay. Croppers and tenants often left debts behind, first because such "debts" were more contrived than real, and hence a normal part of the labor system, and second because these debts were so universal that prospective employers rarely considered them a barrier to hiring new workers. The not-uncommon practice of "debt transferral" simply meant that one employer agreed to assume the "debts" of a worker in exchange for securing his release from his present situation. Assuming that many of these unpaid bills were rather small, transferrals seem to have represented a form of collusion among planters, a gentleman's agreement among competitors for subordinate labor. Thus indebtedness among individual families served as no impediment to shifting and could just as readily be used as an excuse to expel workers as to hold them to a particular plantation. On the other hand, the conclusion that "coercion" of workers played no role in this system would seem unwarranted, to say the least.[21]

In 1916 a USDA official pinpointed the causes of "the very short tenures which are so prevalent in this country": the tenant "naturally hopes by changing from one farm to another to better himself." But this was only one side of the equation: "For similar reasons the landlord is inclined to change tenants, hoping by the change to secure a better tenant." In order to secure a "stable tenantry," then, according to another official, planters engaged in a constant process of "selection and elimination." "Reliable tenants" were those who were "public-spirited and loyal to the planter and who exercise a good influence over those inclined to become dissatisfied." The counterpoint to croppers' "irresponsibility" in moving so frequently was their employer's conviction that the "undesirable ones" should be evicted "as quickly as possible." One planter explained the dynamic that produced a core of subordinate workers and left the others to "drift" from place to place: "If you treat a tenant right and he wants to stay on the place, he will cheerfully do what you want him to do. If he is not a good tenant and is worthless, the only remedy is to get rid of him at the end of the year." Critics of shifting, however, rarely turned their attention to the employers' role in sustaining this practice.[22]

Given the myriad potential sources of conflict between employer and employee, it is not difficult to understand the reasons for December expulsions. In some cases the issue revolved around the specific end-of-year reckoning. On the large Runnymeade Plantation in Leflore County, Mississippi, overseers polled all tenants in November about their intention to remain the following year. For some families the "uncertainties of the upcoming crop settlement" caused them to give "an indefinite answer" to the query, and their response was "considered as a negative [one] and steps . . . [were] taken at once to get a successor[;] this policy has resulted in a more certain supply of tenants." In other words, Runnymeade workers found themselves bound to accept a year-end settlement before the fact, or face the prospect of hitting the road December 31.[23]

When evaluating the causes and consequences of evictions, it is often difficult to assess which departures came as a result of overt pressure and which ones followed more subtle means of discouragement. For example, tenants might voluntarily pick up and leave in disgust when faced with rent increases, continuation of an unfavorable tenure status, or trouble from white neighbors. A similar case can be made on behalf of tenants who decided to leave after being defrauded of their share of the crop at the end of the year. In the early 1930s an Alabama farmer named Dick Richards told an interviewer that he "never got nothing out" of the bale and a half of cotton he had made the previous year; "I worked and dug and never got a thing, and when I told him [the landlord] I wasn't making nothing he said, 'Well you are making money for me, ain't you?' And I said, 'Well, I can quit.' I moved from there, and he didn't know it." Dick Richards left the plantation surreptitiously, but for other swindled tenants, such subterfuge was unnecessary. Croppers might "bolt their debt" with the implicit approval of an employer relieved to see them go and eager to try his luck with new hands fleeing a similar situation on a neighboring farm; in such cases employees rarely asked to see their individual account books, knowing that they would always remain in debt regardless of the size of their crop, the price of cotton, or the extent of their furnishings.[24]

In 1901 George Henry White, a Congressional representative from North Carolina, acknowledged the consequences of these unspoken rules related to labor management: "There is a great deal of fraud perpetrated on the ignorant; they keep no books, and in the fall the account is what the landlord and the store man choose to make it. They can not dispute it; they have kept no account." Recounting his own history, a black man named Barney Alford noted that "I never owned my home; I done public wuk, an den sumtimes I work on de farm fur shares, an' de boss got his share an' left me nuffin. Den I moved on sum war else." In essence, many planters, by the "cajolery of promises never intended to be kept," promises rarely committed to paper in any case, secured a short-term work force that they were prepared to relinquish at the end of each year. This cycle meant that workers had to absorb the costs of a particularly bad year—declining cotton prices, natural disasters—by "loaning" a planter their labor, a loan that was never repaid. More often than not, then, it was the employer who was indebted, eager to default and bring in another "lending agency" (in the form of a new tenant family), people forced to furnish him at a fixed rate for a coming year so full of uncertainties.[25]

Individual planters revealed their own standards for a quality resident work force, while all planters agreed that certain kinds of characters were to be avoided at all costs. As a matter of principle, Alfred H. Stone barred or rid himself of any people whom he could classify as "pistol carriers," "professional crap shooters," "quarrelsome" men, or preachers. Not unsurprisingly, family members suspected of arson or political activities had few opportunities to redeem themselves in the eyes of their employer the following year. For example, when Robert Flagg, a black man, announced his intention to open a school on the Cameron Plantation in Tunica County, Mississippi, the manager of the estate waited only until the year's picking was complete before expelling Flagg, who "under a quiet demeanor stirs up others to mischief." Shifts in migration patterns could affect the availability of workers of one race, threatening the ongoing contract status of members of the other. In Texas around World War I, planters found it possible to hire black and Mexican croppers when confronted with widespread radical political agitation among a host of "troublesome white tenants."[26]

Planters thus based their assessments of entire sharecropping families on the absence or contrariness of the male household head. When a father left during the slack season to work at a sawmill but failed to return at harvesttime, or when a husband died during the year, a family found itself unable to negotiate for the coming year and forced to move. Moreover, whole groups of families could fall out of favor, depending on their age or skin color. Planters rarely hesitated to bid farewell to older tenants, failing in "energy and strength,"[27] to make way for newly formed households. In a strict sense, then, croppers, tenants, and renters were judged not on the basis of their worthiness as field hands but in relation to the household of which they were a part; they labored, and stayed or left, as members of corporate bodies rather than as individuals.

The factor of individual personality remains a highly subjective but significant element in the employer-employee relationship. The traits ascribed to the perfect cropper family changed little over the years from the time Georgia planter David Barrow enumerated them in 1881; the household should be large, industrious, and receptive to advice and direction from a landowner or his manager. Within the confined geographical area traversed by shifting households, word got around about workers' records and about whether they labored best as tenants, croppers, or renters. Particularly prized households might receive for their diligence (and, by implication, acquiescence) special store discounts or additional credits—dubious rewards, to say the least. For example, on Runnymeade Plantation "some negroes whose character is well known, are able to secure small personal credits from the local storekeeper." These "small personal credits" no doubt bound a family more tightly to the plantation, a snare that ambitious workers tried to avoid: "When the devil invites you to a party, tell him you don't want to dance."[28]

Ultimately, the dependent farmer who won favor with white employers enjoyed a highly personal form of success. In his study of black migration during World War I, Carter G. Woodson wrote that the sons of these farmers always had to start from the beginning—that is, at the bottom—to win the "respect" of whites. Any young black man who acted as if he deserved the white community's favor for which his father had worked so hard faced certain disapproval. A 1929 study of blacks in Virginia supported Woodson's view that "The father who is ambitious for his children therefore sends them away and keeps them away." For this reason we might question whether black men ever had the possibility of laboring for a status that they could bequeath to their children, an intergenerational prosperity that relied less on one man than on the ability of that man's heirs to continue in his footsteps. In the eyes of whites, a black father's death also brought to an end his family's "good name."[29]

Within readily identifiable limits, white landowners and their managers also earned reputations that were not transferable to other family members, reputations that ranged from fairness (which had its limits, under the circumstances) to rapacity. At the low end of the scale stood the cheating employers with apparently few redeeming qualities, men who faced annual turnover rates of 100 percent and had to recruit workers from outside the community: "nobody in this part would move in so he got some new folks that didn't know him." Indeed, croppers of both races inevitably focused their frustrations on individuals who wielded power over their daily lives; consequently, in some areas, labor supply depended "largely on the personality of the managers" of the plantations. Yet as Ed Brown soon discovered when he based his decision to move on the basis of one white man's perceived "niceness," appearances could be deceiving. Even a shrewd judge of character like Ned Cobb admitted that he was baffled by the whims of the best employers: "I've studied and studied these white men close. And I've studied em up to many and many a thing that surprises me." Since most planters probably occupied the vast middle ground, they might just as well have kept or frightened off workers on the basis of their personality; the hope that a better employer lived down the road was always balanced by the fear that a family might do far worse if it moved.[30]

Planters could choose to intervene on behalf of their tenants (that is, on behalf of their own interests) in disputes with neighbors or with the law. In Calhoun, South Carolina, landowner J. E. Wannamaker took the side of a black cropper whose cover crops each year disappeared into the belly of a horse owned by "an adjoining landowner and big planter . . . a kinsman" of Wannamaker's. (According to a BAE official, this case "illustrate[s] how interested the landlord is in his tenants and cover crops," a telling observation that linked economic self-interest with old-time paternalism.) According to Thomas B. Davis, the cropper system inevitably encouraged a feudalistic relationship; "The owner refers to 'my man,' even when he is white. It is easier to assume this pose when 'your man' is black. Indeed, blacks so often felt the need of a sponsor in a white-dominated society that they tended to identify with their favorite white for sponsorship or protection." Yet a fine line existed between, on the one hand, such patronage, which might bind a fearful family to a particular landlord for several years, and, on the other, an employer's overweaning arrogance that could push the same family off a plantation in search of a relative kind of independence.[31]

The labor markets of Southern subeconomies then operated on a planter's principle best summarized as the endless quest for the perfect (that is, perfectly subordinate) laborer. It is true that employers competed for uncomplaining, hardworking tenants, but that competition lacked vigor, to say the least. Southern planters faced the delicate task of attracting and retaining workers without disturbing the political system that kept those workers powerless and dependent. Within regions, contracts rarely differed much from one another; employers offered potential workers essentially the same terms, with only modest variations.

Consequently, the system relied on an elaborate set of trade-offs—a smaller share of the crop for a better house (one with screens) one year, an extra $5 for a Christmas bonus attached to poorer quality soil the next. In fact, more favorable contractual arrangments inevitably carried a price tag, hidden or otherwise—the end-of-year bonus charged to next year's account, the garden plot in return for reduced furnishings at higher interest rates. When a planter offered to assume the debt of a family from a neighboring employer, he often simply added the amount to their current statement of charges; at best, he allowed them to begin the new year with a clean slate, that is, "free" from debt, owing—and owning—nothing at all.[32]

Within this small, cramped world of possibilities, the quality of housing became a major issue for dependent workers. Few families invested time or energy in making major improvements on a cabin that might be little more than a chicken coop, and temporary quarters in any case. Although some women took pains to decorate their sparse dwellings and the immediate area outside, "quits" as well as "fires" came too swiftly to make such effort worthwhile in the long run. Indeed, a more livable house had value to the landlord chiefly as a lure for new tenants. For these reasons many families probably concentrated on repairs that were absolutely essential to their own physical well-being. In the case of drafty houses, walls covered with magazine and newspaper pages might serve to insulate as well as decorate a family's living quarters. Still, the primitive state of such cabins, and workers' lack of resources to improve or beautify them, left little room for the play of the imagination.

Under the plantation system, landlords by definition had a monopoly on housing. The situation in southern Louisiana, for example, pertained throughout the South; there, when laborers "refuse to work they have to vacate [the employer's] house, and that is the chief stimulus to make them work . . . [for] they have no other place to go. There are no houses for rent off the plantations. . . . " Given high rates of annual turnover, planters felt that they had few incentives to maintain comfortable homes that would be left in shambles (or so they assumed) at the end of the year. In Texas, an "old [planter's] joke" went like this: "When it is raining, I can't do nothing about the roof, and when it is not it don't need nothing." The generally deplorable condition of tenant housing needs no elaboration here; one Georgia black woman put the case most succinctly when she replied to an interviewer's queries about her own quarters, "'Scuse me, but dis ain't no house." Not surprisingly, then, a great many of the "best" employers "succeed[ed] in keeping their labor, and the better class of them, by making everything around them as comfortable as possible." Of course, comfort was a relative concept. Given the desperate situation of many farm laborers, especially blacks, even modest inducements in the realm of housing could impel a family to leave one employer in favor of another. The possibilities for small improvements were almost limitless—cupboards, shelves, extra rooms, windows, screened windows, a watertight roof, watertight walls, wooden floor, finished wooden floor, functioning chimney, front porch, front porch in repair—the list could go on and on. And physical settings too were marked by infinite variety in terms of proximity to a water source, shade trees, neighbors, roads, cotton fields, churches or schools (or, by the same token, distance from an owner's or manager's quarters).[33]

To suggest that "better housing" was a worthy goal of a "rational" cropper who nonetheless would not make any extra money by moving— that is, to see variations in housing as tangible proof of a competitive labor market—is to ignore the overall low quality of such dwellings in the rural South. W. E. B. DuBois saw the problem primarily in racial terms; textile mill owners could secure their resident work forces only by offering mill housing considerably above rural standards, and that housing was intended for whites exclusively. Black landowners "could build their own homes, roomy and neat. But the rest can scarcely demand what they have seldom thought of." It is probable that the most desirable cabins on any plantation went to workers of highest status, according to race, family size, experience, "trustworthiness," and so forth. But if white croppers and tenants had an undisputed advantage in this contest, the wretchedness of their living conditions in the 1930s, as documented so graphically by Farm Security Administration photographers, testified to the hollowness of their victories. Sixty-five years of "free labor" had not appreciably altered the quality of workers' homes in terms of size, household conveniences, or weather resistance.[34]

The issue of housing suggests that sharecroppers and tenants shifted from one plantation to another for different reasons according to the life-cycle demands of their households. Thus a growing family might seek a larger cabin at the expense of better soil, while newlyweds might content themselves with tiny, ramshackle quarters and a small piece of land as long as the land was fertile. Older families might place a high priority on proximity to kin and worry less about the location of the nearest schoolhouse, in contrast to the parents of many children, who managed to send their youngest offspring to school while the oldest worked in the fields. At the end of any one year, then, families in a neighborhood shifted, but not all in the same direction, as they responded to various contractual arrangements, or other factors over which an employee had little or no control, on the basis of the needs of their constantly changing households.

Exclusive attention to the fate of nuclear families or individual households obscures the prominent role played by kin in determining patterns of shifting throughout the South. In Madison County, Texas, widower Eli Davison lived near all six of his grown children, "all farmin round here"; "I jus' lives round with my children," he said, "'cause I'se too old to do any work." Planters rarely understood the intricate webs of mutual assistance and obligation that kept kin together; but these white men did recognize the significance of such clusters to the extent that they watched extended families leave on their own, in a group, at the end of the year, and they saw the close kin of an evicted family pack up and move as well. On Runnymeade Plantation, "a policy is followed of encouraging a tenant to get his relatives to move on to the plantation and to live near him, as this seems to develop a more stable tenantry."[35]

For whites and blacks, kinship had different meanings as it related to land tenure. Black croppers might draw upon a slave tradition of "mutuality" in establishing networks of self-help. A group "down there together, all connected, kind of kin folks" (in the words of Ned Cobb) might induce a young family to join them. These "corporate or quasi-corporate descent groups" often paid homage to an aged leader, either male or female, and swapped workers at planting and picking time as well as food, money, and child care services. Among whites, who as a group often depended on family connections to landlords in order to advance, a lack of kin in an area could signify a household's particularly desperate situation. A 1922 study of fifty-one white tenant families in North Carolina contrasted the half who were "living on and cultivating family lands" with those who lacked such ties, the latter "pilgrims, strangers, and sojourners in the land, with little or no workstock and farm implements of their own, and a minimum worldly wealth in household goods and utensils with an average of only $426 per family, which is only $17 more than the 66 Negro renters alongside whom they struggle for existence."[36]

Community-based obligations served the same function as blood ties in sustaining households and easing the burdens produced by illness, seasonal crop demands, and old age. Ollie Smith remembered that, on the North Carolina plantation where she lived for many years, sharecropping families rarely thought of themselves as isolated entities; "when neighbors [would] get sick, we'd all throw our work down and go there and help them. Work and iron, clean up the house, work the farm—whatever they needed. They'd do the same to us." Within a subregion, each racial group developed its own set of expectations among neighbors that at once formed the basis of communal life and transcended annual disruptions caused by shifting. In fact, shifting occurred within such a small area that many poor folk managed to retain ties not only to kin and friends but also to local cultural, religious, and educational institutions. A comprehensive study of black and white tenancy in 1923 concluded that "a majority of the moves made by [shifting] farmers are from farm to farm within the community and do not necessarily involve breaking their social connections." Surveyed for the two-year period from 1919 to 1920, at least 56 percent of Kentucky and Tennessee tenants retained "established community relationships" with a trading center, school, or church, or some combination of the three. In 1926 a study of tenancy and ownership among black farmers in eastern Virginia found that, although tenants changed residences more frequently than owners, the former group tended to move shorter distances and retain local ties to a greater extent than their betters. Of the nearly two thousand South Carolina tenant farmers interviewed by federal investigators for a 1933 study, 80 percent of the white, and 88.3 percent of the black, families had remained within the same county since their last move. Apparently, then, charges that shifters had "little interest in community projects, such as the building of a county hospital or the employment of a county nurse" reflected less their high rates of plantation turnover per se and more their lowly economic status, or perhaps (in this case) a vital folk culture that superceded the desire for formal health care institutions, combined with a long-standing mistrust of white medical officials.[37]

Given the routine nature of exploitation under the sharecropping system, a family's decision to leave a place at the end of the year would seem to be the norm, its decision to stay an aberration that demands explanation. Indeed, croppers and tenants often lacked any compelling reason to remain on a plantation for more than one year. Arthur Raper, in *Preface to Peasantry*, wrote, "Anyone who travels extensively in the Black Belt during the winter months cannot but be impressed by the number of wagons and trucks filled with the scanty household furniture of landless and unattached families, white and Negro, seemingly motivated by a vague hope rather than an active expectation of finding something better." As transients within a local political economy that, according to Raper, "insisted that they be landless, that they be servile, and that they be dependent," families could scarcely feel satisfied with a lot that by definition included rundown quarters, institutionalized indebtedness, and close worker supervision that evoked the days of slavery. Indeed, if it is true that the stable farmer acquired a "responsiveness" to his piece of land—a feeling for place that enhanced his farming efficiency as well as his ability to acquire credit—then the long-term tenant remained something of a contradiction in terms. Such a household was by definition unable to better its condition over long years of work, "responsible" or otherwise. No doubt prized by their employers and lauded in theory if not in fact by government officials, members of the Young clan in the late 1930s still resided on the Harrison County, Texas, land owned by their father's master under slavery. But the elderly folk who found themselves living "jus a few yards from de ole [slave] quarters" almost three-quarters of a century after emancipation offered a poor argument for the connection between residential stability and upward social mobility.[38]

An interviewer enamored of James Smith and his masterly command of Smithsonia operations noted without apparent irony that this planter had "overcome the desire of the Negro help to move from job to job." Smith accomplished this feat by employing not only convicts but also "free" workers bound to his estate by five-year contracts. Not all poor folk who remained with an employer were necessarily peons. Some expressed relative satisfaction because they considered their landlord an exceptionally fair man (or so they told federal interviewers), or they enjoyed plenty to eat, or they had experienced some upward mobility (for example, from tenant to renter) while staying on the same place. In any case, tenants stable over a long period proved hard to come by, with planters proud of a work force that included at least a few households that had stayed as long as ten years.[39]

For some of these families, attachment (through the generations) to a single piece of land, whether rented or sharecropped, signified a degree of respectability unmatched by life on the road: "Papa rents from the man what set him free. We have never been nowhere else but right here. Papa died right over there; all of us live on this plantation. None of us ever been in prison or in suits or nothing. We are always in hopes of getting something." But in other cases family members had no illusions about the nature of a long-term employer-employee relationship and its enhancement of a worker's sense of self-worth. Ollie Smith lived for more than four decades on the Woodruff Plantation near Mocksville, North Carolina—"well the same farm cause we changed houses." In 1934, when her father died of pneumonia ("Killed hogs and got too hot over that steam and took under that night in zero weather"), the family asked their landlord "to stand for . . . daddy's coffin" because their gathered crop had not yet been sold and they had no cash. But Will Woodruff, the son of the Smiths' original employer, refused the request for $50, and the family had to arrange for a coffin on credit with a black undertaker nearby. "Now we done been there forty-one years and . . .he wouldn't do it," Ollie Smith recalled. For blacks at least, white landlords, with their pinched sense of obligation, might be patrons, but they could never be kin.[40]

Shifters were not shiftless; more often than not, they remained committed to providing for themselves and their households, and they resisted a fatalistic submission to exploitative employers and landlords. When households rejected working and housing conditions that stripped them of their dignity, when they quit employers who made no pretense of fair-mindedness, when they remained in fact in a state of permanent dissatisfaction, they embraced a kind of idealism, albeit one that the white middle class persisted in claiming as its exclusive domain. As a way of life, then, shifting directly contradicted the notion that croppers and tenants wallowed in a culture of dependency or of poverty. Poor Southerners did not gladly enter into an unsettled way of life; they remained torn between hope for something better and an attachment to home place. In this quest they resembled other Americans at the same time, before, and since. Ultimately, annual plantation turnover revealed not so much a chronic inability among tenants and croppers to apply themselves to hard work and stable employment as much as their persistently thwarted desire for rootedness.

Nevertheless, because shifters did not own land or have permanent addresses, they existed outside the American liberal tradition, a civic culture defined in terms of property ownership and stability of livelihood. The vitality of communities depended to a large extent on generational continuity among homeowners, and though Southern plain folk rarely strayed too far from their kin, they remained on the margins of American public life, beneath the contempt of politicians seeking a predictable constituency—that is, one with the proverbial "stake in society." The political economy that produced transience therefore deprived poor people not only of material well-being but also of their citizenship broadly defined. Throughout the rural South, and later up North too, as the process of dispossession proceeded apace, "the people understand that if you do not have a home place, very little will ever be yours, really *belong* to you in the world."

5

Bound and Free Black and White Laborers Between Field and Factory: The South's Rural Nonagricultural Sector, 1875 to 1930

Around the time of World War I, Florida phosphate workers could rightfully, if regretfully, claim a dubious distinction as the South's most exploited wage earners. For 20 cents an hour for twelve-hour days, six days a week, miners in the Tampa-based industry stood knee deep in mud and water, detonating dynamite charges that blasted barrel-size chunks of rock out of the earth. Once in a while pumps that removed material from the dust-filled pits would explode, burning workers "practically to death."[1] Loaders shoveled the washed and crushed rock into hot, rotating cylindrical dryers that emitted fumes "so strong they take your breath, if you don't hold your breath."[2] At night most men returned from work to makeshift company-owned quarters, with primitive sanitary facilities cleaned only by "an occasional hog."[3] Deprived of any possibility for household self-sufficiency—garden plots were too small and the soil too poor to "raise [anything but] a fuss in"[4]—miners were paid in scrip redeemable only at the company commissary, or in cash discounted at a rate of 10 percent. Even men who toiled up to 150 hours during a two-week pay period owed everything but their souls to the company store. Not surprisingly, to hold on to the workers they had, employers hired pistol-toting guards to patrol the camps.[5]

Like other extractive industries, phosphate mining had always faced difficulties in recruiting and retaining a reliable work force. The seasonal nature of the enterprise—work slackened in the heat of the summer, when the demand for labor fell to one-fourth its December high—meant that employees could expect to work as many as eighteen hours a day during the busy winter, with an "enforced vacation" other times of the year. Pioneer Florida phosphate companies had relied on indigenous white labor, but these "crackers," accustomed to an "indolent life," were, in the words of one observer, "most independent in their views, and as most of them own a homestead and cattle of their own, they like a holiday after a week's work." In an effort to lessen their dependence on local farmers, employers brought in blacks from nearby states and established work camps that rendered their employees increasingly dependent and immobile. By 1919 black family men predominated as miners in the Florida phosphate mines, while white men held all salaried, supervisory positions. At the same time a number of young, single white men toiled alongside blacks in the pits. In 1930 Florida was producing more than four-fifths of the country's total phosphate output, much of it used for commercial fertilizers and exported to Europe. Still, these companies employed no more than 2,200 workers (one-third of them white)—a tiny fraction of the 450,000 gainfully employed men in the state. Due to mechanization, the labor needs of the industry had actually dropped during the 1920s.[6]

The precise economic status of white phosphate miners remains somewhat ambiguous. On the one hand, they lived in close proximity to their dark-skinned co-workers—for example, all of the 170 men who occupied 100 houses owned by the Palmetto Company lived "colored and white together." At this camp some of the houses for supervisory personnel had indoor plumbing, but none of the quarters for "laborers and negroes" boasted such amenities. In 1919 a mine foreman of the Prairie Pebble Company, referring to the difficulties faced by blacks who wanted a portion of their wages in cash, noted that a "low grade white man" encountered the same difficulties in converting scrip to "real money." And yet companies went to extraordinary lengths to enforce distinctions between workers of the two races, no matter how similar their plight in the pits. In contrast to whites, black employees at Prairie

Pebble lacked bath facilities and found their paychecks routinely docked 25 cents each week for "medical insurance," whether or not the resident physician responded to their calls. The children of white employees of a Bartow firm attended a company-sponsored school one mile from their homes, while black youngsters had to trek four to six miles each way to segregated classes.[7]

Despite inequities in their treatment, black and white phosphate workers came together in 1919, when 1,900 of 2,000 men in the Florida industry joined an independent union, the International Union of Mine, Mill and Smelter Workers (often called the Mineral Workers Union) and struck in May of that year. Employers adamantly refused to cooperate with mediators from the National War Labor Board or to negotiate with the union, which demanded higher wages, decent housing, and "immunity from the commissary (company store) system, with no discrimination against employees who trade elsewhere." Tensions escalated in the late summer with the appearance of black strikebreakers imported from Georgia; by the end of August at least five people lay dead as a result of strike-related violence. In September union members defied a district court injunction and set fire to company property and drained the fuel tanks of railroad cars used to transport phosphates from the mines. Nevertheless, the strike and the union collapsed simultaneously the next month, no doubt at least partially because striking workers had been turned out of their homes, a special hardship for the family men, almost all of whom were black. The Mineral Workers Union remained dormant in the phosphate mines until the 1930s.[8]

Throughout the Jim Crow South, rural industries brought blacks and whites face to face with one another in the workplace and at company stores. Although a "constantly changing" color line constituted "a fertile source of friction and bitterness" between the races, it also provided the impetus to biracial union organizing off the plantation and outside of cities—for example, efforts sponsored (successively, but not always successfully) by the Knights of Labor, the United Mine Workers of America, the Industrial Workers of the World, and, in the 1930s, the Communist party and the Congress of Industrial Organizations. Therefore, the political significance of selected rural industries—vegetable and seafood processing; coal, ore, and phosphate mining; sugar refining; lumbering; and turpentine production—goes far beyond the relatively few laborers involved. Between 1875 and 1930 these enterprises claimed perhaps no more than 5 to 10 percent of the Southern region's total labor force at any one time. Yet hidden away in the forests of East Texas and on islands off the coast of Louisiana, or clinging to the mountainsides of Appalachia and deep in the piney woods of Georgia, rural company camps brought into focus the South's dilemma in mobilizing a work force to perform the region's most disagreeable and dangerous jobs. As a white employer in Habersham County, Georgia, noted in the early twentieth century, when blacks and whites refused to work at the pace demanded of them, the ensuing problem of labor management was "not a race question, pure and simple; it is an industrial question, a labour issue," and one, he concluded, "not confined to one part of the country."[9]

In an effort to make a decent living, workers in Southern rural industries faced barriers qualitatively different from those encountered by the millions of "New Immigrants" who settled in the Northeast and Midwest during the same period. Like their sharecropping kin, Southern employees in the extractive sector found it nearly impossible to purchase a home, take advantage of competitive prices for food and consumer goods, acquire skills or formal education, and, in increasing numbers over the years, even quit their jobs. While Northern workers clamored for the steady employment that would ensure survival wages, Southern rural laborers continued to alternate between agriculture and other forms of work, and their efforts to retain ties to the land confounded their employers' attempts to reduce them to total dependency. For their funding and profits, extractive industrial establishments depended on world markets, Northern capital, and natural supply; in contrast to most manufacturing enterprises, many of these rural businesses were small, mobile, and highly transitory. The South's extractive sector thus constituted a kind of colonial economy in its own right; the workers in it supplied raw materials for industrial revolutions elsewhere, at home and abroad, and watched the profits they sweated to produce drain out of their own communities.

And like other colonized societies, the South had a rural work force that was semifree, in contrast to labor relations in the capital-rich North. Although work in rural nonagricultural enterprises was dangerous and ill paid, Southern employers benefited from the fact that landless people had so few options elsewhere within the region or outside it (before World War I). Still, few laborers willingly embraced this type of employment, at least for long stretches of time, and employers had to rely on a certain amount of coercion, depending on the circumstances, to secure work forces sufficiently large and tractable for their needs. In the process, outside Southern towns the boundaries between free labor and bound labor, between agriculture and industry, and between blacks and whites became indistinct, permeable. Deprived of the legal protection and economic independence that flowed from landownership, poor folk of both races found themselves drawn to jobs and then held to them.

For example, in 1911 several "simple mountain boys from East Tennessee, of pure American blood and of good character" were, according to a U.S. attorney investigating peonage cases, lured from their homes by J. F. Smith, an Appling County, Georgia, landowner. Smith set the youths to work on his farm and in his turpentine camp. When they found themselves cheated out of their wages (the promised $1.25 per day) and charged with indebtedness, they fled to Savannah, where they were arrested; there a local judge bound out the six of them to work for Smith until he was reimbursed for his expenses. Chained in two groups of three men each, the young men "were placed in the rear end of the colored coach" en route to Smith's property. Warned an investigating official, "Heretofore, the abuses have been chiefly of Negroes, but this case illustrates clearly how readily they might be extended to white men of excellent character." In the Jim Crow South, at least a few "white men of excellent character" might find themselves chained, "in the rear end of the colored coach."[10]

The history of the South's extractive economy between 1875 and 1930 is the history of successive displacements of rural folk, beginning with fathers squeezed by tenancy, men who began working for modest wages part of the year, and culminating in families pushed off the farm altogether and trapped in company towns and work camps. In the mid-1920s several major Southern extractive industries suffered severe downturns. The consequent contractions and layoffs, combined with depressed agricultural prices, served as the entering wedge of the Great Depression into the South. In 1941, when federal officials documented the plight of small farmers in the area of Hinesville, Georgia, they revealed the final stages in the transformation of rural Southern life. Near Hinesville, paper pulp companies by "the cutting over of large sections [had] reduced the chances of making extra money by hunting or raising cattle on open range." As a result, "The small owners, both white and Negroes, clung to the land. For the latter group the alternative was to join gangs of turpentine workers, travel with them, and live in their villages. Practically the only escape was to be 'sold' (for the amount of the debt) to some other turpentine operator." Well into the twentieth century, then, for these rural Southerners, "landownership—just a place to live and make a garden—was often synonymous with freedom."[11] By this time, of course, the title to a piece of property had eluded the majority of agricultural workers, black and white, most of whom were dependent on planters' furnishings and merchants' stores. But the small farmers of Hinesville may well have understood the bitter existence that awaited them as rural people who lived a life apart from the land.

RURAL INDUSTRIAL WORKERS AND WORK CULTURE

Immediately after the Civil War, when whites relinquished their hold on slave labor, they turned their attention to the riches of the soil rather than the potential of the people who worked it. In the 1860s and 1870s regional boosters could cite "cotton mills, iron foundries, granite quarries, coal mines, saw mills, planing machines [and] salt and sulphur mines" as the basis of "a practical reconstruction." By their very nature, the short- and long-term operations of extractive industries were constrained in a way that manufacturing enterprises were not. Lumbering and turpentining businesses had to push deeper into the pine forests with each passing year, their processing equipment (saw and planing mills, and distilleries) in tow. Sugar refineries and fruit and vegetable canneries stood in the fields, crop perishability a major factor in minimizing the distance between harvest site and factory. Within this subeconomy entrepreneurs faced the task of piecing together a labor force that would sustain development and at the same time preserve basic elements of "the old southern philosophy of living"; the result was a patchwork of foreign immigrants and native white and black men, women, and children, organized as wage earners, contract laborers, unpaid family members, peons, and convicts.[12]

Regardless of the extent of their capitalization or the sophistication of their technology, most rural industries harmonized with the essential principles of plantation management. While Northern heavy industry was shifting into high gear during the late nineteenth and early twentieth centuries, the South concentrated the greatest proportion of its workers in the primary, or extractive, sector. In 1930, 46 percent of all Southern employees made their living from agriculture, mining, fishing, and lumbering, compared to less than 10 percent of Northeastern and less than 20 percent of Midwestern workers. Southern rural enterprises mobilized their work forces and affected the larger Southern society in ways similar to agricultural rather than manufacturing businesses. "Plantation industries" frequently left intact the social structure of their respective communities; as we have seen, the seasonal complementarity of sawmill work (for example) with farming maintained the equilibrium of local economies. In addition, rural enterprises enjoyed a large, subordinate labor pool because of the absence of practical wage-earning possibilities in Southern urban areas. (With their more extensive manufacturing interests, Richmond and Birmingham were the exceptions that proved the rule.) The same kinds of low-wage, unskilled, seasonal jobs characteristic of the rural nonagricultural sector prevailed in villages and towns as well; "public work" went primarily to teamsters, ditchers, and construction laborers, men who could count on employment in any one job for no more than a few months each year.[13]

A survey of rural establishments enumerated in the 1880 federal manufacturing census shows that the wages paid to unskilled hands varied little across state lines, among different industries, or within the same industry. Adult male wage earners received about 75 cents of $1.00 for a full day's work whether they labored in a flour mill near Abbeville, South Carolina, in Henderson County, Texas, or Augusta County, Virginia; or in a sawmill in Accomack, Virginia, or Bordeant Township, South Carolina; or in a cotton gin in Allandale Township, South Carolina, Avoyelles Parish, Louisiana, or Grayson County, Texas; or in a sugar refinery in Louisiana's Ascencion Parish, a stoneware factory in Shaw, South Carolina, a fish oil factory in eastern Virginia, a marble quarry in Tennessee, turpentine works in Chesterfield County, South Carolina, or phosphate mines near Charleston. These wage rates held steady in absolute terms into the twentieth century. Increases in compensation during World War I were hardly sufficient to keep pace with the inflated cost of living, and unskilled wages remained depressed after the war, despite the upward trend in Northern pay rates at the same time. After 1900 wage differentials between North and South had taken on an added dimension of severity, as more and more family men in the South sought full-time employment in rural industries that mainly employed single workers elsewhere. For example, in 1900 married laborers in the Southern lumber force outnumbered single men by a ratio of 49 to 42, while in the Far West and Midwest unmarried men predominated in the same occupation, two to one.[14]

Exposure to the elements and natural hazards made work in Southern extractive industries particularly dangerous. Coal mining, logging, and sawmilling had the highest rates of occupational accidents, far in excess of those in textile mills. The most dangerous of all jobs, coal mining, became even more so as the industry mechanized and expanded after 1900. In terms of annual casualty rates, ordinary cave-ins were more devastating than mine explosions. For example, national statistics reveal that, of the 48,000 miners killed between 1906 and 1935, fewer than one-sixth fell victim to explosions, while the rest died from roof falls and other kinds of accidents. Less publicized and spectacular than mine disasters were the everyday dangers that lurked in the South's lovely longleaf pine forests. Of the lumbering industry, historian Thomas D. Clark writes, "Laborers, black and white, were subjected to the same harsh demands as were the galled and bleeding animals they whipped into and out of mudholes." Besides the inevitable (and at times fatal) mishaps with razor-sharp axes, workers in the woods found themselves in mortal danger while hauling logs on land, sending them crashing into a river or pond, and then rafting them into place. In the forests of the Texas-Arkansas-Louisiana region in the early twentieth century, "the environment itself added to the mayhem," with hungry reptiles and insects a constant menace: "All that was in addition to hot, humid, and occasionally stifling summers and frequently bitter winters, cold enough to freeze water, but not cold enough to bring work to a stop." Even food processing jobs were hazardous to workers' health. In vegetable canneries tomato peelers labored in open-air sheds, bent over a "merry-go-round"; this was "wet work at best," with many women "soaked in juice" while standing in the "accumulation of waste and drippings on the floor." Oyster shuckers developed arthritis and other muscle ailments as a result of their cold, damp working conditions, exacerbated by long hours during peak season.[15]

And finally, the exploitation of natural resources on land and in the sea provoked violent territorial battles, the consequences of which workers came to view as occupational hazards. The sparkling waters of the Chesapeake Bay set the scene for bloody confrontations when, in the 1860s, tongers resisted the introduction of the efficient but rapacious mechanical dredger that removed even the youngest specimens from their beds and hastened the depletion of supplies throughout the bay. A generation later armed poachers and pirates from Maryland and Virginia confronted each other over territorial rights, with citizens from their respective communities firing on boats as they plied the waters near the shoreline. Around the turn of the century the Greek spongers of Tarpon Springs, Florida, took a chance when they ventured too near Key West, where black Bahamian "Conchs" (also spongers) retaliated by setting fire to the interlopers' boats. During their journeys downstream log rafters in the Appalachian Mountains had to contend not only with rapids and sudden spring storms, but also with the murderous intentions of landowners protective of their own water interests, and rival parties that vied each night for a safe place to anchor.[16]

Once ensconced in a camp, no matter how insistent their employers' complaints about labor shortages, employees inevitably experienced lay-offs and shutdowns—not just those stemming from swings in the market or periodic crises (fires, explosions, and so forth), but also normal weather conditions and seasonal rhythms of work. Rainstorms kept lumber sawyers; turpentine boxers, dippers, and chippers; and phosphate miners indoors. Oyster shuckers, vegetable packers, and sugar mill hands stood idle when their suppliers could not work because of bad weather. Business located along rivers came to a halt if water levels were too low to transport their product downstream. The sap ran into turpentine boxes only from March until November. The fortunes of oyster canners mirrored those of the oyster harvesters, who kept busy during months that contained the letter "r." The three-month winter sugar harvest and grinding season was marked by frantic activity, "a time when even the best efforts of all hands [fell] short of accomplishing the many tasks in a satisfactory manner." Cotton gins remained in operation the same amount of time, in the late fall. Sawmill employees dependent on rafters could expect a burst of activity in the spring, when swollen rivers safely accommodated large numbers of logs. Carried on above ground, phosphate mining ebbed in Florida's hot, rainy summer and peaked between October and April. A small farmer might safely shrug off a few days lost to a midsummer storm: "Some days it would rain and I couldn't work. I was sorry I couldn't work, but not too sorry. I rested a little and then went back at it again." However, men and women in isolated camps frequently lacked the opportunities for trapping, hunting, and fishing that might serve as a hedge against slack times; hence these workers depended as heavily on a cash wage as any Northern worker.[17]

The development of extractive industries and their related processing operations led to population dispersal and migration. All over the South small lumbering businesses "cut out and got out," and small sawmills functioned only as long as slender profit margins, and the surrounding timber, lasted. Area farmers who had depended on nearby, slack-season jobs might respond to their disappearance by returning to their fields or ranging over a wider area in pursuit of wage-earning possibilities. After the hurricane of 1893 deprived them of work, the Sea Island men who had wielded pickaxes in the phosphate mines near Charleston took advantage of proliferating Georgia sawmills. Similarly, workers in the North Carolina turpentine forests found themselves in demand farther south, as Georgia and Florida assumed the lead in naval stores production by the late nineteenth century. After the Chesapeake oyster industry peaked in the 1880s (the result of depleted beds), Polish packers and canners began an annual, seasonal migration southward where they worked in the same kinds of jobs. Contractions in the coal industry after World War I sent miners from the southern Appalachians into Virginia tobacco factories and Piedmont textile mills, and up to Chicago and Detroit. The Southern lumber industry, originally the beneficiary of its exhausted Northern counterpart, eventually suffered the same fate; the largest company mill towns in Mississippi, Louisiana, Arkansas, and Texas began to close in the mid-1920s, stimulating migration to Southern and Northern cities. In these cut-over areas, farming was hardly an option for town residents who now lacked the know-how and financial resources to return to the agrarian way of life of their parents, a way of life that was fast disappearing all over the South in any case.[18]

Like sharecroppers, employees in the South's extractive and food processing industries lived within an essentially cashless economy. Many were brought into camps "on transportation," the isolation of the work site "necessitating" employers' advances for this purpose. Thus single men and families owed money to camp owners as soon as they boarded a train many miles, or many days, from their prospective jobs. Attracted to a phosphate mine, seafood cannery, or turpentine farm by the promises of cash wages, they soon found themselves "compensated" in the form of promises of payment. Alabama coal miners were paid in "clacker." During the grinding season, Louisiana sugar workers took home each night a "token representing a day's work"; if not spent by the fifteenth and thirtieth of each month, these "chips" were redeemed in cash. Florida phosphate miners received trade checks—"aluminum change . . . the company's own kind of money." These men, like lumber workers, who were paid in "paper and brass, called 'batwings' and 'cherryballs,'" faced forced deductions for medical care, sometimes called a "hospital fee"— $1.50 per month for a married man, $1.00 for a single worker. Coal miners spent their scrip, or credit, at the company store; whether they were working or not, they had to eat. In fact, most employers generally conceived of the store as a cushion against hard times; food and merchandise advanced during layoffs helped to tie workers to the town once business picked up again. Of the yellow snake emblazoned on a docked paycheck, one black Appalachian coal miner recalled, "Grown men would stand there and cry after receiving a check that had been so tagged. . . . It was virtually slavery."[19]

Just as rural nonagricultural workers followed seasonal work patterns more akin to agriculture than manufacturing, and just as they were eternally beholden to cropperlike "furnishings," so they shared a "traditional" work culture that more resembled farming than factory labor. Rural industrial technology in the South remained primitive, and for four or five decades after the Civil War, a number of industries used essentially the same production techniques as their antebellum antecedents. Until 1910 or so, when gas-powered winders came into general use, oyster-men faced "back breaking work standing over those [hand] winders from sunrise to sundown." This most basic, and most arduous, task associated with oystering "was almost like pulling in an anchor while the vessel was sailing," and, according to one experienced boat captain, "it was difficult getting crews for this kind of work." The phosphate industry reduced its labor demands after 1905, when steam shovels manned by three workers began to replace pickax crews of up to eighty men each, and again in the 1920s and 1930s, with the use of electric draglines to remove the over-burden. Loggers relied on little more than axes, cross-cut saws, skid-poles, and mules before 1900; even later only the largest operations could afford to construct the rail and tram lines, or install the mounted cranes, that facilitated getting out the lumber. Until 1915 a crop of boxes, or 10,500 trees, continued to form the basis of contracts for tur-pentine workers, a standard set by operators in slavery days.[20]

Through the 1920s even the coal that powered the North's second industrial revolution was extracted by labor organized along essentially preindustrial lines. In his classic account of traditional mining, *The Miner's Freedom: A Study of the Working Life in a Changing Industry*, Carter Goodrich extolled the "indiscipline" characteristic of this "cot-tage" industry throughout the nineteenth century. Goodrich quoted a black miner in West Virginia who contrasted the routine of factory work with the "free lance" nature of coal digging; in the mines "they don't *bother* you none." Only infrequently did a foreman venture under-ground to the "rooms" where men, paired in "buddies," worked just as long and as hard as they wished, day to day. Paid by the ton, a man might reach a self-imposed quota by midday—for a father of seven, nine load-ed cars, one for each member of his household—and then head for home; "early quits" were routine. However, mechanization subjected deskilled workers to closer supervision. By the late 1920s machine oper-ators driven to perform routinized tasks were held strictly accountable for a full day's work. Throughout the coal fields, the time was rapidly dis-appearing when a miner might counsel his young assistant, "Always sit down when the boss is around."[21]

In some extractive industries subcontractors enjoyed relative freedom from foremen and supervisors. The farmers who cut wood in their spare time and then hauled or rafted it to a sawmill reported to no one but themselves, and their work routine reflected the needs of their own fam-ilies and the limits of their own resources rather than the dictates of employers. The history of manganese miners in Arkansas illustrates the general attitude of these independent workers. Some men agreed to work for a daily wage ($1.25 around the turn of the century), but many others supplemented farm work with mining; members of the latter group received $4.00 per unwashed ton for excavating and then separating the ore, which was then transported by mule-drawn wagons to town. (Bulldozers did not affect the work itself until the late 1920s.) Mining was an uncertain business at best, but it had its appeal, recalled one old hand: "We'd work ten, maybe fifteen hours. Then I went to minin' agin the next day, you get tired of minin.' But there was lots of these old fellas, they never get tired of minin'; always lookin' for that one big strike and long rest they'd rarely find." At the same time, subcontractors of this sort engaged in a brutal form of self-exploitation; though they could, strictly speaking, set their own hours, they were not free of the economic imperative that also kept their factory-based counterparts in mills and on assembly lines. "You worked hard all year," recalled an Arkansas man who farmed in the summer, mined in the winter, and cut wood and sold chicken pens, grapes, and possums besides; but "we was all poor then."[22]

In certain enterprises, at specific times and places, black workers tried to insist that work assignments be parceled out by tasks and not by time. In the 1860s and 1870s blacks in the South Carolina phosphate industry proved unsatisfactory laborers when worked in gangs paid by the day. Their employers finally acquiesced in their demands by switching to a task system similar to the one these workers had known in Sea Island rice and cotton culture. "Each 'task' was to dig a pit fifteen by six feet, and the worker was paid twenty-five to thirty cents per vertical foot excavated. Thus it was the amount of work, not the volume of phosphate produced or the time involved, that was rewarded, and this allowed workers some control over the pace of work and daily wages paid." As we have seen, the operators of Florida mines felt bound by no such traditions, and they instituted an hourly wage, one that workers in 1919 resisted violently but unsuccessfully.[23]

The residents of company towns were especially vulnerable to close monitoring. Clustered together in small spaces, their labor performed under the watchful eye of a boss, seafood cannery workers endured a killing pace during short seasons. In shellfish canneries that lined the Gulf Coast, resident workers of all ages were roused by a 3:00 A.M. whistle to begin their workday, twelve to fourteen hours, "or however long it takes to process the catch." The paltry wages, combined with parents' anxiety over supporting their families, enforced a rigid discipline among all who filled buckets with shucked oysters and shelled shrimp, and cans

with the steamed product of both. In contrast, cannery workers indigenous to the area could rely on patch money from their gardens, or day
work in domestic service, to free themselves from exclusive reliance on a
piecework wage. For example, in Warsaw, Georgia, the oyster industry
used Poles imported from Baltimore as well as the wives of black oyster-
men. According to an investigator, "The Bohemians were employed, it
was said, not because of their greater skill, but because, being imported
from Baltimore and living in factory quarters, they could be worked for
longer hours and more regularly than the Negroes." Living outside the
work camps, black women shuckers tended to appear in the canneries
"only irregularly," their hours set by a variety of family considerations
outside the purview of their employers. Though disagreeable, the work
thus had its advantages over domestic service; "Most of the women prefer to shuck oysters at higher wages with shorter hours of service and
greater personal freedom." In the vicinity of New Orleans, French
Creoles exercised the same prerogatives when they quit at midday to go
home to cook and wash, leaving their Baltimore co-workers obligated to
remain until the last whistle.[24]

The case of seafood processing, as well as other businesses, reveals
that the rural nonagricultural sector retained a remarkably diverse work
force in terms of its racial, ethnic, and, to a lesser extent, gender characteristics. The shape of this force differed from its agricultural and manufacturing counterparts in several ways. First, it consisted of a higher proportion of immigrant workers than elsewhere in the South; indeed, the
employees' small numbers contrasted with the many different ethnic
groups at work in the coal mines, seafood packing plants, sugar refineries, turpentine camps, and public works construction projects all over
the South. In addition, this sector of the economy stimulated, and relied
on, the interstate and interregional migration of workers to a degree
greater than cotton plantations, textile mills, and urban industries.
(However, with the possible exception of the coal industry, these population movements stemmed in large part from coercion or fraudulent
labor recruitment practices.) And finally, under certain circumstances,
members of the two racial groups proved fungible to rural industrial
employers, producing novel situations in which blacks and whites lived
in close proximity to one another and shared tools and tasks.

In the early twentieth century the following story, presumably apoc-
ryphal, made the rounds in the Southwestern railroad "tie woods":

> Two [white railroad] tie makers went to a house in Arkansas to inquire
> about some timber, and were told by the woman to await her hus-

band's return. They took seats upon the gallery and soon a big negro passed through the yard and around to the rear of the house. After a while the woman reappeared and one of the tie men said, "Your husband seems to be long in returning."

"Oh, no," she replied, "he has already returned."

"We saw no one but a negro, who walked through the yard."

"Well, that was my husband."

"What!" they exclaimed in surprise. "A good-looking white woman like you married to a negro!"

"Yes, indeed," she replied, "and I think I did far better than my sister, who lives down the road a short way."

"Why, what did your sister do?"

"She married a tie maker."

Certainly in every joke there is a little humor, but the words of sympathy expressed by the "good-looking" white housewife for her sister must have had a peculiar ring in the Jim Crow South.[25]

It is possible to outline several general principles that informed the racial division of labor within rural industries. Provided with more employment alternatives than blacks, whites in some areas of the South managed to avoid the least desirable kinds of jobs; in 1901 the Georgia state agricultural commissioner noted, "We have [cotton seed] oil mills and a guano factory; but of course, that is not very pleasant work for whites, and they do not like it." Consequently the South was sprinkled with such mills that employed blacks in all positions, skilled as well as unskilled, with much smaller numbers of white supervisors. In any case, black people never oversaw the work of whites in any industry. Throughout the region blacks performed the worst jobs, though locational and political considerations created pockets of similarly situated whites. Also, as we have seen with Atlantic and Gulf Coast seafood cannery workers, a white labor force housed in labor camps might be considered superior to black "commuters"; here the ease of supervision affected employers' preferences rather than the workers' race per se. Resident-nonresident issues took a somewhat different turn within the tie-making industry. All over the South farmers of both races cut ties in their spare time, but in parts of Texas, where the activity assumed the form of big business, most employers eschewed the use of ax-wielding black "thumpers" (apprentices) in favor of cheap, plentiful white labor: "Some men employ negro thumpers, but the majority of makers do not fancy them. They are all well enough to have and load the ties, but it is not well to encourage them to use the broadax."[26]

The cases of sugar refining, lumbering, and coal mining suggest the difficulties in generalizing about the racial division of labor in the rural nonagricultural South. As sugar mills underwent a process of consolidation, the cultivation of cane became more decentralized. By 1930 over one-third of all sugar farms were worked by tenants, almost all of whom were white, while black people made up the preponderance of day labor on large plantations and in the refineries themselves. For example, in 1900 only 900 of the nearly 4,000 sugar farms in Louisiana were operated by blacks. Thus cane workers remained organized along different lines (as tenants and field laborers) according to race, though they followed the same routines in planting and harvesting. During the forty years after the Civil War, Louisiana planters conducted short-term, successive experiments with Chinese and later Scandinavian and Italian immigrant wage workers because few local native whites felt a compelling economic need to subject themselves to the whims of their wealthier neighbors offering wage work.[27]

In the lumber camps of the South, black men performed the heaviest work. According to one authority, "in the woods, they fell and buck the trees, handle the hooks or tongs, form the labor gang in the skidder crew, work on railroad construction and do the heavy work in the loading process. In the mills, they ride the carriage or haul and stack lumber while white workers handle the machines." Yet these task assignments varied by state and region, with some areas reserving the job of sawyer for whites. White men outnumbered blacks in the woods of Arkansas and Texas by a ratio of three to one and two to one, respectively. The largest businesses consisted of greater proportions of black workers, while small operations drew their laborers from the surrounding areas; in the Piedmont, mountain, and wiregrass regions, timbermen and sawmill owners relied on white farmers who shifted between field work and wage work during the year. In 1910 approximately equal numbers of blacks and whites worked as common laborers in the Texas lumber industry, though blacks were dramatically underrepresented in the more skilled positions of operators and sawyers. In fact, of even greater significance than their concentration in the lowest-status jobs was black men's chronic inability to secure better positions in the industry through either talent or seniority.[28]

The policies of Southwestern lumber barons reveal the potentially profitable malleability of a racially divided work force. When starting up a camp in Texas, Louisiana, or Arkansas, mill owner William Buchanan followed a policy of importing large numbers of blacks and settling them in isolated forest areas sparsely inhabited by whites. Thus in 1894 Buchanan transformed the tiny crossroads of Barefoot, Louisiana, into the company town of Springhill, with a mill force of four hundred men and a production rate of 125,000 board-feet a day. A few whites were clustered in senior administrative jobs; the rest of the workers were black. Buchanan's black workers demonstrated a kind of "loyalty" to their employer mandated by their outpost status in enemy territory. Not too far away, for example, the huge company town of Urania, owned by one of Buchanan's rivals, remained off-limits to blacks; the company employed whites exclusively, from the most exalted supervisory positions down to the lowest water boy. A young black worker from Springhill who innocently stopped into a Urania store for a pack of cigarettes realized just in time that he would be lucky to escape with the pack (it cost him $2.00 instead of the usual 15 cents) and his life.[29]

Between 1875 and 1930 the drama that unfolded in the coal fields of the South revealed an ever variable, ever shifting line that divided black and white workers. In fact, during the militant strikes of the United Mine Workers of America (UMW), members of the two races perceived the line itself as receding, if not disappearing altogether. An array of factors shaping the demographic profile of the Southern labor force—including geographical location; in-migration and importation of men of both races and many ethnic groups; the use of convict labor; mechanization; large-scale strikes; and the demands pressed by a progressive, biracial labor union—all coalesced in the history of coal mining. In the process, the industry and its organization challenged some of the South's time-honored principles shaping the position and prospects of black workers.

Blacks found employment in the coal mines in two distinct regions of the South—the Birmingham mineral district of Alabama and the southern Appalachians. Drawing workers from the nearby Black Belt, the Birmingham region maintained a steady and consistently high proportion of blacks, a little over one-half of the total number of workers in the mines through 1930. (In the mid-1880s a Birmingham mining engineer asserted that the qualities that made blacks such good cotton pickers— their ability to withstand intense heat, arduous physical labor, and long hours on the job—made them good coal miners as well; on the same theme, he noted, "It is quite common in 'open work' on ore veins or in quarries, for the colored laborers to enliven the monotony of their task by singing some melody, keeping time with their hammers, picks, and shovels to the music.") In the Appalachians, a predominantly white area, the proportion of blacks in the coal industry varied by state (Kentucky, Tennessee, Virginia, and West Virginia) and by year, according to fluctuations in labor demands and the recruitment of foreign immigrants as well as the use of blacks as strikebreakers. While the percentage of black workers gradually diminished in the mountains after 1900 or so, the largest group of them remained concentrated in southern West Virginia, accounting for more than one-fifth of all black miners in the South through 1930.[30]

In Alabama employers instituted discriminatory policies aimed at black workers, including less pay for equal work and job assignments based on both race and ethnicity, with former slaves at the lowest end of the hierarchy, after native-born whites, Northern European immigrants, and Southern European immigrants. When blacks joined the UMW (usually in segregated locals) and went out on strike with fellow workers during sporadic uprisings between 1880 and 1921, local citizens watched with apprehension as black strikers confronted black scabs, a novel sight in the South to be sure. In the great strike of 1920 (the continuation of a nationwide rebellion begun in 1919), three-fourths of all Alabama miners who stayed out of the pits were black. Still, the weight of public and political opinion, combined with the companies' liberal use of strikebreakers and convict labor, defeated the union's biracial coalition and ultimately left intact a traditional Southern social structure as replicated in the mines, aboveground and underground.[31]

Black workers fared better in the states north of Alabama and south of Pennsylvania. In West Virginia in particular, black men entered a workplace that was relatively egalitarian and at times even revolutionary in its implications. The mines paid higher wages than work in the cotton fields and in almost all other rural industries; mine operators worked hard to recruit sharecroppers and tenants from depressed areas, and these newcomers often encouraged their kin to follow, setting off a chain migration. Although blacks received the same pay as whites for equal jobs in this region, their fortunes as a group depended largely on labor demands as affected by the expansion and contraction of the industry. Between 1910 and 1920, a time of peak labor demand, some blacks secured the coveted job of machine cutter, though transportation jobs reflected a higher degree of racial segregation. During the early 1920s, when technological innovations proceeded apace, black men already at work in the mines suffered when their jobs as mule drivers were eliminated by motormen. Gradually, as the industry sought to cut labor costs by mechanizing, a disproportionately high number of "black jobs" were eliminated. James E. Millner and other black miners "felt let down by John L. Lewis [head of the UMW] after we all worked so hard and sacrificed so much to get the union where we did." Once again, according to Millner, "Blacks felt the brunt of the change caused by another curve in the road to industrialization." The number of black men at work in the West Virginia mines fell off precipitously after 1930 and every decade thereafter; in 1980, 97 percent of the state's miners were white, reflecting the outmigration of blacks over the years.[32]

Southern Appalachian mine owners followed a conscious policy of encouraging foreign immigration in order to inhibit unionization, and between 1900 and 1915 the coal towns boasted a polyglot unmatched by other types of Southern communities. A survey conducted by the West Virginia Department of Mines in 1909 covered 207 different operations with a total of 33,202 workers, half of whom were native-born (10,910 whites and 8,750 blacks) and the rest recent immigrants from Italy (3,161) and Hungary (1,758), with smaller numbers of Polish, Lithuanian, Swedish, English, Austrian, Russian, German, Scottish, Greek, Irish, Slavic, Syrian, and Romanian workers. As in Alabama, these men at times shared liabilities with blacks (both groups predominated in inside jobs, which were more dangerous than those outside the mines), but as the immigrants and their sons became assimilated into the company towns they came to enjoy more of the benefits that accrued to native workers with white skins. And in racially segregated towns, Lithuanians and Italians, together with Kentucky and Tennessee hill people, stood apart from blacks in all matters social.[33]

In general, foreign immigrants who settled in the South (no matter how short their stay) remained outside the cities, which afforded them few jobs. Some groups established permanent settlements and plied a modest trade—the Greek and Bahamian spongers of Florida, Chinese fishermen in Louisiana (no doubt descendants of coolies imported after the Civil War for work in the cane fields). Some Poles and Slavs stayed on in the West Virginia coal mines after their countrymen returned home right before the United States entered World War I. Members of other communities, attracted by the promise of high wages, expressed disappointment in their new jobs by fleeing from them when the first opportunity presented itself. In the 1880s Irish, Polish, and Italian workers ventured south from the tenements of New York City to railroad camps and then, in some cases, to the phosphate mines of South Carolina, but they seemed unwilling to acclimate themselves to either the heat of the pits in summer months or the peculiar Southern diet year-round. A description of an encampment in the vicinity of Charleston, with immigrant workers biding their time between jobs in the phosphate mines and on railroad crews, suggests their lowly circumstances:

Hit was the roughest kind of men come in to work there—Irishmen, Italians, Polacks and all—and some kind of furriners hit was. Couldn't hardly undertand em when they'd talk. They had what they'd call *kittle* [kettle?]. A big pail or somp'n, and they just cooked out in the woods. Camping out. They even eat buzzard. They catch and eat a buzzard just as soon as you er me'd eat a turkey. That's the way they was. Knock down a buzzard with a shovel er a rock, set up three sticks into the ground to hang up their kittle, build a fire and cook him right there. Hit was a rough mean crowd—most too bad for these Edisto colored to work with.

Bubberson Brown, the elderly black man who recounted this exotic scene, made certain to distinguish the interlopers from blacks native to the area, poor people themselves who nonetheless rarely if ever resorted to a repast of buzzard meat.[34]

The Italian families on Louisiana sugar plantations fared better than their unattached countrymen on the East Coast and in the process offered a lesson in the paradoxes of New South labor relations: Employers disdained workers who were able to find a way up and out of the plantation system. Unlike most Europeans who disembarked in New York City, these immigrants followed established trade routes between Sicily and New Orleans to work in the *zucarata,* or harvest season, of the sugar parishes. At first many came only for the duration of grinding time (the last three months of each year) and then returned to their home-land. Others settled in the United States permanently but bought land or small businesses in a bid for independence from planters. The direc-tor of the Louisiana Experiment Station indicated that the immigrants' greatest virtues as workers were also the cause of their fall from favor in the eyes of their employers: "Those [planters] that have stores prefer the negro, because the negro will spend 95 cents out of every dollar he gets, while the Italian will hardly spend a nickel. He keeps everything he can get." A modest truck farm in the country, a small vegetable market in New Orleans, cash to send to kin back home—these aspirations meant that most Italians perceived of the sugar plantation as a temporary money-making venture and not a way of life. Planters expressed disgust over the counterproductive consequences of all that hard labor. The Italian population of Louisiana sugar parishes peaked in 1900 at 10,273; thereafter the state's Italian community continued to increase, but at the expense of the sugar industry.[35]

Most rural nonagricultural enterprises were highly gender-segregated. Cotton gins, grist mills, and sawmills used black women, along with (black) children, only in such peripheral jobs as water-toting, sweeping, and other forms of custodial maintenance. The sexual division of labor at times reflected the nature of the labor supply—as affected by long-standing household and cultural considerations—as much as by employers' subjective judgments about the proper nature of black and white women's work. Some black women toiled as turpentine dippers, though it would be difficult to ascertain whether or not they entered into, or remained in, that kind of work voluntarily. Women and children served as "whackers" harvesting sugarcane, and the mills employed a mixture of black women, men, and boys.

Women of both races represented a significant proportion of food-processing workers. Oyster shucking was a traditionally female (and children's) task, with individual workplaces organized along racial lines. Some businesses kept black women on as the unskilled shuckers of steamed oysters, while white women predominated in the more skilled jobs of shucking raw ones. Vegetable canneries and packinghouses also employed women, the social structure of their work forces dependent on the labor supply and on the overarching principle of strict racial, gender, and age segregation. In the 1920s the Delaware tomato canneries that employed migrants from Maryland and Virginia assigned men to wash the tomatoes, older (more experienced) women to sort them, and younger women to peel them. Establishments that used the hand-filling method used women for that task; on the other hand, men invariably tended filling machines. The predominance of Eastern European women in the Baltimore oyster-packing industry, and the way that tradition had complemented their husbands' wage earning, influenced seafood and vegetable processing in the South once the Chesapeake supplies began to dwindle in the mid-1880s. The Poles and Slavs of Baltimore had worked in fruit and vegetable canning in the summer and oyster packing in the winter; later these same women, along with their children, would make seasonal migrations east to Delaware and New Jersey and south to the Georgia and Gulf coasts, where they were prized for their skill and their compliance.[36]

World War I upset established patterns in the Southern social division of labor. The draft and other forms of military manpower mobilization drained large numbers of younger, unmarried men from the region, and so husbands and fathers came to play an even larger role in rural industries than previously. The exodus of approximately half a million blacks out of the South during the war years signaled a long-term trend, and in pockets of the Cotton Belt employers of all kinds had to contend with a real, and now permanent, labor shortage for the first time. Some industries, such as zinc and manganese mining, expanded in response to increased wartime demands, as farmers and "floating laborers" gravitated toward small towns transformed overnight into booming work camps. In contrast, the difficulties associated with transatlantic trade led to a temporary collapse in the world market for phosphates, and Florida companies could barely retain their work forces, even at reduced levels.[37]

During the war Southern lumber businesses prospered as the federal government bought up as much wood as businesses could produce for defense-related needs, including the construction of wooden ships. In response to an acute labor shortage, the industry raised wages and recruited more blacks and white women than in previous years. The Southern Pine Association, a trade group sponsored by the largest companies, even established a recruiting office in Chicago to encourage return migration among blacks. By the end of 1918, 5,000 women complemented a male work force 120,000 strong. Predictably, black women replaced black men and boys as hostlers, teamsters, signalmen, yard and road workers, and woodchoppers ("they handle an axe with great proficiency"). White women tended to accept work close to their homes, in small enterprises, and at tasks "limited to the occupations [they] consider above a negro's job." For example, in planing mills, white women were praised for their "application and concentration . . . on the job" while operating machinery; on the other hand, black women were "utilized in tieing bundles, sorting items and lengths, and similar work." White women were also deemed suitable, and in some cases even superior to men, as timekeepers and checkers; "their sheets are always much neater and cleaner than those made up by the men."[38]

In piecing together their work forces, New South employers in the countryside felt free to transgress previously sacred racial and gender boundaries if the success of their enterprises depended on such innovations. Consequently they departed from the principles of their antebellum fathers and grandfathers, men who showed little interest in exploiting whites the same way they exploited blacks—that is, by reducing them to slavery. After the Civil War foreign immigrants occupied a social limbo of sorts, sometimes treated like blacks, other times like whites, as shaped by local labor demands and human geography. In the rural New South the color line was not so much a fixed and eternal verity as it was an ever-changing uncertainty. Postbellum employers thus showed considerable progress, if that is the right term, in making room for white people at the lowest reaches of the labor force.

THE SLIPPERY DESCENT INTO PEONAGE AND CONVICT LABOR

From the viewpoint of the rural industrial employee, the difference between a free laborer, a peon, and a convict lessee was at times a semantic one at best; all too often the legal status of a man or woman changed overnight without any appreciable effect on their miserable condition. Alerting authorities to the plight of fifty Greek immigrants held against their will in a Ferguson County, South Carolina, sawmill, the indomitable crusader Mary Grace Quackenbos warned that if the men tried to escape, they risked arrest under the state's vagrancy laws; after that, as prisoners of the state or county who had undergone a legitimate sentencing procedure, they would be extremely difficult to liberate. A 1906 exposé of a Georgia sawmill and lumber business revealed that its work camp housed fifty convict lessees and fifty "free laborers." The camp's owner paid the state $200 per year for each convict, while the free workers served under ten-year contracts. The convicts were incarcerated each night and apparently punished in a more arbitrary manner than their co-workers. But both groups labored at the same tasks each day, and at the end of their ten years, "free" workers found themselves in debt to the camp commissary and summarily transferred to the prisoners' quarters.[39]

Throughout the South convict labor depended on the type of racial subordination that had undergirded slavery. The convict lease system, enacted state by state with such unseemly haste after the war, gradually gave way (under economic, not moral, pressure) to public works projects manned by city, county, and state prisoners. An overwhelming proportion, perhaps as many as 90 percent, of these prisoners were black, concentrated in those enterprises that had the most difficulty in securing and retaining labor—extractive industries and road, levee, and railroad construction. White Southerners rarely bothered to justify or defend the exploitation of black "criminals" on grounds other than the immense profits that went to the state. A few observers did argue that the state had simply assumed the vital responsibility of disciplining recalcitrant blacks, *in loco* slaveowners, and the classification of workers—as full hands, half hands, or dead hands—evoked the days of legal bondage. Extraordinarily high mortality rates among convicts, combined with institutionalized, ritualized forms of torture (the use of "sweat boxes" and whipping straps encrusted with sand) suggest that officials operated on the basis of an almost limitless supply of labor and lacked any incentive to prolong the lives of prisoners through treatment even remotely humane or decent.[40]

Background information about convicts provides some clues to the racial dynamics at work in arrest and sentencing procedures. Black offenders tended to be young men (in their late teens and early twenties) picked up in urban areas on charges that ranged in seriousness from murder to petty theft, loitering, gambling, and bootlegging—hence the effort to channel some of the "idle" labor on city street corners out into the countryside. Case studies showed that the men most at risk were youths who had ventured into town, only to be arrested on some minor charge and shipped back to the plantation or turpentine still, this time in chains. In the Upper South, for example, "men and women who get into trouble represent raw recruits from the country, forced out by population increase and attracted by opportunities for work in the tobacco factories." Compared to whites, of course, blacks in general could less often pay the court costs that might have saved them from a long sentence of hard labor. In the 1920s attempts by two North Carolina social scientists to find a common denominator in the life histories of black men serving on county chain gangs yielded only a predictable litany that included broken homes; previous arrests and convictions; venereal disease; and a fondness for drugs, prostitutes, fast cars, and easy money—in other words, according to the study's authors, chronic "anti-social behavior."[41]

When faced with decisions about the disposition of convicts, authorities sent a disproportionate number of whites to prison and blacks to the most dangerous work sites, especially coal mines. Personal background information on white prisoners is lacking, but the group apparently included men convicted of capital crimes, together with those found guilty of moral turpitude and public drunkenness. In any case, investigators and reformers routinely focused on the abuses endured by white prisoners (as they did with white peons) to magnify the horror of the system. After describing the sadism that pervaded Texas state prisons, members of one committee reported, "We have seen white men who have suffered all these acts of cruelty and men who have suffered even more." Several white men, including a "big, gaunt cracker" named Thomas Nix, brought to justice for incest, figure prominently in J. C. Powell's accounts of "thrilling chases" (and even more thrilling recaptures) during his years as head of various convict work camps in Florida.[42]

Within these biracial camps and chain gangs, guards and foremen maintained racial distinctions between many blacks and a few whites only with the greatest difficulty. White workers themselves responded to close contact with blacks in various ways. Florida's state prison supervisor reported in 1914 that one facility in particular was foul and lice-ridden;

furthermore, black and white prisoners ate at the same table and slept with only a small partition dividing their respective quarters. A white convict from the camp in question made the complaint more specific and revealed a situation even more dire: Apparently the camp laundry mixed the uniforms of white and black prisoners indiscriminantly, "and I was forced to wear clothes that the negroes would wear the week before which would never fit. . . . " He concluded his letter, "I pray you in the name of the great state of Florida and human decency to hurry an adjustment of conditions there. In the forty days I had to serve I never had a change of underwear and no negro took a bath while there yet I had to live with them in that filthy condition." Few camp supervisors ever bothered with the sensibilities of whites by improving sanitary conditions for blacks. On the other hand, J. C. Powell recounted the case of a white woman prisoner (convicted of infanticide) whom he removed from the company of black women, "thinking to do her a kindness," only to have her pine for her former prison mates; once she returned, they "treat[ed] her with the greatest consideration."[43]

Descriptions of living conditions in these camps sound a strikingly similar note, best characterized by a barn, or stable, analogy. Men were treated like animals and housed like animals. This charge was literally true in the case of chain-gang convicts who were transported around Georgia and Alabama back roads in cages that were identical to (or, in the opinion of some observers, inferior to) those used to hold circus bears and tigers, with "one open side covered by heavy iron bars and a canvas for cold or wet weather." "Tied together like beasts" during the day, they remained confined to these cages and prone in bunks all through the night and up to thirty-six consecutive hours, from Saturday afternoon until Monday morning. One investigator reported that the mules at a Kinston, North Carolina, camp "were better housed and better treated in every way than the convicts." Quarters for free laborers were certainly better, though it is doubtful that many residents gave thanks for their relative blessings. Mexican and black workers in the mosquito-infested lowlands of Georgia and Florida lived in "house boats built over the swamps" and in "'match box' shacks or box cars, segregated from white workers in the towns and in the camps." Lumber operators also favored portable railroad-car dwellings, cramming them with single men of either race.[44]

Unlike slaveholders, camp operators and beneficiaries of the convict lease system replenished their labor forces through arrests and convictions rather than natural reproduction; separated from their families, men had no reason to stay and every reason to try to leave. In fact, the greatest threat to these camps came not from federal officials (and certainly not from local authorities) but rather from family members who initiated attempts to secure the release of loved ones. The U.S. Department of Justice Peonage Files document the hundreds of cases of mothers who tried to smuggle train fare to their sons and daughters held hard at work, fathers and grandmothers who wrote and petitioned law enforcement agents, urging them to act on behalf of their kin. Thus while the camps sought to exploit the helplessness of workers separated from their kin, those family members retaliated in kind. In analyzing the management of these camps, then, comparisons with slavery go just so far; although slaves and convicts might have engaged in similar kinds of resistance—work slowdowns and the pilfering of pigs and eggs, for example—the institution of bondage relied on families, both to keep people on a plantation and to produce more workers, while the postbellum work camps did not.

Convicts were by definition rigorously "supervised," but in most instances their jobs were organized in ways not unlike those of free workers. Prisoners in the Tennessee coal mines were "tasked" each day, according to the industry's tradition; but for these men, failure to complete a stipulated amount of work resulted in a beating rather than a dock in pay. A convict-lease camp in the turpentine forests of Florida turned a tidy profit each year by preserving conventional aspects of naval stores operations; according to the camp's owner, squads of men working under the task system were "the means of getting good work out of the men without punishment." A Northern reporter explained the nature of their "good work": "If there is any loss in earnings from year to year, it is generally the pine trees that are at fault and not the men who work under the task system. Their stint for the day or week is about the same, rain or shine, sick or well. The treatment, of course, depends very much upon the captain, who sometimes has an interest in the business." These convicts had an incentive to finish their assigned jobs as soon as possible, usually no later than Friday afternoon or Saturday morning. One Saturday afternoon the Northern visitor was treated to the incongruous spectacle of an "uproarious" baseball game between two teams, men who, just a few hours earlier, had been wading waist-deep in the swamps, their "constant and heavy work" monitored by guards and "cur dogs."[45]

Similarities in the task assignments and working conditions did not, of course, imply fellow feeling between blacks and whites, imprisoned and free laborers. To the contrary, some of the most bitter strikes in Southern history pitted free men against convict coal miners, or at least against their bosses. East Tennessee's great "Convict Wars" in the Coal Creek–Briceville region spanned the last quarter of the nineteenth century, culminating in the insurrections of 1891–93 when strikers staged several raids on the prison stockade and liberated convict laborers leased by the Tennessee Coal, Iron, and Railroad Company. Begun in 1871, the use of (black) prisoners in the mines and coke ovens immediately depressed the wages of free workers, at the same time offending their dignity as gainfully employed breadwinners. One white man later recalled, "When the convict trouble came we was only gettin' one day work a week. And the convicts were workin' fulltime. . . . Yes, Lord, I saw 'em kill 'em in the mines. The mine boss, that is, for not getting their tasks. And maybe they was sick. It was shameful." Interviewed in 1937, a local woman revealed how convict labor could dramatically alter patterns of wage earning among male and female residents. Mrs. S. O. Sanders recalled that fathers and sons had lost their source of livelihood because the operators "brought in seven or eight hundred free niggers to run the coke ovens. White men could not stand the heat to pull coke. Paid 10 cents an oven. A good hustlin' nigger would pull four or five a day. Seventy-five cents a day was the best any of 'em made. Convicts were here at the same time, seven or eight hundred convicts. White men could not get jobs. No Lawd no." Gradually, employers became more reluctant to risk strikes by free white workers, men who could vote and express their outrage over the system in a way that the black community could not. In contrast, public works crews challenged no identifiable, organized group of white working men; the "good roads movement" thus symbolized a "progressive" South's investment in internal improvements while the state served as neoslaveholder.[46]

Treated like convicts, peons (that is, workers held against their will, by force) fell victim to individual enterprises in direct proportion to the unpleasantness of the work involved. Turpentine extraction provides a case in point. In reflecting back on his own days as the head of a turpentine labor camp during the 1880s, J. C. Powell remarked that "The work is severe to a degree almost impossible to exaggerate, and it is very difficult to control a sufficient quantity of free labor to properly cultivate any great number of trees. The natives follow it more as a make-shift than a vocation, and are only too glad to abandon its hardships for any other character of work that comes to hand." Turpentine workers toiled in "palmetto scrubs and swamps, wet to [their] shoulders," weak from pneumonia, rheumatism, or consumption, and emerged from the woods with the sticky ooze smeared on their clothes and bodies. Around the turn of the century, industry officials were still complaining that blacks were "content with merely enough to keep soul and body together," and so they turned to peonage and the convict-lease "market" to secure the labor unavailable otherwise. Despite the heartfelt outcries of reformers, turpentine work depended on various kinds of unfree workers well into the 1930s, when, according to federal agricultural economists, "needed labor can be obtained only with difficulty in many cases, [and so] operators sometimes use their police power to restrict freedom of movement in the [naval stores] belt." The conclusion to be drawn: "These conditions are hardly conducive to retaining workers or encouraging workers to return to the industry."[47]

The more remote a camp, the bleaker the existence of the people who lived in it, the more desperate their desire to leave, and the more difficult their escape from its confines. Time and again federal authorities investigating peonage cases cited the inaccessibility of the work site as a major element in both hiding abuses and preventing their eradication. In 1912, near Macon, Georgia, a U.S. attorney reported, "the conditions in some of the counties of the State, more remote from larger centres of population, seem to be very serious, the negro being regarded as a species of chattel." Turpentine camps near Pensacola were "a long ways from railroad transportation and the negroes are held in the camp against their will and if they leave, they are forcibly returned." Efforts to aid the immigrants hard at work in Ferguson, South Carolina, were impeded by the "wild and difficult nature of the country where they are being held." Such cases were not limited to the Southern interior. In the early twentieth century a group of Chinese fishermen located their camps in the Baratoria district marshes south of New Orleans. The laborers' quarters, constructed on platforms supported by stilts, were surrounded by water. Once they charged individuals $2.50 for their transportation, their mosquito netting and mattresses, the Chinese had no reason to restrain the men by force; "but simply, by reason of the physical conditions and location of the camps, the men are unable to go." Obviously, such conditions "necessitated" company commissaries and housing, and workers' indebtedness provoked the threats that forced many of them to remain. Others simply could not find their way out of the forests or swamps on their own. In the end, workers need not be formally classified as peons in order to feel trapped in a work camp; the lack of nearby alternative employment possibilities, combined with the absence of an information network that would have encouraged long-range migration, conspired to keep many workers in exploitative situations. Camp owners seemed to have little trouble controlling the operations of the U.S. postal service within the limits of company towns.[48]

Predictably, the peonage camps of the South harbored more than their fair share of black men and women. The peonage files of the U.S. Justice Department bulge with the records of cases reported to the attorney general, beginning in 1901, and reveal the pervasive use of non-free black labor in the South's rural industries. The naval stores workers in the exhausted forests of North Carolina boarded trains bound for the distilleries of Georgia, only to discover weeks later that their wages would be withheld to pay for transportation and board expenses. Though young men and fathers in search of wage work were most susceptible to the blandishments of labor recruiters, black women at times fell prey to ruses of varying degrees of subtlety. Lured by a promise of marriage, Gertha Haigs followed her would-be suitor twenty-five miles into the Florida woods, where she was held against her will and beaten by the men who oversaw her work cutting cord wood and dipping gum. "Importations" of blacks fresh off the farm into lumber camps and strife-torn coal mines routinely involved fraudulent promises from employment agencies, transportation authorities, and operators alike. Thus the fact that some, and perhaps a large number, of these workers remained in a camp, or in its general vicinity, for an indefinite amount of time is less a testament to viable "long-distance" markets for wage hands than it is evidence of their lack of options either to leave or to find another job elsewhere.[49]

In their account books, some sugar planters distinguished among "Dagoes" (that is, Italians), blacks, and whites, suggesting the ambiguous position of workers who were neither former slaves nor native-born whites. More often than not, immigrant workers in the South—especially those who were Asian or darker-skinned Mediterranean peoples—found themselves classified as "others" and reduced to peonage, victims of a combination of circumstances. Secured through Northern employment agencies, legitimate or otherwise, or at times recruited right in the halls of Ellis Island, groups of Greeks ended up in barren railroad camps on the coast of Florida and in remote South Carolina sawmills, Russian Jews in Gulf State turpentine orchards, and Hungarians in shacks owned by Mississippi lumbermen. In 1907 an investigative reporter for *Cosmopolitan Magazine* tracked down peons in the Florida camps, reputedly the most brutal, and noted, "this new form of slavery places white and black on a plane of perfect equality, and enslaves them both with generous disregard of ancestry or complexion." Truly, this was an intriguing bit of American-style egalitarianism tucked away in the Florida swamps. And there were many others: Caught in the snares of one of the "shark" employment agencies of New York City, a batch of immigrant whites was transported to North Carolina and taken on a forced march to an isolated railroad construction camp: "Here they were quartered with negroes in miserable shacks." Foreshadowing the flurry of publicity that would eventually accompany the gruesome deaths of white peons, the writer for *Cosmopolitan* noted, "The monumental error made by the employers of Florida was in going beyond the black man with their slavery. Had they stuck to the racial division they might have escaped castigation, as they have for a decade. But insatiate, and not finding enough blacks to satisfy their ambitious wants, they reached out and took in white men."[50]

In Southern rural industries, methods of labor deployment assumed a seamlessness that indicated the crucial distinction was not between black and white workers, or between free workers and peons, but rather between men who were secure in landownership and men who were not. Indeed, the color line wavered and then disappeared when three cooks in a convict-labor camp, two black and one white, conspired among themselves to escape, under the pretense that "they were going to a neighboring house to get some eggs." Deep in the piney woods, New South employers manipulated categories of workers in an attempt to crush instances of biracial unionism; such was the case at a Merryville, Louisiana, sawmill in the early twentieth century, when in the face of an uprising staged by black and white members of the Brotherhood of Timber Workers (BTW), camp owners imported black strikebreakers and then incarcerated them each night within a stockade. Caught up in what one historian has called "one of history's most perverse vocational training programs," black convicts put to work in the coal mines later (after they were "released") continued to perform the same tasks in the same way— at times for the same person in the same place—but now as "free" workers. Together, then, blacks and whites in the extractive sector served as a testament both to how much the South had changed, in its efforts to mobilize nonslave black and white labor off the plantation, and to how much the region had remained the same since the days of bondage.[51]

ASSAULTS ON FAMILY LIFE IN RURAL WORK CAMPS

Rural industrialists manifested a deep and abiding interest in the political uses of family feeling. Between 1875 and 1930 various configurations of family labor in the South's rural nonagricultural sector testified to the persistent efforts of employers to locate the perfect nexus between labor subordination and family life, by exploiting the desire—and, in many cases, the desperation—of kin to provide for each other. From an employer's perspective, different kinds of households served different purposes. Farmers who commuted to mills and distilleries depressed the wages of laborers resident in work camps. The lack of employment opportunities for wives in extractive-industry communities kept them dependent on the wages of their menfolk. In contrast, camps that employed women and children reduced their labor costs by means of a meager family wage. And finally, the counterpoint to these examples was the all-male camp, a "little man-made hell," where men were stripped of all dignity and of the hope that flows from the nearness of, and contact with, family members. For even the poorest men of the South, "Families were important then, and they were important not because the children were useful in the fields. . . . No, they were important because a large family was the only thing a man could be sure of having. Nothing else was certain." In the work camps, life's certainties vanished into the thin air of pine forests and cypress swamps.[52]

Throughout this period, single men straight from the farm provided a significant proportion of the "floating" labor demanded by these seasonal industries. Primarily young black men, these were the "tramps" so familiar to Southern employers. Men in the timber industry especially were "notoriously itinerant"; moreover, sawmills and tie and lumber camps that "cut out and got out" by definition produced "hoboes" flitting "about the country like a bat at dusk." These men also comprised the bulk of employees on railroad construction projects and in turpentine and lumber work. A native of Edisto Island, South Carolina, Sam Gadsden recounted his early days as a young wage earner:

> I worked a little around the island, then about 1898 I left and went to follow construction work over on the mainland. I was in my teens and early twenties. We built all in the swamps in Georgia and Florida. I did all kinds of construction work. If I came to a place and liked it and could make a few dollars, I would stay. If I didn't like it, if it was a wild place, I wouldn't stay. I would go back to town and by the next Sunday I would be back home again. Sometimes the contractor would take us forty miles down a little railroad track, deep into those swamps and out of the way places. When the train stopped, I would look out, and if I didn't see a church anywhere, I might not even get off the train. Or if I did get off and couldn't find a church anywhere around there, I would not stay long.

It is impossible to tell how many other men, black or white, avoided churchless places for more civilized surroundings. By all accounts, most camps were full of men like Harry Crews's father, a white man "who believes in his bones that anything worth doing is worth overdoing. His is the gun that is always drawn; his is the head that is turned back under the whiskey bottle." On a work crew cutting a railroad right-of-way through the Everglades, Crews resented the continuous harassment from the camp manager and finally reclaimed his honor with the help of a "ten-inch steel ringbolt in the pocket of his overalls which he used to break the man's skull."[53]

The tie-making business depended on family farmers and men in work camps. Subcontractors hired as many as fifty laborers at a time, primarily unattached black and white men. These boarding camps staked out "restricted territories" located deep in the forests, as near to the source of timber as possible. Men who committed themselves (at least temporarily) to the life of a tie-maker were "nomads, the very nature of their calling makes them so, and being nomads, they are spendthrifts. They wander to every point where railroads run and where timber grows." If a man refused to adhere to even the loose strictures of boardinghouse existence, he became a "batcher," living in a tent and cooking for himself, leading a "sort of hermit existence" apart from his more sociable coworkers. In contrast, farmer–tie-makers remained at home and enlisted the help of other family members in an enterprise that caused only minimal disruption to the household's routine. Nanny Suttles, who lived all her life in North Carolina's Blue Ridge Mountains, later recalled:

> We needed all the extra money we made because we farmed in the summer, and Daddy'd cut railroad ties because it'd give him something to do. He didn't make much out of it, so he told us, says, "Girls, come and help me; we'll get out and cut." Well it'd be in the fall and in the wintertime; sometimes snow was on the ground, but not bad cold. You can't cut down trees if it's bad cold, you know, frozen. And he kept a good cross-cut saw and about two or three double-bit axes, good and sharp. So he'd help us get a tree cut down. Then Mother and me, we would saw it; and he would trim the limbs off and trim us a trail down the log. And we'd saw it as he would trim it up and trim out us a trail to it, you see, and mark off the logs. And we'd go right ahead and do it back over on the side of those mountains. It'd be rough getting them out.

Similarly, the farmer-miners of Arkansas's manganese ore district also avoided the rowdy camps, where single men lived in tents and caves and reveled in late-night bouts of gambling and drinking. Fathers who contracted with the mining companies set their sons to work, hauling and digging the ore, without incurring the expense of a paid helper.[54]

Over the course of the history of the South's extractive and food-processing economy, workers who alternated between the family farm and wage work gradually disappeared, replaced by black and white women and men who gave themselves over totally to the lumber town, the coal-mining camp, or the annual odyssey of the truck migrant. This process was by no means a predictable or even one; the move from farm to rural industry took place in steps, over the generations. As a landless farmer in Wolfe County, Kentucky, Melvin Profitt's father responded to a reduction in his share of the crop one year by telling the landlord, "I'll see you in hell!" He moved away from that farm and on to another one, where he could dig coal for 50 cents a ton and also sell the rail fences he had made. During World War I the elder Profitt "would sneak out and get him a job . . . in a coal mine. . . . He comes back every three or four weeks and his neighbors would find out about it, maybe get them a job so they could follow the same pattern." Faced with a shortage of compliant croppers during the war, Profitt's landlord began to sell off his property to coal miners and returning soldiers. But as a young boy Melvin Profitt decided to parlay his physical strength into a man's job, full time in the mines; "I'm going to tell you I's as big as any man then, don't think I wasn't." He worked in the coal mines all his life and expressed few regrets about missing life back in the hills, where "there has been a number of people to starve and almost went naked." The reason he decided on a kind of job that eventually felled him with black lung was simple: "I had to do that [mining] in order to support the family."[55]

Another type of controlled residential work setting, managed by owners of seafood- and vegetable-processing plants and sugar refineries, operated on the principle that large families should stay together and work together. These enterprises systematically used the labor of women and children for brief periods each year, usually no more than three to six months or so. Consequently, their employees regularly migrated between alternative kinds of work on an annual basis. These migrations yielded gainful employment, but employment that was chronically "shabby"—that is, highly unpredictable. Of families that worked in the oyster industry during the winter and fished and peddled seafood during the summer; or those that tilled cotton in the Delta during most of the year but earned wages on sugar plantations during the grinding season, it could be said, "There is . . . no distinct class of the unemployed."[56]

In canneries and sugar mills, the pitiable wages accorded to individuals necessitated that parents retain control of their offspring as long as possible; on the other hand, the ability of youngsters to earn money at an early age tempted them to strike out on their own much sooner than the sons and daughters of sharecroppers. This tendency lessened the economic pressure on the household head, no longer the family's sole support, but at the same time it intensified the need for younger children to become productive workers, and forgo schooling, as early as possible. According to a study of black oyster workers in Georgia, "Since almost all the wives and mothers in the Warsaw group do other work, and the children begin at a very early age to earn money by shucking oysters, the father, mother, and children above ten years of age are to a large extent economically independent of each other. This economic independence causes much disorganization in the home life." Likewise, teenage sugarcane cutters of both sexes felt free to marry. Still, though hardworking newlyweds might make ends meet, they would necessarily fall on hard times once children started to arrive and the household's income either remained the same or declined with the mother's withdrawal from wage earning.[57]

The intense economic demands on these families help to account for the apparently unseemly haste with which they ushered their small children into the workplace. Confined to oyster cannery camps (and without their black co-workers' opportunities for gardening and foraging), Polish families were lauded by their employers for their willingness to evade (laxly enforced) child labor laws. With fathers only sporadically employed other times of the year, and with work for mothers and children virtually nonexistent in their hometown of Baltimore, parents expressed both pride and urgency as they showed off their five-year-olds who had "learned the trade." One mother said of her seven-year-old daughter, "She kin beat me shuckin'—an she's mighty good at housework too—but I mustn't praise her too much right before her." A lack of child-care facilities, suitable or otherwise, together with the belief that idle children were too prone to mischief for their own good, created a perverse harmony of interests between parent and employer; contrasting his Baltimore-based work force to indigenous blacks, one employer remarked, "There is no comparing them. The whites work harder, longer hours, are more easily driven, and use the children more."[58]

This migratory, piecemeal existence frequently demanded that family members be separated for months at a time. Louisiana sugar planters characteristically employed larger numbers of men than women, except during harvesttime, when wives who lived in other parts of the state joined their husbands to help with the grinding. Among the earliest Italian immigrants to the cane fields were men who would work only during the busy season and then return to their native Sicily for the rest of the year. Later, immigrants came from New Orleans and as far away as Chicago and New York City to spend their winter months in the fields. Black families along the Atlantic and Gulf coasts took advantage of their nonresident camp status and showed great resourcefulness in allocating tasks among family members; in the winter fathers and sons remained at home to tong for oysters or fish, while mothers and daughters found temporary quarters near the canneries. In the summer the women of a household might work as domestic servants, while the menfolk farmed and the children picked and sold berries. Around the turn of the century, among the 3,500 Baltimore Poles to go south each year were fathers who found employment on the boats or wharves near plants; but other men stayed at home in the city year-round, if not to work, then to look for work, while household members went back and forth between Southern canneries in the winter and the truck farms of Maryland and Delaware during the summer.[59]

On sugar plantations and in cannery camps, the quality of housing for families revealed their position as marginal workers. Cane cutters lived in cabins clustered near the mill; Chinese and Italian laborers had no previous association with such dwellings, but to blacks they too closely resembled the old slave quarters. In describing Southern coastal cannery camps, investigators for the U.S. Department of Labor Children's Bureau compared the living conditions to those of animals; with as many as eight people to a room—and lacking closets, cupboards, screens, and indoor plumbing—the shacks bred disease and demoralization. On Avery Island off the coast of Louisiana, native-born whites and Polish alike, all "fooled out of Baltimore under false promises," victims of "this terrible fraud," found themselves compelled to sleep at night on bare floors without coverings of any kind, the stench of rotting seafood in their nostrils. When, after the death of a baby in the camp's so-called nursery, a mother appealed to the mayor of a neighboring town, she was told that the bosses had a free hand in their operations, "and there is not much law for them."[60]

Of course, neither child labor nor the family wage system was unique to Southerners who toiled in the rural nonagricultural sector. Textile mills and tobacco factories in the Piedmont region and the Upper South depended on large families to keep wages low. Many working-class families in Northern cities set children to work in textile mills (the "Rhode Island system"), shoe and candy factories, and sweatshops; at home, under the putting-out system; and in the streets, to scramble for small jobs the best they could. Among the children of a particular family, the chances for schooling changed over the life cycle of a household, with the youngest in a more favorable position if older siblings' work permitted. The departure of these older wage earners from the household might, of course, signal the abrupt termination of a child's formal education.

However, families in the South's canneries and on sugar plantations experienced a fundamentally different set of demands on their energies. These Southerners were by definition migratory laborers. As searchers for work, household members routinely separated in the course of a year, with fathers and older sons, on the one hand, and mothers, older daughters, and young children, on the other, forced to go their separate ways in order to help support the family. Such migrations and separations undermined the nuclear family as a unit of cohabitation—for example, an unemployed father in Baltimore might stay at home all year to look for work, mandating that his wife and children journey to Biloxi canneries during the winter and pick Maryland tomatoes during the summer.

In contrast to all-male work camps and systems of migratory labor, the coal towns of southern Appalachia and the Birmingham district and the large lumber towns in Mississippi, Texas, Arkansas, and Louisiana were populated with both single men and families that remained (or rather, theoretically could have remained) rooted to one place from year to year. Although both coal mining and lumbering enlisted the services of boys and young men, first as odd-jobbers and then as apprenticed workmen, neither industry utilized the family wage system or systematically exploited child labor (or women's labor either, for that matter). Nevertheless, these settings eroded family integrity in a number of different ways, indicating once again the political purposes to which employers could put various forms of household organization.

The following discussion focuses on the family lives of miners and lumbermen. The largest lumber camps and coal towns contained as many as two or three thousand people, though most were much smaller, and showed marked similarities in the organization of households within them. Still, these two types of communities differed from one another in racial and ethnic composition as well as company management; some evolved over time, from rude pioneer camps through a transition phase and finally into stable, planned villages; and variations in size and patterns of labor unrest revealed that each place had a social dynamic all its own, one not easily dismissed by sweeping generalizations about a generic "company town." Hence lumber and coal towns hardly had parallel histories; in 1930 the vast majority of the former kind were "temporary establishments," [61] in contrast to the permanent (or at least longer-lasting) coal-mining camps. The brief, bitter life of the Brotherhood of Timber Workers contrasted with the tenacious existence of the United Mine Workers of America, a union marked by uneven successes to be sure, but an enduring organization nonetheless. Despite difficulties in comparison, however, it is possible to delineate certain similarities in lumbering and coal-mining operations that reveal larger truths about the fate of black and white workers isolated together in settlements that developed only because of their proximity to certain raw materials.

As newcomers to lumber or coal-mining towns, men, women, and children might appreciate the opportunities for a new life of conviviality among their own kind, in contrast to the loneliness of farm households in out-of-the-way places. Born in the Blue Diamond mining town of Perry County, Kentucky, Marvin Gullett believed that, in the early part of the twentieth century, "Most people felt they was going to paradise when they moved to the mining camps. It was a way of life that they liked." He cited the higher wages and modern conveniences that contrasted with the endless struggle back on the farm, and added, "There was a feeling of neighborness. Everybody lived close to one another [and] there was a great population. I guess five thousand people [lived] at Blue Diamond at one time. Once they was in close proximity to one another they become like a tribe." These workers thought of themselves as members of a great extended family (within their own racial or ethnic group) in ways similar to those of residents of Piedmont textile mill villages. The largest coal towns, with their several churches, baseball teams, and YMCA activities, more nearly resembled their textile mill counterparts, but only a handful of lumber towns approached this degree of associational and cultural organization.[62]

As the most dangerous of all occupations in the South, lumbering and coal mining gave rise to everyday fears from which no family member was immune. Descriptions of the Banner mine explosion in 1911 are notable for their emphasis on the indifferent curiosity of the crowds that gathered to witness rescue operations; the victims, mostly convict laborers, had no nearby kin to keep vigil or mourn for them. Yet lesser misfortunes than those that claimed the life of a miner or sawyer could throw a household into turmoil. Families of fathers who suffered a disabling accident, fell ill, succumbed to alcoholism, got into trouble, turned out to be "sorry" providers, or just plain grew too old lacked any kind of company-sponsored insurance or protection: "John, I'm sorry. You've done all you could for the company and we appreciate it, but we have to send you home. You're not able to work any more."[63]

Moreover, even regular paydays were not always sufficient to keep a family together when only one person was working. A black lumberman recalled of the hard times in the industry, "I was working for $2.25 and [the white worker] was getting about $3.00 and something. They didn't know how I could live on that, . . . how a black man could feed a family of seven children and a wife." Within these one-industry towns, among mothers and older daughters, only black women had a reliable source of employment—domestic service in the households of supervisors and managers, emptying toilets and washing clothes for the families of ordinary white workers. A few white women managed boardinghouses or took in lodgers in their own homes. In contrast, men in these camps could at times head for the hills to fish, trap, and hunt—traditional male pastimes that in hard times could mean the difference between a well-fed and a starving family. This is not to suggest that the introduction of low-wage "women's industries" in these towns would necessarily have propped up households always perched so precariously on the brink of financial disaster. But the relative lack of petty-trade opportunities for women, and the reliance on one male breadwinner exclusively, served to highlight forms of gender segregation new to former farm families.[64]

With the introduction of mechanization and routinized work days—when lumbermen rose early in the morning to board tram cars that took them into the forests for a total of sixty hours each week, and when coal miners returned home each night in the darkness, fourteen hours after they had left—women spent much time alone, with their own children, and in the company of neighbors. Gone were the wifely duties of household production, the women's role in handicrafts, canning and preserving, bean stringings, corn shuckings, and molasses boilings. The town store eliminated the time and challenge intrinsic to shopping in more diversified communities, though miners' wives contended with a new kind of chore that never ended—scrubbing the floors, clothes, and children forever coated with coal dust: "It was something you lived with day and night." Patterns of socializing on front porches and baseball fields, at the store and union meetings, in pool halls and saloons also reflected a line more tightly drawn between men's and women's worlds. A housewife accustomed to such a life—that is, a woman who had grown up in the camps—might acquiesce in it more readily than the farmer's daughter, a new bride who preferred the country "where the air was clear like wine" and where she could have a more direct hand in providing for the family's economic welfare.[65]

Of course, gender segregation was only part of the story; lumber and coal towns instituted separate and unequal facilities for members of the two races. Whatever was judged to be the most desirable section of town in topographical terms—the level center of a coal town, wedged between the hills, or the raised area of a lumber town, away from the malarial swamps—remained off-limits to blacks. White miners' families were also clustered according to class and ethnic origins, with "silk stocking row" set apart from the Italians in Yellow Flats, Poles in Hunkie Town, and mountain folk and other "Americans." The more elaborate a town's recreational facilities and services, the more intricate its code of racial separation, on sports teams, in movie theaters and schools, at the company store. Black communities sponsored their own newspapers and sustained their own voluntary associations, they celebrated "Emancipation Day" on August 8 and prayed in their own churches. On the Fourth of July they honored the principles of freedom in the afternoon, following ceremonies for whites in the morning, and they advanced the cause of economic justice in "colored" locals of the BTW and UMW.[66]

Black neighborhoods were subject to the predatory impulses of white men, especially at night. Though brothels, speakeasies, and gambling parlors located in black sections of town might appear on the surface to be racially "integrated," in fact the location of such places revealed the contempt with which whites regarded the sanctity of black family life and particularly the efforts of black mothers and fathers to safeguard their children against the temptations and violence that inevitably pervaded these "red light" districts. Like their Northern counterparts who went "slumming," white men in Southern company towns felt free to venture into black quarters to drink, play craps, seek out prostitutes, dance, and listen to music. As a result, "many legal altercations stemmed from whites invading the privacy of the black compounds and behaving in a fashion unacceptable in the white sections of town. Not surprisingly, the blacks occasionally fought back." And also not surprisingly, more blacks than whites found themselves caught up in the dragnet of police raids. The involvement of black children in numbers-running and bootlegging enterprises was indicative less of some antisocial proclivity among blacks, or a race-based tendency toward household disorganization, than of the concentration of these kinds of activities in black neighborhoods—a concentration that spared white households from the larger, bitter consequences of their own fathers' illicit and criminal behavior.[67]

Within the extractive sector of the Southern economy, the best efforts of parents to earn a living and make a home could not stave off disaster for their children, who would bear the brunt of economic collapse.

During the mid-1920s contractions in the coal industry led to bankruptcies by the hundreds and propelled some people northward to Midwestern cities, others into Piedmont textile mills, while still others decided to hang on and adjust to straitened circumstances as best they could. Competition from Brazil wiped out the Arkansas manganese mines; cheap labor in other countries, coupled with cane diseases in the Louisiana fields, led to reductions in the American sugar business; and the depression in Southern agriculture set in motion a chain reaction that devastated the Florida phosphate industry for the next quarter century. On the eve of the Great Depression, perhaps one-half of the rural population in West Virginia, southwestern Virginia, eastern Kentucky, and eastern Tennessee made their living from extractive industries that could no longer support the offspring of growing families. For the thousands of blacks who had migrated to Appalachia at the turn of the century, the coal fields offered only a "generational stopover" on their way north. At the same time, the Southern lumber industry suffered a sharp decline, pushing blacks and whites out of Mississippi, Arkansas, and Alabama as well as Appalachia; the largest, most reckless companies ravaged hundreds of thousands of acres of timberland and left in their wake "abandoned mills and dying communities." The Southern Pine Association, an operators' group, opened a "Cut-over Land Department" to encourage stranded workers to return to farming, but the stump-filled, eroded lands held by member companies hardly encouraged agricultural production of any kind. In a throwback to the antebellum period, small mills grew up to cut down new stands of trees as they matured; but the days of the largest mills towns were over.[68]

The hardships faced by industrial workers in the rural South were by no means unique to them or to this period; as one observer noted of displaced coal miners in 1933, "Here, in miniature, is a cycle which technology seems to be working out in America at large." A crippled coal industry meant that "Some of these children must be the next generation of coal miners; the rest will be surplus hands in a region which has no other ways to use their energies."[69] Large families, so integral to a rural culture common to blacks and poor whites in the South, produced the "surplus hands" who would eventually journey to Northern cities and find another way of life, this one also vulnerable to business contractions and fluctuations in world markets. Until families moved north, though, many would continue to move around in the South, undergoing various forms of fragmentation in the process, as they tried to make a living.

The histories of households thus charted the process of dispossession in the rural South. The cotton staple-crop economy relied on families, but not for the whole year. Consequently, married as well as single men sought out work in extractive industries, although the jobs were short term and the wages low. Over time, as the price of cotton declined, whole households had little choice but to adopt a seminomadic way of life, following their menfolk into forest and mining camps. The culmination of this process was the system of East Coast migratory labor, for truck-farm operators not only exploited landless men, women, and children working together but also forced them into perpetual transience. And so, in the early twentieth century, when the cotton staple-crop economy began to falter, East Coast fruit and vegetable growers began to expand their operations and thus capitalize on the adversity faced by families in the South and, eventually, families from the far corners of the world.

6

"A Golden Florida Made Ready for Them Too": East Coast Migratory Laborers, 1890 to 1990

Situated at the southern tip of Lake Okeechobee, in the heart of Florida's fertile "winter garden," lies the town of Belle Glade. Home, or rather "home base," for thousands of men, women, and children who work every summer on truck farms along the eastern seaboard, Belle Glade exists as a community of impoverished agricultural wage earners between December and May, and then dwindles to a remnant of that community through the summer and autumn. Over the years chroniclers of life in Belle Glade—journalists and novelists, anthropologists and epidemiologists—have highlighted the connection between the residents' hard work in the fields and their hard living in town. Beginning in the 1920s Georgia sharecroppers were lured to the Florida Everglades by promises buried in the muckland, "ground so rich that everything went wild."[1] These black women and men came to Belle Glade to pick beans and cut sugarcane all week and "cut loose" Saturday night, when work tickets were transformed into cash that was quickly lost to crap games and "Joe Louis" (whiskey strong enough to knock a grown man down). By the late twentieth century half of the town's population hailed from Haiti, migrants in pursuit of one more variation on the American dream. Yet regardless of their cultural heritage, parents and children in Belle Glade, "on the muck" in the winter and "on the season" in the summer, endured the backbreaking rigors of stoop labor by day and experienced big-city street life by night. In Belle Glade, then, a Southern rural past and a Northern urban future formed a most revealing nexus.

Through the 1980s, Belle Glade the agri-ghetto claimed a wintertime population of 17,000 souls lodged in a congested concrete jumble of low-lying buildings intertwined by streets paved poorly if at all. Located in south-central Florida, the town was many miles from service jobs provided by the motels, high-rise condos, and luxury estates of Palm Beach to the east and Fort Myers to the west. The only winter work available was secured through an early-morning "shape up" (described by observers as "the daily buying and selling of labor")[2] that parceled out any number of workers to "day haul" trucks, depending on the size of the crop that week. The approach of summer signaled the cessation of virtually all agricultural work in the region, but even during the height of the winter and spring growing season, wage earning was contingent on the forces of nature, always variable and unpredictable. In the town, workers paid high rents for shabby quarters and poor services. Bars and pool halls offered a cool, dark sociability, but also the drugs, alcohol, and games of chance that served to distract people of all ages from the heat and glare of the Florida sun. The streets were mean enough that parents and older siblings took pains to keep young children off them. Interviewed in the 1980s, a thirteen-year-old Haitian girl, responsible for paying the household bills and translating for her non-English-speaking mother, said she refused to let her younger brother and sister go outside after school. "Don't let them go in the streets and play and stuff . . . just put them in the house, don't let them go out there, just cut on the TV . . . too many crimes around. . . . People get shot."[3]

For such a small town, Belle Glade attracted a great deal of national media attention, all of which stressed the sociopathological aspects of migrant life. Residents received more pity than scorn from outsiders when, in 1960, the CBS News documentary *Harvest of Shame* exposed their persistent poverty and year-round underemployment. Thirty years later a PBS sequel, *New Harvest, Old Shame,* revealed that not much had changed for the town or its people. In the mid-1980s the community became a laboratory for the Centers for Disease Control, when it was reported that Belle Glade had the highest per-capita rate of AIDS in the nation; exacerbated by crowded living conditions, the disease afflicted homosexual men, intravenous drug users, prostitutes, and their children. Stigmatized by their "Godforsaken town where AIDS was spreading rampantly," Belle Glade shoppers had to watch as store clerks routinely sprayed their checks with Lysol before accepting them. During the winter freeze of 1989, journalists' accounts stressed the workers' desperate plight and documented their reliance on an inadequate and haphazard patchwork of social services, including government aid and private charity. From the perspective of beach-bound tourists on either coast, sipping glasses of orange juice over a morning paper that featured photos of hungry and dejected black and Chicano workers, Belle Glade must have seemed remote indeed.[4]

Yet Belle Glade was also a community of hardworking people of color; and as such it had a different face, one rarely seen by the rest of the world. The town was originally settled by displaced sharecroppers who exhibited their own brand of initiative in seeking wage work. During the Great Depression, some husbands and fathers who entered the brutal world of Everglades sugarcane cutting earned $3.00 daily and at the same time paid "a home-town boy to do the early work on their cotton acreage at $1 a day." Once sucked into the Atlantic Coast migrant stream, Belle Glade families often demonstrated a commitment to hard labor that was perversely disproportionate to the meager compensation they received. In 1954 a single mother of four could work seven days a week, up to twelve hours a day, picking beans and chopping peppers, and receive a total ("less transportation costs") of $20.60.[5]

For at least seven months out of every year, Belle Glade offered a relatively settled existence for such folk, a place where they stored their belongings and left babies in the care of older kin, while they made the summertime trek up North; a place where social relations, no matter how difficult or troubled, rather than paid employment, served to define people's sense of themselves: "I might pick, but I ain't no picker." In the 1930s and 1940s the largest growers, along with federal investigators, noted with dismay that workers preferred to live on their own in the home-base towns of Belle Glade and Immokalee, avoiding Federal Security Administration (FSA) camps (called "the projects") and company towns. Some married couples quite pointedly turned their backs on Harlem, a subdivision of Clewiston managed by the U.S. Sugar Corporation, and on the largest FSA camps of Okeechobee, Everglades, and Canal Point, which offered "a nice two- or three-room house with lights, water and electricity furnished . . . and a gymnasium for kids, school, recreational facilities." Apparently, wives liked to shop in the stores of Belle Glade and surrounding towns; no matter how limited their resources, these establishments seemed more appealing than the camp commissaries. Workers of both sexes also wanted to avoid the close supervision of camp guards and managers; "in town" households had more latitude in deciding which family members would go to the fields on which days.[6]

Belle Glade suggested an essential continuity between the Southern sharecropper and the Northern ghetto dweller, both groups plagued by chronic underemployment, even when times were good. The path that led farm families from Georgia to Florida revealed a continuum of marginalized labor from the countryside to the city. In the 1930s some croppers were retained by cotton planters, only to be worked "through and through" the fields, in gangs, stripped of their household allotments of land. Replaced by tractors during the planting season, all family members were reduced to a single task, and fathers lost much of their authority; "Because the jobs are all alike, the man no longer can set himself apart as the head of the family by reserving for himself a distinct job." A few families migrated to nearby towns, to await the day when they would be hired back on as wage labor by former employers; others tried to eke out a living in the rural nonagricultural sector, and the decision to explore possibilities in Florida was a natural consequence. Once in Belle Glade, workers soon realized that the winter garden would not feed their families year-round, and they accepted the routine of transience for part of the year, every year; after that, their hope and ambition eroded gradually. The people of late-twentieth-century Belle Glade constituted an "underclass" in the sense that they lived and worked outside the standards established by an advanced consumer society allied with a modern welfare state; still, as the members of hardworking families, they defied classification and shared much with both their slave forebears and their inner-city contemporaries.[7]

THE EAST COAST STREAM AND ITS SOCIAL DIVISION OF LABOR, 1880 TO 1990

Agricultural migrants were by definition the most marginal of all American workers. Systematically alienated from every level of the body politic ("no one's constituency"), excluded from basic worker-protection legislation of the New Deal, and for many years shunned by major labor organizations, they subsisted "at best . . . hardly above the thin edge of distress, without margin for health, education, or other family needs." An anachronistic method of labor deployment under the direction of independent operators called crew leaders guaranteed that most migrants well into the 1970s and 1980s would continue to labor under exploitative conditions similar to those encountered by sharecroppers and phosphate miners a century earlier. In fact, the added "costs" of transportation (in addition to housing and food) docked routinely from a worker's pay, coupled with a seminomadic existence that precluded families from foraging on a regular basis, magnified the evils of "furnishing." Nevertheless, in contrast to its changeless quality as a method of organizing labor, the system thrived on a constant infusion of new groups of workers. The ebb and flow of a variety of racial and ethnic groups into the East Coast stream resulted from local employer prejudices as well as global market and political forces, all factors that contributed to the process of economic marginalization in twentieth-century America.[8]

The development of the Atlantic migrant stream had its roots in the long-suppressed demand for fresh fruits and vegetables among residents in the largest Eastern and Midwestern cities. Until the late 1800s that demand went unfulfilled for two reasons—the lack of adequate transportation and refrigeration facilities, and the lack of a large pool of easily accessible, seasonal labor for harvest operations. During the 1880s technological innovations such as the railroad refrigerator car and the extension of improved rail (and later trucking) routes coincided with the beginning of a long series of natural and man-made disasters that devastated rural economies, both in this country and abroad, and propelled people off farms to find other jobs. Around 1900, for example, the collapse of the seafood-processing industry in the vicinity of Baltimore "freed" blacks and Polish immigrants for labor on Norfolk and Eastern Shore truck farms, and some black workers began an annual seasonal migration to New England fruit orchards. About the same time, the demise of Louisiana sawmills and logging camps provided the necessary labor for expanding strawberry fields located in the southeastern part of the state. In addition, the migration of Mexicans into Texas, and planters' increased reliance on them as cotton pickers, contributed to the decline of sharecropping there, creating a whole new class of dispossessed folk, some of whom headed west to new cotton fields while others turned east to seasonal fruit and vegetable work. Noted a presidential commission on migratory labor in 1951, "We depend on misfortune to build up our force of migratory workers and when the supply is low because there is not enough misfortune at home, we rely on misfortune abroad to replenish the supply."[9]

During the 1930s agricultural economists calculated the collapse of the cotton sharecropping system under the combined weight of farm mechanization, federally sponsored crop reduction programs, and declining prices. Simple equations expressed the mechanistic nature of cropper displacement. Every tractor represented the expulsion of two to four (or, according to some observers, three to five) families. The Agricultural Adjustment Act of 1933 cut cotton acreage by one-third in the course of the decade. Estimates of the number of cropper and tenant household members expelled from plantations ranged from 500,000 to 1 million. From the mountains of Appalachia and the hills of the Missouri Bootheel, families of both races migrated to swell the ranks of day labor, a "floating and dispossessed army" that remained in the countryside, unable to find jobs in cities. By this time the widespread ownership of cars and trucks made possible the long-range migration of families, in contrast to the earlier prototypical migrant, the hobo who rode the rails. It was during this period that the summer south-to-north migration route became organized and routinized.[10]

World War II defense industries absorbed at least some excess labor from the countryside, and migrant workers on both the East and West coasts (whites in particular) eagerly "settled out" as soon as other job options presented themselves. By midwar the number of Atlantic stream migrants had dropped from a depression-era high of 30,000 to 10,000. (Later observers would note that wartime growers somehow managed to salvage their crops with a labor force only a fraction the size of the one they had recently characterized in terms of "shortages.") In 1943 the federal government, overreacting to employers' alarms, initiated the *Bracero* program (in effect until 1958), which admitted Mexican workers into the country on a temporary basis. Over the next few years Mexican immigration spilled out of the relatively narrow confines established under this program, as workers south of the Texas border responded to increased demand for farm laborers in all areas of the United States; in 1949 at least half a million illegal aliens were at work, most of them on the West Coast.[11]

Over the next four decades the federal government followed this general strategy favorable to growers' demands for foreign-born and off-shore agricultural workers. In the late 1940s and early 1950s, increasing numbers of Puerto Ricans and British West Indians were encouraged to migrate to the mid-Atlantic region, under a contract system negotiated directly between employers and their native country or, in the case of Puerto Rico, territory. A 1970 study of interstate agricultural workers along the eastern seaboard found that 40 percent were native-born black, 31 percent Puerto Rican (black and white), 15 percent Mexican, and 11 percent (presumably native-born American) white. The number of workers probably peaked (estimates range from 66,000 to 100,000) around this time; thereafter mechanized harvests in certain crops would require fewer hands and lead to more intense job competition among outcasts and newcomers. Political upheaval in East Asia and Latin America during the 1970s and through the 1980s left its imprint on the Atlantic stream. By the end of the twentieth century, Haitians, Mexicans, Guatemalans, Salvadorans, and Jamaicans chopped Florida cane, grubbed for North Carolina potatoes, and picked New York State apples, while Laotians, Cambodians, and Vietnamese toiled in New Jersey blueberry fields. Moreover, the stream itself lengthened to include the northernmost parts of the East Coast, as Jamaicans and Mexicans from Texas now joined Canadian Indians in Maine, raking blueberries, harvesting broccoli, and packing eggs.[12]

The term migrant "stream" is misleading, for it implies that workers moved in a regular and continuous pattern up the East Coast, following various harvests northward as they matured week by week. Harvest schedules for different crops would seem to confirm this pattern; for example, theoretically a worker could begin "in beans" in Florida from January through mid-April, then find work in North Carolina potatoes from June through July, and move on to Virginia tomatoes (August), and into New Jersey potatoes and a variety of New York State fruits and vegetables as late as October. In fact, however, several studies reveal that most migrants labored in only one or two states each summer; though hardly sedentary, they avoided a life of constant transience as well. Patterns of mobility up the eastern seaboard reflected not an unbroken chain of truck farms but rather clusters of truck-producing areas; the largest (in addition to Florida's sugarcane, citrus, and vegetable sites) included Charleston and Beaufort, South Carolina; Aurora-Bayboro and Elizabeth City, North Carolina; Norfolk, Virginia, and the Eastern Shore of Maryland; Kent and Sussex counties in Delaware; middle New Jersey; Long Island; and upstate New York.[13]

In general, the Atlantic stream consisted of migrants who varied their routine in response to changes in job opportunities (or rumors thereof) as well as those who followed the same path to work each year. Interviewed by Congressional investigators in 1942, William Yearby, a black native of Georgia who had lived in Belle Glade for nine years, reported that he worked in New York State each summer for three or four months, some years in Long Island potatoes and cauliflower and other years in beans near Syracuse. He preferred to stay in Florida year-round; "If I can get work I want to stay here. If I can't, I will go back up." At the same time, an exceptionally large crew of 350 persons left Florida at the end of each May and went directly to Kings Ferry, New York, until fall. When profiled in 1945, this crew had existed for fifteen years and consisted of an inner core of repeat workers, surrounded by "a fluctuating membership" that changed every season. These irregular members probably included people like Yearby, who joined the crew at the last moment in the absence of better prospects. Moreover, many crews attracted new workers and lost original ones en route north. And finally, some laborers joined the stream only when truck harvests complemented the slack seasons of their own staple crops. For example, Louisiana rice workers also cut sugarcane and picked strawberries at different times of the year, and cotton hands in the Deep South states could harvest Florida sugarcane in late summer and return home in time for their own picking season.[14]

The wretched living and working conditions among migrants, made notorious through various exposés and investigations over the years, gave proof of the lowly position of these workers. African-Americans remained a constant presence in the Atlantic migratory stream from its inception onward. Noted a Georgia grower in 1885: "Truck farming being but a branch of the general agriculture of the South, it is to the same God-given instrument, the negro, the farmer must look for his labor." Nevertheless, throughout the history of truck farming, employers up and down the eastern seaboard utilized a number of different groups whom they categorized and judged according to racial and ethnic characteristics. More to the point, growers felt compelled to distance themselves socially and psychologically from the hands they hired. Accounting for the rise of Mexican migrant labor during the 1920s, historian Ruth Allen noted, "Living conditions could scarcely be worse unless with greater congestion, and one of the factors that is making the Mexican a welcome laborer in some sections of the State is that the American landowner and his wife dislike to see 'white people living that way.'" In 1984 state initiatives to provide migrants with a minimum wage and protection from routine, exorbitant deductions for food and housing prompted this response from the manager of a corporate orchard in New York State: "these people have no care in the world," and, he added, they did not necessarily share the same "values" as people like himself—"a car, a house . . . this or that." Such views echoed from the nineteenth into the twentieth century and perpetuated the notion that poor workers of all kinds lived apart from middle-class American life because they lacked aspirations to join it.[15]

Native-born white migrants constituted a significant presence in the Atlantic Coast stream only during the Great Depression. After 1941 the supply of these workers withered in response to defense industry demands and, later, Northern industry in general. In the 1930s, though, Salisbury, Maryland, growers could witness workers, "combined white and colored mixed," emerging exhausted from a single truck after a one-stop journey from Concordia, Virginia. The few whites who were based in Florida during the winter were less likely to follow the crops up the coast and more likely to join the Midwest berry stream, where they were joined by other former tenants and sharecroppers. Some of these latter folk labored near their own homes only during the harvest, while others followed the summer migration that led to the orchards of Michigan. Compared to blacks, whites often journeyed longer distances, and outside crews, because they were more likely to have access to private automobiles and they were less likely to be harassed by law enforcement agents on the road. For example, in 1911 fifteen-year-old Frank Collins, the son of a North Carolina farmer, went to Georgia on his own in search of work. Five years later he was in Texas, and during the next decade he picked cotton in New Mexico and grapes and lemons in California. The Great Depression pushed Collins back east, where he tried his hand at farming in Georgia one more time; soon after he established winter residence in Florida. After the Everglades vegetable season he would move on to Kentucky strawberries and Indiana tomatoes, finally ending the fall in Michigan cherries. By this time Collins had a wife and three children; they traveled together, by car, each season, but managed to keep the children in Florida public schools during the winter: "Well, we don't travel while school is going on; the school is in the same season of the [Florida] work."[16]

To a certain extent, then, the economic crisis of the rural South challenged a long-standing racial division of labor based on the principle that "there were jobs known as Negro jobs at which the white man would not work." The result, according to one rural sociologist in 1940, was that "the labor problems of the two races have more or less converged, and although the problems of the white and colored agricultural laborers are not identical they are similar in essential respects." In Florida this essential similarity in some cases meant that, although blacks and whites might be assigned different tasks within a single establishment, "the [living] conditions are equally bad" for both groups. In other cases members of the two races worked at similar kinds of jobs but clustered apart from one another. On the eve of the war blacks outnumbered whites on Belle Glade truck farms by three to one, while the Lakeland citrus district employed whites exclusively. Blacks in the Sanford area and whites in the Okeechobee area both harvested celery, though blacks got only 50 to 60 percent the hourly pay of whites for the same work. Until well into the 1960s, white men and women could claim as theirs alone the more desirable cannery and packinghouse jobs, upholding the adage of rural-industrial employers, "You can't work whites and Negroes together." For migrant laborers, work under a roof of any kind was evidence of a relatively privileged status; in contrast to field workers, these employees enjoyed minimum-wage protection under the Wagner Act, and they received steadier work (that is, relatively uninterrupted by inclement weather) during the harvest season. White men also filled the more desirable year-round jobs in sugar mills, because, according to one black worker in the late 1960s, "They want the black man out in the field. They want him to inhale the dust."[17]

Growers near large urban centers north of the Mason-Dixon line more often employed foreign-born whites than former sharecroppers. Around the turn of the century, Eastern European immigrants lodged in Northeastern and Midwestern cities began to seek seasonal work on the countryside near their homes. Groups of Slavs found relief from periodic contractions in the Ohio steel industry by working on local fruit and vegetable farms in the summer, at the same time Russian immigrants entered the sugar beet fields of Colorado and newcomers to Chicago formed part of the Midwest berry stream. On the East Coast, Polish families from Baltimore, together with Italians from Camden and Russian Jews from Philadelphia, adhered to a sexual division of labor that sent wives and children to nearby truck farms while husbands who could find work at home remained in the city. The Italian labor contractor or crew leader (called a *padrone*) "always prefers to engage the large family with many children for this means many pickers and of a sort more easily satisfied with the low rate of wages." Although they did not become part of the north-south migratory stream, these desperately poor workers shared with their Belle Glade counterparts the occupational hazards of seasonal agricultural work—low, sporadic earning dependent on climate and crop conditions, poor housing, and a low standard of living mirrored in the gaunt faces of malnourished children.[18]

Migrants competed among one another for the lowest positions on the American job hierarchy, and growers predictably sought to manipulate ethnic rivalries to their own advantage. As early as the 1880s Florida

C. Children of the Dispossessed

The children of landless rural Southerners were deprived of the advantages that more fortunate youngsters all over the country took for granted—sustained schooling, a settled homelife, and freedom from backbreaking labor. During the busy harvest season, the cotton crop claimed the energies of boys and girls (1); during the late nineteenth century, and in the 1920s and 1930s, declining cotton prices forced households to put more of their members to work picking, at earlier ages, and for longer hours. Around the turn of the century, along the Atlantic and Gulf coasts, the seafood processing industry employed indigenous black families (2) as well as Polish immigrants imported each season from Baltimore (3). The need to process the day's catch quickly meant that small children were roused from sleep before dawn and spent the day wielding sharp knives, surrounded by dampness and the stench of rotting shells. New Deal legislation banning certain kinds of waged child labor provided respite for some children (4) and placed added pressure on mothers to join the work force. However, few sons or daughters from poor families were ever completely relieved of responsibility for helping to provide for the household; youngsters foraged, hunted, scavenged, and fished in an effort to add to the family larder (5). Migrant workers remained outside federal labor and social-welfare legislation in any case, and their children continued to toil alongside adults in the fields, sharing with them all the occupational hazards of an essentially unregulated industry (6, 7). White migrants, who more often than blacks owned their own cars, tended to travel exceptionally long distances in search of harvests during the course of the year (8). A hard life on the road kept workers and their children isolated from the good schools and decent jobs that might have enabled them to "settle out" of the migrant stream.

C1. Son of migrant farm hand picking cotton in Calvert, Texas, 1941. Photo by L. C. Harmon. National Archives.

C2. Oyster shuckers at Apalachicola, Florida, 1909. Photo by Lewis Hine.
Florida State Archives.

C3. Canning factory, Bayou La Batre, Alabama, 1911. The eight-year-old on the right had been shucking oysters for three years. Photo by Lewis Hine. National Archives.

C4. Children of coal miners, Scott's Run, West Virginia., ca. 1936. Photo by Lewis Hine. National Archives.

C5. Miner's son, barefoot in the snow, digging coal from mine refuse on the side of the road, Scott's Run, West Virginia, ca. 1936. Photo by Lewis Hine. National Archives.

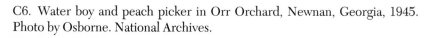

C6. Water boy and peach picker in Orr Orchard, Newnan, Georgia, 1945. Photo by Osborne. National Archives.

C7. Migrant laborer and son picking carrots, Maricopa County, Arizona, 1942. Photo by L. C. Harmon. National Archives.

C8. Children picking sugar beets, Hall County, Nebraska, 1940. Photo by L. C. Harmon, National Archives.

citrus growers tried to recruit a mixed labor force of foreign immigrants, native-born blacks, and local white farmers in order to avoid work stoppages that might be coordinated by one group or another. A Women's Bureau survey of Delaware canneries in 1924 found that employers provided steadier work for Baltimore Poles and Philadelphia Italians compared to Norfolk blacks. According to a 1922 study conducted by the U.S. Department of Agriculture, New Jersey employers seemed "to prefer Negro labor. In spite of this, Italians in some instances have been forcing out the colored workers by offering to work for lower wages, but once thoroughly established and with competition overcome, the Italians have not hesitated to demand higher pay." On the other hand, during the 1930s an abundance of idle workers inflamed racial animosities to the extent that some growers could not deploy their work forces in an orderly way. For example, poor white Florida field hands demonstrated their contempt for the "lower standard Negro farm laborer," so great was their own humiliation at having to accept such work until they could find other jobs "paying a higher rate of pay and requiring less physical exertion to do." Employers reported that tensions between the two groups were too high to work them in the same crews. Even a booming national economy could not eliminate bitter competition among workers. In the 1960s Florida sugarcane growers ordered Jamaican men to work "in the midst of the [black] natives," including women, in order to set a pace that the women could not match. The consequent withdrawal of African-Americans from this type of job produced the "shortage" of domestic labor that growers needed if they were to justify the importation of offshore workers.[19]

European immigrants and native-born whites disappeared from the East Coast stream when New Deal worker-protection legislation and World War II offered them and their children a release from stoop labor. By the late 1930s workers of Italian descent living in Philadelphia could subsist on unemployment insurance of $8.00 a week and "when strawberries come in, they may pick them"—or not. According to one observer, these workers "came with the greatest reluctance and only because they had no alternative jobs." Defense work provided these men with an entrée into the industrial economy, and they and their offspring never returned to the New Jersey fields. Moreover, by stretching wartime budgets, their wives managed to retire from the summertime work force. This development suggested a larger trend that affected the sexual division of labor within the truck-farm labor force. During World War II New Jersey truck and packing plant employers complained that, because "husbands were making good money," wives who worked as sorting operators had to be replaced, by men who were "inefficient" by comparison. About the same time, North Carolina strawberry growers in the vicinity of Fort Bragg and Fort Davis reported that their regular employees were staying at home: "When the head of a family is making good wages, as the men employed on defense work did, the economic pressure on the family is eased, and the women and children do not go to low-wage jobs a long way from home." In contrast, native-born black women never left the migrant stream; they were employed in the most arduous field jobs, and the growth in their numbers after the war testified to the relative worsening of the economic well-being among blacks in general.[20]

To East Coast growers, foreign-born migrant laborers had several obvious advantages. A yearning to return home with a pocketful of cash after a season, or several years, of harvest work, combined with an ever-present fear of deportation, made Mexican and Caribbean workers particularly vulnerable to the power that employers sought to wield over all their hands. Contracts negotiated between employers and the governments of Jamaica or the Bahamas, or with the territorial governor of Puerto Rico, served to guarantee workers a set number of days employment, at a set pay level—guarantees denied to domestic laborers. At the same time, these contracts depressed wage levels for all workers and prohibited hands from negotiating for a better deal once they arrived on the mainland. Mexican and offshore workers could exercise little choice over the jobs they accepted; those under contract were bound by law to perform a certain type of work, while those without contracts sought any kind of job that would pay the dollars they could stretch so much farther at home. Illegal aliens, of course, feared arrest should they express discontent of any kind. Mexican labor proved accommodating when it came time to attend to the sparse second round of picking beans and cotton; domestic workers moved about more freely in quest of first harvests. When, in the early 1970s, African-Americans refused to work on a Florida "muletrain," a corn-picking machine that paid $11.33 for eight and a half hours of work, they demonstrated their distaste for this kind of exploitation and in the process opened up jobs for Haitian immigrants. Noted a vice president of U.S. Sugar Corporation, "If I had a remedy comparable to 'breaching'—that is, firing and deporting—an unsatisfactory worker which I could apply to the American worker, they'd work harder too."[21]

As refugees from a poor, overcrowded land rent by political upheaval, Mexicans began to enter the United States in the early 1920s, when restrictions on European immigration heightened the demand for railroad construction workers as well as agricultural laborers. Moving across the border into Texas, and carrying with them low expectations in terms of pay and housing, large families established their home base in the lower Rio Grande Valley and quickly found favor among rural employers all over the United States. Consequently these men, women, and children displaced successive groups in their seasonal treks northward— native-born black and white sharecroppers in Texas; urban immigrants at work in the fields of Ohio, Michigan, and Colorado; and blacks on the eastern seaboard, all paths that veered off from the "Big Swing" through the winter garden and cotton-growing regions of Texas. In the 1930s the Texas intrastate migration alone claimed the energies of 300,000 Mexicans (along with 40,000 blacks and 60,000 native-born whites). By the early 1950s Mexican migrant labor consisted of two types of workers—legal aliens, who were single men, and illegal aliens, who tried to move unobtrusively from place to place, their kin in tow. Around this time the children of original Mexican immigrants began to seek work as American citizens; most remained based in either Texas or California, but a few found their way into the Atlantic migratory stream, where they were "most readily distinguished from other Florida migrants by the nature of [their] family ties"—a "family cohesiveness" that kept young and old, male and female "together on the road, in the camps, and in the fields." Growers particularly prized young single men who boasted of "keeping strong" by picking fruits and vegetables; these migrants were known for their willingness to work hard to make as much cash as possible so that they could return to their families in Texas or Mexico, or establish households themselves.[22]

Puerto Rican workers entered the United States in large numbers between 1947 and the late 1960s; by 1969, 21,000 labored under contracts negotiated by growers with the territorial government of Puerto Rico. Recruited from the arid inland section of the island, the migrants considered themselves a fortunate few, men who supplemented agricultural work in their homeland, busiest between March and June, with employment in the mid-Atlantic region during the summer and then in Florida's winter garden. Some returned to Puerto Rico in the fall, when outdoor work was scarce in all three regions. Like their young Mexican counterparts, Puerto Rican workers were deemed "a godsend to the farmer" because they "want to work and get ahead and save money and send it home." But as American citizens, Puerto Ricans enjoyed a favorable legal status that allowed them to take advantage of educational and welfare services without fear of reprisal. In the early 1980s the Mexicans who picked Pennsylvania mushrooms and New Jersey tomatoes were more destitute and less educated than the Puerto Ricans who worked side by side with them in the fields; these Mexican families needed every dollar their children could earn in order to repay the "coyotes" who had slipped them across the border. Yet American citizenship guaranteed Puerto Ricans only relative advantages, for in the 1980s much better educated young people (even some with a few years of college) began to seek out mid-Atlantic migrant camps as an alternative to the bleak future they faced back home.[23]

In 1941 a Florida grower named L. L. Chandler proposed that the Immigration and Naturalization Service admit large numbers of "Nassau or Bahama Island Negroes." Chandler offered a succinct rationale for tapping this new pool of labor: "the cold fact remains yet that the domestic or Florida producer, already harassed and suffering from severe competition with foreign-produced vegetables where cheaper labor prevails . . . [now could make use of] these Negroes in the Bahama Islands [who] are without employment, and it would really be a favor to them if permitted to simply fill in the slack. . . . " Apparently, if foreign labor harvested for starvation wages abroad, they could work during their own off-season for slightly higher compensation in this country, thus restoring some balance to a domestic industry suffering under the weight of foreign imports. During World War II and thereafter, British West Indians (Jamaicans and Bahamians) and Haitians entered the United States as migrant workers. Though often grouped together under the heading "offshore foreign workers" to distinguish them from Puerto Ricans and Mexicans, these groups varied in their demographic characteristics and in the role they played within the Atlantic Coast migratory stream. For example, in the post-1945 period, Bahamians found jobs with Florida fruit and vegetable growers, while a large proportion of Jamaicans went directly to the U.S. Sugar holdings near Belle Glade. Thereafter Jamaicans would constitute the largest offshore group at work on the eastern seaboard, single black men who slept in the stark barracks of Clewiston, lonely men who were too exhausted to watch TV at night: "The White Man Does Steal Us Very Bad." However, by the late 1970s it was the Haitian refugees who existed at the very bottom of the Atlantic stream's compressed scale of human misery. Non-English speaking, subject to arbitrary arrests and summary deportations, Haitian families had little recourse if "the boss never paid me a cent" for "back-killing work." Few had illusions about returning to the state-sanctioned terrorism of Haiti, and yet no haven awaited these refugees in America, though they followed in a long line of immigrants who believed that everyone here owned "cars, pretty clothing, jewelry, boats, and lots of dollars." As one woman put it: "*Ou Kouri Pou la pli ou tonbe nan la rivie*: "If you run due to the rain you'll fall in the river."[24]

Migrants differed in their willingness to transfer their loyalties from their home place, wherever that might be, to Florida. Interviewed in 1988, a sixty-five-year-old white widow named Ruby Holland, "who talks with the dialect of the Ozark hills where her father was a sharecropper," recounted the odyssey that had led her to poverty-stricken Immokalee: "I've picked peppers and tomatoes from Florida to California and chopped cotton all over the South. . . . I quit when I couldn't take the chemicals coming off the plants on my hands. They'd swell up on me every night, and I'd go to sleep clawing them." While other more fortunate Social Security recipients basked on terraces of coastal condominiums, Ruby Holland scrounged for aluminum cans to redeem for cash at the rate of 30 cents a pound. "For me," she said, "I want to die back home in Arkansas. You make a living out of this Florida dirt, but it ain't never going to be home." Other migrants managed to preserve ties to the place where their forbears had lived for generations. During the depression workers from Georgia and Alabama, now transplanted to the muckland, "traveled in family or kinship groups and retained connections at home who arranged for their work at home during the slack season in Florida." Living in Belle Glade in 1942, one black woman told investigators that she considered her home to be Dawson, Georgia; "When I go to Georgia I am going home, that's Dawson, Georgia." Asked "why do you consider Dawson your home?" (since she had moved away in 1937 and usually stayed there no more than two weeks out of the year), she replied that she "had a little place" in Dawson, where the father of her children still lived; "We have been parted 7 years, but still that's home, all my things are there."[25]

"THEY DON'T HAVE ADDRESSES": THE ISOLATION OF MIGRANT LABOR

Within the migrant labor system, instances of forced labor were not uncommon. In the 1940s officials of the U.S. Sugar Corporation brutalized their workers with such impunity that even the Federal Bureau of Investigation confirmed the existence of peonage: "There does not seem to be any dispute as to the fact that those men who have attempted to escape from the plantations and are picked up on the highway or shot at while trying to hitch rides on the sugar trains are returned to the plantations and forced to work." A cutter from Barbados described the work as "partially slaving yourself. It was what I call a kind of way a man had to do all that he could in his body to make a dollar." Yet growers need not have indulged in criminal excesses to preserve the essential features of a postbellum Southern political economy. These men relied on crew leaders, for whom the raw profit motive reigned supreme, unmediated by the so-called paternalism practiced by slaveowners who had a long-term, vested interest in keeping their workers alive and functioning. Moreover, the family wage system remained intact in seasonal migratory labor long after it was abandoned in other sectors. (Government officials often had difficulty assessing wage levels because "The earnings, especially of younger children and wives, were frequently pooled with those of the family when farmers paid them off, and thus were unknown.") In fact, migrant farm workers were remarkable for their isolation from the rest of American society, and from any meaningful government intervention. Even in the late twentieth century, various public agencies seemed intent not on dismantling the system but on propping it up by "reforming" it.[26]

Like sharecroppers and the residents of rural industrial work camps, migrants were beholden to employers for shelter as well as employment; a "good job" could either pay well or provide relatively decent housing, but usually offered some combination of the two. In response to the question of a congressional committee member, "How much do you receive there [Salisbury, Maryland]?" one worker replied, "20 cents an hour and good living quarters." Poor housing conditions were inextricably linked to poor health among migrants. Tin shacks and ramshackle barracks were cramped quarters for families, too hot to enter until after sundown on a blistering summer day. Leaky walls and roofs in drafty quarters and primitive sanitary facilities, combined with poor nutrition and arduous field work, took their toll in the form of respiratory and intestinal diseases. Predictably, the corollary of ill health was inadequate and, too often, inaccessible medical care; as a result, migrants accepted readily identifiable forms of sickness as their "normal" condition. A study conducted by the Florida State Board of Health in the mid-1950s found that the parents of babies with diarrhea believed that was "just the way babies are ..." Concluded the investigator, "It isn't just a matter of economics, or of the clinic being available. These people just haven't learned what being sick means." Or perhaps more accurately, "these people" felt they just could not afford to give in to illness.[27]

In their outrage, migrant workers who lived and worked under inhuman conditions often defined their plight as no better than that of animals. These included the Baltimore Poles reduced to living "like cattle" and "like hogs," they said, in Maryland vegetable fields; the blacks hauled "like livestock" in trucks up the East Coast and treated "like dogs" in the Florida cane fields. Employers countered that their workers deserved no better, more resembling pigs and roving, "wild Florida range cows" than people at all. Reformers pointed out that most states were more likely to lavish funds on the protection of fish and wildlife than on the welfare of migrant children, who enjoyed "no closed season." By the 1940s federal regulations stipulated that truckloads of livestock must be watered and unloaded routinely, in transit, but no such laws applied to the workers like those crammed into a single truck, without room to lie down during a virtually nonstop, fifty-five-hour journey from Palm Beach to Delaware. In 1970 devastating floods in the vicinity of Belle Glade reduced thousands of migrant workers to starvation; but public outcry focused on the uncertain fate of Everglades deer affected by high water levels. These comparisons of people to animals were more than mere hyperbole. Up and down the eastern seaboard migrants actually lived in barn stalls, chicken coops, and geese structures; "catters" slept outside, on porches, under trees; and horses received the care of veterinarians more often than babies saw physicians. Migrant men and women remained sensitive to such indignities but helpless to eradicate them. In 1914 a representative from the National Child Labor Committee found that the Polish immigrants subsisting in shanties on the Maryland countryside refused to let him take a photograph of their quarters, so ashamed were they that they had to "live like hogs": "Do you think we like to live that way? Ach—they treat us like cattle out there." Of her crowded conditions on the road, Johnnie Belle Taylor observed in 1942, "We just put up with most anything, just to be working, trying to live."[28]

Out of sight in isolated areas, migrant camps were small, self-contained entities where workers were forced to purchase supplies from a commissary or "jook joint"; the lack of cooking or refrigeration facilities hindered families' efforts to preserve their own food or prepare their own meals. One camp in the Florida Everglades went so far as to keep "its water supply locked up except for 2 hours a day . . . [in] another . . . water was sold at a penny a bucket." Crew leaders had an incentive to sell workers cigarettes, alcohol, drugs, and various forms of "entertainment." It was not unusual for workers to find themselves indebted to a crew leader for transportation before they picked even one hamper of beans, and each rainy day in camp brought added living expenses that a shrinking paycheck could not cover. Because of myriad deductions, accounts of end-of-week and end-of-season pay sounded suspiciously like annual reckonings on cotton plantations. Some workers considered themselves fortunate if they broke even at the end of a backbreaking season of picking cabbages or grubbing potatoes, and some, in the words of one crew leader in Maryland, "didn't make enough money to pay expenses to get back to Florida and were disappointed. . . . " In the 1960s a fruit packer could earn $52 for five days' labor but receive a paycheck of only $7, "and if he wanted to stay in one piece, he had to accept it."[29]

At the center of this labor management system was the crew leader. Part employer, labor contractor, transporter, creditor, and provider, the (Florida-based) crew leader assembled a group of workers at the beginning of the northern harvest season and made arrangements with employers to deliver a certain number of hands at a certain time of the summer. The relationship between crew member and leader was a highly personal one, and turnover from one year to the next exhibited the same kind of dynamics that affected shifting sharecroppers. As one crew leader noted, "In this migratory labor you never have a crew that you can depend on. You may work them a week and maybe he is with someone else the next week. You know how it is." Caught between a grower's need for many hands to harvest as quickly as possible and his own inability to retain workers from year to year, or even week to week, the crew leader understood that it was in his (or her) natural interest to create a labor surplus on the road, whenever possible. The leader might manage a tight-knit group welded together through indebtedness, dependency, and kinship; but no matter what the basis of his authority, he exercised absolute control over which workers performed which jobs for how long—a form of power that depended on cajolery or threats or, more often, some combination of the two. Usually located far from law enforcement agents, migrants rarely had any recourse if mistreated; and even persistent workers might have difficulty locating any kind of legal official sympathetic to their grievances. In 1969 a black crew member named Newlon Lloyd reported that the year before, "a crew leader threatened to stomp me to death because I was trying to go away to the bus station. He said if I take the bus, he would stomp me to death." In response to Lloyd's complaint, a local police officer tried to talk him out of having the would-be assailant arrested: "You know, tomorrow you will forget all about this. I don't think you want to arrest no crew leader. It's kind of dangerous for a migrant worker to arrest the crew leader."[30]

Local officials depended on crew leaders to keep their workers confined to the camp so that they would not have an incentive to patronize local movie theaters, bars, or grocery or department stores. Dressed in work clothes, often darker in skin color than townspeople, migrants were quickly recognized by apprehensive merchants. Consequently communities up and down the East Coast engaged in a variety of tactics to keep migrants at work in the fields but outside their boundaries; "His labor is welcome but he is not." En route from Belle Glade to the Eastern Shore of Maryland in the mid-1950s, one crew in search of a meal was turned away from a diner (Fort Pierce, Florida); forbidden to use the toilets at a gas station where the bus had refueled (Melbourne, Florida); forced to remain near their trucks at a small grocery store (Bay Harbor, South Carolina); intimidated by state police officers during an hour-and-a-half rest for sleep; and, the next morning, kept inside the ferry house while awaiting transportation across the Chesapeake Bay (Norfolk, Virginia). These instances of harassment shaded off into cases of unconstitutional search and seizure whenever state and county law enforcement officers fined northbound truckloads of migrants that passed through areas of labor-hungry truck farmers. As late as the 1960s, state troopers between Florida and New York State "lay in ambush waiting for the migrant cara-vans to prey on them and drain from them whatever small savings they might have in the form of fines."[31]

Migrant labor was even more exploitative than work in the manufac-turing and service sectors, no matter how poorly paid. Throughout the twentieth century, migrants consistently received wages that amounted to from one-third to one-half the annual pay for unskilled factory jobs, but even these figures were generous, since up to 40 percent of their earnings consisted of nonmonetary compensation in the form of trans-portation, food, and housing. Minimum-wage reforms in the 1960s and 1970s were limited to hourly wages (most migrants worked on a piece-rate basis) and applied only to the largest farms (in 1980, 2 percent of all farms with migrant laborers). In general, pay scales bore little pre-dictable relation to the larger commercial crop market. Although grow-ers up and down the Atlantic coast bemoaned a shortage of laborers each season, migrants fell further behind in their pay, compared to industrial workers, as the decades passed. In fact, "prevailing wages" reflected a "historic economy" based on traditions and assumptions quite apart from any putative competition for labor. For example, a former General Motors official transplanted to Clewiston quickly adapted his labor management techniques to Southern tradition as interpreted by the U.S. Sugar Corporation. M. E. Von Mach explained his policies before a USDA wage hearing in 1937: "I would say that if we were to pay 1 cent more to these men it would be disastrous to the laborers. Now, that sounds funny coming from me, being a northerner and used to high wages and good living conditions; but if you were to give the 'nigger' more money than he gets now he would leave 2 months sooner because he has too much money to spend." Within neighborhoods, employers often colluded with one another before the picking season and set wages well before the first truckload of workers from Belle Glade appeared on the horizon. Hence migrants' compensation might not reflect their employers' profits at all.[32]

For migrants, work days necessarily came in fits and starts; long "enforced vacations" were punctuated by frantic days of picking at all hours of the day and into the evening; recalled one resident of Pearl City, Florida, "During the gathering time there wasn't no off days. . . . it was dark when the last one get out of the field." This extreme unpredictability characterized all levels of commercial food production. Year-to-year routines showed little continuity; in 1934 the Arkansas strawberry crop used 20,000 mostly "outside" workers, and three years later, local labor harvested a much smaller crop. Individual seasonal migrations depended on a precarious harmony of harvest peaks, and a delay in the ripening of Florida beans ate away opportunities awaiting workers in Delaware melons. A day's worth of rain, cold weather, or high winds could throw as many as 5,000 men, women, and children out of work in a single area. Difficulties in coordinating transportation for crews, combined with the perishability factors of various crops, often left workers waiting in trucks and buses, and in the fields, for hours on end—a part of their "work day" for which they would receive no pay at all. It was not unusual for Florida bean pickers to arrive in the fields at 8:00 A.M. and find the fields too wet to pick for four hours. According to their crew leader, they would "just sit there and wait, get their breakfast," and, in the process, of course, run up their tabs for sandwiches and soft drinks. To wile away the time, "they might be playing poker, blackjack, I don't know. I don't pay any attention to that. The native Negro does that wherever he is, you know." Once started, work under the sun had no set hours: "You go home when the man tells you." Under these conditions, laborers made no clear distinction between work and nonwork days, and the concept of "vacation" had very little meaning to them.[33]

Insecurity of employment was compounded by the disagreeable nature of the work. Years of stoop labor produced chronic fatigue as well as curvature of the spine and a whole host of other kinds of muscular ailments and bone deformities. Sugarcane cutters in the 1980s, like those in earlier centuries, suffered from wounds inflicted by razor-sharp knives and needle-sharp stubble. In addition, laborers in the Florida cane fields contracted skin rashes and in some cases even blindness from contact with the silt-fine muckland; "Dat muck'll itch yuh lak ants." Increased efficiency in crop production brought only new dangers, not respite from old ones; citrus and vegetable migrants labored in the midst of deadly insecticides "applied indiscriminately by airplanes and field carts, even the day before harvest." Less dangerous perhaps but no less representative of the migrant's lowly status were everyday forms of discomfort that came from long hours out-of-doors, in the heat and mud. One migrant mother complained bitterly about the bug bites that caused her children so much pain, and her own consequent emotional distress: "The worst thing, if you ask me, is the bites they get. It makes them unhappy, real unhappy. They itches and scratches and bleeds, and oh, it's the worst. They must want to tear all their skin off, but you can't do that."[34]

Government complicity in the migrant labor system assumed many forms. For all practical purposes, until the late 1960s (when Title I funds were allotted for the education of migrant children), the federal government made no move to monitor working or living conditions; but it did play an active role, through the U.S. Employment Service and the Farm Placement Service, in recruiting migrants and matching them to growers. Announced one Florida state employment official, in his quest for workers, "I need a hundred hungry people." In the 1920s and 1940s federal officials yielded to the entreaties of growers and admitted hundreds of thousands of foreign workers. Government-grower collusion was explicit in the Everglades, where, in the 1930s, local officials withheld Works Progress Administration jobs from field hands; "closed out" households (that is, cut them off from relief benefits) at the start of the winter harvest season in order to minimize grower criticism of relief efforts; and actively promoted the establishment of "jook joints" that provided areas (through, for example, the Palm Beach County collector of amusement taxes) with much-welcomed revenues. Sheriffs in South Florida enforced "vagrancy laws," but only when the beans needed picking and the cane needed cutting; and school boards, "in cooperation with the local growers," sponsored "a summer term in the Negro schools in order that the bean pickers of school age may work in the fields . . . without neglecting their education." During World War II, especially, the labor shortage prompted planters and sawmill and turpentine operators to seek aid from law enforcement agents in stemming a slack-season migration southward; as a result, "local police, sheriffs, and constables . . . pick up people en route here [to Florida] with such labor on one charge or another, threaten the Negroes who are on the truck, and the result is that such Negroes leave the truck and go to work in these areas where they are stopped." States throughout the Lower South revived laws prohibiting labor enticement, Reconstruction-era legislation enlisted to meet twentieth-century needs.[35]

Beginning in the 1960s local, state, and federal officials aimed a variety of programs at migrants; some were merely ameliorative, providing health care and entertainment to residents of labor camps, and only efforts in the areas of job training and formal education (usually carried out on a small scale) seemed to have much promise. Entitlement and income-transfer programs in the form of Social Security, unemployment compensation, Aid to Families with Dependent Children (AFDC), and food stamps allowed elderly people and single mothers to stay in Florida year-round, but without the good wages and steady jobs needed to lift them above the poverty line. By the 1980s the Reagan revolution had so diminished federal funds for specific initiatives, and local areas felt so compelled to divert scarce resources to more pressing issues, that concerted measures on behalf of migrants seemed increasingly unlikely.

Excluded from New Deal social welfare legislation, migrants had never received their fair share of federal programs. On the one hand, Hispanic and native black households continued to rely heavily on their respective kin groups for aid; they retreated into a prideful self-sufficiency that sprung from suspicion of white welfare agents as well as from their own lack of information about various programs and eligibility requirements. In the 1970s and 1980s the constant flow of "new immigrants" into the Atlantic Coast stream meant that a large number of workers— for example, 40 percent of those toiling in the Florida Everglades right before the killer freeze of 1989—could not meet the residency requirements for assistance. On the other hand, many migrants eligible for aid failed to apply for it. Crew leaders might refuse to allow workers to apply for food stamps, even when they were subsisting on raw sweet potatoes. In the summer of 1985 near Laurel, Delaware, only 10 out of 150 needy migrants received food stamps, mainly because of the stipulation that they travel fifteen miles to Georgetown and pose for a photo identification card that would then be sent to them through the mail. Noted one social worker, "Some live in boarded-up homes, while others live in cheap hotels. They don't have addresses." On the road, a day spent puzzling over mysterious application forms meant the loss of a day's wages and not necessarily the guarantee of help. The connection between work and welfare remained problematic in any case, with a good week's picking likely to disqualify a worker from aid altogether, or cut his or her benefits proportionately.[36]

In 1970, in a "crumbling three-room shack" in Lake Hamilton,

Florida, lived a black woman named Netti Hayes, the single mother of eight children. For Mrs. Hayes, the Great Society and the war it waged against poverty seemed quite distant from her own daily efforts to keep her family together. She received $179 per month from AFDC, plus food commodities, and managed to shop "outside the ghetto" where she could find better prices at discount stores in nearby Haines City. But her landlord charged $60 a month for her house, and she had to buy all of her appliances and furniture "on time" at exorbitant interest rates. She tried to make ends meet by "picking fruit, cleaning house, whatever she can do and whatever she can get"; in response, ever-vigilant welfare officials took care to reduce her benefits, even though she could not find regular employment. For this woman, the opening of popular tourist attractions, such as Cypress Gardens to the south and Disney World (in 1972) to the north, would not have much of an impact on her financial well-being, for she had no means of transportation that might allow her to take advantage of new jobs in cafeterias or hotels. And so each summer Netti Hayes bade farewell to her two oldest children who left home to seek out employment on Northern truck farms; she also sent north some of her younger children in the company of their grandmother. Thus did the Atlantic Coast migratory stream extract from black people their sweat and their fondest hopes born of the desire for a better way of life.[37]

FAMILY AND CULTURE AMONG AFRICAN-AMERICAN MIGRANTS

In 1940 a Farm Security Administration official lauded a lesser-known chapter in the "Florida legend"—a chapter "not set forth on the glossy pages of tourist circulars" but rather one that reached "by word of mouth from cabin to cabin" across the South; hearing the message, "landless people, white and black, learn that there is a golden Florida made ready for them too," where "the beans, the tomatoes, the celery and the sugarcane" will all bring them "big money." Indeed, for most migrant laborers, the lure of the place was very real—"Big Lake Okeechobee, big beans, big cane, big weeds, big everything"—and the harsh reality that awaited them in Belle Glade and its environs seemed strangely at odds with the hopefulness of people grown restless on crumbling cotton plantations and tobacco farms. Once in Florida and drawn into the migratory labor stream, families continued to reenact a cycle of optimism followed by disillusionment, as young people recapitulated the struggles of their parents and as parents readjusted their sights on the future according to lessons learned "on the season." Black people tried to carve out for themselves and their families a measure of autonomy within a labor system that offered few rewards for hard work; these strategies reflected their resistance to field-work servitude, twentieth-century style.[38]

Many croppers abandoned the plantation only after engaging in heroic efforts to eke out a living from the land. Throughout the Cotton Belt black and white households pilfered fence posts for firewood, foraged for berries and fished in streams, and used small plots of land retired from cotton production in order to grow food and feed livestock. One family of Alabama tenants sought out work in a Delaware cannery, but only when they could not become self-sufficient—through gardening, bean picking, and "odd jobs on farms at $1.50 or $2 a day." In some cases, of course, migrant labor itself was a form of supplementary employment for sharecroppers who managed to cling to a piece of land. Entry into the migrant labor stream often occurred incrementally, by stages, and represented the culmination of attempts by fathers and older sons to find wage work in the rural nonagricultural sector. The South was littered with small communities, scattered remnants of mine or mill towns now defunct; North Carolina, for example, included a "residue population or island population which used to be around a sawmill. . . . The industry has disappeared and it has left those people there. . . . " For other blacks, who had annually shifted their families from one plantation to another and who had relied on Georgia turpentine stills or Florida phosphate mines for slack-season employment, a move to Belle Glade seemed to be the next best step in a journey that had begun with emancipation.[39]

Households "frosted out once and drowned out again" responded to the positive inducements offered by truck-farm work; in the words of one black cropper from South Carolina, a father of five, "I got to the place where I couldn't hardly make a living so I had a chance to try to do better." For large landless households that toiled in the cotton fields but still accumulated less that $200 per year, even the piece-rate wages for berry pickers seemed munificent in comparison. In turn, truck-farm workers who migrated each summer up the East Coast made more money than their friends who either remained in Florida year-round or those who returned to their home state in the summer months. A black squatter named Richard Mitchell in Del Ray Beach lost his entire tomato crop to floodwaters one year and then heard that he could make $6 or $7 a day in Swedesboro, New Jersey; "It wouldn't cost anything to come up. I didn't have anything to start with. I said, 'Well I can do that.' I'd try to make myself something. So I just swung on the truck and came along." Mitchell traveled with more than forty men in the same truck from Florida to New Jersey expecting to find a job in a factory, but he realized too late he would get only "Farm work—we haven't heard anything about the factory."[40]

For Georgia men and women, kin provided the information and lodging necessary to sustain a classic form of chain migration. Born around 1950, a black woman named Laurine Pickett lived with her sharecropping parents, "the only family living on The Man's place" by that time. One Christmas reckoning time, her father returned from "the big house" and reported once more, "We ended up in the hole again this year." The family scratched and scuffled; Laurine Pickett remembered that her father "was always trying to find an outside job to help us get along." The four children, along with their mother, would "all of us work the garden, and if we see any bottles or scrap along the road, we'd save it. We'd do all we could to keep from using The Man's money. We all worked so hard at it we kind of got silly about savin' and scrimpin'." Then an aunt in Belle Glade urged the family to join her. To pay for the trip, the next fall they surreptitiously transported basketloads of cucumbers they had grown to a nearby market. When that venture failed to yield sufficient cash, Laurine Pickett's father "stole all the corn he could stuff into that truck" and then he "used the money for bus tickets to get us all out. My mother was scared, because there were a lot of stories about what a farmer would do if he caught you stealing and running." This act of desperation won for the Pickett household a life in Belle Glade and on the season.[41]

As black Americans became more settled in Florida, they began to devise strategies that would provide them with some latitude to parcel out opportunities for schooling and obligations to work among various household members. A family's financial well-being directly affected the ages and number of family members sent out to the winter day-work ritual that took place on street corners throughout home-base towns; the poorer the family, the more likely wives and children would show up for the 7:00 A.M. "shape up." Unlike Mexicans, native-born black family members often separated from one another at the end of the Florida harvest. Mothers and fathers might leave their children at home, with elderly kin, rather than subject them to life on a New York apple farm; "the camp's not for children," said one mother, whose two remained with her parents in Florida for the summer. She and her husband could count on more sustained schooling for their offspring, and her parents could count on a more settled life for themselves, no doubt due in part (by the early 1970s) to Social Security payments. These considerations, as they affected the generations, help to explain the relative dearth of the very young and the very old among migrants, especially after seasonal laborers began to qualify for welfare payments of any kind in Florida.[42]

Work routines varied according to different crops, and each season migrants sorted out a matrix of factors related to the regularity of employment, method of payment, and nature of supervision and crew organization. Choices often reflected the efforts by poor people to avoid committing themselves to the most arduous and dangerous jobs on a long-term basis. For example, sugarcane cutting provided "powerful regular work"—"they work all day and they work every day"—but native-born blacks resisted going into the cane fields if they could help it. "Because of the danger and the tedium and the piece rate, Americans have shunned work in cane," reported journalist Alec Wilkinson in 1989, and as a result imported Jamaican workers came to dominate a job in which "more than one in every three [workers] cuts himself or is cut by someone who has lost control of his knife, or wrenches his back, or suffers an attack of some kind in the heat, or steps in a rabbit hole and turns an ankle, or is bitten by fire ants, or pierces an eye or an eardrum with a sharp leaf of cane while bending over and grabbing a stalk."[43]

When native-born cane cutters deserted the sugar fields, they did so gradually, during World War II, often after meeting "some of these other Negroes who tell them how much easier it is to pick beans 4 or 5 hours a day and only work 2 or 3 days a week and make what they want to" (that is, very little, in the eyes of cynical U.S. Sugar officials). In fact, American-born blacks resented not only the hazards inherent in cane cutting but the way tasks were assigned and supervised. These laborers also preferred beans to celery, because celery work was organized in a manner similar to sugarcane; moving down the rows together, crew members divided into cutters, strippers, and packers had to work together, and maintain the same pace, so it was easy for a supervisor to dismiss a worker who held the whole crew back. In contrast, bean pickers worked by themselves and earned according to their inclinations as individuals (or according to their ingenuity, when they stuffed the bottom of the basket full of vines, as "filler"). Nevertheless, a bean farmer who consistently "busted the hamper" (that is, forced pickers to pack containers more tightly than usual) would have to raise his piece rates to attract people to his field.[44]

The legacy of slavery cast a long shadow over twentieth-century truck farms. According to sociologist Dorothy Nelkin, who studied black apple pickers in New York State during the 1960s, workers were not averse to sharing with one another access to a particularly bountiful row or tree, but they were likely to express their resentment toward an enforced system of gang labor, by working more slowly than growers thought they should. During World War II traditional forms of labor resistance in the fields—now called "sitdowns" and "slowdowns"—struck growers as downright unpatriotic: When a worker "begins picking at 11 o'clock and picks 'til 2 and then quits, I guess he's on a sit-down strike too, because he's made $3 and that's all he wants. When he's got a misery (from too much 'jooking' the night before) or when he's got a sick grandmother or a friend in jail he must see about, yes, I guess he's on a sit-down or a slow-down." To some extent, these tactics, based more on individual than collective action, reflected the wartime labor shortage; and yet they also evoked postemancipation days in the rural South, when freedpeople of both sexes withheld from white men their full productive energies.[45]

The migrant labor system depended not so much on the hopelessness of workers as on their stubborn belief that a better deal was bound to appear on the next farm, or up north. In assessing the initiative of families in seeking out work, then, it is necessary to consider the institutionalization of fraudulent recruiting practices—promises of "soft jobs at extravagant wages" that proved so effective in ensnaring hopeful people. To meet the demand for over fifty thousand winter workers in the Everglades in 1940, growers placed ads and distributed flyers (primarily in Georgia) that stressed the seasonal complementarity between cotton picking and truck-farm work. A "cane cutter's special" ranged as far afield as Mississippi, gathering up workers with promises of free transportation, the chance to "Enjoy Florida Sunshine During the Winter Months," along with "Cash Issued Every Day . . . Free House Rent, Recreation, and Medical Attention." In the mid-1980s a woman five months pregnant with her third child could flee back to Florida and away from from drought-stricken cucumber fields of the Eastern Shore of Maryland, "clinging to a promise of one or two months' weeding work at $3.35 an hour." For her co-workers on the road, however, a crew leader's decision to head to New York tomato fields revealed the summertime truism, "I guess all you can do is keep heading north." Indeed, hopes of all kinds had always paved the way to Florida and the way north, hopes that spanned the grand ideal of self-sufficiency—"six rooms just for my family. . . . Chickens. Ducks. I would like to have a cow if I could get one"—to the more modest expectation that the week's bean crop would be full enough to pay for the truck ride back to Belle Glade at the end of the season.[46]

As migrants, families sought to provide for their traditional needs in ways suited to their new circumstances. Women continued to assume primary responsibility for cooking and child care; but unlike farmers' wives, they contributed little direct income to the household unless they performed field work. Gone were the usual tasks of gardening and dairying. On the road housekeeping tasks, reserved for rainy days, became even more difficult now that camp quarters were even more temporary and congested than those of sharecroppers. Some wives and mothers had to improvise with open-pit fires and with bed tickings stuffed with moss. Many households resorted to time-honored methods of "scrambling" and "scrimpin' around" outside the confines of the paid labor force. In Florida a sudden winter freeze that brought a halt to wage work sent family members out to the Glades to trap rabbits and catch catfish. One grower, noting that black migrants would rather remain in Florida year-round than go "on the season" up the coast, reported that fifty men could share summertime jobs intended for twenty-five of them by each working three days a week and then "they can get out and knock a rabbit in the head and catch a few fish. It's remarkable how cheap they can live." Other men and women sought temporary employment outside of agriculture, usually in Florida but sometimes up north as well.[47]

Native-born blacks demonstrated certain household strategies and cultural values that their employers hailed as evidence of their "instability" and "irresponsibility." To most whites, Johnnie Belle Taylor, based in Farm Security Administration camp near Belle Glade in the 1940s, appeared to be a typical black single migrant mother of five. In fact, she was at the center of an extended family that carefully parceled out tasks to its several members. Her husband was in Key West "trying to work down there, so he kind of hated to leave since they needed men so bad on the water line and all." The two youngest children remained in the care of their grandmother during the day, while an older daughter assisted her mother and the middle two children "go to school some and help" at home some. The family spent its summers in Georgia working in tobacco first and then harvesting peanuts and cotton in the fall. The willingness of the Taylor household to explore new opportunities and abandon old employers was part of a general tendency among blacks to avoid continuous work for an unscrupulous grower, if possible; in the words of one white man, "if he [the worker] doesn't trust you he is not going to stay long, not if he can get some place else to go."[48]

Migrants could only rarely win better jobs or higher pay on the basis of work well done. Crew leaders remained at the top of the camp hierarchy, and these men often chose bookkeepers, row checkers, cooks, and basket leaders from among their kin and friends. Only camp cleaners were below pickers in pay and prestige. The piecework method of payment meant that if a household wanted to earn more money it must pick faster or for longer hours, with more family members in the fields, compared to the day before. Turnover among and within crews precluded any sort of seniority system, and employers had little incentive to raise wages from one year to the next. In the end, with most workers engaged in a number of different, highly temporary tasks during any one season, compensation ultimately reflected the "quality of fields" more than skill or on-the-job initiative. Regardless of a grower's chronic complaints about shoddy work, few suggested that skill was really the issue. In recruiting Jamaicans, the U.S. Sugar Corporation liked to suggest that "black men in America simply lack this skill [of cutting], just plain don't have it, but no wonder, it's an *exotic* skill, and we have to go to an exotic (and backward) place to obtain artisans still capable of performing it." In fact, the vast majority of Jamaicans had never stepped foot in a cane field, and they had to undergo a training period when they arrived on the mainland—a period for which they were poorly compensated, if at all. The swiftness with which unsatisfactory workers were breached suggests that even highly experienced cutters were less valuable to the corporation than more compliant workers.[49]

Confined within a system that discouraged personal industry and ambition, some migrants hoped to become crew leaders themselves, while others just wanted to become free of them. Conducted by the USDA, a 1952 study of Atlantic Coast migrants revealed that, of a sample of thirty crew leaders (two white men, three black women, and the rest black men, all in charge of all-black crews), "More than half had risen from the ranks of the migratory labor group." Of course, only a tiny percentage of workers ever found their way into this powerful, and often lucrative, position. "Freewheeling" was a more realistic goal, and not an inconsequential one, for migrants who owned a car increased their earnings to the extent that transportation costs would have otherwise depleted them. The 1952 USDA study also found that one-fifth of black Atlantic stream migrants were freewheelers. During the 1930s on the East Coast, and thereafter in the Midwest berry stream, white migrants managed to avoid dependence on a crew leader to a greater extent than blacks. At the same time, this form of "independence" was relative at best and bought at the price of social attachments that might provide support and continuity to families ever on the move. In recounting several years' worth of peripatetic travels from a farm in Missouri to Arizona, then back to Missouri and into Pennsylvania, on to St. Louis and Wyoming, back to Arizona and Missouri again, through Texas and into Florida, one white woman declared that she saw many others like her family "travelling to look for work," but "we didn't have very much time to associate with many people. We were going too fast ourselves."[50]

Education provides an intriguing case study of migrants' priorities, for systematic, sustained schooling was as effective a way out of the stream as it was difficult to achieve. As late as 1970, 90 percent of East Coast migrants had not graduated from high school; but this figure may be comparable for other kinds of dependent, more sedentary agricultural workers as well. It would be tempting to divide migrant families into two groups, with one extreme represented by the families who arranged to have their children start school on time in the fall and remain in classes until summer vacation, either by leaving them with kin in Florida or by heading north late and coming back early. (This latter choice was not available for crew members.) At the other extreme were, of course, those parents who, for whatever reasons, financial or otherwise, followed the path of least resistance and forced their children to forgo schooling in favor of picking. In the words of the superintendent of education for Palm Beach County (Lake Okeechobee), "Education is in competition with beans in this county, and beans are winning out."[51]

Yet such radical contrasts would be inaccurate for a number of reasons. Structural and political constraints often made formal education inaccessible even for those parents who desperately wanted it for their children. Until well into the 1960s, local school districts mandated regular attendance for resident children only. Even after states passed compulsory attendance legislation, parents were at times unable or reluctant to present the requisite documentation (such as birth certificates) or to pay for books and other supplies; and truant officers were less than diligent in pursuing offenders. Especially in Northern camps, families remained outside the boundaries of stable communities that might have provided the encouragement and social context that made schooling possible. Too often, then, parents fended for themselves as they tried to balance the short-term disadvantages with long-term gains that inevitably accompanied schooling. Certainly the household's earning power was often a primary consideration, but so too was the dignity of their children, poorly dressed, and in some cases "feared [by resident parents and their offspring] as possible sources of physical and moral contagion." Public school classes offered lessons in shame and humiliation—lessons that inevitably overshadowed the acquisition of literacy skills. Held back, "retarded" year after year, ridiculed by resident children often lighter skinned than themselves, migrant youngsters became resentful and resistant to going to school at all. Ultimately the work camp served as a refuge, a more appealing place by virtue of its familiar faces and routines. And so, while many migrants clearly understood the value of education in the face of extreme financial pressure and relentless discouragement, some gradually gave up a commitment to schooling, and so did their children. As children grew older, they became more sensitive to the hostility of their teachers and classmates, and more self-conscious about their appearance, even as their earning power was increasing. The decision to drop out, then, was often made by a twelve-year-old who announced one day, "I ain't going back," to the mixed relief and chagrin of careworn parents.[52]

In their work and family lives, black migrants followed a routine that blended some of the characteristics of slavery against the cultural backdrop of a modern metropolis. From all accounts, when Southern-born black men and women entered the East Coast migratory stream, they left behind them the field hollers and call-and-response work songs that they had sung as sharecroppers, that their grandparents before them had sung as slaves. While whites had heard in these songs the happy voices of contented field hands, the music had in fact offered a collective lament and protest that stretched back into a West African past. Now, on the road, older women kept alive traditional gospel music, but their impassioned solos became increasingly difficult to hear over the radio sounds of James Brown and Aretha Franklin, later superceded by Michael Jackson and 2 Live Crew. Elderly black migrants might harken back to their simple Southern homes, but younger people identified more with the city, its music and street culture.[53]

At the same time, migrants carried with them the remnants of the African-American slave community when they sought to care for themselves and eschew contact with whites. A distrust of white physicians preserved the practices of root doctors specializing in herbal medicine; the U.S. Sugar Corporation in Clewiston found that their employees sooner appealed for aid from "quacks and healers, midwives, and Indian herb doctors" than the company's "hospitals and free medical service for its employees." Many workers feared to venture far from their own quarters, and an unexpected encounter with a curious anthropologist or persistent government official would often provoke a worker to respond *"with the answers he thinks the questioner desires,"* a variant of the deference ritual practiced under slavery. In camp, migrants regaled each other with folktales laced with "a thread of luck or fate," or jokes in which, "through cleverness and earthiness rather than status or power, the underdog wins out in the end and the white man, or the dominant figure, becomes a fool."[54]

Observers readily drew comparisons between the rigidly segregated quarters and mind-numbing labor of migrants on the one hand, and housing and working conditions in the urban North, on the other. Home-base towns rivaled the nation's worst slums in terms of over-crowding and lack of sanitation, and produced similarly debilitating effects on the residents' morale. As early as the 1920s "jook joints," most of them owned if not operated by whites, introduced rural blacks to big-time vices that had rarely intruded into croppers' cabins on cotton plan-tations. Whether in Pahokee, Florida, or Pocomoke City, Maryland, the "roaring" nightlife in migrant communities—"all them drunks shoutin' and yellin' an' trying to break into cabins"—left tempers on edge, par-ents and children fearful. Out in the fields, in the "rural sweatshops" and "factories without walls," the seemingly placid scene of a migrant picking beans obscured the "job stress akin to factory work" that stemmed from a piece-rate system as vicious as any endured by successive waves of immigrants in New York's garment industry. Migrants, like factory work-ers, had little or no contact with their employers; they did not harvest potatoes "for Mr. Brown" so much as they "worked in potatoes."[55]

The constantly changing, unpredictable employment situation gave rise to a kind of raw anxiety that permeated camp life, especially since "migrants spend both leisure and work time within a single limited social group." This enforced closeness might prompt migrants to retreat at night behind locked doors, to protect some semblance of privacy; but more often they sought out the company of others and engaged in vari-ous social rituals designed to ease uncertainty and affirm their member-ship in the group. For younger men, masked behind nicknames and a swaggering bravado, these rituals might include "playing the dozens"—a verbal game "the aim of which is to defeat an opponent by attacking his mother"—or brandishing knives and picking fights. Card games and gambling, drinking and "bickering," all served as a means for migrants to "kill time" and cope with disorder, even as these activities fueled the dis-order that permeated camp life: "All day Ah'm pickin' beans. All night Ah'm pickin' mah box and rollin' dice. Between de beans and de dice Ah can't lose."[56]

Of course, by itself, the process of "settling out" promised neither the eventual eradication of the migrant labor system nor the redemption of individual families. Most black migrants craved a year-round home in Florida, a house near Belle Glade they could call their own. Finding a job outside the migratory stream required cash savings (to make up for wages lost during the job search), information about possibilities, and decent clothes to make a good first impression—not to mention the edu-cation, skills, and "credentials" that became increasingly important as the twentieth century wore on. The most logical source of jobs for migrants was, of course, the agricultural sector, but, according to the President's Commission on Migratory Labor (1951), "for the migrant to settle down as a nonmigrant farm laborer will not help him much financially."[57] In some cases, "settling out" signaled the ultimate failure, one more form of displacement endured by workers affected this time by the introduction of mechanical harvesters in certain crops. But more generally, as long as commercial growers found profit in pleasing the Northern palate with fresh fruits and vegetables during the winter months, and as long as most picking operations remained unmechanized, migrants who escaped the stream would inevitably be replaced by new ones.

In the early 1990s the precariousness of the Immokalee pinhookers served as a reminder that, for migrants who worked to "settle out," the structure of the local political economy could overshadow personal ambition and enterprise. The pinhookers were former migrants, mainly of Mexican heritage, who worked for themselves by picking near-ripe tomatoes in the fields southwest of Belle Glade and then selling them to restaurants and food services in the area. Thus within Immokalee, described as resembling "a densely populated, inner city ghetto far more than a rural town," the spirit of hard work and upward mobility remained alive and well. For example, Cande and Cristina Vasquez, who arrived in Florida from Mexico via Texas, managed to take themselves out of a migrant labor stream that extended "to Michigan, Indiana, Ohio, picking cherries, strawberries, cucumbers, red tomatoes"; he worked as a pinhooker, she opened a beauty parlor, and they bought a home. Nevertheless, a growers' association, the Florida Tomato Committee ("a legal cartel"), feared losing their local market to the entrepreneurs and urged the Department of Agriculture to extend certain packing standards to the pinhookers, thus making it more difficult for them to sell their produce cheaply. In the midst of these efforts, tomato farmers began to limit their sales to pinhookers, who faced the loss not only of their business but also of their dreams, their "American" dreams.[58]

If familiarity with a region and, within it, personal contacts and social networks were all prerequisities to locating a job, then Florida would appear to be the most likely permanent home for migrants. And yet since the south-central Florida economy could not absorb large numbers of year-round workers, migrants who settled out there continued to live in poverty. Originally from Cordele, Georgia, Elnore Jackson pieced together a life in Belle Glade, but only by working in the fields in the winter and washing and ironing for wages in the summer. Her husband labored "in the celery, getting beds ready"—"not always [steady work], but some days"—while their neighbors went up north. They had made the move to Belle Glade because "they say you can make good, and by coming down here we could do better than at home." For other migrants who settled out on the road—the Haitian family just barely managing to scrape by in Raleigh; the pregnant Puerto Rican teenager who followed her boyfriend to New York City, where the unemployment rate among Hispanic young people was 25 percent; the Immokalee blacks who found a precarious foothold in the Delaware poultry industry—the act of leaving the migrant stream offered little in the way of material comfort or economic security. And so, reduced to a life of perpetual, circular movement up the East Coast and down again—as much as two thousand miles each season—migrant laborers took shifting to its logical, albeit extreme, conclusion.[59]

The town of Belle Glade exhibited a certain timelessness striking in the midst of worldwide political and economic upheaval. Yet by the late twentieth century, small, conservative migrant-host communities up and down the eastern seaboard were registering the effects of larger structural transformations in American society. For example, until the mid-1980s Seaford, Delaware, was "the kind of small rural town where just about everyone knows everyone else, . . . an Ozzie and Harriet kind of place." And then, according to one resident, "Satan himself, out to kill, steal and rob our town," migrated to the Sussex County town in the guise of Haitian immigrants who, the town fathers charged, created among black laborers and white middle-class "solid citizens" an insatiable market for crack cocaine. As the "outsiders," Haitians became the scapegoat for a phenomenon that affected both races and all classes in Seaford. With the coming of crack, the number of syphilis cases and crack babies, as well as arrests for robberies, assaults, murder, and prostitution, showed dramatic increases in the community, but the drug had a more sinister side that statistics could not reveal, "almost as if the poison had been dumped into the drinking water." Women found the smokable crack more appealing than injections of heroin, for instance, and lost themselves in daily highs that left them oblivious to their dependents; recalled one recovering addict, "I couldn't think right. I didn't care about my kids, my grandkids, my father, my sisters and my brothers. All I thought about was the pipe and the next hit." The ensuing epidemic overloaded Seaford's court system and medical services, its employers and police officials, with no end in sight. Whole groups were devastated; the first to feel the drug's effects were poor blacks employed in the town's poultry industry, but no one seemed immune. Remarked one woman: "If there is crack in Seaford, you're not safe anywhere," as the small town reeled from the big-city scourge.[60]

In the 1930s, when bank failures in the urban North hastened the demise of the sharecropping system in the rural South, the organic wholeness of the American economy became manifest, and the fate of farmers became inextricably linked to that of city folk. Half a century later the lines that had earlier divided the rural poor from the urban poor, agricultural workers from industrial workers, Southern blacks from Northern blacks, receded and blurred. Rather than characterize this process as one that "harmonized" the conditions of all marginal persons in American society, perhaps it would be more accurate to stress the violence that infected a body politic now torn between postindustrial capitalism and a "historic economy" still rooted firmly in the institution of slavery. There was crack in Seaford, and no one was safe anywhere.

PART III

THE SOUTHERN DIASPORA IN THE TWENTIETH CENTURY

7

Separate Ways: Deep South Black and Appalachian White Migrants to the Midwest

The great migrations out of the South and into the North represented a twentieth-century social transformation of revolutionary proportions. Between 1910 and 1960 about 9 million people, whites slightly outnumbering blacks, left the South; most of them headed for the Northeast and Midwest, where they profoundly altered housing patterns and electoral politics, and helped to strengthen the industrial labor-union movement. During these years the geographical and political-cultural locus of the black population underwent a dramatic shift; in 1910 fully 90 percent of all blacks lived in the South, but half a century later the population was evenly divided between the South and the urban North. Interregional migrations had longlasting effects not only in terms of the structural changes they initiated but also in terms of the judgments that more fortunate Americans made about the character of the migrants themselves. Poor folk who deserted the farm in favor of a new (and presumably better) life elsewhere carried on a grand tradition of opportunity-seeking in America. Nevertheless, policy-makers and journalists too often saw only evidence of degradation, rather than determination, in the weary faces of people who moved north. These judgments ultimately served as the basis for a uniquely American ideology of race, one that shaped the idea of a Northern black "underclass," as well as notions of poverty in general, during the late twentieth century.

When people left the Southern countryside, the paths they followed into cities and up North were circuitous ones, some reserved for members of one race and others traversed by blacks and whites alike. In effect, the migration histories of the two groups ran together, shaped by common forces of displacement and dispersal, and then apart, as a result of contrasting circumstances and historical consciousness. Many people of both races clung to the hope of a life on the land and left only as a last resort, and as migrants, many mourned the loss of a home place of kin and community. But for blacks, northward migration represented a continuation in their historic quest for freedom. White employers might condemn the various waves of black out-migration in the twentieth century as final proof of "the irresponsible and roving disposition of this race of people," an assessment that echoed the frustrations of Reconstruction-era cotton planters; but a migrant to Chicago likened his sojourn to shifting by noting "Before the North opened up with work all we could do was to move from one plantation to another in hope of finding something better." If Southern blacks were "like plants that were meant to grow upright but became bent and twisted, stunted, sometimes stretching out and running along the ground, because the conditions of our environment forbade our developing upward naturally," then the North beckoned as a place that would nurture their quest for "independence" defined in terms of good schools and steady work at fair wages.[1]

Many migrants hailed from the rural South, but they often engaged in a frantic search for day work within the region, in nearby villages, remote company towns, and large urban areas, before heading for the Midwest or Northeast. The history of the John and Virginia Crews family from York, Alabama, tells a larger story about the twisted byways that ran northward. For this black sharecropping family, reckoning time in December 1911 brought the shock of bitter disappointment; the white plantation owner paid the three adults in their household only $11.00 for a whole year's labor. But cries of outrage would not put food on the table, so in January Virginia hired on as a strawberry picker for a neighboring farmer, and John "was riding for miles each day checking out any rumors about public work, road repair, anything," in the vicinity of their

home. Daughter Burniece later recalled that her father "had a philosophy that if he worked hard and treated his fellow men fairly, in due time
God's blessings would be showered on him and his family." And so, convinced that justice would continue to elude him on the Alabama countryside, this black man left his family in the spring of 1912 and traveled
to the city of Bessemer, where he learned of jobs for coal miners in far
away Virginia. John Crews summoned his family, and together they traveled by company-sponsored train to the town of Embodin. Over the next
six years the family sought steady work and refuge from exploitative
employers, first in a small settlement in the hills above Embodin; then in
Cincinnati, where John could find only irregular construction work and
Virginia labored as a domestic; and after that in Logan, West Virginia. In
Logan the family felt keenly the lack of schools and churches, and in
1917 a disastrous flood forced them to leave. Finally they settled in
Detroit, so that John could take advantage of the wartime boom and
work for American Car and Foundry, a job he lost after the armistice.
Over the next half century he would scrounge for work of any kind,
whether pushing a broom or a junk cart, in an effort to make good on a
vow Virginia had made to herself one wintry night in Alabama long ago:
"Stars, I promise you that I won't stop until I get a home of my own . . . a
REAL HOME!"[2]

The chronology of intrarural and rural-urban movements within the
South, and of south-north migrations, reveals the interplay between
Southern economic change and Northern job opportunities as those
developments affected different groups of Southerners in different ways
over the years. Some Southerners went willingly, grateful for the possibility of work elsewhere, while others were forced off the land by landlords, faceless government policies, and new kinds of technology, all promoting "progress" and "modern living." Rural whites from regions other
than Appalachia tended to move to Southern cities or, especially during
the 1930s and 1940s, to the Far West. Thus, in order to explore systematically class and racial factors as they affected patterns of migration out
of the South beginning in 1916, it is helpful to compare the characteristics and motivations of blacks and Appalachian whites. During the 1930s
and later, the growing impoverishment of the Deep South and
Appalachia led observers to single out the two regions as emblematic of
rural distress nationwide; both areas were characterized by high rates of
fertility and illiteracy and by "families [who] live on farms that are so
small, or on lands so poor, that they cannot make a satisfactory living."
(Congress officially, if belatedly, recognized the plight of Appalachia in
the mid-1960s with the creation of the Appalachian Regional Council

[ARC], and later lawmakers implicitly acknowledged the similiarities between the two regions when, in 1988, they established the Lower Mississippi Delta Development Commission, based on the ARC model.) In discussions of the links between Southern rural and Northern urban poverty, links established through migration, scholars predictably focus on both sharecropping blacks and coal-mining or subsistence-farming whites: "The concentration of Negro rural poverty in the Core South and the white rural poverty in the Appalachian South are conditions that lead to important consequences for the metropolitan North." These consequences reflected at once the initially similar class status of the two groups and their unequal prospects based almost solely on skin color.[3]

White migrants from the hills of Tennessee and the hollows of Kentucky, where coal-mining machines replaced men and where lumber barons and strip miners pushed farmers off their eroded land, expressed their longing for a modest homestead in terms that Virginia Crews would have understood: "our own land . . . where we can keep ever bite we raise an don't have to be a moven ever year, we can git ahead a sight faster . . . " But deprived of that possibility in the South, they crossed the Ohio River and went to Chicago, or Cleveland, or South Lebanon, Ohio, all because "The mostly thing I want for my kids is a home, which I don't know if I'll ever have. Cause I've been drug from here to there with em so much that I would really like to settle down and have a home where I wouldn't have to go no more." For poor whites, going north revealed a deeply felt economic imperative, but individual decisions lacked the political and moral urgency that elevated black migration to the level of myth and allegory. Many transplanted Appalachians dreamed of the time when they could return to their birthplace with enough money to bask in the beauty of the hills for the rest of their days. In contrast to Deep South blacks who moved far distances to Detroit or Chicago, natives of Kentucky, West Virginia, or Tennessee who found work in the lower Midwest, and especially southern Ohio, managed to visit home-bound kin frequently, and in the process kept alive a dream of landownership.[4]

For one family that had to "scuff around" for day work in Virginia and then "scuff around" for day work once they moved to Newark, New Jersey, in the early 1960s, the way north seemed a less dramatic move than most "detached" observers might have imagined. Throughout this period of migration, displaced croppers and tenants, some of them huddled in miserable slums on the outskirts of Southern towns, others adrift and seeking work apart from other family members, became ever more like city folk. Increasingly, then, migrants from the rural South to the urban North exchanged "rural insufficiency" for "urban insufficiency";

D. Displacement and Dispersal in the Twentieth Century

World War I marked the first time in American history that Northern employers opened their gates to significant numbers of rural Southern folk. The large cities of the Midwest, with their sprawling factories and steel mills, attracted blacks from the Deep South (1) and whites from Appalachia. The migrants were farmers fleeing from the exploitative sharecropping system, as well as wage earners eager to escape from the company towns that extracted coal, lumber, and phosphates. World War II provided large numbers of Southerners with an entree into the industrial work force, and workers of both races and both sexes eagerly sought out jobs that offered steady work at good wages (2). The beneficiaries of discriminatory hiring practices, many white (male) migrants gradually worked their way up through semiskilled and into skilled positions; in contrast, the vast majority of similarly qualified black men and women were limited to the unskilled and service sectors of the economy (3). After World War II, the Appalachian mountains, and rural areas throughout the South, suffered economic and demographic upheavals when millions of families, black and white, were replaced by machines—and in particular, by advances in mechanical cotton picking and in mechanical coal mining (4). More and more groups of Americans became stranded in depressed communities that lacked good schools and good jobs—whites in the Southern mountains, blacks in the rural South and in northern inner cities (5), and members of both races in the decaying mill towns of the Midwest. The thread of continuity linking the southern slave past with patterns of northern postindustrial poverty was most apparent in the East Coast migrant labor stream (6). By the late twentieth century, the stream relied on a core of African-American workers, and a constant infusion of people representing distressed populations from around the world.

D1. Migrant family arriving in Chicago, ca. 1916. Schomburg Library.

D2. Riveters at work in a Douglas Aircraft plant, World War II.
Photo courtesy of Douglas Aircraft.

D3. Railroad dining car waiters, ca. 1940. Schomburg Library.

D4. Waiting in line for food stamps in Nashville, Tennessee, January, 1975. Photo by Kit Luce.

D5. McDonald's worker, ca. 1990. Photo by Alan Dorow.

D6. Central (and only) camp kitchen, presided over by the the wife of the crew leader, migrant labor camp in Dover, Delaware, July, 1990. Photo by Joseph Sorrentino.

gone forever were the days when a modest patch of land could yield economic or political self-determination for any group in any area of the South. To some degree, the issue turned on gender, race, and timing; for example, in the 1920s Charlottesville domestics bound for New York City would find few other kinds of jobs open to them. On the other hand, male wartime migrants might experience a more drastic break with their past jobs, as they began to "leave off tending green growing things to tending iron monsters." Yet regardless of the individual characteristics of the migrants, or the time of their departure from the South, they yearned to make a decent life for themselves, in an effort to claim dignity and well-being as their American birthright.[5]

THE DEMOGRAPHY OF DEPARTING POPULATIONS

Southern migrants to Northern cities, in the words of two scholars who studied the phenomenon, were "born into a certain migration system." This observation, which implies the generational continuity between specific Southern places and specific Northern destinations, also highlights race-based differentials. A survey of the chronology of population movements from World War I through the beginnings of a return migration half a century later illustrates the intertwining of black and white streams and reveals the individual household strategies that produced these streams. In terms of the two respective racial groups, the black migrations were proportionately larger than those of whites, accounting, perhaps, for the disproportionate attention accorded them in the historical literature; for example, in the 1950s, the decade of greatest out-migration from the South, 15 percent of the total white population of Kentucky and West Virginia left, while 25 percent of all blacks from the Deep South states of Mississippi and Alabama headed north. Nevertheless, the dynamics of black and white migrations were similar in the sense that kin relations served as the vital link sustaining self-generating patterns of movement.[6]

Migrants carried north with them traditions of household resourcefulness characteristic of the rural poor from all over the world, but these traditions reveal little of the dependence or fatalism modern-day observers often attribute to the "underclass." Although the vast majority of Southern out-migrants had rural roots, they were not necessarily too "ignorant" or "ill-equipped" (in education or training) to "adjust" to Northern life. Much confusion has arisen from the fact that migrants often listed the names of towns or cities when queried about their Southern origins by census takers or scholars. To the question Where did you come from? interviewees of both races might provide technically accurate but ultimately misleading answers that revealed their point of embarkation, but not a true sense of either their home or their community attachment. Migrants who hailed from remote backcountry areas or from tiny sawmill settlements that had no name might list the nearest town as their "home" to clarify matters for an inquisitive stranger ignorant of Southern geography. The fact that some blacks fled from phosphate camps or lumber towns led contemporary observers (and recent historians) to assume, mistakenly, that Southern wage earners were by definition both urban dwellers and industrial laborers.[7]

In a related vein, the problem of selective migration is too often cast in terms of formal education. The vast majority of Southerners who moved north during the twentieth century, white and black, came from poor areas where local school systems in general were underfunded, to say the least—the grading of classes haphazard, the lessons rudimentary at best. An individual's grade-level attainment, though easily quantifiable, is a less useful indicator of intelligence and "preparation" for life in an industrial society compared to more subjective qualities we might consider under the broad label of "gumption." In fact, as mentioned earlier, within rural households children's school attendance was more likely a reflection of sibling rank and temporary family fortunes than of native ability and determination. When a black child named Maggie Comer was growing up in Memphis (she called herself a "country girl" because her family came from a sharecropper's cabin in Woodland, Mississippi), she and her siblings received very little schooling; Maggie herself did only six months' worth of classroom work her whole life. (However, she always remembered that her real father had "more education than the white man he was working for.") Her stepfather expressed his violent opposition to formal education of any kind, and yet Maggie managed to study on her own, quickly coming to realize that "I'm not too much at education, but with my fingers I could beat some people with a pencil." Though an abusive man, a "drifter," and a poor provider for his family, Maggie's stepfather refused to curry favor with, or even labor for, a white man—"No, I don't work for anybody," he declared—and the young girl probably in some fashion imbibed his spirit of defiance toward the caste system. At the age of seventeen she moved on her own to East Chicago, where she lived with her half sister Carrie and her family. Other migrants told similar stories—of dropping out of school at an early age to "go to work and help out with the rest of the kids," all the time admiring a mother who "couldn't read or write, but you couldn't cheat her out of a penny. She could get on the ground and make marks. She could count down to the last cent that anybody owed her, but she didn't know to write her name when she died." Buried in the biographical details of many migrants, regardless of whether they found a good job and a settled life in the North, is evidence that these people chafed under their employers' authority.[8]

The problem of the migrants' "training"—their ability to make the transition from farming to factory jobs—is, of course, more related to both their work experience and again their natural abilities than to their formal education per se, especially between 1916 and the 1960s. Through the 1920s, the North, and especially the industrial Midwest, offered unskilled jobs and other entry-level positions that required of applicants little in the way of craft skills or book learning. Black migrants were, of course, identical to poor-white Appalachians—and to immigrants from villages in southern Italy and shtetls in Poland, for that matter—in terms of their ability to master unskilled and semiskilled tasks quickly and easily, whether those tasks were performed on an assembly line or at a construction site. After the massive contraction in the economy during the Great Depression, World War II once again opened the way north for migrants of little skill; but by the early 1950s automation in heavy industries throughout the North had begun to erode the job opportunities of all migrants, and especially black men, lacking formal education or nonagricultural work experience.[9]

Gender issues reveal the similarity and dissimilarity in the motivations of black and white migrants. For most landless men regardless of race, life in the rural South consisted of "just work and pay up and work and pay up and keep the family goin. . . . " Yet given the legacy of slavery and white people's historic contempt for the sanctity of black family life, black men's sense of inadequacy as providers for and protectors of their households carried with it a special resonance. Though black women might have lacked a life mission strictly equivalent to that of their menfolk's search for "manhood," they had their own distinctive, and distinctively powerful, reasons for wanting to leave the rural South. Some female migrants (like some white women) expressed an aversion to the isolation of rural life and to a household economy that forced mothers and daughters to toil in the fields well into the twentieth century: "I daydreamed and said when I grow up I'm not going to marry no boy that lived on a farm because I was raised on a farm. And I don't want to pick no cotton." Other women resented the additional domestic burdens imposed on them by husbands who went off to work temporarily in sawmill camps or on port-city docks. As a group, however, black women found it difficult to articulate the specific reasons that might have affected their decision to move north. One reason was that all these women were the potential, and some were the actual, victims of sexual abuse and harassment from white men. In addition, a tyrannical father, husband, or lover might set in motion for any woman a series of moves culminating in her migration out of the South. In the mid-1930s Sara Brooks finally mustered the courage to leave her husband of five years, a violent man who beat and burned her and courted more than his fair share of outside women: "He was very cruel to me, very cruel." Together with her children, Sara Brooks moved in with her brother, a sawmill worker in Bainbridge, Alabama, where she worked at a series of domestic service and factory jobs. Within a few years her brother had moved to Cleveland and Brooks left Bainbridge for Mobile, to be with her sister. At her brother's suggestion—"Why don't you come up here? You could make more here"—Brooks went to Cleveland in 1940, returned South for a while shortly thereafter, and, with her three sons, relocated permanently to Cleveland in 1944. Later she told the story of her odyssey in a way that began with her decision to leave her husband and ended with her reunion with her children: "But after I got away from my husband and from Mobile, Alabama, and got here in Cleveland, I started to progressin' and then my kids came."[10]

Demographic patterns of migration fragmented kin groups and communities, severing bonds of mutual dependence and obligation. Movement off the countryside drained neighborhoods of a precious resource—the strength and energy of their young people. In the Kentucky counties of Bell, Perry, and Harlan, and in Mingo County, West Virginia, 40 percent of all residents left during the 1950s. In some cases out-migration produced unbalanced sex ratios (most often in favor of women); in almost all cases elderly people remained behind, adding to the burdens of younger adults. Fertility rates dropped with the departure of childbearing women, and mortality rates increased, reflecting the increasing proportion of aged persons within the community. Too, a father gone north could unintentionally wreak havoc on extended-family relations, with his wife now forced to seek wage work away from home and a grandmother left alone with a passel of "grands" to mind for days or weeks at a time. The flight of kin, and the burdens shouldered by those who stayed—some hoping to win "a star in [their] crown in glory" as a reward for their sacrifices—in turn provided the incentive for more people to leave. Stripped of traditional family and neighborly support systems, an Appalachian factory worker might consider a pink slip an unmitigated disaster. As one woman described the plight of a co-worker who had just been notified that she would be laid off, "She has no family left in the country. . . . All of her people have gone to the city, and they have no garden."[11]

Though patterns of northward migrations evolved over the decades in response to changes in the nature of "pushes" out of the South and "pulls" into the North, the characteristics of the migrants themselves demonstrated marked continuities. For the most part, these men and women were young, many possessing the energy and optimism of youth. Though most grew up surrounded by poverty and hardship, they did not necessarily consider such surroundings their inevitable fate; in fact, the act of migration in and of itself belied charges that they were, by culture or temperament, passive and dependent.

FORAYS NORTHWARD DURING WORLD WAR I AND THE 1920s

Numbers and place names provide the skeletal basis of migration history. The origins of large-scale black flight out of the South sprang from a specific event—the efforts by the Pennsylvania and Erie Railroad to recruit black (male) workers in the summer of 1916. Labor agents initially targeted Florida cities, though some of the migrants (out of a total of 12,000) came from Georgia as well. Meanwhile, Chicago-based railroad recruiters issued similar appeals to sharecroppers in Mississippi and Alabama. Northern labor agents soon found themselves out of a job, for during the war years alone half a million blacks moved north, the vast majority relying on advice and information from kinfolk rather than prospective employers. Migration along the two routes would swell and recede in response to Northern labor demands for the rest of the century. Each path pointed almost due north, up the East Coast to such seaboard cities as New York and Philadelphia, and up the Mississippi Valley to the strongholds of Midwestern manufacturing—Detroit, Cleveland, Milwaukee, and Chicago. Between 1916 and 1927, 1.2 million black people fled the South. These early migrants found unskilled war jobs in the nation's largest cities; after a few years the existence of vital black communities in those cities would to some extent compensate newcomers for the lack of diversified economic opportunities.[12]

Although just slightly more whites compared to blacks left the South between 1916 and 1930 (1.3 million), their migrations early took on a different character. Rural whites from the Deep South tended to move west when they moved out of the South at all, and this group also contributed greatly to the process of Southern urbanization in these years. During the first three decades of the twentieth century, for example, over three-quarters of all white Southerners who moved a substantial distance stayed within the region and headed cityward. Most prominent among white Southerners who went directly north were Appalachians. These out-migrants were not a homogeneous group; they came from different kinds of economies—mining towns, subsistence farms, commercial tobacco farms—and responded to local economic crises; for example, as a source of employment, the coal industry peaked in Tennessee in 1907, but not until 1923 in northern West Virginia and Virginia, and 1927 in southern West Virginia and eastern Kentucky. As early as 1915 groups of Kentuckians had made their way to the town of Hamilton, in Ohio's Miami Valley, and in the 1920s Chicago and Detroit developed clusters of migrants from Tennessee. Yet it was the small-town destinations in southern Ohio that made Appalachian migration distinctive from its black counterpart. The locations of these towns, not too far across the Ohio River, allowed short-term visits back home, and few blacks lived there to compete for low-paying, unskilled jobs. Moreover, such towns in general afforded these migrants opportunities to acquire small, cheap patches of land—a seemingly modest goal, but one central to the collective identity of people in, and from, Appalachia.[13]

Although only 10 percent of the nation's population, black people accounted for 20 percent of all interstate migration during the 1920s. The larger, political meaning of the war lingered on in the consciousness of black Southerners long after the last cannon had been stilled. U.S. army officials feared that social disorder would ensue should the black soldiers who had helped conquer the Kaiser decide to forgo their humiliating return to Jim Crow; consequently, blacks were mustered out of the service in their home states rather than in a central northeastern location (New Jersey), as was the case for whites. Still, this bureaucratic maneuver was only partially successful in keeping black veterans down in the South on farms; for example, a study of black migration out of middle Georgia counties in the early 1920s found that seven out of ten local white landlords reported that at least some of their field hands "left the farm after their return" from the army. As fathers, brothers, sons, and neighbors, these men expanded the networks that provided the wherewithal for other kin and community members to take their leave of the South in the 1920s, and later.[14]

At the same time, young black women, especially in the South Atlantic states, discovered that the demand for domestic labor in large

Northeastern cities had intensified with the gradual disappearance of Swedish maids and Irish cooks. To some extent, similar considerations drew Iowa farm girls and the black daughters of Sea Island phosphate miners from the wearisome toil of rural life. One twenty-year-old who left St. Helena for New York City in 1925 told an interviewer that there was "Nothing for a colored girl to do down there. Only thing a girl could do is to work in the oyster factories, and that's considered men's work. Too nasty for a girl, too." She and other coastal women comprised a unique migration stream by virtue of its long history (instigated by Northern teachers who had come south in the 1860s) and its reliance on information exchanged among young single women, north and south.[15]

Though implicit political protest and explicit economic hardship might form the catalyst for a family's decision to migrate, changes in household composition often proved to be the precipitating factor. It was in the early 1920s that Lucy Benson headed for a place she came to call a "strange country" (Newark, New Jersey), because she feared for the safety of her children in rural Georgia. Her story was not unusual; she grew up without a father in a one-room cabin that housed nine other children. At an early age Lucy was put to work minding her younger siblings while her mother labored for 35 cents a day as a domestic servant. Later, as a young widow with four sons of her own, she tended a small vegetable patch, cooked, sewed clothes, and plowed with a mule in the fields in a frantic effort to provide for her family—"Many a day I fell on my knees and asked God to help me, to give me the strength to get my children away." In her poverty and in her concern for her offspring she resembled countless Southerners; but it was the death of her husband that made migration an imperative and not just a distant possibility: "The reason I hurt so bad when my husband died 'cause I had nobody to help me with the children."[16]

In the 1920s rural Southerners were in the midst of a dress rehearsal for the Great Depression. Tariff increases led to more costly consumer goods, and a drop in cotton prices put the squeeze on croppers and small owners alike. In addition, the decade ushered in a downturn in the cotton textile industry, eliminating the mill town as a haven of steady employment for poor whites from either the Piedmont or the mountains. In 1923 a Louisiana Bureau of Agricultural Economics statistician reported a general dispersal of 10 percent of the rural population (two-thirds of whom were black people), with about six out of ten of the migrants moving elsewhere within the state—"to oil fields in northwest Louisiana, to carbon plants in the northern part of the state, to work in sawmills and on the public highways now being constructed. Near large cities some farm labor has gone to work on city streets." One of his Texas colleagues noted a similar trend, exacerbated by the influx of cheap Mexican labor, and added, "more whites than blacks are going to town," the result of a discriminatory urban racial division of labor that encouraged Deep South native whites to remain loyal to the region of their Confederate grandfathers. In the absence of a way north, the grandchildren of slaves more often than not had no choice but to cast their lot with kin clusters in the country; in the 1920s, in an effort to earn money without relying on whites, the blacks of Greene County, Georgia, tried unsuccessfully to engage in the commercial farming of rabbits living in abandoned buildings, but the experiment ended when the animals succumbed to disease en masse. Although rural blacks would continue to migrate to Southern cities, the predominance of whites moving in that direction led to a gradual proportionate decline in the black urban population.[17]

The images and values of a national consumer culture penetrated the South in the 1920s, highlighting the apparent drabness of rural life. As mass-communication and mass-marketing techniques improved, as radios and department store catalogs appeared in the rudest of cabins during the 1920s, as the style and size of the family automobile became a preoccupation among men all over the South (and country), and as Hollywood offered tantalizing glimpses of knobby-kneed flappers, poor Southerners realized that the level of their deprivation had increased proportionately. North Carolina–born Mary Mebane noted that "the black working poor do not scorn the trappings of the middle class. . . . to *have* to walk five miles for any reason is not invigorating; it is a chore and an inconvenience. Black folk don't want the simple life. They've had that, they know all about it; they want to try some other life for a change." When Northern kin returned home to show off new clothes and big cars, they inspired envy in people who, according to Harry Crews, a white man, "loved *things* the way only the very poor can." Only in the North could black people share in a general American indulgence in things. Southern poor whites might be forgiven their spendthrift ways, but the scorn heaped upon black families for seemingly innocuous purchases—"a battery radio, a sewing machine, some bright-knitted caps for the children, and some oranges"—assumed ominous political overtones on the plantation: "They'll buy automobiles and radios and won't work for hell." A matter of pride among whites, conspicuous consumption among blacks amounted to a red flag of defiance; driving the wrong kind of car—"a white man's [fancy] car"—could leave a black man beaten and bloody on the side of a Southern highway, proving the timelessness of the observation, "You know, black folks who had money had to be kind of careful then."[18]

The post–World War I booms in the Chicago steel, Akron rubber, and Detroit auto industries began to empty the "stranded populations" of the Appalachian mining districts by the late 1920s; during the last seven years of the decade, 3,400 mines closed and 212,000 workers lost their jobs. Although two-thirds of all southern Appalachian counties suffered population losses during this period, continued high fertility rates replenished the local labor supply. By 1928 the first interstate bus lines and the first surfaced highways leading out of the region had hastened the departure of whole communities—for instance, one-quarter of all the people in eleven eastern Kentucky counties. Born in 1916, Effie Saylor grew up in a traditional large family in rural Lincoln. When her older brothers moved to Ohio, her father had no one to help him farm, and in 1928 he followed them north. It was a painful decision for the older man; later his wife would blame his premature death on the Cincinnati Milling Machine Company, which had "cooped [him] up" for nine years.[19]

THE GREAT DEPRESSION: FAMILIES THROWN INTO MOTION

The Saylor family would have been hard-pressed to see much difference between their plight and that of equally unfortunate neighbors who struggled a few years later during the Great Depression. Throughout the 1930s the commercial agricultural export trade continued to decline precipitously, and by mid-decade farmers nationwide had reduced their acreage 70 percent compared to 1920–21 levels. Within individual households the loss of a father or older sons meant unmitigated hardship for families too large to sustain themselves on small and worn-out parcels of land. Nevertheless, during the 1930s the processes of displacement quickened and deepened, fueled by forces new to the Southern landscape, New Deal policies foremost among them. National Recovery Act minimum-wage legislation spurred the mechanization of the tobacco industry and threw large numbers of black women and men out of work. The crop-reduction programs of the Agricultural Adjustment Administration (AAA) severely cut the demand for farm labor and, as "God's gift to the tractor people," provided ready cash for planters to invest in labor-saving machinery. In myriad ways then federal policies served as a stimulus to migration and displacement. Congressional

hearings at the end of the decade yield glimpses into the painful relocation of small settlements to make way for public works and forest and
parks-service projects throughout the South. The immediate and long-
term consequences of major development programs such as the
Tennessee Valley Authority are well known, but the fates of groups such
as the isolated Santee-Cooper (South Carolina) farmers, located in the
flood plain of a proposed dam, are all but forgotten. These 841 families,
"for the most part Negroes living on small tracts, as owners or squatters,
which they had occupied in a remote section for generations," endured
"enforced movement" at the hands of federal officials. A relocation project that benefited forty of the families was regarded as a "model" community.[20]

In response to various upheavals, poor families regrouped. Households
"split" by their employer, or evicted from the land altogether, combined
with neighbors in an effort to pool their resources and care for each other.
A Federal Emergency Relief Administration (FERA) study of relief recipients in rural Alabama found that about one-fifth of all poor families had
consolidated; "the size and nature of the added family gives strong indication that a great many of these combinations were forced by the cotton
reduction program." On the other hand, family fragmentation was not
uncommon either. A comprehensive survey of two Southern cotton
areas, encompassing almost two-thirds of all rural blacks in the country, reported that on the "open countryside," in villages and in towns,
black households on relief were two to three times more likely to have
no adult men compared to their poor-white counterparts. The relatively high proportion of female-headed households among Southern
blacks during the Great Depression, a trend caused by widespread
unemployment among black men, foreshadowed a similar development, caused by similar forces, in Northern cities three decades
later.[21]

Blacks and poor whites alike engaged in time-honored forms of
resourcefulness and developed new survival strategies as families
broke up, kin came together, and whole communities scattered or
relocated. Some black men, such as the fathers of Maggie Comer and
Mary Mebane, men who "didn't like white people" and would not
work for wages under them, embraced a life of hunting, fishing, trapping, foraging, and kin cooperation, and shed few tears over lost croppers' contracts. Indeed, a diet of fish, birds, nuts, berries, and whatever vegetables came out of a patch was bound to be more appealing
than the high-carbohydrate, low-protein fare of tenants and sharecroppers. On the other hand, an unemployed, landless black man was

a man inherently at risk within the rural South, and he and his family were likely to lead a precarious life.[22]

Ultimately, the hallmark of depression days was migration. Among blacks, long-range movement slowed but did not abate, and more than one-half million of them embraced the North as a land of "relative opportunity" during the 1930s. An equal number of white Southerners left their ancestral homes, many from Texas and Arkansas heading to the West Coast in the company of similarly displaced refugees from Oklahoma. Yet even more dramatically, intraregional migration intensified, providing a measure of a latent migratory spirit that in better times would be channeled northward. Families forged new paths, or followed in the footsteps of kin, or retraced the journeys of their elders in an effort to stay together and stay alive. In the early 1930s rural folk in Alabama moved to the Muscle Shoals and Wilson Dam area to take advantage of government-sponsored construction jobs. The state's southern counties saw an influx of migrants during potato-picking season—men, women and children who next moved on to work on truck or fruit farms or in Louisiana sugarcane. Some "family groups" sought out daily wage work or coal-mining jobs, either as a permanent solution to their woes or as a temporary expedient during the winter. Men like David A. Griffin, a white farmer from Fair Oaks, Arkansas, led unsettled lives; during the 1930s Griffin went from farming to working as a railroad carpenter and repairman, then back to sharecropping. Soon after that he took a job in an Oklahoma paint factory, but returned to Alabama cotton fields. His sons scratched for local day work—berry picking in the hills, cotton picking in the swamps. These generational and temporal combinations of farm, factory, and day work were not unprecedented, of course, but the depression made every form of labor more insecure to an unprecedented degree.[23]

During the 1930s the militance of biracial union coalitions such as the Southern Tenant Farmers Union and the United Mine Workers testified to the straitened circumstances of the poor of both races. Yet within squatters' camps and urban-fringe settlements, the racial caste system continued to make invidious distinctions and to separate out white families deemed worthy of aid or employment, no matter how paltry the benefits. The case of evicted sharecroppers in the Missouri Bootheel region (in 1939) reveals the cross-currents that affected rural blacks and poor whites suddenly and violently thrown together. Driven off plantations as a result of crop-reduction programs, several hundred families staged a "roadside demonstration" in January 1939, though state highway police attempted to disperse them and segregate them by race in the process. A camp established in June housed eighty black and fifteen white families, but provided little relief for pregnant women of either color, all of whom suffered from a lack of food and medical care. Within a few weeks the whites "found better opportunities and moved off, as did a few of the colored families," leaving a virtually all-black community by the end of the summer. Local white landowners expressed extreme hostility toward the interracial settlement; and elsewhere, throughout the region, black demonstrators faced more brutal forms of police harassment compared to their white counterparts living separately down the road and "over the hill."[24]

Clustered outside Southern cities, quasi-rural slum dwellers tried to combine cotton picking in the fall and gardening in the summer with day work during the rest of the year. A 1940 federal report revealed the blurring of distinctions based on urban and rural life, agricultural and wage labor, dependency and self-sufficiency within these communities. The poor population in the vicinity of Fort McClellan, Alabama, consisted of "the usual group of relief, squatter, and 'marginal' families found around cities. Probably not more than half the group depended entirely on farming for a living. On the other hand, well over three-fourths of them depended on farming or gardening for at least a part of their living." In 1941 a fatherless white farm family from Bacon County, Georgia, moved to one of these enclaves in Jacksonville, Florida. They came out of a way of life shared by other "subsistence farmers—tenants out on the fringe of things—[who] moved a lot, much more than most people would imagine, moved from one patch of farmed-out land to another, from one failed crop to a place where they thought there was hope of making a good one." Fleeing a violent husband, Myrtice Crews had gathered her two children together and they "left in the dead of night, daddy behind us, silhouetted by the kerosene lamp and raving in the doorway." The next day they boarded a bus bound for the Springfield section of Jacksonville, a bus filled with other "tired people savaged by long years of scratching in soil already worn out before they were born." Harry Crews's mother "went straight to King Edward Cigar Factory for a job and got it." While she was at work he and other six-year-old boys occupied themselves—"We stole and we sold"—all the while trying to avoid the browbeaten mothers who dominated the settlement: The women who "smelled, stunk, of tobacco, their hair, their clothes, their skins, probably even their hearts"—and the women who also, incidentally, tried to preserve these exceedingly fragile families.[25]

During the 1930s whites more often than blacks tried to start anew on the South's cheapest lands in the mountains or on sandy flats. Mill towns and mining camps offered workers only reduced hours at cut wages, sending them back onto "submarginal lands," small plots of land eroded after generations of farming and lumbering. Hard times in the North indicated that many Appalachian migrants' attachment to that region was tenuous at best, and, given similarly poor employment conditions north and south, family members might as well return to a familiar world of kin. Between 1930 and 1934 the Southern white population of Flint, Michigan, declined by 35 percent (Southern blacks left the city in proportions only half as great, though their job status was lower than that of white migrants). The back-to-the-land movement and north-south migrations composed of such men as Denver Mattingly, a Kentucky native laid off by the Hudson Motor Company of Detroit, represented the reversal of a long-standing pattern, a reminder of the "well-established principle that each migration current is accompanied by a counter-current." These trends, combined with the high fertility rates of white rural women, resulted in a slight increase in the Southern white farm population (by 6.6 percent) while the percentage of black farmers declined (by 4 percent) during the same period, despite their similarly high fertility rates.[26]

The operation of federal relief programs during the Great Depression revealed how and why blacks and whites might perceive public assistance in different ways. For the small farmer of Appalachia, reliance on the dole constituted an abrupt break with the past. Writing in *The Survey* in 1930, Kentucky social worker Mary Breckinridge drew a picture of white mountain men "proud as Lucifer" now waiting forlornly in Southern relief lines (she called them "corn-bread lines"). Roscoe Ledington had lost his regular job as a loader at the Blue Diamond coal mines near Hazard, and he was now eking out a living by "working on timber" during the winter. When spring came, he had no money to buy seeds to make use of a small patch of rented land and eagerly accepted the small amount of money he could make by doing odd jobs around the local relief office. George Morgan, a carpenter, was thrown out of work on the railroad when "better men hungry for work" returned from Northern cities such as Hamilton, Ohio, and Detroit because of layoffs in auto factories and paper mills. Modest local works projects offered aid to a few of these men, but in the absence of adequate relief resources, Breckinridge wrote, "a free and hospitable people are sharing their corn-meal with returning neighbors and kin, and sheltering them in their one- and two-room cabins." In their willingness to hunt for work, to migrate in search of opportunity, and to continue to aid others in even more desperate straits, Appalachian whites engaged in a variety of household strategies common to the poor of both races. And yet Breckinridge prob-ably used the term "a free . . . people" to underscore her white clients' heritage of pride and self-sufficiency. For the Kentuckians, reliance on government aid represented a new and insidious source of humiliation.[27]

Among the black population, federal relief policies preserved tradi-tional Southern forms of enforced dependency and contributed to the forces of social dislocation. Not surprisingly, blacks failed to receive their fair share of either outright relief or federal works programs. For exam-ple, in 1935 black South Carolinians represented one-half of the "relief population" (a suspiciously low proportion in any case), but only one-third of public works employees. Blacks throughout the Cotton South consistently received smaller monthly aid checks compared to similarly (or less) distressed whites. Just as significant, however, were the efforts of some federal officials to collude with Southern landlowners in main-taining a dependent rural labor force. Indeed, no sharp line separated private employment from public relief when federal funds were used to shore up the sharecropping furnishing system. In the Delta, planters preserved the time-honored custom of the "eternal debt" and at the same time actively discouraged individual households from demonstrat-ing even modest forms of initiative, such as raising chickens and vegeta-bles to eat and sell. Planters were "fearful of any governmental program that promises to bring independence to the sharecroppers," according to one federal official, and they withheld from workers their share of AAA crop-reduction subsidy checks.[28]

In some cases planters and administrators agreed among themselves (of course, the two groups overlapped in many locales in any case) that needy families should qualify for relief only during the slack season; in this way the FERA provided families with a minimal amount of support during the winter and late summer but cut them off from aid when the first cotton bolls appeared in the fall. A 1934 FERA survey entitled "Landlord-Tenant Relations and Relief in Alabama" found that, although the "conventional attitude" was that the landlord "is expected to 'take care of' the tenant when the latter needs aid . . . now . . . many landlords are shifting the responsibility to the relief agencies. Approximately 30 percent of the tenants interviewed stated that their landlords had helped them get on the relief rolls." In the cotton county of Monroe, Mississippi, some landlords simply cut off furnishings altogether on the assumption that federal relief would tide their workers over until reck-oning time. Throughout the South relief recipients were systematically denied aid during the cotton planting, chopping, and picking seasons; this practice amounted to a federally funded policy of keeping only "households without employable persons on relief during the work season." Moreover, the availability of federal aid encouraged some landlords to "split" families and furnish only individual, able-bodied field workers, instead of entire household units which invariably contained young, ill, and elderly members.[29]

In a more general sense, federal programs enabled employers to retain a reserve army of agricultural laborers without assuming year-long responsibility for them; as the possibilities for rural nonagricultural work disappeared, government aid subsidized planters during the slack season. Reductions in crop acreage pushed increasing numbers of blacks out of sharecroppers' cabins and into towns, where they subsisted as cotton-picking day laborers at the beck and call of white employers. In the North Carolina tobacco belt, federal investigators noted the "emptying of tenant houses and the concentration of displaced tenants in nearby towns and villages where they seek casual or Works Projects Administration jobs until the crops which they have not planted or cultivated are ready for harvest. The picture is completed when the farmer at harvest time recalls his displaced workers for a few weeks' temporary employment." This pattern persisted into World War II; for example, one planter praised government-sponsored construction work at Fort Bragg because "landlords are not having to furnish them [tenants] now. . . . they'll all come home when the time comes"—that is, for picking season.[30]

Families such as the Moshers of Russell County, Alabama, could confound welfare workers who assumed that blacks would automatically and predictably react in a certain way to either the offer or the withdrawal of relief, no matter how meager. Left behind by large numbers of their kin and neighbors who had moved to Chicago during World War I, in 1933 the Moshers (a family of ten), decided that they too should relocate, when they found they could not live on the small amount of public aid allotted them that year. After Mrs. Mosher traveled with two of her children to attend the funeral of a brother in Chicago the following year, she remained there, and by September 1935 six of her other offspring had followed her. Alarmed Chicago social workers informed the mother that she would not receive any public assistance, assuming that that threat would dissuade her husband and the two other children from coming north. Instead, the recent migrants determined "to try not only to stay in Chicago but also to bring the rest of the family North to join them." The Moshers' household strategy signaled their eagerness to move north, to preserve family ties, and to scorn local and federal efforts designed to keep them literally in their place by means of various public assistance programs.[31]

MIDCENTURY WAR WORKERS AND REFUGEES

World War II produced Southern population movements that both resembled and differed from their pre-1940 precursors. If, as some observers suggested, all Southerners, and young people in particular, were "dammed up" on the countryside and within the region as a whole, their numbers increasing at an alarming rate despite shrinking economic opportunities, then the war opened the floodgates of migration once again, the torrents spilling over the region as well as flowing northward. The collapse of the sharecropping system and the subsequent mechanization of cotton picking in the rural South, combined with the consolidation of coal companies and introduction of the "continuous miner" coal-cutting machine in the Appalachian Mountains, left millions of blacks and whites with little choice but to move. The effects of these technological advances deepened and expanded in the 1950s; between 1940 and 1960 more than 5 million Southerners left the region, although the Northern urban job structure was becoming increasingly less hospitable to men of modest educational levels.[32]

The war effort as well as its aftermath (especially in the form of the GI Bill), at home and abroad, introduced to Southern soldiers and workers straight off the farm a new world of places and life possibilities. For black Americans as a group, in particular, the war years represented a watershed of massive proportions. By the end of the 1940s, for the first time in history, the total black urban population exceeded the number living in rural areas. Blacks were twice as likely as whites to move long distances (that is, to noncontiguous states), and the Far West at last became a viable destination for growing numbers of migrants—a total of 258,900 during the decade. The largest numbers of black migrants went to New York (211,153), Chicago (166,322), Detroit (130,272), and Los Angeles (112,648), with male newcomers outnumbering females by almost two to one. For both black men and women, the drama of life on the home front is perhaps best captured by the transcontinental journeys of Southern families that left their rural homes and migrated to Seattle (for example), only to endure cramped living conditions in makeshift public projects and the degrading, racist policies practiced by the shipbuilding unions.[33]

Certainly much of the literature on wartime migration focuses on the south-to-north trek and the political implications of that move; but an equally compelling and telling story was unfolding within the South itself, where government-sponsored construction of factories and army installations hastened the process by which agricultural workers lost their ties to the land. Though released in 1942 and dealing specifically with the Huntsville, Alabama, area, a study of the impact of national defense on various rural communities applied equally to households displaced throughout the depression years and earlier: "The family which worked at odd jobs, tilling a few acres in a haphazard manner, and augmenting earnings through scouring the woods for sassafras roots, picking dallas grass seed, trapping coons and skunks, snaring fish in baskets, and poaching on game reservations, etc., could not be dumped into another community with the expectation that the resourcefulness of the family would enable it to get by."[34]

Private and government-sponsored building projects spurred much intraregional mobility among unskilled wage seekers. Black men especially remained thwarted in their desire for Northern defense jobs until the war was well underway; therefore, they eagerly pursued employment opportunities within the South, though few men of either race secured stable jobs in the process. Army construction projects, such as the Triangular Division Camp near Ozark, Alabama, could put eighteen thousand men on its payroll during its peak season; but half of these employees fell into the category of unskilled, and they had to move on once the work was completed—in this case, in 120 days. Skilled and relatively well-educated white men received permanent positions in these installations. The Tennessee Valley Authority, for example, relied on local farm workers for construction work, but operations and maintenance jobs more often than not went to outsiders. Though in 1939 the South contained 61 percent of the nation's low-income farmers, the area received less than one-fifth of all defense contracts, a proportion that remained essentially unchanged throughout the war years. Located along the eastern seaboard or the Gulf Coast, or in the Piedmont, many of these projects proved inaccessible to large numbers of agricultural laborers, especially blacks concentrated in the Deep South. Moreover, even for whites, new jobs were expensive to seek out ("Most folks don't know how much it costs to travel around like this," noted one white man who had just moved from Columbus, Georgia, to Tallahassee), and temporary at that ("'If you don't save at least half what you make,' his wife put in, 'you'll be having to beg as soon as the job gives out'").[35]

Migrants quickly recognized the relation between poor living accommodations and strains in family relations. In many cases workers spent their "big wages" on tiny quarters. Housing was so scarce around some of the larger projects that employees had to make do with the most primitive conditions; about 3,000 of the 19,400 construction workers at Florida's Camp Blanding set up tents in the nearby woods southwest of

Jacksonville. Because the children who followed their fathers to these temporary work sites were deprived of schooling, and whole families suffered from a lack of medical care, many men opted to live in barrackslike structures during the week, near work, and commute home on the weekends. In the space of a few months, W. M. Jennings of Alabama worked at Camp Blanding, then in DuPont's ordnance plant at Childersburg, and finally at the Seibert arsenal near Huntsville. For this last job he traveled by car back and forth between the plant and his family in Gadsden, a distance of 156 miles a day (for four weeks), thus extending each work day by several hours. Contemplating his next move, Jennings observed, "If I don't find some place where I can bring my family over here, my wife's gonna quit me and my kids are going to get so they don't know me." In Newport News, inadequate housing for black male workers led to high turnover rates among employees who quit in order to go back home to be with their families periodically; this trend prompted white employers to denounce blacks as "irresponsible" war workers. Moreover, a father's absence often forced family members left behind to adjust to a new division of labor: "If the man is working away from home there is very little work he will do at home other than that which seems absolutely necessary, such as planting and cultivation." Lola Joiner, together with her two teenage sons responsible for all the harvesting of their crops since her husband, Henry, found a job at Seibert arsenal, did not seem to mind; coming from a long line of black landowners, she said, "All my family likes to work. We likes to plow and we likes to hoe and we likes to spread our arms out and grab hold of something." But other wives and children reacted to these household disruptions with less equanimity, and some families were irrevocably shattered.[36]

During the war, in the South, as in Detroit or Chicago, whenever black men did find employment, a traditional racial division of labor held sway: "It wasn't just the Army, it was all jobs. If a white man and a black man walk up for an opening, and it ain't no shovel in that job, they'd give the job to the white man, but if he got a opening and there's a shovel in it, they'd give it to the black man." Moreover, gender conventions fell to wartime necessity sooner than racial caste considerations. A planning meeting of a U.S. Employment Service Regional Labor Supply Committee (comprising representatives of six Southern states) revealed that, when the labor market was particularly tight, employers were more likely to recruit white women than blacks of either sex. In 1942 the Bell Aircraft Company informed government officials that "upon completion [the new plant near Atlanta] will employ approximately 40,000 people, of which it is estimated that approximately 75 percent may be women." This policy left little hope for the 13,500 black people in the area, people "available for work." A study conducted of the Atlanta work force about this time showed that blacks suffered from an unemployment rate nine times that of whites (43 percent versus 5 percent). At work sites throughout the South—for example, the Atomic Energy's Oak Ridge, Tennessee, plant, and textile mills now roaring to produce clothing, tents, and linens—employers managed to preserve their discriminatory hiring policies throughout the war, despite the jawboning of an understaffed and ineffectual Fair Employment Practices Commission. Thus when Macon defense industries sought out "a considerable number of displaced [white] women from textile industries . . . women [who] are considered to be desirable employees by reason of their previous experience," when former coal miners returned home to partake of the coal boom, and when dairy farmer job-seekers were classified as "skilled" in contrast to cotton tenants and croppers, virtually no black people benefited. It was no wonder then that the belated opening of Northern war-industry jobs to blacks (in 1942 and 1943) caused so many to leave the South so hurriedly, and desperately; in a relative sense, at least, they would not benefit, either politically or economically, from wartime mobilization in the home of their slave grandparents.[37]

Appalachian migration northward intensified during World War II and the rest of the 1940s, when between two and three out of every ten residents left the region. This trend continued through the 1960s; between 1940 and 1970, 3.2 million Appalachians moved away, most to the Midwest. By the 1950s migrant communities scattered throughout the Midwest, in small towns and big cities, had solidified their connection with individual hometowns; eastern Kentucky folks tended to head for Cincinnati, Hamilton, Middletown, and Dayton; while southern West Virginia sent its young people to Columbus, Akron, and Cleveland. All of the southern Appalachian states—Kentucky, Tennessee, Missouri, and West Virginia—contributed to the flow of migrants into the largest urban areas, the men finding jobs in Chicago's light industries and in Detroit's auto factories. Reporting on the case of one migrant household that followed the "Southern grapevine" to Chicago's Uptown district in 1968, a reporter noted, "Thus the Blands go to Chicago because that's where most migrants from the Clarksburg, West Virginia, area go."[38]

John C. Turner moved from Breathitt County, Kentucky, to Middletown, Ohio, to work in an airplane factory for the duration of the war; "I had a daughter who lived up there, and I stayed with her and her husband."

Yet "that was just temporary. Turner's Creek was home." From the same community, another Turner, Henry, left behind his twelve children and thirty-three-acre farm to take a job with the Reliable Castings Corporation in Cincinnati; he went home on weekends for over a decade before finally bringing his whole family north. Meanwhile, the average hours and wages offered by the coal mines more than doubled in the course of the war, opening up long-overgrown paths into mining towns. After the war in 1945, the automation of the coal industry combined with cutbacks in demand would once again hasten the departure of miners to the north, and these men and their families were joined by returning soldiers who could find no jobs. But not all Appalachian migrants were former or would-be miners. From eastern Kentucky came whole clans of tobacco farmers, renters who lost a considerable portion of their income when the federal government reduced commercial crop subsidies, and subsistence farmers who had had little experience with wage work of any kind.[39]

The war left a fundamentally different legacy for white Appalachians compared to blacks, for several reasons. Most significantly, Northern defense industries welcomed Southern whites early and, for the most part, enthusiastically. Moreover, for returning white soldiers and workers, their hometowns in the mountain hollows or mining districts might offer little in the way of modern comforts or resources, but rarely did they assault one's sense of justice or mock sacrifices made in the war. In contrast, the black GIs who went home to the South encountered a corrupt plantation system, a system rife with fraud and threats of violence, where feudalistic traditions of white intimidation and black deference "seem strange in a civilized world." In 1946 a black man from Promiseland, South Carolina, sought help in finding a job through a Veterans Administration office in his state. Told to apply for an unskilled position in a nearby mill, Isaac Moragne angrily recalled later, "I was a staff sergeant in the Army. I travelled all over England. I sat fourteen days in the English Channel. And I wasn't going to push a wheelbarrow." In contrast, Jim Ryan, a white man from the mountains of North Carolina, described his migrant neighbors' motivation in more explicitly economic, rather than political, terms. Commenting on the reaction of servicemen who had seen much of the United States, and some of the world, he noted, "And the jobs weren't here. You know, if you want to drive a big car, you have to have enough money to support that habit; and the jobs just weren't here. And then the people weren't satisfied with what essentially had been subsistence farming, and loggings." For black GIs, the South lacked jobs, but it also lacked the resources that would support their self-respect.[40]

And finally, while black migration out of the South is and was portrayed by scholars and participants alike as a liberation movement of sorts, the relocation of Appalachian families more often than not seemed to have an elegiac quality, as many white migrants grieved for a way of life cherished and then lost. According to Ernie Mynatt, when he was a youngster in Breathitt County, Kentucky, in the 1950s, "no one even mentioned to me the possibility of staying. It was assumed all through my childhood that when I grew up, I would move north." Mynatt testified to the ambivalence of his fellow (white) migrants, many of whom were hit hard by the mechanization of the coal industry in the 1950s: "When automation took over the coal fields, they had to come [to Cincinnati]. They didn't want to come, they had to. Machines allowed six men to take the place of 60. It emptied out the coal fields." For other Cincinnati-bound migrants, and for Appalachian poor whites in general, the forces that pushed them out of their home place loomed larger than any putative appeal of the industrial North, and some left only with the intention of returning home as soon possible.[41]

The images of migration presented in Harriet Arnow's classic novel *The Dollmaker* contrast the lush beauty of the Kentucky hills, and the dream of Gertie Nevels for a piece of land to call her (family's) own, with the grim existence that awaited them in Detroit, where they lived in prisonlike, low-lying public housing among a bizarre collection of neighbors who gave violent expression to regional, religious, and ethnic prejudices. In the North Gertie loses her dream and two of her children—a son runs away, back home to his grandparents, and a daughter is killed by a fast-moving train. Throughout the novel the tone is one of unmitigated suffering and harshness; the North seems to have no redeeming qualities, except in the eyes of her weak-willed and ineffectual husband, Clovis, a factory mechanic.[42]

The postwar return migration south among white workers had no counterpart among blacks. At times gender differences surfaced in unpredictable ways when white families contemplated their future in a demobilized North. Over the bitter opposition of his wife, Clovis Nevels makes it clear that he prefers tinkering with machines in Detroit to pursuing odd jobs in Kentucky. But a white Southerner named Teddy Davies, who was among 24,000 people thrown out of work when Ford's Willow Run plant was closed in Detroit, observed, "The wife likes it here. She likes the indoor plumbing, and the kids like the school. We'll stay as long as we can." On the other hand, one of Davies's co-workers, Tennessee's Jim Bones, was looking forward to moving back home, no matter what the future might hold in store: "Damn sick and tired I am of being called a hillbilly. You make more money here. Sure! But they bleed all hell out of you just as fast as you can make it." For this man, and even for the others who remained in the North, the South would always be "home."[43]

Fifteen years after the war the widescale introduction of the mechanical cotton picker had eliminated the need for 80 percent of the South's sharecroppers. During the late 1940s and through the 1950s, Southern black people continued to leave the South. One out of ten (1.5 million) of all black Southerners abandoned the region between 1950 and 1960, almost all bound for the largest Northeastern, Midwestern, and (increasingly) Far Western cities, despite the decreasing demand for black labor all over the North. Meanwhile, southern Appalachians continued their trek due north, especially to the small towns of southern Ohio. Once in the North, they contributed to the gradual "bleaching" of the suburbs. In the 1950s the southern Appalachian counties of West Virginia lost 25 percent of their population; those in eastern Kentucky, 35 percent. In some areas of the latter state, jobless rates reached 80 percent, with the precipitous decline in mining, rail, and agricultural employment. It was during these years that Less Caudill acquiesced to the wishes of his wife and children that they remain in Ulvah, Kentucky, as he began a more or less permanent commute between a factory in Indianapolis and his Kentucky home. The family as a whole supported this arrangement despite the burdens it placed on his wife, Barbara. She noted, "I've had to be father, mother, and the one to pay the bills, the one to buy the coal and see that it was hauled into the house, and I've had to be the one to get up in the mornings to build the fires. I've had to be everything and that is more responsibility than any one person can live and bear up under."[44]

By the mid-1960s Southern out-migration had slowed, at least partially in response to a changing Northern economy that had less use for unskilled laborers of either race. On the other hand, magazines, popular music, movies, and television promoted the notion of personal "style" attainable only through the single-minded devotion to brand names and fashionable entertainers. This view of the "good life" lured Southerners out of towns and villages and encouraged Appalachian youth to depart because "of this stigma attached to being a mountain person." The end of the decade provided some evidence that a significant return migration was in the offing; for whites, the migration was due to the decline in heavy industry (especially steel, autos, and rubber), the revitalization of the Southern coal fields during the Vietnam War, and their disillusionment with life "in the places where the mountains are gone." Black people responded to changes wrought in the South by the civil rights revolution and in the North by the deterioration of ghetto communities wracked by drugs and crime. Some inner-city folk decided to try to make a go of it on a small piece of Southern land that had been in their families for generations, while others decided to send their children to live with Southern kin, away from the mean streets of the North. In these ways, black people at last sought to reclaim the South as their homeland too.[45]

Interviewed in the early 1970s, a white man named Richard Jackson, a native of Henderson County, in western North Carolina, spoke about a lost vision of the good life in Appalachia. Time was, he asserted, when people in the mountains could tell the difference "between wealth and money; they aren't the same thing. . . . Wealth was having enough land to feed you and tools to work it. Now we talk about [wealth] in terms of money. That's a lousy salad; coins are not chewable at all." Jackson made a distinction between, on the one hand, the physical deprivation of an impoverished existence, and, on the other, the conscious embracing of a physically arduous but plain life, outside the mass culture of twentieth-century materialism. He noted, "There is nothing beautiful [or] romantic about an enforced marginal existence. There *is* something beautiful about people who have decided that in order to live in a pretty good place they are willing to make some sacrifice in terms of convenience."[46] Jackson's comments referred specifically to the people of the Blue Ridge Mountains struggling to make ends meet in a low-wage tourist economy during the 1960s, but his words pinpoint a central tension in the history of migration out of the South throughout the twentieth century. Southerners defined "a pretty good place" in different ways; for some, such a place was in the countryside or deep in a mountain hollow, somewhere in the vicinity of the home of forebears from bygone generations and kin today, a place where the soil fed a family but also supported a way of life—or at least, that was the ideal. Other Southerners saw Northern cities, with their more diversified job structure, their better schools, and their vibrant cultural and associational life, as pretty good places, well worth the price of uprooting their families and starting all over again.

For both black sharecroppers and white farm folk from the mountains, the journey north actually originated in the late nineteenth century, when their bid for economic self-sufficiency, through landownership, failed. Set adrift in the Cotton South, moving from one plantation to another, or drawn into coal and lumber camps, they began to realize that they would never again see the day when a patch of land alone would provide the kind of life they or their children wanted or deserved. And so, thwarted in their desire for a homeplace in the country, they ventured northward, some more eagerly than others, into radically different kinds of surroundings, and found that in the process of resettlement, some things changed mightily and others, not at all.

8

Ghettos and the Lack of Them: Southern Migrants in the Midwest

Waiting in line for a job at a Detroit defense plant in April 1943, a black man named Charles Denby found himself standing next to a white migrant from Tennessee. The two struck up a conversation. The white man, who had "never been North before or in a plant," mentioned that he had no idea what kind of job he should request. Denby, though raised on a cotton farm in Lowndes County, Alabama, had had considerable factory work experience—in a Detroit auto plant, a Pittsburgh steel mill, an Anniston, Alabama, foundry, and a Memphis machine supply company. He had heard from a friend in Detroit that "the best job was riveting" and that it paid $1.16 an hour. When it came time for him to talk to the employment officer, Denby said he knew all about riveting ("I was lying to him but I wanted to get the job"). The officer replied that Denby's "experience wouldn't apply" and offered him the choice of attending riveting school, which paid 60 cents an hour, or taking a "laboring job" that paid 27 cents an hour more. With a family to support, Denby decided to accept the latter position. Shortly thereafter he learned that the Tennesseean had also asked for a riveting job, but that no one had inquired about his work history or insisted that he undergo a period of low-paid training. Denby later recalled, "He said they had given him a job, riveting." The white man marveled, "And I just come in from the fields." In contrast, Denby was assigned to the dope room, where "the odor of glue made the average person sick" and labor turnover was high; gradually black men took the places of the white men who departed, but in the course of the war, black women came to predominate in the small, suffocating space.[1]

If Charles Denby's encounter with the personnel official indicated how difficult it was for a black man to get a good job in wartime Detroit, then the efforts of his wife, Christine, revealed how hard black women would have to labor during the postwar period to secure any position outside a cafeteria or the kitchen of a white woman. Christine worked as drill press operator in a Chevrolet plant until the company "laid off the women, all the women, white and colored, on VJ Day." She heard that Chrysler was hiring, but the officer in charge told her that there were no jobs—at least "not for *you*," while the "white women were just going in." Challenged later for its discriminatory employment policies, Chrysler announced "that the reason they didn't hire colored women was because colored women didn't apply for work," an assertion that prompted Christine to "hop . . . on a bus right away" and go down to the plant to ask for an application form, which she was denied. Observed the black woman, herself a migrant from the South, "I like it up North and I wouldn't go home to stay. But I don't like the Northerners."[2]

For black migrants, Northern workplaces often seemed to recapitulate historic Southern patterns of racial prejudice. In 1936 Frank R. Crosswaith, a black Socialist and chairman of the newly formed Negro Labor Committee (based in New York City), argued that "finding work" for migrants obscured the larger issue—the invariably demeaning, irregular, and ill-paid nature of that work: "For nearly 300 years the slaveholders and their overseers 'found work' for the Negro, but he received no pay for the labor performed. Shall we build monuments now to the slaveholders because they 'found work' for the slaves?"[3] Crosswaith's angry query amounted to more than just rhetorical hyperbole. To compare the twentieth-century urban North to an antebellum slave plantation raises the issue of a deep continuity underlying the experiences of blacks over the generations, a continuity that transcended region, economy, northward migration, and to an extent, at least, even history itself.

In the Midwest, countless Southern black migrants watched poorly educated whites from Kentucky or Tennessee take advantage of skin color and kin ties to secure jobs, confirmation of the fact that all blacks would be prevented "from making our fullest contribution—not for lack of ability but for lack of whiteness." Black job seekers told of the grim determination necessary to secure the most menial job, and the luck necessary to retain it; for the vast majority, promotions were simply out of the question. And even the migrants' children who struggled into the professional middle class labored under a kind of socially reinforced system of expectations unknown to their rising white counterparts: "being the best, being perfect, became very important—too important." Understandably, then, some black people believed that the urban North offered only a variation on an old theme played in the rural South; one black man described his move from Memphis to Cleveland by suggesting that all blacks needed a "racial survival kit," and "of course as you move North, the contents of your survival kit change; you begin to be a little more sophisticated. But the kit is still there."[4]

At the same time, the move north offered black Southerners a new arena for struggle, one centered around jobs, and within this arena they helped to forge a powerful, biracial labor movement for the first time in American history. Black workers in the auto, steel, railroad, and meat-packing industries earned wages that they had hardly dared to dream about in the South. In the 1930s and 1940s the Congress of Industrial Organizations, with its "culture of unity," took concrete steps to break down barriers of mutual distrust between the races and among ethnic groups, and encouraged workers to see themselves as equal partners on the picket line and equal citizens in the nation. Caught up in the early, heady days of CIO organizing, black men and women experienced a new form of collective and personal exhilaration. Sylvia Woods, a black woman who hailed from New Orleans and worked in Chicago, recalled that, as a result of her commitment to labor activism, "I learned that the average white worker wanted the same identical things that I wanted. . . . A decent home . . . an education for their children. . . . I learned who the enemy was. It was the man who owned the plant and kept us separated." Woods served as a local official of the United Automobile Workers (UAW) union in an airplane plant during World War II; and at one point, through her efforts, the UAW waged a successful fight to reinstate a white migrant from Tennessee who had been fired from his job. Because he understood that Sylvia Woods was working on his behalf too, the man not only became an active union member but reevaluated his attitude toward blacks in general. According to Woods, "We threw a party one night and he came—this southerner who didn't want a black to do anything—he brought his wife and children. We used to call him Tennessee. I danced with him that night. It was really something." In the 1930s, a liberal Democratic president broke the Republicans' historic hold on the political loyalties of the descendants of slaves. Yet even Franklin Roosevelt felt constrained about denouncing the lynching of blacks. Within such a repressive climate, the policies of the CIO placed that group in the forefront of national institutions promoting racial egalitarianism.[5]

The history of black migrants suggests that many failed to succeed in the "promised land" of the North not because of their poverty but because of white attitudes toward their race. A comparison between the experiences of two groups that migrated to the Midwest, Deep South blacks and Appalachian whites, helps to sort out the factors of color, class, and culture as they affected the prospects of Southern newcomers to Northern cities. A considerable body of scholarly literature examines both foreign immigrants and Southern black migrants; several scholars have argued that black people found themselves at a disadvantage in the North compared to their Eastern European predecessors because transformations in the Northern economy (beginning in the 1920s) gradually eliminated the need for large numbers of unskilled workers.[6] If that had been the sole reason for the growth of poor black inner-city communities, then Southern white migrants, who started their northward trek in earnest in the 1940s, would have fared even worse in the race for good jobs and decent housing. And yet in fact, as a group, Southern Appalachians prospered early, and steadily, compared to their black counterparts, primarily because they gained easy access to semiskilled jobs, and they had the freedom to move around within urban areas, or at least as far as their fortunes and family loyalties allowed. Encouraged by Northern factory owners and personnel officials, Southern kin-based communities continued to regroup across the Ohio River, and together white migrants gained a foothold in the Northern industrial economy.

This comparison, which holds class factors (strictly defined) constant and highlights the issue of race, is not without its difficulties. For example, it is important to consider exactly when discrete groups of Southerners moved north, recognizing that both job opportunities and the political implications of those opportunities changed over time. The black Mississippians who signed up with Henry Ford in 1919 believed themselves fortunate to be working for such a (relatively) progressive employer. Yet by 1942 the Ford Motor Company, which steadfastly refused to recruit blacks of either sex for the war effort, was under bitter attack from black labor and community activists. To cite another example: The timing of a move could greatly affect the housing options of Southern white migrants, many of whom sought out kin and neighbors from home as soon as they arrived in the North; while the first migrants formed clusters in inner-city areas, most of them (or their children) eventually moved out of these "ports-of-entry," and their kin who came later joined them in the suburbs or in stable working-class neighborhoods.

Observers often contrasted the "individualism" of Appalachian white migrants with the "group-mindedness" of blacks in the ghetto; but such labels were misleading. In effect, Southern white families could afford to fend for themselves, to put their faith in the ability of a father or older son to hold onto a semiskilled job in a factory, and to move out of the inner-city or back south whenever it was in the household's interests to do so. This relative freedom depended both on specific institutional supports and structures that worked in favor of whites, as well as on the ambition and talent of individuals. For example, holding better and more secure jobs compared to blacks of equal (or greater) ability and schooling, white migrants in larger proportions gained the seniority advantages that derived from union membership. Within the limits of their personal finances, whites, unimpeded by laws, restrictive covenants, and zoning policies that might have inhibited their movement, had a large measure of residential mobility. In effect, the head start and permanent benefits they were accorded in the labor and housing markets rendered group action based solely on skin color or "culture" unnecessary. In contrast, all black people, regardless of class status, labored under certain constraints; as Charles Denby suggested, racial consciousness originated with whites and "has been hurting us for three hundred years in this country. I wasn't the first to write the word. Since I can remember it has been hurting me."[7] Under such conditions, a black corporate ethos amounted to a fait accompli, the inevitable result of whites' racial ideology and the laws and policies that sustained it.

The 1940s and 1950s, when the greatest migrations out of the South took place, coincided with changes in the Northern economy that fundamentally altered the status of unskilled wage workers. Before 1930 or so, black field hands were integral to the Southern staple-crop economy and Appalachians provided the necessary manpower for labor-intensive work in the coal mines. Both groups, serving as a "reserve army" of sorts, played a necessary part in World War II defense industries. However, by 1950, workers displaced by the decline in demand for labor in both the agricultural and extractive sectors of the South found fewer and fewer comparable opportunities in the North. Automation and firm consolidation—trends frequently associated with the 1970s— began to erode the jobs of black fathers and sons as early as the mid-1950s.[8] Thereafter, a declining number of employers, north or south, would seek out the poorest folk of either race for manual labor jobs or, indeed, for jobs of any kind; and slowly but surely black families trapped in the ghettos began to register the devastating effects of their economic redundancy.

OUT OF THE DELTA AND OUT OF "PARADISE": MIGRANTS TO THE MIDWEST

In Midwestern towns and cities, one particular group of Southern migrants encountered a somewhat less than enthusiastic reception among the powers-that-be. Municipal officials considered them lazy, promiscuous, rapidly proliferating welfare-seekers, a drain on the public treasury, a stain on the city's image. Educational officials tracked their children for failure in the public schools, and medical authorities decried their persistent superstitions in all manner of ailments, such as rinsing out a child's mouth with urine to cure a rash called thrush. Employers expressed mixed feelings; the migrants provided cheap labor, but they were unreliable, inept at any kind of machine work, slow on the job, and unambitious. Landlords told them that they need not apply, citing their large families, allegedly deplorable housekeeping practices, and presumed violent proclivities (with the knife as the weapon of choice). Their neighbors native to the North soon developed a repertoire of jokes that focused on the migrants' ignorance of city ways, their primitive Southern origins, their slovenly appearance and demeanor. The migrant woman was likely to be careworn and distracted, accompanied by her ne'er-do-well, painfully thin mate: "he moves with a somewhat listless, slouching gait; his face bears a wooden inscrutableness, a slightly melancholy aspect, and his eyes meet you at a sidelong angle, with long, distrustful looks of inquiry." Shiftless, evasive, and untrustworthy, they supposedly lived for the moment and squandered their weekly paychecks on trinkets and drink. Once in their new homes, they apparently remained willing and able to tolerate the most degrading living and working conditions, "immune to discomforts that sorely try other Americans."[9]

These comments, all directed at native-born, Protestant, English-speaking whites—men and women who hailed from the southern Appalachian Mountains—are, of course, striking for the way they resembled stereotypes of African-Americans. Some observers made explicit the similar nature and tone of prejudice directed at the two groups; asked whether established Cincinnati homeowners evinced more opposition to an influx of blacks or Appalachians, one community activist observed, "It depends on who's invading the neighborhood." In the 1940s some Chicago employers even compared Southern whites unfavorably to blacks, citing the whites' habit of taking trips of indeterminate duration back home to the South at all times of the week or year. One real estate agent went so far as to make class distinctions among blacks while lumping all Southern whites into a single, damnable category: "We'd rather rent to a Negro, a Mexican, or a Filipino than to a white person from the South. . . . A good clean colored person is a better tenant than a southern white anytime." Disdainful Northerners charged that poor whites' compulsion to spend their money on alcohol, games of chance, and inflated credit-card purchases made them "nigger-rich"— that is, unable to save or handle money in a responsible way. Nevertheless, as a group, Appalachian migrants to the North managed to overcome prejudices against them, prejudices that were superficial in their focus on speech patterns, clothing styles, and personal demeanor. In contrast, black migrants could never shed the liabilities associated with their skin color.[10]

Despite their poverty and the (at least initial) hostility they encountered from Northerners, Appalachian whites did not necessarily adhere to a distinctive folk culture comparable to (at least for analytic purposes) African-American culture. The whites came from a variety of local economies—subsistence farming, commercial tobacco production, coal mining, or some combination of the three—and not until they arrived in the North did people from these different backgrounds think of themselves as members of a homogeneous group; they had never used the term "Appalachians" (let alone "briars" or "hillbillies") to identify themselves. Moreover, it is not possible in all cases to posit a radical break between a bucolic rural past and a grimy urban future in the course of migration. For example, descriptions of Harlan County, Kentucky, coal-mining towns in the 1940s reveal the family dissolution, high rates of alcoholism and crime, slumlike housing, and general social demoralization associated with big-city living. The view that Southern whites, as migrants from an "isolated," "changeless culture," were completely unprepared to make their way in an urban industrial economy (a "culture of change") ignores the rapid developments that had transformed Appalachian life from the 1880s onward. Few Appalachian whites (or Southern blacks) came directly from a way of life devoted exclusively to the tilling of the soil. Through rural nonagricultural work and intraregional migration they had gained wage-earning experience; poor housing and poor schools were hardly a shock to them; and they had many precedents (whether in the form of poaching or moonshining) for making a living outside the mainstream labor market. In the 1950s and 1960s Appalachians living in the "shallow rural," somewhere between the suburbs of large towns and the remote backcountry, were well integrated into a consumer wage economy driven by chain stores and national corporations.[11]

Social workers and scholars alike have spent much time and effort trying to define a distinctive Appalachian culture without realizing that many of the traits ascribed to this group of people were common to rural folk in general, including Southern blacks. The effort on the part of households to combine wage work with patch farming and to rely on kin for financial support in good times and bad was less a "Kentucky way" than a rural way of life. When mountain folk deferred to their betters, they practiced a kind of deference ritual that blacks had practiced under slavery. Even musical forms considered the core of a "pure" Appalachian culture included elements of Southern black influence (the blues and gospel music) and changed rapidly over the generations, in the process attracting loyal fans throughout the country. (Noted one black woman, "I . . . know that if you listen to a real good hillbilly song, they have that same feeling that the Negro has. It's a deep sensitive feeling.") And finally, the "backwardness" of Appalachian life was belied by the strenuous efforts of a considerable proportion of the population to leave it, at least temporarily. Commented Rosalie Van Houton, a Kentucky native who had moved with her husband to Detroit during World War II, "They think we're dumb just because we come from outside. They're a whole lot dumber than we are. They've never been outside their own little community."[12]

Once in the North, southern Appalachians exhibited few of the traits that would qualify them as an ethnic group; their extended families, rather than precisely defined cultural bonds, served as their primary-group reference point. A significant number of Appalachians chose to distance themselves from their fellow migrants and to blend into the population at large. For the upwardly mobile of either sex, it was possible to leave the "ridgerunner" taunts behind forever by losing their accents, adopting Northern dress fashions, switching the radio dial from Hank Williams to Frank Sinatra, and grabbing the first chance to move to a modest house in a working-class suburb. The children of migrants saw little reason to tout themselves as the kin of hillbillies—hence the irony of a Northern social worker or teacher strumming Old English folk ballads on a guitar, or building a model of strip mines for classroom display, all in an effort to honor an Appalachian "culture" that restless, rock-and-rolling youngsters hoped to forget as soon as possible. Thus over time class and generational factors could erode even the longing for home that many migrants had originally expressed, a longing that was their initial, and in some cases only fleeting, common denominator.[13]

Beginning with the World War I era, Southern migrants sought employment within a Midwestern industrial job structure that bore similarities to the racial division of labor imposed by the Southern cotton plantation. In both places black people remained confined to the lowest jobs, though they received the same wages (or contract provisions) as the disproportionately few whites with whom they shared those jobs. In some instances—for example, in a Northern steel plant or on a Piedmont plantation—blacks faced stiff competition from whites and counted themselves lucky if they managed to get hired at all. Large manufacturers (through centralized personnel offices) might or might not abide by industrywide conventions in terms of hiring blacks, and smaller establishments gave individual shop foremen a great deal of latitude in indulging their preferences for co-workers of their own religious or ethnic group. (Unions might protect the principle of seniority on the job, but they could not serve as "gatekeepers" and control the hiring of black people in the first place.) When employers considered upgrading their hands to semiskilled positions, blacks invariably fared less well than whites. A recent study of the hiring practices at Ford Motor Company in the 1920s suggests that the personal attributes that would win higher positions for white workers—their marital status, education, and experience—counted for little when employers contemplated assigning blacks to certain jobs. Clustered at the lowest rung of the industrial tenure ladder, black workers were the first to be displaced (by whites) in the event of depression in the 1930s or the restructuring of an entire industry such as autos in the 1970s.[14]

Within this economy, Southern whites gained a crucial advantage over blacks in two ways; first, they received preference for semiskilled jobs, and second, they received the on-the-job training necessary to upgrade their positions more often. Certainly in terms of work skills, southern Appalachians were not superior to blacks in any meaningful way. A Bethlehem Steel Corporation official's comments about blacks could just as well have applied to Appalachian whites: "coming as they did from rural agricultural sections of the South, bringing with them their old traditions and superstitions, they presented to us many new community problems." Labor in the extractive sector bore little resemblance to assembly-line or skilled factory work; noted one observer, "Cincinnati is a skill town, and coal miners have no skills. They were hung up here." Despite a fondness among some for tinkering with auto engines, white migrants arriving in the North in the late 1950s and 1960s found themselves at a disadvantage in the job market, compared to workers with more formal technical experience; said one Chicago factory maintenance worker in 1964, "You can't buy a job these days if you don't know how to run a machine. I worked at just any job I could get, but there isn't much in West Virginia." Thus later Appalachian migrants were less likely to establish a niche in heavy industry, and either alternated between low-skill jobs up north and back south, or settled into depressed inner-city neighborhoods and took day work as they could get it.[15]

The experiences of Southern migrants in both small Midwestern towns and the area's largest cities reveal the interplay of racial and class factors in their patterns of adjustment. In southwestern Ohio and the small towns scattered throughout the Miami Valley (Butler County), Appalachians became the primary labor force for manufacturing businesses. In contrast, blacks were confined to the largest Midwestern and Northeastern cities. By World War I the region just north of the Ohio River was an established center of high value-added industries, producing a wide variety of products from machinery and paper to cash registers and iron, steel, and chemicals. Well-developed transportation networks, the proximity of raw materials, and a cheap labor supply (primarily subsistence farmers from Kentucky) continued to make the area an attractive one to industrialists through the 1960s. In 1950 more than one-third of all workers in Hamilton were Kentucky-born, while five east-central Kentucky counties dominated the in-migrant labor force of Middletown. Over the next two decades the depression in the Virginia and Tennessee mine industry sent more Southerners to the Miami Valley; by 1970 the proportion of Appalachians in Ohio towns ranged from one out of six in Cleveland and Cincinnati to one out of three in Columbus; one out of two in Hamilton, Middletown, and Norwood; and virtually all the residents of South Lebanon. Conspicuous in their absence from the valley were significant numbers of foreign immigrants and Southern blacks.[16]

The initial World War I Kentucky migration to Ohio, notable for its "clannishness," perpetuated itself over the years through kin networks eagerly exploited by Northern employment officers. Before 1960 about one-third of all Southern Appalachian migrants were illiterate, and they eagerly accepted unskilled and semiskilled jobs throughout the region.

In Middletown during the post–World War II era, one-half of all employees of the Inland Container Corporation hailed from Wolfe County, the home of a company superintendent who combined job recruitment with periodic visits to relatives back south. In the same town, the Armco Steel Corporation as a matter of policy granted hiring preference to the children and relatives of workers; consequently, migrants from certain Kentucky counties came to predominate in individual departments. Asked about the hostility of native Ohioans toward Kentucky folk, one migrant said that he had encountered "no trouble" in his entry-level job, because almost all his co-workers shared the same roots and "there weren't no buckeyes [that is, Ohio-born people] to get along with." In the early 1980s the vice president of Cincinnati's Reliable Castings Corporation reflected on his quarter century with the company and noted, "We started hiring these people [Kentuckians] before my time, and whenever we needed help, they'd bring their brothers and cousins. Somehow, the employees would know we needed help before we did, and they'd have people up here." A Pulaski County, Kentucky, native testified to the simplicity of the hiring process when he recalled that, in 1956, at the age of twenty-one, he heard from a friend that "they were hiring at General Motors. I came up here on a Sunday and went to work on Tuesday. . . . They asked me what my name was, and they let me right in. My friend had given them my name."[17]

Within this regional job market, then, native-born whites dominated manufacturing jobs, including those that in other areas of the country (the South, the largest Northern cities) went to blacks. Unskilled white workers for Cincinnati Time Recorder labored "in what amounted to a steam dust. Our eyes were red; our throats, noses, and lungs were irritated to the point of fatigue due to conditions." As late as 1976 the sandstone miners at Cleveland Quarries Company in South Amherst (some of whom lived in company housing) worked without a lunch hour and without the benefit of company toilet facilities. According to one observer, "This is a low-wage, dangerous-occupation company which tolerates high turn-over in order to keep profits high, and wages and benefits low." Complaints that southern Appalachians led a highly transient existence because they returned south often obscured the fact that they held undesirable jobs that historically had had high rates of turnover and absenteeism among all racial and ethnic groups. In general, turnover by industry and within individual plants was correlated with type of job and not with the race of the person who held it.[18]

The relatively few black migrants in the Miami Valley suffered unemployment rates up to four to five times greater than Appalachian migrants; when they were lucky enough to enter the work force, they entered at the unskilled level and then stayed there, although recent white migrants moved more quickly into semiskilled positions. In 1940 the long-term effects of these hiring practices were already clear. A study of Hamilton revealed that assembly-line plants such as Fisher Can and Ford Automotive Parts offered unskilled jobs that "are in many cases simplified so that less than one day is required for complete mastery of the requirements." Moreover, it was common for "plants such as the foundries and paper mills [to] follow a policy of making all promotions in the shop from the ranks, which makes it possible for the uninitiated to be inducted slowly into the demands of any responsible position." The result was an "ease of occupational adjustment" on the part of former farmers and miners and also, not insignificantly, a regional labor force that had little need for black workers at any level. In the 1970s Cincinnati blacks were more than twice as likely as southern Appalachians to hold unskilled or service jobs.[19]

Despite their history of chronic layoffs and, after 1960, their declining job opportunities at the entry level, over the generations Appalachian migrants and their children established a number of different kinds of communities for themselves in Ohio. East Dayton, Cincinnati's Over-the-Rhine and Lower Price Hill, and Hamilton's Armondale and Peck's Addition represented classic port-of-entry communities for the first migrants and for some of those who followed. Yet these poor neighborhoods were characterized by high rates of residential turnover, as migrants and their relatively successful offspring explored other housing options—stable working-class or lower-middle-class areas such as Mill Creek, near Cincinnati, or Wrightview, outside of Dayton; or small towns such as South Lebanon, where families could tend some corn and hunt and fish as well; and finally, pleasant suburbs where well-to-do whites settled and quickly blended into the middle-American landscape. A migrant family might logically progress from Peck's Addition to a better area of the working-class Belmont district, and finally move out to Fairfield Township, where they could enjoy "at least superficially some of the isolation of the hollow . . . set up a vegetable patch and . . . find some of the [ethnic and racial] homogeneity still preserved in the Kentucky hills." On the other hand, other white migrants, depending on their own background and the location of their Northern kin, might move directly from the South to a stable suburb and stay there.[20]

Because of this relative residential openness, and because few poor Appalachian communities were composed exclusively of white migrants, the term "cluster" (rather than "ghetto") is an accurate description of their concentrated patterns of settlement. Unlike black ghettos, Appalachian ports-of-entry were often located near factories so that blue-collar workers had an economic incentive as well as a familial imperative to locate there, where "the folks there were 'a heap more obligin'." Compared to poor whites, blacks in the lower Midwest and in Northern cities in general had a consistently higher index of residential segregation, though Appalachian migrant clusters might remain geographically somewhat isolated from other neighborhoods. For example, the topography of Lower Price Hill produced "an enclaved community since a steep, unpopulated hill encloses it to the north and highways, major thoroughfares, and a viaduct spanning the Mill Creek Valley surround it in other directions." As a result, residents might replicate hometown patterns of kin relations and continue to lack access to good schools and modern medical care.[21]

In the largest Midwestern cities, where substantial numbers of both black and white migrants congregated, racial disparities in work and housing options became manifest. For southern Appalachians, a modern metropolis might turn out to be either a sanctuary of middle-class respectability or the "capital city of Hell."[22] To some extent, of course, the range of social mobility enjoyed by migrants and their children depended on their backgrounds and commitment to schooling; but an individual's "adjustment" to Northern life also reflected indefinable qualities, such as a yearning (or lack thereof) for a Southern home place. In contrast, Southern black migrants to Midwestern cities faced a much narrower range of choices in terms of employment, housing, and community—choices that were shaped more by an urban infrastructure of institutionalized racism than by the migrants' formal education or hard work. This is not to suggest that the black ghetto arose out of impersonal historic forces; to the contrary, it was the product of conscious decisions on the part of individual employers, real estate agents, city councilmen, and housing authority administrators. Nevertheless, the structural factors that created such a large class of inner-city black poor are somehow easier to measure and analyze, compared to the more amorphous personal characteristics that kept the white poor in poverty.

As a means of chronicling the emergence of black ghettos in the North, a comparison between Southern black and white migrants to Chicago, Detroit, and Cleveland (during the period from 1940 to 1970) is instructive for several reasons. First, the two groups migrated to these cities in significant numbers. Between 1955 and 1970, for example, Appalachian whites accounted for about 10 percent of all in-migrants into these cities; by 1970 approximately 200,000 Appalachians lived in

Detroit, 169,000 in Chicago, and 144,000 in Cleveland. The black populations of these cities were larger (Detroit: 660,428; Chicago: 1,102,620; and Cleveland: 287,841), though these figures represent not only migrants but in many cases their children and grandchildren as well. Second, because both groups left the rural South at the same time, they entered the urban labor market together, unlike Eastern European immigrants, most of whom arrived in this country before 1920. And finally, although the historical record is spotty, it is possible to make meaningful generalizations about the respective fates of Southern blacks and Appalachian whites in these cities.[23]

These generalizations are not meant to obscure differences among the three places or to ignore the complex histories that characterized the growth and development of their ghettos. For example, Detroit, as a one-industry town, differed from Cleveland, with its more diversified job structure. In Chicago (by far the largest of the three municipalities, with a population of almost 4 million in 1940), the South Side soon after 1916 assumed all the classic characteristics of a ghetto, in contrast to the early, more open, and less rigidly segregated working-class black communities of Cleveland. Nevertheless, for many years—from the 1930s until the mid-1950s—Chicago could boast an incorruptible housing authority that was committed to the ideal of residental integration. Each city had its own separate history of machine politics responsive to various permutations of racial and ethnic diversity; and these histories have been told in detail, and well, elsewhere.[24]

At the same time, there are basic similarities among the three cities in the ways that black ghettos evolved and grew over the years. Beginning in the 1950s, whites fled from the city limits of all three metropolitan areas, reversing generations of population growth and leaving blacks increasingly concentrated in areas with declining tax revenues. (One Southern white man could hardly conceal his glee when he noted that the migration of black people out of the Delta had now exposed the self-righteous hypocrisy of Northerners: "The displaced sharecroppers moved to the Northern cities and the liberals moved out."[25]) In 1980 black people represented 40 percent of Chicago's population, 63 percent of Detroit's, and 44 percent of Cleveland's; all three cities had suffered losses of manufacturing jobs in the 1960s and 1970s. When black men and women violently rebelled against their subordinate status—in Chicago in 1965 and 1968, in Cleveland in 1966, and in Detroit in 1967—they gave collective expression to a perverse symmetry of long-standing forces that converged on the ghettos of all three cities. By that time racial discrimination had so thoroughly corrupted fundamental urban institutions that even the political process, under the guidance of black city councillors and mayors (in Cleveland, Carl Stokes between 1967 and 1972; in Detroit, Coleman Young, beginning in 1974; in Chicago, Harold Washington, from 1983 to 1987), could do little to undo the damage. Though banks might be purged of redlining practices that denied mortgages and other types of loans to ghetto residents, suburban real estate agents sued for their unlawful dealings, and downtown employers pressured to hire more blacks in low-paying service jobs, the fact remained that inner-city people lacked access to the growing employment opportunities outside the cities because they lacked the money to commute to or live near those jobs. These trends in ghetto formation were not unique to Midwestern cities, of course, but rather represented patterns in the growth of poor black populations throughout the Mid-Atlantic, Northeastern, and Far Western states as well.

An examination of inner-city poor whites reveals that an emerging "underclass" was not composed entirely of blacks and that the huge black ghetto was not a necessary or inevitable accompaniment of twentieth-century urban growth. In large Midwestern cities, as in small towns, white Appalachians demonstrated a wide range of responses to their new surroundings. One group put into practice the observation of a Chicago social worker, who declared that the typical migrant faced "just a one generation problem": "All he has to do is lose his southern accent and move out of the migrant community and nobody recognizes him any more." In 1970 less than one-half of all Southern Appalachians in Cleveland (most of them natives of West Virginia) were concentrated in the city, where they could be studied as an identifiable cultural group; the rest were scattered, and for the most part absorbed, throughout the Standard Metropolitan Statistical Area. Outside of center cities, enclaves of migrants were too small to be considered population "concentrations," one of the major defining characteristics of the "underclass." In addition, some migrants' constant shuttling back south and up north meant that they too would remain hidden from decennial census takers. The chronically poor migrants who stayed in ports-of-entry constituted a much smaller group compared to black residents—probably only 10 to 25 percent of the number of poor blacks in the same city, with Chicago at the lower end of that range. In 1960 between four and five out of ten poor whites in Detroit, Chicago, and Cleveland lived in the suburbs and working-class neighborhoods, rather than in the central city. For the children of migrants, their parents' move into a stable working-class area, either directly or eventually, probably represented their best chance for upward mobility; generational continuity spelled disaster in

Chicago's Uptown, Cleveland's 25th and Lorain, and Detroit's near West Side district, where residential and job turnover was high and respect for formal education weak. According to one Cleveland resident, people remained "real good hillbillies before they moved to the suburbs."[26]

Northern host communities differed over time in the degree to which they received Southern white newcomers. In the late 1930s large numbers of migrants to Detroit entered a constricted job market and found themselves limited to jobs in restaurants, ice cream parlors, and carbonated beverage plants; it is uncertain whether military mobilization lifted them en masse out of these positions and into the auto industry. Certainly the migrants to wartime Detroit considered themselves to be persecuted outcasts; though jobs were relatively plentiful, housing was not, and class, ethnic, and racial tensions were an integral part of the city's boom years. In any case, by the late 1960s auto jobs went to "people who've got friends and relatives," and the lowest positions throughout the city remained reserved for blacks. In contrast to the Detroit case, Southern whites who moved to Chicago during World War II faced little hostility from resident workers, because the migrants were such a small percentage of the city's total population and there seemed to be plenty of jobs for all. These migrants replaced drafted men in the city's light manufacturing and wholesale commercial establishments, though "the foothold they have obtained is an insecure one." By this time the steel, construction, and meatpacking industries were dominated by Eastern European groups.[27]

The interrelationships among education, housing, and job status differed for white migrants compared to blacks. More often than their black counterparts, Appalachian whites arrived in Chicago, Cleveland, and Detroit with a car, which facilitated job hunting and commuting; they relied on kin networks for their first job, which they found relatively quickly; and they received the on-the-job training, promotions, and upgrading that eventually lifted them out of entry-level positions. The fact that whites regardless of nationality tended to live in close proximity to major urban employers (in contrast to blacks confined to central cities) put them at an advantage in terms of attending union meetings and benefiting from company-sponsored community outreach and welfare programs. Residential stability and education yielded little in the way of material gain for blacks. In the mid-1960s an extensive survey comparing the options of Southern black and white migrants to Cleveland found that although black women and men who had been in the city five years or less were better educated than whites (and although long-term black residents had similar levels of schooling compared to whites), whites were more likely to move into operative jobs and bypass unskilled work. Black women, again though better educated than white women, remained concentrated in service positions, in contrast to the factory, clerical, and sales jobs of white wives (or more often, white single women). A Chicago researcher reported that both blue-collar and white-collar white applicants got jobs faster than blacks equally qualified for those positions: "The Negroes' skills did not suffice to overcome racial barriers, evidently." Most employers who hired any black people at all did so only because they served as a particularly cheap labor supply, or because white workers could afford to avoid jobs that were too dirty and dangerous. Compared to working-class whites, blacks suffered from higher rates of unemployment, part-time as opposed to full-time work, and layoffs during war mobilization and economic downturns; and lower rates of overtime, upgrading, and promotion.[28]

It was no wonder then that black migrants consistently displayed a deep sense of disappointment over their jobs in the North. Not only did unskilled blacks resent the sight of whites (as a group) prospering at their expense, but early on, in cities such as Detroit, black college graduates who worked as department store elevator operators had to content themselves with their role as "ambassadors of the Negro race." Still, a few black families managed to parlay the slimmest of means into a stable and relatively privileged middle-class existence. For steel mill laborers, railroad porters, janitors, teachers, and semiskilled autoworkers, even a modest salary and a modicum of employment security (with the help of working wives and much scrimping and saving) could serve as the ticket to homeownership and a college education for their children.[29]

Like blacks, white migrants from the rural South who remained poor had histories of chronic underemployment or unemployment. In the 1950s and 1960s numerous day-labor agencies operated in Uptown, where about one-half of the 100,000 residents hailed from the southern Appalachians. These agencies matched unskilled workers with temporary employers, for a fee. The men who milled around agency offices either daily or periodically were by definition marginal and by personal characteristics readily identifiable. Day workers possessed neither savings nor cars; they were frequently older men with medical or mental problems, or alcohol and drug dependencies. In some cases they had made a good start initially but then an on-the-job injury, or a precious car battered in an accident or repossessed by the bank, proved to be their undoing, the first in a series of disasters—the loss of a job, then drinking problems, the dissolution of a marriage. Some migrant couples had difficulty accommodating themselves to Northern ways; Bill and

Amanda Carter, from Atlanta, felt that wherever they moved the "niggers [were] tryin to move in." Though their baby had recently died because of Amanda's poor prenatal care (she never got enough to eat) and the couple had been evicted from their apartment, Bill disdained work at a television-tube plant because of its large number of black employees and because "it's so damned hot in there." Noted Amanda philosophically, "with Bill it's day to day." Other men shunned low-paying jobs as intrinsically demeaning: "I wouldn't work for no sonofabitch for no dollar and a quarter an hour. Shit, I'd steal off the street first. Can't pay your rent on it. Now down home I'd work for a dollar and a quarter an hour, but that's different." And finally, for men whose "hearts were elsewhere" (that is, determined to move frequently between North and South), even a modest commitment to a low-paying job was too much.[30]

Clearly, then, not all Appalachian migrants—or their children—moved smoothly into the middle class or even the stable working class. Despite the successful assimilation of southern Appalachians as a group into Northern society, by 1970 a small class of the persistent poor had emerged throughout the Midwest. Some Appalachians living in southern Ohio seemed to form an identifiable subgroup due to their poverty, their low educational achievement, and their tight-knit kin clusters. A constricted job market promised to perpetuate such clusters into the foreseeable future. Because of their large families and uncertain paychecks, blue-collar Appalachian whites faced discrimination in housing, and consequently suffered from overcrowding in dilapidated tenements and single-family dwellings. White slums differed from stable working-class neighborhoods by virtue of their disproportionate numbers of malnourished and lead-poisoned children and female-headed households. In the early 1940s the "four concentrations of Kentuckians in Hamilton" all had "in common a proximity to the corporation limit, a dump, and a railroad." Peck's Addition contained more than its share of one-room shacks with dirt floors, some of them "renovated chicken coops." In the 1970s Cincinnati's poor white neighborhoods ranked high in poverty and social disorganization. Lower Price Hill had the highest rate of functional illiteracy (53 percent) of any area—black or white—in the city, reflecting the fact that two-thirds of all sixteen- to twenty-one-year-olds had dropped out of school. Over-the-Rhine had similar proportions of poor families and female-headed households compared to black areas such as the West End. The large number of bars in Southern white migrant neighborhoods, favorite hangouts for husbands and older sons, hardly helped to redeem a population already prone to ritualistic knife-fighting and drinking. How and why certain children managed to leave the slums is something of a social-scientific mystery; a worried mother, a sympathetic teacher or social worker, a love of learning—all or any of these factors could provide an entrée into the middle class for one son or daughter, while neighbors and siblings automatically followed in their parents' footsteps, up North or "back home." In the early 1980s up to a third of all (6 million) Appalachians in the Midwest lived "lives of extreme hardship in an innercity world that can destroy body, mind, and soul."[31]

The reluctance or refusal of some poor Appalachian migrants to apply for local or federal assistance prompted sympathetic observers to glorify their tradition, or "culture," of self-sufficiency: "My people don't want 'help.' They don't like the idea of someone standing over them and saying, 'Poor souls, I feel sorry for you, and let me give you something.' They are a very tough people; they've survived hard winters, one after the other, and they've learned how to take care of themselves." Nevertheless, welfare statistics provide a somewhat different picture, one that indicates, for example, that recent migrants needed a certain amount of time to find their way through a bureaucratic maze of interviews and application forms in order to qualify for aid. In 1940, 43 percent of all persons on relief in Hamilton were Kentucky-born (though they represented only one-fifth of the total population), and by that time disgruntled welfare officials were already complaining that this group had become "demanding" and manipulative in their efforts to gain more benefits, such as clothing and medical care. Two decades later, with the War on Poverty and blacks' increasing supervisory roles in welfare offices and job training programs, some white migrants resisted applying for aid not just because welfare departments were "highly bureaucratic, impersonal, with a lot of paperwork," but also because they resented dealing with black social workers and administrators. Moreover, media attention fostered the impression that "social programs [were] oriented toward blacks." A 1975 study of Appalachian migrants to Cincinnati, who together with their children made up 20 percent of the city's population, found that fully 55 percent of a sample population had "either received welfare benefits [including workmen's compensation] in the past or was receiving them at the time of the survey"; 20 percent of the city's black and 35 percent of the city's white population were on some sort of welfare at the time. These statistical profiles contradict the stereotype of the sturdy mountaineer who eschewed aid as a matter of principle.[32]

Some Appalachian migrants, like some rural migrants in general, continued to admonish their children, "Don't get above your raising," in deference to traditional values that prized kin obligations over individual achievement. Persistent concentrations of poor Southern-born whites highlighted the alienation of some of these people from formal educational institutions. With their high dropout rates and their poor attendance records, white youths remained immersed in a traditional culture—one reinforced by parental approval, inadequately funded school systems, and peer pressure—that kept them from acquiring the schooling that might have assured them passage into the suburbs. Indeed, the poorest migrants, and their children who remained in these slums, were distinctive (compared to their counterparts in the black ghetto) for their general lack of commitment to schooling; according to two Cincinnati studies, blacks as a group stayed in school longer than young people in Appalachian neighborhoods, but blacks as a group failed to receive the requisite "payoff" in the form of better jobs.[33]

Changes in gender roles, like attitudes toward schooling, provide an indicator of the ability, or willingness, of migrants to embrace an urban way of life. In general, in the North, Southern white migrant women worked outside the home in lesser numbers compared to blacks, simply because of the advantageous position of their menfolk—a position that was purely relative. Like black women from the plantation South, Appalachian women were accustomed to performing a variety of tasks related to household maintenance, but through the 1950s, few of these white women had extensive experience with wage earning in general or machine work in particular. For a woman who had never seen her mother or aunts responsible for work outside the home in addition to the routine chores within it, an apparent unequal division of labor between wage-earning wives and husbands could come as quite a shock: "I thought to myself that I'd been away from home as long as he was, that day and every day, working as hard as I knew how. So I deserve a little respect too." Observers often commented on the strains in marital relations that resulted when the family needed a wife's earnings but her husband could not reconcile himself to his own sense of inadequacy as breadwinner.[34]

Descriptions of poor white women, careworn mothers with too many children, wives who contended with "alcoholic bums" for husbands, and "good women who did their best and worked themselves to death" evoke the "black matriarch" stereotype. Observers commented on the networks of mutual support that sustained kin and neighbors: "all the women have some other women who are on welfare or very poor and they sort of follow each other around the city [Chicago]. They have this one friend who always lends them money, they are always in debt to each other, there is a circle of two, three, four people who are always lending each other money because the check is late or they have to take a taxi and there is nothing left for that." (As documented in Carol Stack's anthropological study, *All Our Kin*, similar kinds of networks bound together poor black women in a Midwestern town.) This female ethos of mutuality was often juxtaposed to a street-corner culture that glorified a masculine sensibility of individualism, physical aggression, and raw misogyny. When a white wife remarked of her husband claimed by the tavern, "He's lost in sin now," she articulated a mighty disappointment that, unknown to her, joined her in sorrowful sisterhood with like-minded black women. Nevertheless, the experiences of even very poor white women might diverge from those of their black counterparts; as migrants from Southern households that had tried to maintain some semblance of foodstuff self-sufficiency (through the ubiquitous vegetable patch), these women might feel a loss of domestic productivity that black women back south had never known. Moreover, even poorly educated white women found jobs as sales clerks, office receptionists, or factory workers while black women remained segregated in institutional or personal service.[35]

A white husband mortified that he was unable to provide for the family on his own might decide to return south, either with or without the entire household, and seek comfort from his kin. For white migrants, family ties in the North could facilitate the search for housing and employment, but family ties in the South could also offer a support system readily available in hard times; black migrants were at a disadvantage in both respects. Indeed, what some critics called maintaining a "biresidential family" or a "stumble around kind of living"; or working the "treadmill of never-ending transiency" affected almost every aspect of the poor Appalachian migrant's experience. Unable to make their way fully into the Northern middle class, some migrants left for home and never returned, while others went south for varying lengths of time, depending on their needs and inclinations. Weekend visitors to Kentucky could take advantage of discount flea-market sales and enjoy Sunday dinner with grandparents; laid-off operatives returned to work in the fields for seasons at a time; bachelors might venture "back to Kentucky to get a wife." This tendency soon worked its way into northern Appalachian folklore: Upon passing through the pearly gates, one startled angel wondered aloud why so many others were chained to a heavenly pole, and was told that St. Peter feared that they would otherwise all return to the mountains on the weekend. Apparently the locus of "paradise" was a matter of dispute.[36]

The combination of poverty and the perpetual lure of home (in the South) fragmented white families. At age thirty-two, Charlotte Gibson, the mother of ten children, aspired only to have a home of her own. Married in 1950 to Harold Gibson, eight years her senior, she and her children would spend the next decade and a half hungry, in transit between Logan, West Virginia, and Chicago's Uptown neighborhood, then back to live with her kin in and around Logan, only to return to Chicago, worn down by a series of round trips to despair. An abusive man, and unable to hold a steady job, Harold would disappear for months at a time, leaving his wife to rear their children in rat-infested apartments and to beg for help from disapproving landlords, truant officers, welfare bureaucrats, social workers, and private charity agencies. Much of the family's moving between West Virginia and Chicago reflected Charlotte's efforts to follow the whims of Harold's job quests. Bad luck seemed to dog his every step—a sudden layoff, a repossessed car. One promising stint as a coal miner in Logan came to an abrupt end soon after creditors started to garnishee his wages; he quit out of spite. When Uptown community activists recorded Charlotte's story in 1966, she and the children were on the verge of starvation, and Harold was drinking heavily, with not a shred of self-respect left; noted one interviewer, "The unmistakable self-esteem [he had] in West Virginia, his brandishing of pay stubs, his expansiveness as breadwinner and householder, his pride in arduous work, all decayed with disuse." The welfare officials who considered Charlotte Gibson's case saw only an irresponsible white woman unable to maintain steady contact with any agency or keep her children in school for any length of time. At least as long as the Gibson family resided in Uptown's slums, they were part of Chicago's white "underclass."[37]

WHITE FAMILIES AND THE BLACK COLLECTIVE

Despite their similarly low material condition, black and poor white migrants differed in their associational impulses because of past experience and current reality. Forcibly held in slave quarters or within a neoslavery plantation system since the early colonial period, black people had developed a sense of group solidarity; in contrast, Appalachians remained worshipful of the "farm freedom" they (or more likely their ancestors) had enjoyed down through the generations.[38] As a source of collective identity for the vast majority of migrants, the Appalachian Mountains represented slippery terrain. The poorest white migrants were neither here in the North nor there in the South, and their upwardly mobile neighbors considered themselves only temporary residents of the clusters in any case. Consequently, the lure of home for the poorest and the lure of the suburbs for the ambitious left community institutions in Appalachian neighborhoods weak and ineffectual.

One journalist observed that recent Appalachian migrants to the North lived in a ghetto that was "geographical" but not "social," a reference to its striking lack of formal cooperative effort of any kind. Religious affiliation offers a case in point. Appalachians in the North tended to favor ephemeral storefront churches over more sedate, established congregations. The storefronts led a precarious existence, totally dependent on the whims of individual pastors, some of whom, such as a Detroit religious leader in the 1950s, might find success in offering a "big city version of hill-billy religion in a rock-and-roll age." "'Guest preachers' from the southland" served as constant reminder to worshipers of their divided loyalties and had the added benefit of keeping "the people from gettin tired of" their regular minister. Researchers who studied these churches in Cleveland, Detroit, and Chicago drew a careful distinction between religious belief and church attendance; in Detroit three-fourths of all southern Appalachians interviewed for one study "retained a firm belief in faith healing," yet not one of them went to church on a regular basis.[39]

Scholars who have studied the group life of Appalachian neighborhoods invariably comment on the lack of political activity as compared to that of blacks, or of religious or ethnic groups. Unlike Italians or Greeks, Appalachian whites had no distinctive rituals or holidays (or, for that matter, a separate language or national tradition) that distinguished them from other native-born American Protestants. The poorest Appalachians evinced little enthusiasm for group membership in general; associational activity increased with class status. Until the early 1960s kin-oriented inner-city Appalachian clusters developed few if any advocacy groups that focused on housing or employment issues. Then social workers and community activists began to form organizations, such as Dayton's Our Common Heritage, Columbus's Central Ohio Appalachian Council, Hamilton's Appalachian People's Service Organization, and Cincinnati's Urban Appalachian Council; their purpose was to upgrade neighborhood conditions and to promote pride in an Appalachian heritage defined primarily in terms of music and folk crafts. Nevertheless, organizers remained torn between the issues of "cultural awareness" on the one hand and "social change" on the other, reflecting the scattered and fragmented nature of migrant settlement. Slum dwellers lacked the energy to become involved in these groups, and suburbanites tried to shun identification with "hillbillies," though they might create their own class-specific groups, such as the O'Tucks (Kentucky-born Ohioans).[40]

In fact, Southern migrants could claim no distinctive political organizations as their own. Conducted in the late 1969, a comparative study of the effects of "lower-class culture" on political participation focused on the Belmont neighborhood of Hamilton, along with two black ghettos (north central Philadelphia and the east side of Detroit); Summerhill, a black area in Atlanta; and a Mexican enclave in San Jose, California. Belmont was exceptional among all of these working-class communities by virtue of its "political indifference," expressed through low membership rates in "any kind of organization." The Appalachian migrants and their children who lived in Belmont had failed to develop a "class ideology"; they were poor but they lacked class consciousness. Since most poor whites were by definition nonhomeowners, they formed no "neighborhood improvement associations" used by other classes of whites to keep blacks out of their communities. An exception to this rule was South Lebanon, Ohio, where, in 1981, one resident acknowledged of his community, "if the people get excited about something, it's usually so that they can oppose something." A white youth gave an example when he defined the threat of black in-migration as a galvanizing force: "We gotta stay together to keep them out," he said. "That may be the one thing we do best—keeping the blacks out of town." Of course, in this respect, at least, the South Lebanese from Appalachia were probably not much different from other all-white neighborhoods in other parts of the country.[41]

Described as "the salvation shops which today are Detroit's second-great industry," some wartime Detroit churches that catered to Southern whites built vast tabernacles on the rock of racist demagoguery. It is not clear, however, that these organizations qualified as protopolitical movements formed in the service of any putative economic or social interests shared by Appalachians exclusively; indeed, it would be difficult to pinpoint such interests distinct from those of other poor whites. "Guest roof raisers" such as the Reverend Harvey Springer, the Cowboy Evangelist from Denver, could enthrall a congregation at the Christian Temple by lambasting gasoline rationing in one breath and excoriating Jews, Catholics, and blacks in the next. Nevertheless, responsibility for the city's racial and ethnic tensions went beyond the hate-mongering promoted by these churches. Nativist groups such as the Ku Klux Klan and the Black Legion enjoyed widespread support among a cross-section of Detroit's native-born Protestant population and included the city fathers as well as blue-collar auto workers.[42]

Appalachian migrants in the Midwest seemed to maintain a self-conscious individualism, as indifferent to appeals to their class consciousness as they were to the ballot box. Scholars and residents alike offered a variety of reasons—that their lack of spatial concentration failed to win them the favors of machine bosses or ward-level politicians; that steady employment for fathers and free school lunches for children "take the edge off the extreme poverty and brutality these people experienced" in the South; that since they worked so hard and for such long hours, during night shifts and overtime, they had little time to devote to larger political issues. A sociologist who studied Chicago's southern Appalachians in the early 1960s reported that full-time wage-earners considered themselves relatively successful in the North and resented political activists' attempts to portray them as either members of an oppressed proletariat or as simple, romantic mountain folk. Employing the former approach, Uptown's New Left organizers in the 1960s found the "Southern white culture . . . a very difficult one to organize in." Poor whites, with their high rates of (north-south) mobility, professed little interest in the need for either local or national long-term political change. Rennie Davis, a member of Students for a Democratic Society and organizer for a project called Jobs or Income Now (JOIN), believed that young jobless men, "with a tradition of violence in their families and most of them very anxious to maintain that tradition," represented a "potential revolutionary force"; but Davis also acknowledged that in trying to keep up with their streetwise ways, he felt compelled to "drink all day" on the corner with them. For Davis and his youthful comrades, staying "virtually drunk all week" hardly helped to focus their minds on grassroots organizing.[43]

When faced with classified housing advertisements that proclaimed "No Southerners need apply" or with restaurants that refused service to all "hillbillies" and "ridgerunners," poor whites might be tempted to follow the lead of the Detroit man who, according to one fanciful story, went straight to the local chapter of the National Association for the Advancement of Colored People (NAACP): "We ain't got nobody to take up for us, so do you think the NAACP will do something to these folks for us?" In 1958 an urban sociologist at Wayne State University called southern Appalachians the city's "most voiceless and the most scapegoated" people; "They have no NAACP or Urban League, no B'Nai B'rith or American Jewish Committee, no Hiberian League or Polish Refugee Association. Yet they are refugees—displaced persons—from our own blighted south. . . ." Later, in the mid-1960s, poor inner-city whites would pay the price of their own voicelessness as poverty programs quickly became identified with blacks

exclusively, at least partially because of ghetto leaders' political sophistication bolstered by a critical mass of black voters. For example, originally a German immigrant neighborhood, Cincinnati's Over-the-Rhine
became a port-of-entry for Appalachian migrants in 1940, when the area
"was in an advanced state of physical and social deterioration." Two
decades later another group moved in—"blacks, mostly displaced from
large scale improvements in the West End." Noted one observer, "They,
unlike the Appalachians, wanted a stronger voice in their own destiny,
and the Federal government gave them the opportunity," through the
Model Cities and other New Society programs—though to little longlasting effect.[44]

About the only similarity between the political orientation of white
slum dwellers and black ghetto residents was the lack of class ideology,
or rhetoric, that emanated from their respective communities. For
blacks in Chicago's South Side, Detroit's Grand Boulevard neighborhood, or Cleveland's Central Avenue area, race, and not class, was the
standard by which all political activity was measured. This is not to suggest that social-class differences were nonexistent, or insignificant, within ghettos. In all three cities, the National Urban League (NUL) served
as a nervous mediator between white employer-benefactors and poor
blacks, Southern migrants and long-term residents alike. The NUL's
impulse for integration and middle-class respectability, and its efforts to
place blacks in any kind of jobs at all, contrasted with the black nationalist campaigns of Marcus Garvey (black Chicago was second only to
Harlem in its organized support for him) and the Black Muslims. These
efforts suggest the dilemma faced by black elites who depended on
whites for money, political favors, and jobs that might in turn be doled
out to their less fortunate brothers and sisters; racial issues overrode, but
could never completely obscure, class relations between blacks and
whites, and among blacks, within the urban political economy.[45]

Curiously, some observers have seemed intent on focusing on patterns of so-called black dependency (as revealed, more specifically, by
Aid to Families with Dependent Children recipients), while ignoring
black collective efforts that ranged from settlement houses to charitable
and benevolent societies, workers' organizations, housewives' leagues,
and church day care centers. It is not the purpose of this discussion to
chronicle the political achievements—and setbacks—of black communities in the urban Midwest. Rather, it is worth noting the vast number and
variety of black advocacy and self-help groups that touched almost every
aspect of ghetto life in the post–Great Migration period. These groups,
some well funded and enduring, others makeshift and short-lived, aimed

to fill the gap left by the discriminatory policies of public and private welfare agencies (from Travelers Aid to the United Way) and to press for black civil rights in the courts, in the workplace, and in the schools. The stories of these organizations play a prominent part in the memoirs of individual men and women, in scholarly community studies, and in institutional histories for Detroit, Chicago, Cleveland, and other major American cities as well. Whether sponsored by the NAACP or the Congress for Racial Equality, the African Methodist Episcopal Church or the Communist party, a segregated Y, ad hoc neighborhood groups, or a lone, inspired individual, these groups reveal a tradition of group resourcefulness, a tradition that originated in the slave quarters, continued in the postbellum rural South, and found a new, if similarly harsh, home in the urban North.

The role of blacks in organized labor in particular reveals the strong collective impulse that characterized the historic black community, an impulse sharpened and focused by Jim Crow, Northern-style. When migrants encountered racist employers in the Midwest, they drew on a Southern legacy and language of struggle that informed their response. In the eyes of Jesse Reese, a black worker at the Youngstown Sheet and Tube tin mill, a new, mean-spirited boss was a "slave driver" as well as a member of the Ku Klux Klan—in other words, a late-1930s Northern incarnation of Southern racial prejudice. In contrast, Appalachian whites had little in the way of historical experience to prepare them for the hostility they faced from other workers. One woman auto worker in Detroit seemed at a loss to account for the stereotyping of hillbillies; she used the analagy of racism as a result: "People fight against us Southern whites. We are on the same basis as Negroes."[46]

To blacks, labor activism was part of a larger mission, one intimately connected with their new home in the Democratic party, and labor unions and broad-based civil rights organizations were logical, if not always comfortable, allies. Neither white women nor Appalachian migrants organized advocacy organizations that could in any way compare to the efforts of African-Americans through the 1960s. During World War II discrimination in the West Coast shipbuilding industry in general and the boilermakers' union in particular called forth the efforts of the NAACP in cooperation with the Shipyard Negro Organization for Victory (Portland), the Shipyard Workers Committee for Equal Participation in the Unions (Los Angeles), and the Bay Area Council Against Discrimination (San Francisco-Oakland). Between 1925 and 1972 a whole host of national black labor groups pressed for the end of discriminatory policies; though these groups ran the political gamut from Communist-backed black congresses to committees of conservative trade unionists, they were all responding to the overt barriers that excluded blacks from various unions and denied them their fair share of decent jobs throughout the nation.[47]

When black people could play an active part in molding a labor organization, they gained a sense of pride and control over their own destiny. An all-black union such as the Brotherhood of Sleeping Car Porters (BSCP), founded in 1925 by A. Philip Randolph, instilled in its members the self-confidence that came with being part of a larger group, part of a well-defined cause. Rosina C. Tucker, the leader of a BSCP Ladies Auxilliary, later recalled, "Not only were these men helped financially, they were helped educationally. They grew in knowledge, and they were able to do things that they never dreamed of doing before. . . . It was a benefit in almost every area of life, for these men. It was wonderful." Progressive, racially integrated unions went further in rewarding blacks for their strong ethos of worker solidarity. In particular, the labor militance and racial egalitarianism of the CIO in the late 1930s inspired men and women who had long distrusted white unions as one more instrument of oppression. Present at the violent birth of the CIO-affiliated steelworkers union in Youngstown in 1937, Jesse Reese found himself ducking to avoid the blows wielded by a policeman; he was amazed when he "saw that people were getting beat. I'd never seen police beat women, not white women. I'd seen them beat black women, but this was the first time I'd seen them beat white women—with sticks." In female auxiliaries affiliated with the UAW in Flint, Michigan, and with the Steel Workers' Organizing Committee in Chicago, black women came together with white women of various ethnic backgrounds, white women who had felt estranged from each other as well as from wives and mothers of a different race. Black women labor leaders' "sass" and "feistiness"—in the tradition of the verbal outspokenness practiced by their slave foremothers—now helped to advance the rights of all workers. In 1939 a black packinghouse worker in Chicago could claim that the CIO "done the greatest thing in the world gettin' everybody who works in the yards together, and breakin' up the hate and bad feelings that used to be held against the Negro."[48]

And yet in the mid-1950s, Cold War politics caused Big Labor to draw back from civil rights; by that time, according to historian Herbert Hill, "the CIO commitment to racial justice had become abstract and ritualized." Over the next few years the decline of heavy manufacturing would leave black workers persistently vulnerable, whether or not they were union members. Nevertheless, nearly fifty years after the founding of the CIO, black blue-collar and white-collar workers continued to put their faith in the labor movement to a much greater degree than their white counterparts in similar job categories.[49]

It is more difficult to generalize about the role of Appalachian migrants in the great labor battles of the 1930s and 1940s. In some instances migrants took north with them a lifelong dedication to union activism as a result of their earlier support for the United Mine Workers, which launched organizing drives in West Virginia and Kentucky just as bloody and bitter as any sponsored by other unions in the North. On the other hand, a case study of one UAW local (in Hamtramnck, a Polish community in Detroit) reveals that labor activism appealed to white Southern migrants according to their job status and their residential stability. Among the more highly skilled workers who rarely returned to their native state, an "evangelical commitment to the UAW was for them a commitment to an urban way of life as much as it was to trade unionism." Less skilled Southern white migrants proved exceptionally reluctant to cast their lot with collective action of any kind, and ultimately, "the act of joining was highly individual." If Appalachian migrants recoiled from the prospect of fraternizing with blacks in a tavern or at a union meeting, they probably did so in the same proportion as members of various white ethnic groups, whether in Ohio's Mahoning (steel and iron) Valley, in a Cleveland rubber plant, or on a Detroit auto assembly line.[50]

Throughout the Midwest, the residential segregation of blacks solidified their status as second-class citizens, even as it facilitated their political organization. Between 1940 and 1970, black people in Detroit, for example, had abundant reason to see themselves as a group apart from the white working class. On the job, black auto workers were the targets of hate strikes initiated by whites, recent migrants from the South as well as ethnic groups that "had acquired negrophobia as part of their Americanization." Blacks, confined to the worst jobs, charged that the dangerous speedups they endured were more accurately a form of "niggermation" than "automation." Outside the workplace, they lived in congested neighborhoods hemmed in by white-instigated terrorism, restrictive covenants, zoning restrictions, and a complicitous Federal Housing Administration. In one black neighborhood, the particularly "tight-knit" East Side, leaders scornfully denounced UAW influence in the community as "plantation politics." If Representative John Conyers's impression of the Detroit Riot of 1967 was correct—that it constituted "a war of the haves against the have-nots"—then it was no surprise that city policemen found a few poor whites caught up in their dragnet of looters. Nevertheless, the physical concentration of blacks made them more vulnerable to the depredations of power elites, in contrast to their more dispersed fellow migrants, Appalachian whites. In 1971 the police department formed a special law enforcement unit called STRESS (Stop the Robberies; Enjoy Safe Streets), and in the process gave license to police brutality toward black citizens.[51]

It was no wonder, then, that over the years black people in Detroit formed a series of their own labor organizations, from the Trade Union Leadership Conference in 1957 to the Black Power–inspired League of Revolutionary Black Workers (LRBW), an umbrella group that included the Dodge Revolutionary Union Movement and other company- and plant-based associations, in 1969. Nevertheless, internal tensions prevented black workers from presenting a united front in opposition to white authority, especially when a distinct class or gender group presumed to speak on behalf of "the black community" at large. Some of these tensions were long-standing—for example, conflicts between, on the one hand, the integrationist-minded National Urban League, with its white patrons, and, on the other, militant nationalist and labor groups. During this period the Black Power Movement in general highlighted gender and age differences within the black working class. In the course of the LRBW's brief life, for example, some older black women workers expressed their fear of young black men who were more preoccupied with asserting their manhood than with addressing the grievances of all employees regardless of sex or seniority.[52]

By the late 1960s, with invidious racial distinctions expunged from job descriptions, union apprenticeship programs, and the bylaws of "neighborhood improvement associations," black advocacy groups could declare their mission accomplished, without much tangible evidence to prove it. Meanwhile, ghettos in the largest Midwestern cities were undergoing structural changes that sapped strength from institutions based on place as much as race. When whites fled to the suburbs and working-class fringes, they took jobs with them; and new businesses had few incentives to locate within "decaying" inner-city cores. Chicago, Detroit, and Cleveland ranked high among all the cities losing employment opportunities from the late 1950s on. Detroit's loss of 100,000 jobs during the 1970s and early 1980s signaled only the last stages in the precipitous decline of a blue-collar sector for blacks, a decline that had begun fifteen or twenty years earlier. The percentage of black female-headed households began to rise dramatically in response to these trends affecting the urban labor market. In contrast to the earlier Northern black community, with its full range of classes, including a large proportion of strivers, the late-twentieth-century ghetto contained mainly impoverished people, few of whom had the resources or where-withal to press for reversals in the deterioration of local job markets, housing, or schools. The black middle classes, for the first time in American history able to pursue residential and employment opportuni-ties outside their own communities, could hardly have been expected to forgo the reality of a dream that promised not only rewards commensu-rate with their talents but also neighborhoods safe enough for children. It was during this time too that demographers noted the beginnings of a return migration to the South among relatively well-educated blacks headed for the Sunbelt. In the end, given the opportunity, few would choose to live in an area where a housing project such as Chicago's Cabrini-Green determined the health and welfare of neighborhood resi-dents. Once again the South would serve as a safety valve of sorts, this time for black people who measured the North against the expectations of their Southern parents, and found it wanting.

Born in 1903 in Mississippi, Howard Spence knew life in the twentieth-century rural South at its very worst and very best. The oldest of nine chil-dren in a father-absent family, he picked cotton and cut railroad ties as a youth before moving north to Chicago in 1920. There he worked at a vari-ety of jobs, as a shoe shiner, a candy-store operator, a chauffeur, and a factory laborer. During World War II he went back south to serve as an NAACP organizer in voter registration drives; later, he was instrumental in drawing media attention to the murder of fourteen-year-old Emmett Till, the symbol to many Northern blacks of the South as an enduring no-black-man's-land. In the 1950s Howard Spence went back north, this time to Sacramento, but in 1975 he became "part of the pilgrimage back South" when he decided to move permanently to Verian, Mississippi, where he had lived earlier. Active in town politics, impressed by the fact that in Verian now "They don't call me Uncle Howard, Preacher, or boy no more," Howard Spence offered this observation on life in the urban North:

> You couldn't *give* me a place in Chicago. You couldn't *give* me a place in Detroit or New York or Philadelphia . . . I got people up there [in Chicago]. If they die, well, if they don't bring them home I don't go to the funeral. See, I was there when you could sleep in the park all night and nobody wouldn't bother your pocketbook. . . . Now my sister's house is barred up like a jail. You go through about three iron doors before you can get inside the house. And they still come in. . . . And you mean to tell me I want my last days to be like that? When I can

sleep with my doors wide open and the birds wake me in the morning and [I can] smell the flowers?[53]

Howard Spence's comments hardly suggest that the small-town South was a latter-day paradise for blacks; as an older, retired man his interests were different from those of younger people in town who were trying to find good jobs for themselves and good schools for their children. But Spence's comparison between urban North and rural South in the late twentieth century does reveal the elusive nature of the "promised land." By that time the vulnerable status of inner-city blacks was revealed most starkly in their relative immobility, for they lacked the most basic resource possessed by even the poorest of their forebears—the hope for a decent life elsewhere.

In 1980, when the Seiberling plant of Firestone Tire and Rubber Company closed its doors, 1,200 workers in the town of Barberton, Ohio, lost their jobs, and the United Rubber Workers local there ceased to exist. Throughout Summit County, a total of 20,000 men and women were unemployed due to plant closings in the rubber industry. Two years later only one-fifth of the former Seiberling employees had located jobs that paid as well as their previous work; the rest had taken low-paying service jobs or remained out of work altogether. For four decades before the Seiberling shutdown, Barberton, with its unionized rubber, glass, and brass plants, had boasted a comfortable standard of living for blue-collar workers who reaped the benefits of high labor demand. Migrants had arrived in large numbers from West Virginia, Kentucky, and Tennessee, giving the town a distinctive "country identity." But in the 1970s the local rubber industry, like other heavy manufacturing interests in the Midwest, had fallen victim to two related developments—foreign competition and the quest for cheap labor; in 1972 Sun Rubber of Barberton had tried to cut costs by cutting wages, and responded to an ensuing strike by joining the parade of "runaway shops" to the Sunbelt—in this case, to Georgia.[54]

An observer of Barberton in the early 1980s pronounced it full of "detritus, decay, a social garbage heap." Unemployed workers harkened back to their Appalachian roots of "making do" and tried to hunt, fish, and forage, but widespread industrial pollution had rendered the surrounding rivers, marshes, and forests noxious and lifeless. Older workers in particular found it difficult to relocate elsewhere; many were homeowners, unable to sell their property; they could not afford moving costs; and they were loath to sever kin ties and start anew alone. In the community where so many people were stripped of their livelihoods and their personal dignity, crime, illegal drug use, alcoholism, teenage pregnancy, and other manifestations of stress and despair multiplied and festered. The attempt to organize a council of unemployed workers foundered because of a high turnover rate among the group's leaders.[55]

The son of a West Virginian who had come to Ohio to toil in the "gum mines," Mark Burke had worked at the Seiberling plant for a decade before he was laid off in 1980. Over the next few years he would work at an "under the table" job for two tax-free dollars an hour, journey to Florida for a brief stint as a construction worker, and ferret out a number of odd jobs in the vicinity of Barberton—doing yard work, chopping wood. Once the proud member of the rubber workers union, he now spent much of his time trying to drown his own bitterness and shame in the bottle. He said to a sympathetic listener, "There's a big difference between what I could be and what I am."[56]

Throughout American history, groups of black and white workers had found themselves side by side—working together in a seventeenth-century Virginia tobacco field, or later as cotton choppers, phosphate miners, or bean pickers; or applying for entry-level jobs at wartime defense plants. Invariably, the histories of these particular groups of workers diverged according to the color of their skin, though sooner or later other groups in different places would continue to mock the color line by their sheer proximity to one another. In the late twentieth century the children of Southern migrants to the Midwest still lived in racially segregated communities, but the inner-city ghetto and "rust belt" full of displaced steel, rubber, and auto workers began to show similar signs of social breakdown. The preoccupation of middle-class white America with the pathology of the black ghetto only served to hide the plight of people who knew all too well that whiteness was never an absolute, or final, advantage.

PART IV

POSTMODERN POVERTY IN AMERICA

9

American "Underclasses" in the Late Twentieth Century

In the late twentieth century, in absolute terms, the locus of poverty in the United States was not black, Northern, or urban. Census data for 1990 revealed that poor whites (21 million) outnumbered poor blacks (9 million) by a ratio of two to one. Black people constituted a minority (39 percent) of all Aid to Families with Dependent Children (AFDC) recipients. A majority of poor Americans lived outside central cities—in rural areas, small towns, metropolitan areas, and suburbs. Measured in terms of actual physical want, poverty was greatest in the states of Texas, South Dakota, and Missouri, which together accounted for one-half of the nation's 150 "worst hunger counties"; poor people there lacked access to the federal food stamp program, and "large numbers of residents face[d] nutritional deprivation." Southerners living below the poverty line (13 million) were more numerous than their counterparts in the Northeastern and Midwestern states combined (a total of 12 million persons). The South had the highest proportion of poor children (26 percent of its population under six years of age) of any region in the country. Less than half (46 percent) of poor children lived in inner cities. A higher percentage of black female-headed households in rural areas fell below the poverty line (64 percent) compared to similarly constituted households in the inner city (51 percent).[1]

Given these figures, the fact that many Americans continued to associate poverty primarily with the Northern, urban black "underclass" calls for an explanation. The disproportionate number of blacks living below the poverty line and the historical roots of their persistent poverty help to account for at least some of the attention they received from the news media and national policymakers. In the early 1990s, the poverty rate among black Americans was 28 percent, compared to 8.8 percent among whites. Nearly half of all black children lived in poor households (the comparable figure for whites was 13 percent), and nearly three-quarters of these children lived in female-headed households (as opposed to 46 percent of poor white children). About half of all black families were headed by a woman, but only 14.3 percent of white families. Of all poor black people, six out of ten lived in central cities, but only one out of three poor whites lived in these areas. Clearly, then, poverty was not an exclusively black problem, but it did affect black people to a disproportionate degree, a fact not unrelated to the system of slavery that pervaded the southern United States until 1865.

Still, black ghettos seemed to attract more than their fair share of pity, or scorn, for reasons that reflected contemporary American values and priorities. More particularly, sensational stories about the "underclass" (defined rather narrowly in terms of persistent, concentrated poverty) resonated within a white middle class caught up in its own fascination with sex, violence, and alcohol and drug abuse. A focus on urban areas simply made the poor, in their "concentration," easier to count by census tract.[2] Moreover, this focus seemed to confirm traditional American beliefs that poverty on the countryside was somehow cleaner, healthier, more wholesome, and less degrading than its inner-city counterpart.[3] Ghetto street life, though hardly representative of African-American culture or community values, assumed a threatening cast, but in a perversely appealing way, to a society that condoned the widespread ownership and use of firearms; routine substance abuse;[4] and the blatant exploitation of female sexuality. In the late 1980s, in a series of widely publicized cases involving attacks and alleged attacks by young black men on young, white, middle-class women, that street culture seemed to spill out of its own boundaries and affect the safety and security of privileged Americans. The pathological sin-sex-race "tangle" described by Lillian Smith as long characteristic of Southern life now came to pervade the national consciousness in the form of "emblematic violence on the [Northern] streets."[5]

Accordingly, the claim that ghetto life represented a bizarre subculture of pathology and social deviance not only objectified the black poor as "others" but also missed larger issues. First, stories of ordinary black people who tried their best to make do with very little in the way of material resources became lost amid generalizations about the "exotic" quality of black inner-city life. Second, even ghetto youth street culture reflected certain "mainstream" values, although in a particularly violent way. Finally, violence perpetrated by teenage youths was common to poor neighborhoods throughout the country, and not unique to ghetto streets. In any case, the grip of the black "underclass" on the American imagination served to obscure the historical and economic processes that by this time had created a multitude of "underclasses," people who were neither black nor the residents of Northern cities. By the late twentieth century a growing population of immigrants from Latin America, the Philippines, China, India, and Southeast Asia, combined with structural transformations in the American economy that affected the previously secure white working class, revealed the political—and moral—limitations of a continuing focus on race and urban residence as the defining characteristics of the poor.

The problem of poverty in America was a problem endemic to the national economy and embedded in the country's history and political culture. Ever since tobacco planters in early-seventeenth-century Virginia expressed their "contempt for both the poor and the black,"[6] by setting Africans and English indentured servants to work in the fields, the profits enjoyed by a few have been extracted from the toil of many. But exploitation of labor tells only part of the story; over the generations employers and, ultimately, the imperatives of a worldwide commercial market not only drew workers into a national economy, albeit at a lowly level, but also, more recently, expelled them from the economy altogether. Such was the nature of technological progress, of regional development, of business efficiency, all bought at a price—the impoverishment of various groups through chronic underemployment, culminating in a late-twentieth-century process of marginalization that left increasing numbers of people outside the world of gainful employment. Submerged under these global forces of integration and consolidation lay the struggles of ordinary people to labor for their own well-being and keep their families together in the process.

The dispossession of various groups then was an inevitable consequence of American economic growth. Neverthless, in the minds of many more fortunate Americans, the issue of poverty remained inextricably linked to morality. Here, productive labor formed the crux of the issue, though "work" was defined in exceedingly narrow terms, as steady, long-term participation in the paid labor force. For example, Social Security, an entitlement program for older citizens regardless of race, sex or class, won general favor among Americans, because assistance was contingent on employment or dependence on someone who had been employed. The result was a program that, in a fifty-year period, dramatically cut the poverty rate among Americans over sixty-five.[7] Aid to Families with Dependent Children payments, which in 1988 went to less than 5 percent of the American population (10.8 million individuals, almost all of them women and children), were stigmatized as "welfare," while Social Security was not. The federal funds committed to AFDC represented less than 2 percent of the national budget; over a seventeen-year period (1970–87), real benefits fell by 37 percent.[8] Many poor households were, of course, entitled to more assistance, from various programs, which they never received; red tape was a form of moral authority that discouraged the needy from pressing their claims through an impersonal bureaucracy.

In any case, by the 1990s much of the widening gap between the rich and the poor resulted not from the growing ranks of the unemployed but from the worsening relative position of two-parent families that could not earn a living wage. In a global economy that depended on highly credentialed workers in specific technical fields, employees in the traditional service sector, as well as those in manufacturing pursuits increasingly dominated by computers and robotics, suffered a drop in wages during the 1970s and 1980s. Therefore, poverty became more and more a problem of gainfully employed persons; employment per se was less an issue than the kind of employment available to people without formal education.[9]

Twenty-five years after the start of the federal antipoverty initiative known as the War on Poverty, American voters (and the two major political parties that represented them) expressed their reluctance to commit more tax monies to measures that had produced so little in the way of tangible results. In the 1980s the Reagan administration was successful in shifting part of the burden for a whole host of human services away from federal responsibility and onto already beleagured state and local governments; under conditions of fiscal constraint few lawmakers at any level dared to think boldly about the plight of displaced workers and their children. A plethora of scholarly research demonstrating (in the late 1980s, for example) the positive effects of even relatively modest programs, such as prenatal education for pregnant women and early childhood programs for their offspring, had little effect on the priorities of national policymakers. Though popular in principle with the electorate, "workfare" programs remained underfunded and shortsighted. Mothers often had no economic incentive to train for clerical jobs that would prove counterproductive to the welfare of their children; most of these jobs were low-paying and insufficient to raise a household out of poverty, and also deprived workers of the medical benefits they received from AFDC.[10] For inquiring congressional committees, richly textured ethnographies of poor communities provided an entrée into the supposedly curious lives and rituals of the poor but offered no specific solutions, while massive compilations of data on narrow issues were always vulnerable to criticism on methodological or statistical grounds. Thus a deep malaise afflicted the national will to act to eradicate the causes of social and economic distress, causes that were multiplying and intensifying in a postindustrial society.

In effect, poverty programs and policies enacted during the New Deal and afterward reflected less the objective situation of families at risk than a specific political ideology. At the heart of that ideology lay the issue of race—a problematic notion in any case—rather than the more relevant issue and more meaningful analytic concept of class. Given the limited enthusiasm with which most Americans contemplated poverty and its possible solutions in the first place, it was no wonder that the intense scrutiny accorded the black "underclass" came at the expense of attention and concern for other poor groups. And yet comfortable Americans were living in a world, and not just a nation, of many "underclasses," groups and communities sharing certain vulnerabilities that transcended race and culture.

WHAT'S NEW IN THE NORTH:
OR, KIDS KILLING FOR CRACK AND SNEAKERS

For Southern migrants to Northern ghettos, the racial prejudice and institutional restraints they encountered in their new home were hardly new; in certain significant respects, Southern society served as a prototype for its Northern counterpart. The urban poor tried to make do with the little they had, at times in ways that eluded the scrutiny of officials paid to monitor their behavior, and they continued to demonstrate high rates of job and residential turnover in ways reminiscent of their "shifting" forbears. Nevertheless, by the late twentieth century ghetto neighborhoods had fallen victim to the twin plagues of drugs and guns; now residents feared for their lives not at the hands of Klansmen, but at the hands of their own children—teenagers and young men who, either singly or in gangs, preyed upon people of their own race. However, this fact alone revealed little that was distinctive about African-American culture. A small number of youths participated in muggings or "wildings," leaving the vast majority of black men to deal with the residual effects—that is, the fear and suspicion with which whites and blacks alike greeted almost any black man on the streets, especially at night. Moreover, crime patterns in all places, not just black ones, reflected to a great extent a community's peculiar social ecology, consisting of available jobs, educational resources, and physical layout as well as the attitudes of adults toward various kinds of crimes and their youthful perpetrators. Comparative data on crime therefore suggest that black ghettos were but one kind of crime-ridden neighborhood, and that Hispanic and poor-white communities confronted their own problems in this regard, though with variations based on their respective mix of job and schooling opportunities. Still, this particular perspective offered cold comfort to the black people who lived in dread of youths with their "quasi-military swagger," youths who sought to "act right" by peer-group standards.[11]

Northern urban cores deteriorated dramatically after 1960 or so—the result of urban renewal projects that displaced and dispersed ghetto residents, the flight of the black middle class, and declining entry-level job opportunities for the poor who remained behind. In the late 1980s, for example, "nostalgia [was] rampant" among older black residents of New Haven, Connecticut, men and women who had worked hard at service and manufacturing jobs in the 1940s and 1950s and had walked the streets at night in safety. But now gangs of youths, murderous "posses," held their neighborhoods hostage. Coming of age at a time when commercial TV and rap music, and sports and movie stars, set the standards for success and self-satisfaction, at a time when "the idea of the dignity of labor has come to seem quaint at best," some ghetto young people of New Haven saw, in the words of one observer, "washing dishes or frying burgers for a risible wage . . . [as] an act of either blind faith or sheer desperation." Some of them preferred hustling over "scuffling" for "the Man." Beginning in 1985 the appearance of crack cocaine in several major U.S. cities (most notably Washington, D.C., Detroit, and New York) had signaled the death of culture within affected households—

most of them poor, and many of them black—"When they got on that stuff, they don't even know their own mother."[12]

In practical terms, working definitions of the word "underclass" hindered rather than advanced an understanding of these particular issues in the ghetto. Scholars tended to focus on racially segregated, "hyperghettoized" areas and to suggest that the "concentrated" poor were by definition "isolated" from mainstream society. In fact, even the poorest urban census tracts consisted of some people who were blue-collar workers (postal and transit employees, for example) and others whose wages were insufficient to raise them above the poverty line. These residents took pains to distance themselves from the youth culture that surrounded them and too often invaded their own homes. The mother of a young black man accused of murder could declare: "I'm a working person, and a working person doesn't know what's going on on the streets." Most youths understood that they followed a way of life condemned by their elders, especially elderly women. The ghetto abounded in plenty of role models who pointed in the direction of decent behavior; but too often they went unheeded.[13]

The definition of the underclass in terms of "antisocial" behavior was especially misleading. The entrepreneurial impulse that led some youths into selling newspapers and others into selling stolen goods was less inherently "destructive" than the context in which it was carried out. The life cycle of families suggested that such behavior in any case was not an unvarying characteristic of certain deviant individuals. Perhaps the grandmotherly antidrug activist was once herself a teenage mother. The public laments of older black women in particular—the long-suffering caretakers of grandchildren and, in some cases, of their own drug-using or drug-dealing children—highlighted generational and gender issues. These issues, while assuming a special poignancy in the AIDS-afflicted, crack-addicted 1990s, had roots in the rural South, when righteous-living women railed against the demons of dance and drink that consumed their menfolk and their offspring of both sexes. Moreover, the lines between moral and immoral behavior were never clearly drawn in the lives of single individuals—the crack-dealing father who plied his trade on the mean streets of Harlem in an effort to pay the rent and provide for his wife and young son; the welfare mother who tried to escape from a bullet-scarred housing project for the sake of her family; the drug dealer who shielded her small children from the sight of narcotics agents tearing through their apartment; the young prostitute who refused to participate in a "freak show" (a sex show for crack users) because she could not find a babysitter for her child. These parents mourned for the lost innocence of their sons and daughters, but "around here the devil's always knocking on the door."[14]

Among the poor, household strategies for survival assumed a number of different forms, but usually the goal was a predictable, ordinary one—to care for children and maintain ties among the generations. Thus the charge that the underclass had priorities quite different from the middle class confused means with ends. Like the sharecroppers forced to scrounge for wage work to supplement their inadequate "furnishings," inner-city folk faced the undeniable fact that one minimum-wage job was insufficient to feed, clothe, and house a mother and her children. Hence individuals and groups of neighbors and networks of kin devised diverse ways to survive. They rearranged their households, pooled their resources, and parcelled out tasks on the basis of age and sex. Income came from "working off the books"; negotiating around, or manipulating, the welfare bureaucracy; part-time jobs; and soliciting aid from friends, parents, and former boyfriends. The adults who worked in fly-by-night sweatshops with false Social Security cards did so not because they were criminally inclined but because they knew that, if they reported extra income, their welfare payments would be docked in proportion to their own initiative in supporting themselves.[15]

In Northern ghettos, the South of the past and present loomed large. A chain migration out of the South replenished ghetto neighborhoods and encouraged continuous visits between New York and North Carolina, Mississippi and Chicago. As the economic infrastructure of places such as Shelby, Mississippi, became indistinguishable from that of places such as inner-city Cleveland, the North's dangerous but highly lucrative underground economy offered inducement for some young people to catch a ride out of the South. In the late 1980s on the wall of a Detroit crack house was posted a notice that promised enterprising and hopeful employees: "[with] hard work and dedication we will all be rich within 12 months." Such a prediction seemed to be confirmed by the spectacular careers of the owners of the business, the Chambers brothers of Arkansas, who left Lee County (one of the ten poorest in the nation) in the 1970s and soon emerged as the "Lee Iacoccas of the Lower East Side." For the brothers, plunged into the maelstrom of a drug underworld and eventually arrested and convicted on a variety of charges, the way north brought only fleeting glory, a momentary triumph that mocked the more modest, but equally unfulfilled, aspirations of the men and women who went before them.[16]

Just as emancipation from slavery was not sufficient to ensure political equality for black Americans, so the Civil Rights Acts of 1965 failed to reverse historic patterns of economic inequality that kept large numbers of black people impoverished and politically powerless. In the late nineteenth century and on into the twentieth, registrars in the rural South perfected the technique of the bluff in intimidating potential black voters, and in the late twentieth century, urban Northern welfare workers badgered and insulted aid applicants who deeply resented patently unfair rules and regulations in the first place. The belief that black people should accept any kind of employment so they could work for the sake of working evoked the principles espoused by postbellum cotton planters, prompting ghetto men to chide their peers stuck in ill-paid service jobs as "slaves." Private-sector workers, of course, remained ineligible for health care and child care subsidies; the problem lay not with an overly generous welfare state but with the paltry wages and benefits that were the hallmark of "free enterprise." The erosion of employment opportunities in heavy industry meant that in 1988, black people were overrepresented in the following jobs (by a factor of two to three times their proportion of the total population): nursing aides, orderlies, and attendants; cleaners and servants; maids and housemen; taxi cab drivers and industrial truck and tractor equipment operators. Black mothers continued to make a relatively greater contribution to the family income compared to their white counterparts; the steady decline in job options for their menfolk held constant certain underlying patterns in the household economy that had long mandated the labor of women and children. The oft-repeated charge that the poor in general and welfare recipients in particular were lazy and shiftless proved tenacious in the face of evidence that most were continually in and out of the paid labor force, and stayed out for understandable reasons—ill health, child care responsibilities, inability to find a job that would compensate for high commuting costs.[17]

In the ghetto, foraging assumed a number of different forms—rummaging through trash cans for food and redeemable aluminum cans; looking for coins in pay phones; tending a vegetable garden in a vacant lot; grabbing apples and oranges not from a landlord's tree but from the shelves of a neighborhood fruit stand; hustling neighbors and strangers for cash, drugs, and cigarettes. Self-employed workers ran the gamut from hairdressers to card sharks—anyone offering goods and services (including entertainment), for pay. A strong cooperative ethos among kin meant that middle-class black professionals in the suburbs continued to support informal systems of income redistribution on behalf of their needy relatives left behind in the inner city; the demands for help, especially in times of crisis, seemed infinite, while white-collar paychecks were finite: "Your brother's sick. He needs to see somebody. What are you going to do?"[18]

Neoconservatives might make much of constitutional guarantees of political equality for all Americans and the equal economic opportunity that allegedly flowed from basic rights; but in a society of radically unequal places, poverty negated the notion of "opportunity." Poor people moved around within the urban economy a great deal, while high housing prices outside (and even, in the case of gentrified blocks, inside) the ghetto kept them confined to certain areas. In contrast to the late-nineteenth-century cotton South, where planters eagerly sought after field hands, Northern urban employers drastically lessened their reliance on black labor as the twentieth century wore on; and yet, in both places, the result was shifting, high residential and job turnover within a narrowly circumscribed area. Throughout ghetto neighborhoods (and the nation at large), employment instability remained highest among the poorest workers—people who lacked full-time or minimum-wage jobs, people in poor health without medical benefits, mothers with intractable child care problems, employees who would not or could not show "loyalty" to employers who regarded them as unworthy of decent pay and decent working conditions. A 1983 survey of Chicago recipients of Aid to Families with Dependent Children revealed that nearly one-third of the respondents had moved at least once within the last twelve months; some had suffered a loss of income, or eviction, while others had sought out a larger, or safer, place. In the late 1980s Madeline Cartwright, a school principal in North Philadelphia, told an interviewer that the single mothers of the children in her school could barely meet necessary household expenses with bimonthly welfare checks of $130: "So they just move and move. They live in these abandoned houses, no running water, with an electric wire that came from next door to their house. The kids take a two-liter soda container and go borrow water. That's how our children live." Cartwright pointed out the connection between poor housing and a marginalized existence: "Many of our children don't have addresses. They don't have anything."[19]

Like the localized plantation economy, the ghetto consisted of an enclosed area where educational and employment resources were limited. In the 1970s and 1980s native-born young black people made impressive gains in terms of finishing high school; by 1989 their dropout rate had fallen from 27 percent in 1968 to 15 percent, about the same level as whites and half the rate for Hispanics. However, these gains yielded little payoff in terms of entry-level and low-skill job opportunities, more and more of which were located in the suburbs. Consequently, an increased black "commitment" to schooling could not compensate for the loss of jobs that had given previous generations of working-class youth their start in the primary labor force. (In this respect, even poor inner-city white youth who dropped out of school earlier were more successful in finding jobs.) With major retailing establishments in black areas owned and operated by nonblacks—by, for example, Koreans in Brooklyn, Chaldeans in Detroit, and Arabs in Chicago—black customers patronized merchants who plowed profits back into non-black families and community institutions. Blacks as a group lacked role models— neighbors and kin who could provide informal training in retailing—and they lacked access to capital; banks persisted in redlining practices when they reviewed loan applications from black prospective homeowners and entrepreneurs. Within this exceedingly circumscribed world, then, it was no wonder that some people set their sights low; in 1991 a young New Haven black's attitude that (as interpreted by one observer), "If you don't care too much, failing to get it won't hurt so much" sounded much like the Alabama sharecropper who earlier in the century "made up his mind that he weren't goin to have anything . . . after that, why nothin could hurt him."[20]

Analogies between the Southern plantation and the Northern ghetto are suggestive, but not literal. For example, while the underlying structure of black households might remain the same despite the transition from rural South to urban North, patterns of gender relations underwent a fundamental realignment. Through the generations, demands made on the productive energies of all members had caused families to separate or had kept them separate—when slave husbands and wives lived in "abroad" marriages and learned from bitter experience that the normal life cycle of planter families would lead to the separation of parents from children, sibling from sibling; and when sharecropping men went out to find wage work in the nonagricultural sector for days, weeks, or months at a time. In 1990 the number of black female-headed households (1.5 million) nearly equaled similarly constituted white households (1.8 million), though blacks represented only 11 percent of the total population. Within black families, babies came, in or out of wedlock, as a "heavenly gift," but then young grandmothers labored to hold together three or more generations (all under thirty years of age in some cases) as they had in the Delta or on the Sea Islands.[21]

Nevertheless, both the social meaning of childbearing and the familiar obligations of family members became transformed in the urban North; it would be inaccurate to trace certain configurations of family life in a direct line from the sharecropper's cabin to the urban neighborhood. For many American teenagers, regardless of where they lived, sexuality constituted a literally natural and normal act; but in the ghetto, pregnancy played a large part in confirming the value of girls and boys in the eyes of their boyfriends and girlfriends. A young black man might perfect his streetwise persona, with its heavy dose of sexual prowess and verbal (if not actual physical) aggressiveness, to "get over" a girl—that is, to overcome her initial resistance to his advances. But for their part, at least a few girls played accomplices in this game rather than the victims of it. A junior-high school counselor in Washington Highlands, a poor neighborhood in the District of Columbia, summed up the prevailing philosophy: "It's not cool to be an A student. It's not cool to be a virgin. It's not cool to say you're a virgin. You shouldn't be on birth control." Given the eagerness with which young girls—children, really—conceived children, well-meaning calls for sex education and the use of contraceptives among black youth sounded naive. Enough young men learned soon enough that girls had their own anxieties (not unique to one race or class), a fair number of which could be fulfilled by nice clothes and plenty of attention; hence the flow of sexual favors from girls to boys who got "down with the posses" and bought them things "that cost crazy dollars."[22]

Beginning in the mid-1980s, the crack plague drastically reordered family life among a small but highly publicized segment of the black community. The church-going grandmother survived the migration from farm to city, but her sorrows festered and multiplied in the late-twentieth-century ghetto. One elderly black woman who had to stretch her pathetically thin resources for her "grands"—the children of a "crackhead" mother, her daughter—noted that her burden was "not a fond thing, a joy thing." In the past daughters, if not always sons, stood ready and willing to care for the children they bore; but the needleless crack culture, more appealing to women than heroin, proved too tempting to too many mothers and daughters who abandoned their own children, either routinely or periodically, temporarily or permanently, when they went "out there." When sons killed their mothers for drug money and ten-year-old girls prostituted themselves for a dollar, the family as a web of caring individuals died too. News stories abounded about children selling crack to their teachers, pregnant women using it with impunity, family members serving as pimps for each other, and mothers bartering their food stamps so they could get high. In households where children worked as "layaways," couriers, or lookouts, sons and daughters became the breadwinners, and a new form of dependency, mother on child, emerged in the ghetto. The devastating effects of crack engulfed not only the people who sold it and the people who sold their bodies to pay for it, but also the babies born with their systems infected by it and bystanders caught in sidewalk crossfires. It was not surprising then that some observers labeled drug abuse in general and crack abuse in particular as a new kind of slavery—that is, a new kind of enforced dependence; but the institution of slavery had relied on the reproduction of the black community, while crack destroyed it: "There are no old crack-heads."[23]

And there were no old crack (or for that matter heroin) dealers. Within metropolitan regions, ghetto drug dealers catered not only to their neighbors but also to gentrified and suburban customers, in effect confining the consequent bloodbaths to black neighborhoods. By definition, the distribution and sale of controlled substances was a vicious business; crack culture in particular helped to account for the record homicide rates set by several American cities in 1990. For the most part these deaths resulted from gang and turf wars and retribution for individual deals gone sour. The theory that each dealer's demise represented a larger lesson to impressionable youth of course ignored evidence indicating that, according to one undercover agent, "We'll put them in jail, and then someone will take their place tomorrow." The drug trade was a bottomless pit, and some young people, especially young men, appeared ready and willing to jump into it.[24]

The lure of the trade depended to some extent on familiar imperatives associated with poverty-stricken communities, but also on the dynamics of a male street culture. With the black youth unemployment higher than 35 percent in the late 1980s (compared to a white rate of 14 percent), and with the annual volume of drug sales truly astounding—over $750 million in the District of Columbia alone—dealing provided a logical source of employment and cash in the black community. Like immigrant ward bosses and organized crime figures a few generations earlier, crack kingpins indulged themselves in fancy clothes and big cars that captivated awestruck youngsters, and at times they put some of their profits back into the community with great ceremonial flourish. Yet wealthy drug lords acknowledged few larger social obligations of any kind. They "hustled backward"—that is, they spent their money on fat gold chains, "fresh girls," and Porsches.

These dealers were not ordinary American dreamers. Because of its violent nature, drug dealing was as much a ritualized form of street activity as it was a business. In some cities the trade was remarkable for its hierarchical, efficient organization centrally controlled by a few men who communicated via beeper and telephone to a vast corps of more or less disciplined employees, with ten-year-old "runners" doing much of the dirty relay work. The well-publicized and self-evident fact that only a few lucky, short-lived souls could make $1,000 a day at this job—the rest also put their lives on the line, but for much more modest sums of money—hardly discouraged the hopeful from working their way up the organizational ladder. Such upward mobility depended on entrepreneurial skills to some extent, but mainly on a good deal of "profilin'"—the public display of masculine aggression, especially the ability to inflict pain and to endure it without flinching. Thus comparisons between big-time drug dealers and Wall Street inside traders, emphasizing their greed and ruthlessness in carrying out illegal activity, ignored the fact that while white-collar criminals relied on the computer, drug lords brandished Uzi semi-automatics in their customers' faces. Although inside traders on the stock market might also make enormous profits at the expense of other people, they rarely put a bullet though a rival's brain or broke the legs of a recalcitrant underling; neither did they peddle death and misery in small plastic packages as the source of their livelihood. This is not to exonerate white-collar (often white) criminals, but to suggest that drug dealing attracted a few young men (of all races) for reasons other than purely "financial." Selling drugs was a way of life, a way of being in a mean world, and poverty alone could not account for the sadistic impulses among the people who did it.[25]

Black criminals received the most media attention and opproprium when they attacked white people. In fact, of course, black neighborhoods in general and black people in particular suffered more than any other group from inner-city violence. (In 1986 about four-fifths of the crimes against blacks were committed by people of their own race, and about four-fifths of the crimes against whites were committed by whites). Young black men killed each other with guns—nearly half of all black males murdered in 1988 died from gun wounds—but they also killed bystanders—babies in their cribs, mothers on front stoops, elderly men on park benches. In Southern towns and work camps, there had always been men (white as well as black) who cultivated a reputation of hard living, especially when they were fortified by firearms and liquor. But the sixteen-year-old in the Brownsville section of Brooklyn who got his first gun because "There's a party this weekend and I just thought it's good to have one now" represented a new phenonemon. Verbal taunts and insults backed up by a Raven MP-25 semiautomantic took on a whole new meaning. Young men who swaggered or "pimp rolled" down the street were not a menace per se to society; but when they brandished their Taurus PT-92AF's at the same time, no one in the vicinity was safe. Thus what distinguished inner-city blacks from people living elsewhere was not their putative tolerance of crime but rather the climate of fear that surrounded them. Indeed, as one scholar has suggested, we might well define the "underclass" as those persons preyed upon by a few "truly deviant" people who just happened to be the neighbors and kin of their victims. One need not flee from impoverished areas to find the most outspoken critics of the minority of youths and men who plundered and terrorized; said one Boston black woman, a resident of the city's Roxbury neighborhood, "Nobody knows that decent people live here . . . working people. We're dying too. These kids have put us in prison."[26]

These young men were seemingly impervious to all restraints, as represented by law enforcement officials, schoolteachers, grandmothers, and their own consciences. When they turned neighborhoods into battlegrounds that resembled (both in terms of mortality rates and random violence) the jungle warfare of Vietnam, they took a national, historic gun culture to its logical, if horrifying, conclusion. At the same time, the people who feared for their lives at the hands of these young men gave expression to another historic impulse—the desire of people everywhere to move to a better place for the sake of their children. Feature news stories and obituaries revealed the depth of desire among inner-city men, women, and children "fed up with the crime and high rents," people who had for years contemplated moving back South—or just out. Said one sixteen-year-old in a Harlem neighborhood that was more "danger zone" than ghetto, "All I want is to live long enough to move off this block."[27]

Though explicitly "antiwhite," ghetto street culture was also arrayed against women and older persons regardless of their color. On the street, an ethos of brutal bravado reigned supreme, and to the "winners" (ephemeral though they might be) went the shearling coats, gold chains, leather jackets, and BMWs that conferred a purely materialistic status. When drug dealers peddled death, they did so not out of outrage over historic injustices but out of rage against their peers, their parents, and all others who would deny them the "respect" they demanded. Likewise, drug abuse signaled the end of politics, a retreat into a world of despair, a world without culture, obligation, or larger meaning of any kind. Although the late-twentieth-century Northern urban ghetto consisted of an infrastructure similar to that of the antebellum plantation—the confinement of black people to a limited area, where they were systematically denied good jobs and education—young men on the street threatened to undermine the corporate ethos that had sustained the black community under slavery. Indeed, political activity within the ghetto—whether in the form of anticrime neighborhood patrols, tenants' rights groups, clinics for drug addicts, or parental involvement in education—was specifically directed against a street culture that threatened to pull everyone, male and female, young and old, into a pit that was peculiar to postmodern America. Nevertheless, the quiet battles waged by community organizers failed to satisfy the craving of many journalists and news analysts for more lethal fare in the form of stories and documentaries that seemed almost stylized in their presentation of violence and degradation. Being poor, and caring for other people who were poor, was hard work; the "underclass" remained newsworthy, to the detriment of the people who were in it but not of it.

Although this discussion has focused on black Northern urban ghettos, it is clear that, for residents within distressed communities throughout the country, neither skin color nor culture provided immunity from the problems that pervaded inner-city Detroit or the South Bronx. For working-class Mexican immigrants in New York City and Appalachian migrants in Dayton, times were hard and job options slim. And for all of them, Northern city streets represented a new world, a harsh new world of drugs and danger, one that in its outer manifestations bore little resemblance to the one they or their parents had known back home, on the land.

POSTMODERN POVERTY IN AMERICA

In the late twentieth century the faces of poverty were many, and scattered throughout the nation. Some of the poorest regions, such as the Lower Mississippi Valley; the old Cotton Belt in the South; the Appalachian Mountains; and Native American reservations in Oklahoma, New Mexico, and Arizona, had roots deep in the nation's history of slavery, commercial development, and territorial conquest. Other regions of persistent poverty arose from the large-scale migrations of the twentieth century, and included Hispanic communities along the Texas gulf coast, urban cores in the largest Northern cities, and the desolate rural regions of the upper Midwest. Within these poor areas, people defined themselves not only according to their lowly economic status but also according to their kin ties, their shared religious beliefs, and their neighborliness. Hence a classical labor market, in which unemployed and underemployed people would readily move to places where jobs were plentiful, remained theoretical at best. In a postindustrial economy, low-wage jobs proved to be a poor incentive for uprooting one's family. Jimmy Green, who lived in the black section of Natchez, Mississippi, considered himself "proud poor" instead of "sorry poor"; with a sporadic income derived from wage work, handiwork performed for in-laws, and cash borrowed from friends, he yearned for a steady, $6-an-hour job. But as for abandoning Natchez, he could not see the point: "Natchez is Natchez all over the world. The other places are only bigger than Natchez."[28]

In the early 1990s conventional categories based on race, culture, and national origin inhibited discussions of poverty and the "underclass" in modern America. The persistent poverty of black and Mexican migrant laborers, white hill farmers in the Ozark plateau, Tennessee and Kentucky migrants to small Midwestern towns, and chronically under-employed Appalachian folk of both races attracted little attention or concern from policymakers bent on defining the underclass solely in terms of its spatial concentration. Moreover, the plight of the Hispanic population in general, and Puerto Ricans in particular, often disappeared in a debate that defined poverty on the basis of race or national origin. The term "Hispanic," of course, refers to neither category, and statistics on black-white poverty or foreign versus native-born persons invariably obscured the declining status of Spanish-speaking people, a group that included American citizens born either in this country or in Puerto Rico, and people of both African and European descent. Within the *barrios* of Los Angeles, the migrant labor camps of Florida and decaying mill towns of New England, Spanish-speaking workers bore a disproportionate share of the burdens imposed by a new, credentials-conscious labor market. For example, in 1989 an estimated 300,000 Hispanics in Massachusetts included about 160,000 Puerto Ricans and lesser numbers of immigrants from the Dominican Republic, Peru, El Salvador, and Guatemala; it was unclear how many of these were illegal aliens. In Boston the percentage of female-headed households among all Spanish-speaking groups amounted to 79 percent, a clear sign of their extreme vulnerability within the state's recessionary economy.[29]

American corporations created distressed communities when they abandoned their own workers in favor of cheaper ones abroad. In the process, these firms also preserved a number of underclasses throughout the world. For example, the *maquiladoras* located along the northern Mexican border gave rise to crowded workers' communities akin to those in Hong Kong, Taiwan, or Korea. The Mexican workers paid by IBM, Foster Grant, ITT, General Electric, and Chrysler just a few miles from American soil were thus part of the general economic system, and the larger historic process, that created poverty-stricken communities in the United States. The desires of the people caught up in these systems told not a story of cultural distinctiveness so much as a common struggle for dignity. Noted one leader of the workers living in the shantytown of *Colonia Emiliano Zapata,* a new border settlement: "They come with big dreams. Where they come from, there is no work and they're dying of hunger. So they look at their children and say, 'I'm going to the border to work.'"[30]

The parts of the rural South where poor households represented up to 70 percent of the total population remained in a time warp of sorts. The underlying continuity between antebellum slavery days and conditions in the 1980s was palpable. In Alabama, modern state political conflicts played out "the oldest theme" in that state's history: "the corporations and the plantation owners appeal for the votes of working-class whites by convincing them that blacks hunger for their jobs and a disproportionate share of government benefits." Meanwhile, extractive industries continued to prosper to the detriment of property tax–funded public education, especially in the rural areas. Functional illiteracy among adults of both races plagued the South to a degree greater than in the North. "Runaway shops" from the North and from as far away as Japan sought out Southern workers and took advantage of their gratitude for steady work of any kind, no matter how poorly paid. For many rural folk, the choice was between a meager welfare check (the monthly average sent to Mississippi and Alabama AFDC families was $115), and a job similar to the ones offered at Indianola, Mississippi, catfish plants, where single black mothers worked under "neoslavery" conditions.[31]

By the late twentieth century the rural folk of both races who had been left behind by their migrating kin faced a form of hardship that increasingly resembled the way of life in the urban North. Beginning in the 1930s, with the entry of the South into the national labor market, and culminating in the Civil Rights Revolution of the 1950s and 1960s, the Southern political landscape underwent a metamorphosis. By the 1970s black state legislators and mayors residing in showcase Sunbelt cities offered eloquent testimony to the long-deferred "empowerment" of their constituents. In the largest urban areas black men and women with the best credentials found employment opportunities that ensured them a solid and comfortable middle-class life. Nevertheless, in the countryside and in the mountains, Southerners endured hardship brought on by new kinds of industries that engaged in old forms of exploitation—low-wage service, tourism, and nonunion manufacturing jobs. For some people local conditions provided a glimmer of opportunity that would seem to reward rootedness. Through federally subsidized construction projects and community-action programs, the federal government (especially in the 1960s) created at least some new jobs in the Delta and Appalachia, though the menial and temporary nature of these positions failed to bolster a sagging regional economy. More and more, country people were drawn into the "shallow rural," a place between the suburbs and the backcountry, where they remained integrated fully into neither the South's industrial nor commercial agricultural sectors.[32]

Regardless of their racial composition, rural areas in the South continued to suffer the aftershocks of a reorganized global economy. In Appalachia, characterized by "chronic intergenerational poverty," residents outside the major metropolitan areas lacked access to good schools and to good jobs that paid a living wage. Black and white folks alike in eastern North Carolina saw a generations-old way of life slip away with the coming of the mechanical tobacco harvester in the 1960s; "Men and their wives and children were as scarred by the upheaval, as throwed away, as if lightning had struck them. But from lightning they could have taken refuge." Family members separated, some to go off to Norfolk to find work, others to drift from one low-paying job to the other. In the Deep South the growing number of elected black officials proved powerless to change long-standing state taxation policies in favor of industry, policies that stunted public education and other public-welfare programs. Nor could these officials halt the spread of "ghettos" deep within plantation country, towns bereft of retail stores and jobs, with a large number of impoverished citizens lodged in drug-infested public housing projects. In the late 1980s, with one-seventh of the Delta's people receiving food stamps (three times the national average) and more than one-quarter without work, the area rivaled any Northern city in terms of its deep and persistent (if not geographically concentrated) poverty.[33]

In the South old forms of dependency took on new shapes, in the process lessening distinctions between the manifestations of poverty in different regions of the country, in rural and urban areas, in the past and present. In places where ancient patterns of racial etiquette still pertained, only a fraction of the poor received the AFDC or food stamp assistance to which they were entitled, so successful were local administrators in discouraging some applications altogether and rejecting others on technical grounds. In Spartanburg, South Carolina, for example, only one-third of all poor families received aid in 1988. Poor rural families had many of the same characteristics as their urban counterparts—high rates of female-headed households and welfare dependency, alcoholism and teenage pregnancy. The residents of public housing projects such as the one in Marrero, Louisiana, daily endured the police brutality and violent drug culture that led youths to scorn jobs at Popeye's Chicken in favor of more deadly alternatives. Noted Rose Smith, a community activist who lived in the Acres Road Project in Marrero, "When we was coming up, you might hear about one person smoking something wrong. Now you see little bitty kids getting killed for nothing, over drugs. It's real bad."[34]

Throughout the rural United States groups of poor people engaged in time-honored survival strategies that became lost in, eclipsed by, the northern, urban black "underclass" debate. For example, the rural poor of New England stayed "hidden by the trees," though their standard of living approximated the lowest in the nation. Four out of every five people in Washington County, Maine, lived below the poverty line. Here people pieced together a living from wage work in the seasonal fishing, food processing, and tourist industries, from the forests and the soil. Within the region a predictable dynamic of resourcefulness and enforced dependency pertained, with families raking blueberries in the summer and assembling Christmas wreaths in the winter, braiding rugs, shucking clams, and doubling up their families. When sixty-eight-year old Mae Heath in Clarksville, New Hampshire, supported herself with Social Security; help from her daughter, brother, and neighbors; and a game warden who gave her a moose to butcher, she followed ways of rural living practiced all over the country for many generations. Foraging was central to this way of life. In Errol, New Hampshire, in the late 1980s "a man and wife and their children lived for a time on berries, dandelion greens, and horned pout caught nightly on Umbagog Lake." They dutifully reported every bit of income, even the vegetables sold out of the garden, to welfare case workers who reduced their checks proportionately.[35]

In the late twentieth century the global assembly line created whole new groups of poor people in America, at least some of whom had been car owners and homeowners, many of them white, living in small towns and on the fringes of large cities. These were the workers displaced from their jobs in the steel, rubber, and auto industry, men and women replaced by robots and foreign imports. In the Mesabi Range of Minnesota, the steel, taconite, and lumber workers familiar with cyclical downswings now had to confront a more devastating, and permanent, form of underemployment due to the decline of or increased competition within their respective industries. Patterns of labor and residential mobility reflected a host of factors, including the age and experience of workers, the particular industry they had depended on, and the places where they lived. Older homeowners in the Mesabi Range turned to hunting, fishing, foraging, woodcutting, and relying on more fortunate kin in an effort to remain where they had lived for so many years. In Pittsburgh, such large numbers of younger (white) men and women left the region in response to the loss of 90,000 jobs in the late 1970s and early 1980s that the city's overall unemployment rate fell dramatically; but hidden in these optimistic statistics were the black and older workers who, finding it difficult to move to other parts of the country, stayed behind. Joblessness in the city's black neighborhoods in fact reached "catastrophic" proportions. The larger difficulties of retraining and relocating displaced workers proved beyond the reach of most programs, whether sponsored by unions, private employers, or the federal government. The overall health of a local economy determined whether the men and women most likely to lose their jobs—those with the least seniority and formal education, black men, black women, white women, and older persons—would find comparable work nearby, or anywhere. In Pontiac, Michigan, in the early 1980s, some laid-off black auto workers hesitated to leave the area permanently in search of work elsewhere, ever hopeful of a recall that grew more unlikely with each passing month. A 1986 Department of Labor study found that displaced steelworkers were less likely to find alternative employment compared to other laid-off workers, simply because they tended to live in one-industry towns, where steel served as the lifeblood for the whole community. Consequently, unemployment rates in steel regions such as Johnstown, Pennsylvania, and the Gary-Hammond-East Chicago area were significantly higher than the national average.[36]

Thus the decline of heavy manufacturing left pockmarks of poverty on families in America's once-proud heartland. Between 1985 and 1990 Waterloo, Iowa, a factory town of 70,000, lost over 7,000 jobs when Rath Meatpacking closed its doors and the Deere farm machinery plant cut its work force in half. Said one former Rath employee, "We never meant to quit our jobs. They quit on us." The shopping malls and nursing homes, together with a new state-of-the art meatpacking plant owned by IBP Inc., provided 8,000 new jobs in the vicinity of Waterloo in the late 1980s, but those jobs offered drastically reduced wages and health and vacation benefits compared to the ones in the old factories. Men and women who had for decades made good union wages five days a week, eight hours a day, now found themselves trying to make ends meet by working long hours at minimum-wage jobs and by relying on food stamps and the Cedar Valley Food Bank. In the lives of these workers, the working poor, coalesced all the bitter ironies born of American technological progress and an unfettered world market. Families splintered in the course of the day, with employed parents and older children forced to move to the round-the-clock rhythms of drugstores and fast-food restaurants in a service economy. Young people left Waterloo for good as soon as possible; gone were the blue-collar jobs that had enabled their parents to buy homes and take summer vacations. Empty taverns and bowling alleys testified to the erosion of a community once bound together by a set work schedule and by enough money to spend on leisure time. At $4.20 an hour, even in a place where food and housing were cheap compared to the rest of the country, two full-time breadwinners could barely support two children. If the causes of poverty in Waterloo were new, the consequences were all too familiar.[37]

In 1990, to highlight the plight of Chinese sweatshop workers in New York City and unemployed miners in Cranks Creek, Kentucky, was not to ignore the systematic racism that still plagued the American political economy. Rather, a focus on the myriad causes of poverty, and the various groups impoverished, put race in its place as one factor—albeit a highly significant one, along with age, sex, and ethnicity—that shaped a person's chances for gainful employment and, beyond that, for a decent job at a decent wage. The proliferation of the poor in the 1980s testified not to a new kind of national economy more heartless or rapacious than previous ones, but rather to the lessening of government controls that had previously checked to some extent the radical economic inequality which was a natural consequence of agrarian, commercial, and industrial capitalism. The Reagan Revolution was more accurately a counterrevolution; rather than diverting the country onto a new course, toward "greed," it set the country back onto its original course, toward the unfettered pursuit of wealth characteristic of the earliest Southern colonies.[38] Without the countervailing influences of labor unions and government regulatory agencies, the economic process of marginalization that engulfed greater numbers, and a greater diversity, of blacks and whites was bound to continue unabated, spawning more and more "underclasses" along the way.

We are where we live; or, in some cases, more accurately, we are where we want to live. Our immediate surroundings determine the nature of the schooling our children receive, the kinds of jobs we get, the cost of our auto insurance, the quality of health care and police protection available to us, the merchandise we find at local stores and the prices we pay for it. Our sense of ourselves as individuals and family members is reflected in the tranquility of tree-lined streets or the filthy clutter of vacant lots.[39] Certainly the formal, political equality of all American citizens (based on enfranchisement) presents a radical contrast to inequalities among communities; the image of gleaming, downtown office towers juxtaposed to a nearby burned-out ghetto is familiar to us today, an emblem of "normal" patterns of growth and economic development over the years. Some people are rich and some people are poor, and the places where they live preserve their status through the generations.

Neighborhoods are often knit together by class and cultural cohesiveness, by kin and friends, people more or less bound by a historic identification with a particular place and the collective memory that shapes it. Throughout American history, black and white men and women of modest means have alternated between loyalty to their homeplace, attachment to it, and the hope that they and their children would someday enjoy a more just and comfortable way of life, a way of life possible only elsewhere. Individuals and families respond to these conflicting desires according to their own priorities; but in the end, the ability to stay or move according to their own inclinations has always been a luxury of sorts. More often than not sharecroppers, mountain farmers, migrant laborers, and phosphate miners faced choices so constricted as to almost disappear altogether. When workers were fired or laid off from their jobs, evicted from their homes, displaced by mechanical cotton pickers or by coal-mining machines, they had little say in the matter. On the other hand, freedom of movement depends on the money a person has already made, skills and credentials, the color of his or her skin, the viability of kin connections and job opportunities close by or far away. Dispossession, then, is not an exclusively economic process, reversible by balancing dying communities in one part of the country with new jobs in another part. Well-to-do families can afford to explore new job opportunities, sever community ties, and relocate, secure in their decent standard of living; but social networks, more than jobs, constitute the lifeblood of poor communities.

The "culture of poverty" thesis serves a larger political purpose, for it encourages some people to believe that the poor positively revel in their own misery, that they shun stable marriages and steady employment almost as a matter of perverse principle. According to this view, the poor live in a different country, following a way of life that is as incomprehensible as it is self-destructive. Yet even those scholars and politicians sensitive to the structural underpinnings of poverty seem oblivious to the jobs-housing-education nexus, the fact that menial jobs alone are not sufficient to keep families intact or to ensure the self-respect of a breadwinner of either sex. The truth of the matter is to be found in patterns of labor mobility and migration through the years, the stories of families that picked up, moved, and started over again. Some left joyfully and others in anger; but they tried, sometimes successfully and other times not, to act upon values common to most families now and in the past, here and abroad, regardless of class or culture.

As the twentieth century nears its end, the prevalence of racial politics on the streets and in the halls of Congress means that a national ideology—one based on imperatives formulated in the antebellum South—will continue to war against reality in an America of many "underclasses." For African-Americans, to identify one's interests on the basis of skin color is to continue to shoulder the burdens of slavery in a postemancipation society. Certainly a black skin constitutes a permanent badge of "otherness" in American society. At the same time, as the poor population comes to be ever more foreign, native-born white, and even (formerly) middle class, a politics based on race proves ever more self-defeating for blacks and whites alike. In the early 1990s the political leaders who understand this fact are few and far between, so rooted in the national consciousness is the idea of black distinctiveness. That belief is bolstered by research and news stories focusing on a single Northern urban "underclass." Thus does a society conceived in slavery perpetuate itself, and postindustrial America remains colonial Virginia writ large.

Notes

Introduction

1. Thomas Byrne Edsall with Mary D. Edsall, "Race," *The Atlantic*, May 1991, p. 53.
2. Nicholas Lemann, "The Origins of the Underclass," *The Atlantic*, July 1986, p. 59. Lemann, like Ze'ev Chafets, the author of *Devil's Night: And Other True Tales of Detroit* (New York: Random House, 1990), views the ghetto, and indeed all of black history, as bizarre and exotic, outside the "white mainstream." Chafets, for example, notes that the writing of his book constituted "the closing of a circle. As a small boy I had always been fascinated by black people. In the gray monotony of a Michigan car-town they seemed like vivid, foreign strangers. I can still remember my earliest glimpses of the black section of town, ripe with intimations of exotic vitality and mystery" (p. 6).
3. See, for example, Barbara Jeanne Fields, "Slavery, Race, and Ideology in the United States of America," *New Left Review* 181 (May/June 1990): 95–118.
4. See, for example, Judith N. Shklar, *American Citizenship: The Quest for Inclusion* (Cambridge, MA: Harvard University Press, 1991); Linda

Gordon, ed., *Women, the State, and Welfare* (Madison: University of Wisconsin Press, 1991).

5. See, for example, Jason DeParle, "Suffering in the Cities Persists as U.S. Fights Other Battles," *New York Times*, 27 January 1991, pp. 1, 21.

6. Edward F. O'Brien to A. M. Crawford, Mt. Pleasant, S. C., 5 September 1866, M869 (S.C.), Microfilm Reel 34, Bureau of Refugees, Freedmen, and Abandoned Lands, Record Group 105, National Archives, Washington, D.C.

7. Peter T. Kilborn, "Scraping By, Illegally, Mining Kentucky Coal," *New York Times*, 3 March 1991, p. 1.

8. See, for example, John Mack Faragher, "Open-Country Community: Sugar Creek, Illinois, 1820–1850," in Steven Hahn and Jonathan Prude, eds., *The Countryside in the Age of Capitalist Transformation: Essays in the Social History of Rural America* (Chapel Hill: University of North Carolina Press, 1985), pp. 233–58.

9. Quoted in Alec Wilkinson, "A Reporter at Large (Sugarcane): Big Sugar, Pt. II," *The New Yorker*, 24 July 1989, p. 63.

10. See, for example, Chandler Davidson, *Race and Class in Texas Politics* (Princeton, NJ: Princeton University Press, 1990), p. 221.

11. Interviews with Jackson Jordan, Jr., and Ruth Shays in John Langston Gwaltney, *Drylongso: A Self-Portrait of Black America* (New York: Vintage Books, 1980), pp. 98, 101, 31.

12. Interviews with Seth Bingham, Ella Turner Surry, Nancy White, Gordon Etheridge, Bernard Vanderstell, John Oliver, Janet McCrae, and Mabel Lincoln in ibid., pp. 226, 239, 144, 235, 115, 18, 124, 234, 69.

13. Ann Petry, *The Street* (Boston: Houghton Mifflin, 1946), p. 323.

14. Rebecca J. Scott, *Slave Emancipation in Cuba: The Transition to Free Labor, 1860–1889* (Princeton, NJ: Princeton University Press, 1985), pp. 219–22, 239. The quote is on p. 253.

15. See, for example, George Grantham and Carol S. Leonard, eds., *Research in Economic History: Agrarian Organization in the Century of Industrialization: Europe, Russia, and North America* (pts. A and B) (Greenwich, CT: JAI Press, 1989); Jane Humphries, "Enclosures, Common Rights and Women: The Proletarianization of Families in the Late Eighteenth and Early Nineteenth Centuries," *Journal of Economic History* 50 (March 1990): 17–43.

16. Quoted in Charles Van Onselen, "Race and Class in the South African Countryside: Cultural Osmosis and Social Relations in the Sharecropping Economy of the South-Western Transvaal, 1900–1950," *American Historical Review* 95 (February 1990): 123.

17. Benjamin DeMott, *The Imperial Middle: Why Americans Can't Think Straight About Class* (New York: Morrow, 1990).

18. Lionel Rose, *"Rogues and Vagabonds": Vagrant Underworld in Britain, 1815–1985* (London: Routledge, 1988), p. 1.

Chapter 1
At the Crossroads of Freedom: Black Field Workers

1. "in . . . We": Ira Berlin et al., eds., "The Terrain of Freedom: The Struggle over the Meaning of Free Labor in the U.S. South," *History Workshop* 22 (Autumn 1986): 128. I would like to acknowledge Ira Berlin for drawing this material to my attention and for providing its historical context in his lecture, "Rethinking Afro-American History," Harvard University, March 1991. See also Kevern J. Verney, "Trespassers in the Land of Their Birth: Blacks and Landownership in South Carolina and Mississippi During the Civil War and Reconstruction," *Slavery and Abolition* 4 (May 1983): 64–78.

2. "Land . . . be": Berlin et al., eds., "The Terrain of Freedom," p. 129.

3. "We has": quoted in Eric Foner, *Reconstruction: America's Unfinished Revolution, 1863–1877* (New York: Harper & Row, 1988), p. 105; Paul Cimbala, "The Freedmen's Bureau, the Freedmen, and Sherman's Grant in Reconstruction Georgia, 1865–1867," *Journal of Southern History* 55 (November 1989): 597–632; Ira Berlin et al., eds., *Freedom: A Documentary History of Emancipation, 1861–1867,* Series 1, vol. 3: *The Wartime Genesis of Free Labor: The Lower South* (Cambridge: Cambridge University Press, 1990), pp. 59, 253, 297–98.

4. Planter quoted in Francis W. Loring and C. F. Atkinson, *Cotton Culture and the South Considered with Reference to Emigration* (Boston: A. Williams, 1869), p. 5.

5. See, for example, Samuel L. Gardner to Brig. Gen. Wager Swayne, Selma, Ala., 10 August 1865, Series 1040, M809 (Ala.), Reel 18, Records of the U.S. Bureau of Refugees, Freedmen, and Abandoned Lands (hereafter BRFAL), Record Group 105, National Archives, Washington, D.C.

6. Barbara Jeanne Fields discusses the "hybrid" nature of postbellum black labor in "The Nineteenth-Century American South: History and Theory," *Plantation Society in the Americas* 2 (April 1983): 7–28.

7. Gavin Wright, *Old South, New South: Revolutions in the Southern Economy Since the Civil War* (New York: Basic Books, 1986), pp. 17–18; Lewis Cecil Gray, *History of Agriculture in the Southern United States to 1860,* vol. 1 (Washington, D.C.: Carnegie Institution, 1933), p. 565; Sarah S. Hughes, "Slaves for Hire: The Allocation of Black Labor in Elizabeth City County, Virginia, 1782–1810," *William and Mary Quarterly,* 3d ser., 35 (April 1978): 263; John Inscoe, "Mountain Masters: Slaveholding in Western North Carolina," *North Carolina Historical Review* 61 (April 1984): 143–73; Donald O. Whitten, "Rural Life Along the Mississippi: Plaquemines Parish, Louisiana, 1830–1850," *Agricultural History* 58 (July 1984): 477–87; Leila Sellers, *Charleston Business on the Eve of the American Revolution* (Chapel Hill: University of North Carolina Press, 1934), pp. 98–106; Philip D. Morgan, "Work and Culture: The Task System and the World of Lowcountry Blacks, 1700 to 1880," *William and Mary Quarterly,* 3d ser., 39 (October 1982): 563–99.

8. Interview with Berry Smith in the Federal Writers Project *Slave Narratives*, collected in George P. Rawick, ed., *The American Slave: A Composite Autobiography* (Westport, CT: Greenwood Press, 1972), vol. 7 (Miss. Narrs.), pt. 2, p. 13 (hereafter with the name of the interviewee, FWP *Slave Narrs.*, the volume, publication date, and page number); Philip E. Graves, Robert L. Sexton, and Richard K. Vedder, "Slavery, Amenities, and Factor Price Equalization: A Note on Migration and Freedom," *Explorations in Economic History* 20 (April 1983): 156–62; Juliet E. K. Walker, "The Legal Status of Free Blacks in Early Kentucky, 1792–1825," *Filson Club Historical Quarterly* 57 (October 1983): 382–84. See also James Oakes, *The Ruling Race: A History of American Slaveholders* (New York: Knopf, 1982).

9. See, for example, Michael P. Johnson, "Runaway Slaves and the Slave Communities in South Carolina, 1799 to 1830," *William and Mary Quarterly*, 3d ser., 38 (July 1981): 418–41; Gerald W. Mullin, *Flight and Rebellion: Slave Resistance in Eighteenth-Century Virginia* (New York: Oxford University Press, 1972), p. 40.

10. Clarence L. Mohr, *On the Threshold of Freedom: Masters and Slaves in Civil War Georgia* (Athens: University of Georgia Press, 1986), p. 173; Ira Berlin et al., eds., *Freedom: A Documentary History of Emancipation, 1861–1867*, series 1, vol. 1: *The Destruction of Slavery* (Cambridge: Cambridge University Press, 1985), pp. 110, 667, 675; "druv" quoted in Elizabeth Hyde Botume, *First Days Amongst the Contrabands* (Boston: Lee and Shepard, 1893), p. 58; James T. Currie, *Enclave: Vicksburg and Her Plantations, 1863–1879* (Jackson: University Press of Mississippi, 1980), p. 98.

11. "the able-bodied": John R. Dennett, *South As It Is: 1865–1866* (New York: Viking, 1965), p. 259; Berlin et al., eds., *Destruction of Slavery;* James H. Brewer, *The Confederate Negro: Virginia's Craftsmen and Military Laborers, 1861–1865* (Durham, NC: Duke University Press, 1969); John Cimprich, "Slave Behavior During the Federal Occupation of Tennessee, 1862–1865," *Historian* 44 (May 1982): 335–46; Victor B. Howard, *Black Liberation in Kentucky: Emancipation and Freedom, 1862–1884* (Lexington: University Press of Kentucky, 1983); Ronald L. F. Davis, *Good and Faithful Labor: From Slavery to Sharecropping in the Natchez District, 1860–1890* (Westport, CT: Greenwood Press, 1982), p. 172; C. Peter Ripley, *Slaves and Freedmen in Civil War Louisiana* (Baton Rouge: Louisiana State University Press, 1976), pp. 50–53.

12. Ripley, *Slaves and Freedmen*, p. 10; Mohr, *On the Threshold of Freedom*, pp. 113–14; Virginia Newman, FWP *Slave Narrs.*, vol. 5 (Tex. Narrs.), 1972, pt. 3, p. 150; Robert F. Engs, *Freedom's First Generation: Black Hampton, Virginia, 1861–1890* (Philadelphia: University of Pennsylvania Press, 1979), p. 85.

13. "seek": Report of G. D. Robinson, Mobile, Ala. 17 January 1866, S1040,

M809 (Ala.), Reel 18, BRFAL; "magnetic": Edwin Q. Bell, "In Lieu of Labor," *DeBow's Review,* 4, After War Series (July/August 1867): 69; Mary Armstrong, FWP *Slave Narrs.,* vol. 4 (Tex. Narrs.), 1972, pt. 1, p. 29.

14. Berlin et al., eds., "The Terrain of Freedom," p. 116; Turner Jacobs, FWP *Slave Narrs.,* Supplementary Series (SS), vol. 8, 1977, pt. 3, p. 1119; W. L. Bost, FWP *Slave Narrs.,* vol. 14 (N.C. Narrs.), 1972, pt. 1, p. 145; Pike County: Lewis Jefferson, FWP *Slave Narrs.,* SS, vol. 8, (Miss. Narrs.), 1977, pt. 3, p. 1143.

15. Mary Anderson, FWP *Slave Narrs.,* vol. 14, (N.C. Narrs.), 1972, pt. 1, pp. 25–26; Levi Ashley, FWP *Slave Narrs.,* SS 1, vol. 6, (Miss. Narrs.), 1977, pt. 1, p. 81; Henry Bobbitt, FWP *Slave Narrs.,* vol. 14 (N.C. Narrs.), 1972, pt. 1, p. 124.

16. "people": report of F. W. Liedtke, Monck's Corner, S.C., 1 November 1866, M869 (S.C.), Reel 34, BRFAL; "no person": report of H. Sweeny, Helena, Ark., 30 June 1865, M979 (Ark.), Reel 23, BRFAL; "nothing": Cora Gillam, FWP *Slave Narrs.,* SS 2, vol. 1 (Ark. Narrs.), 1979, p. 69.

17. "all have": Berlin et al., eds., *Wartime Genesis of Free Labor,* p. 692; "made . . . where": J. B. Smith to H. Smith, Georgetown, S.C., 7 March 1866, M869 (S.C.), Reel 34, BRFAL; "No shoe": Dennett, *South As It Is,* p. 227; "Highland . . . fotched": John William DeForest, *A Union Officer in the Reconstruction* (New Haven, CT: Yale University Press, 1948), p. 37; "seemed": Dennett, *South As It Is,* p. 227; Louisa Adams, FWP *Slave Narrs.,* vol. 14 (N.C. Narrs.), 1972, pt. 1, pp. 6–7.

18. "to limit": DeForest, *Union Officer,* p. 29; "within": report of G. D. Robinson, Mobile, Ala., 17 January 1866, M809 (Ala.), Reel 18, BRFAL; "gigantic": quoted in Lewis N. Wynne, "The Role of Freedmen in the Postbellum Cotton Economy of Georgia," *Phylon* 42 (December 1981): 313; Lawrence N. Powell, *New Masters: Northern Planters During the Civil War and Reconstruction* (New Haven, CT: Yale University Press, 1980), p. 12; William Cohen, "Black Immobility and Free Labor: The Freedmen's Bureau and the Relocation of Black Labor, 1865–1868," *Civil War History* 30 (September 1984): 221–34; Paul Skeels Pierce, *The Freedmen's Bureau: A Chapter in the History of Reconstruction* (Iowa City: University of Iowa, 1904), pp. 99–100. See also Louis S. Gerteis, *From Contraband to Freedman: Federal Policy Toward Southern Blacks, 1861–1865* (Westport, CT: Greenwood Press, 1973).

19. "Savagest": Carl Schurz, *Report on the Condition of the South* (New York: Arno Press and the *New York Times,* 1969; orig. pub. by Congress in 1865), p. 18; "run off": report of C. W. Pierce, Demopolis, Ala., 24 October 1866, M809 (Ala.), Reel 18, BRFAL; "ruinous": Charles Griffin, report on the Freedmen's Bureau in Galveston, Texas, 1 July 1867, M798 (Tex.), Reel 18, BRFAL; "with . . . any": report of S. S. Gardner, Greenville, Ala., 3 July 1868, M809 (Ala.), Reel 18, BRFAL. See also Edward L. Ayers, *Vengeance and Justice: Crime and Punishment in the Nineteenth-Century American*

South (New York: Oxford University Press, 1984); William Cohen, "Negro Involuntary Servitude in the South, 1865–1940: A Preliminary Analysis," *Journal of Southern History* 42 (February 1976): 31–60; Rebecca Scott, "The Battle Over the Child: Child Apprenticeship and the Freedmen's Bureau in North Carolina," *Prologue* 10 (Summer 1978): 101–19; Oscar Zeichner, "The Legal Status of the Agricultural Laborer in the South," *Political Science Quarterly* 55 (September 1940): 412–28; J. G. DeRoulhac Hamilton, "Southern Legislation in Respect to Freedmen, 1865–1866," *Studies in Southern History and Politics* (New York: Columbia University Press, 1914), pp. 137–58.

20. "blackened . . . for": J. A. Mower to O. O. Howard, New Orleans, La., report of October 1866, M1027, (La.), Reel 27, BRFAL; "organized": W. E. Leighton to R. K. Scott, Greenville, S.C., 5 March 1866, M869 (S.C.), Reel 34, BRFAL; "in terror": report of E. O. C. Orde, Little Rock, Ark., 22 February 1867, M979 (Ark.), Reel 23, BRFAL; Peter Kolchin, *First Freedom: The Responses of Alabama's Blacks to Emancipation and Reconstruction* (Westport, CT: Greenwood Press, 1972), p. 18; Donald F. Nieman, *To Set the Law in Motion: The Freedmen's Bureau and the Legal Rights of Blacks, 1865 to 1868* (Millwood, NY: KTO Press, 1979), p. 45.

21. "bad": P. B. Johnson to J. T. Kirkman, Woodville, Tex., 31 July 1867, M821 (Tex.), Reel 21, BRFAL; "to take . . . overtaken": A. Evans to William Sinclair, Sherman, Tex., 15 January 1867, M821 (Tex.), Reel 20, BRFAL.

22. See, for example, Stephan Thernstrom, *The Other Bostonians: Poverty and Progress in the American Metropolis, 1880–1970* (Cambridge, MA: Harvard University Press, 1973); Paul E. Johnson, *A Shopkeeper's Millennium: Society and Revivals in Rochester, New York, 1815–1837* (New York: Hill and Wang, 1978).

23. Dexter E. Clapp to Fred H. Beecher, Raleigh, N.C., 7 August 1865, M843 (N.C.), Reel 23, BRFAL.

24. "inexcusably . . . to exist": William H. Ross to H. W. Smith, Macon, Miss., 4 September 1867, M826 (Miss.), Reel 30, BRFAL.

25. William Cohen, *At Freedom's Edge: Black Mobility and the Southern White Quest for Racial Control, 1861–1915* (Baton Rouge: Louisiana State University Press, 1991), chap. 3. Cohen argues that the Black Codes' vagrancy provisions were generally ignored or unenforced.

26. "*irregularity* . . . work . . . labor": Berlin et al., eds., "Terrain of Freedom," (letter of Joseph Daniel Pope), p. 112. See also Edward King, *The Great South: A Record of Journeys* . . . (Hartford, CT: American Publishing Company, 1875), p. 272; Loring and Atkinson, *Cotton Culture*, pp. 17–18.

27. "should": Rosser H. Taylor, ed., "Post-Bellum Southern Rental Contracts," *Agricultural History* 17 (April 1943): 123; report of J. S. Taylor, Hamburg, Ark., 14 July–30 September 1866, M979 (Ark.), Reel 24, BRFAL.

28. "signing": A. W. Brobst to T. S. Free, Jefferson County, Miss., September 1865, M826 (Miss.), Reel 30, BRFAL; Gavin Wright, "Postbellum

Southern Labor Markets," in Peter Kilby, ed., *Quantity and Quiddity: Essays in U.S. Economic History* (Middletown, CT: Wesleyan University Press, 1987), p. 111; Prana K. Bardhan, "Labor-Tying in a Poor Agrarian Economy: A Theoretical and Empirical Analysis," *Quarterly Journal of Economics* 98 (August 1983): 501–14; Cohen, *At Freedom's Edge,* chap. 3. Cohen notes that masters often hired out slaves on an annual basis; but these contracts were not labor contracts per se. Federal military officials initiated labor contracts on plantations in the Department of the Gulf as early as 1862.

29. "a degree": Harold D. Woodman, "Post-Civil War Southern Agriculture and the Law," *Agricultural History* 53 (January 1979): 336; Harold D. Woodman, *King Cotton and His Retainers: Financing and Marketing the Cotton Crop of the South, 1800–1925* (Lexington: University Press of Kentucky, 1968), pp. 295–314.

30. "Several": report of Samuel S. Gardner, Greenville, Ala., 18 June 1867, M809 (Ala.), Reel 18, BRFAL; Jerrell H. Shofner, *Nor Is It Over Yet: Florida in the Era of Reconstruction, 1863–1867* (Gainesville: University Press of Florida, 1974), p. 103; A. P. Caraher to E. L. Deane, Unionville, S.C., 31 July 1867, M869 (S.C.), Reel 35, BRFAL; "but": monthly report of William Bernie, Lincolnton, N.C., 31 August 1868, M843 (N.C.), Reel 23, BRFAL. See also Paul D. Escott, *Many Excellent People: Power and Privilege in North Carolina, 1850–1900* (Chapel Hill: University of North Carolina Press, 1985), p. 151; Michael W. Fitzgerald, "'To Give Our Votes to the Party': Black Political Agitation and Agricultural Change in Alabama, 1865–1870," *Journal of American History* 76 (September 1989): 489–505.

31. "Don't": C. H. Smith to O. O. Howard, Little Rock, Ark., 23 July 1867, M979 (Ark.), Reel 23, BRFAL; Donald G. Nieman, "Black Political Power and Criminal Justice: Washington County, Texas, 1868–1884," *Journal of Southern History* 55 (August 1989): 391–420.

32. LaWanda Fenlason Cox, "Agricultural Labor in the United States, 1865–1900, With Special Reference to the South" (Ph.D. diss. University of California, Berkeley, 1942), pp. 106–8; Joseph D. Reid, Jr., "The Evaluation and Implications of Southern Tenancy," *Agricultural History* 53 (January 1979): 153–69. See also Susan Archer Mann, *Agrarian Capitalism in Theory and Practice* (Chapel Hill: University of North Carolina Press, 1990).

33. "labor": contract quoted in James B. Browning, "The North Carolina Black Code," *Journal of Negro History* 15 (October 1930): 461–73; "do all": John D. Moore to James W. Sunderland, Lauderdale, Miss., 30 September 1867, M826 (Miss.), Reel 30, BRFAL; "The necessities . . . extort": Orlando H. Moore to H. W. Smith, Aiken, S.C., 31 July 1866, M869 (S.C.), Reel 34, BRFAL. See also report of F. W. Liedtke, Monck's Corner, S.C., 31 August 1866, M869 (S.C.), Reel 34, BRFAL.

34. Johnson: "Testimony by a Georgia Freedwoman before the Southern Claims Commission," Savannah, Ga., 22 March 1873, in Berlin et al., eds.,

Destruction of Slavery, p. 151; "so many days": G. A. Williams to H. Neide, Charleston, S.C., 6 July 1867, M869 (S.C.), Reel 35, BRFAL. See also Charles L. Flynn, Jr., *White Land, Black Labor: Caste and Class in Late Nineteenth Century Georgia* (Baton Rouge: Louisiana State University Press, 1983), pp. 53–79.

35. Ripley, *Slaves and Freedmen in Civil War Louisiana*, p. 58; "when . . . general": report of James Gilette, Mobile, Ala., 21 May 1868, M809 (Ala.), Reel 18, BRFAL; "as a general": report of J. B. Clinton, Amelia and Powhatan Counties, Va., 31 January 1867, M1048 (Va.), Reel 46, BRFAL; Dennett, *South As It Is*, p. 44.

36. "a supposed": W. G. Roberts to O. Brown, Fredericksburg, Va., 31 December 1866, M1048 (Va.), Reel 46, BRFAL; "Shoats": report of J. A. Yordy, Eutaw, Ala., 22 May 1868, M809 (Ala.), Reel 18, BRFAL; "claiming": Samuel L. Gardner to Wager Swayne, Selma, Ala., 10 August 1865, M809 (Ala.), Reel 18, BRFAL; A. W. Brobst to T. S. Free, Jefferson County, Miss., September 1865, M826 (Miss.), Reel 30, BRFAL; Samuel Hace to R. K. Scott, Sumter, S.C., 10 September 1867, M869 (S.C.), Reel 35, BRFAL.

37. "into": A. S. Collins to W. H. Sterling, Marksville, La., 10 February 1867, M1027 (La.), BRFAL. Added the agent, "[although the defendants would probably be sent to the penitentiary], it cannot be termed a crime, as such things are done frequently—without any thought of wrong in this country." See also Steven Hahn, "Hunting, Fishing, and Foraging: Common Rights and Class Relations in the Postbellum South," *Radical History Review* 26 (October 1982): 37–64.

38. "big": Eli Davison, FWP *Slave Narrs.*, vol. 4 (Tex. Narrs.), 1972, pt. 1, pp. 296–97.

39. "Men": Report of R. A. Wilson, Demopolis, Ala., 30 October 1868, M809 (Ala.), Reel 18, BRFAL; "are willing": A. Geddes to Wager Swayne, Tuskegee, Ala., 7 September 1865, M809 (Ala.), Reel 18, BRFAL; "a disposition": report of Thomas H. Hay, Hillsborough, N.C., 31 July 1868, M843 (N.C.), Reel 23, BRFAL. See also Roger L. Ransom and Richard Sutch, *One Kind of Freedom: The Economic Consequences of Emancipation* (New York: Cambridge University Press, 1977); John Strickland, "'No More Mud Work': The Struggle for Control of Labor and Production in the Low Country, South Carolina," in Winfred B. Moore, Jr., and Walter J. Fraser, Jr., eds., *The Southern Enigma: Essays on Race, Class and Folk Culture* (Westport, CT: Greenwood Press, 1983), pp. 43–62.

40. "driving off": report of J. S. Taylor, Hamburg, Ark., 14 July–30 September 1866, M979 (Ark.), Reel 24, BRFAL; report of Wm. H. Doherty, Elizabeth City, N.C., July 1868, M843 (N.C.), Reel 23, BRFAL; "on the slightest": J. A. Mower to O. O. Howard, New Orleans, La., October 1866, M1027 (La.), Reel 27, BRFAL; "severe": report of C. W. Pierce, Demopolis, Ala., 30 June 1868, M809 (Ala.), Reel 18, BRFAL.

41. "driven . . . to reap": A. W. Brobst to T. S. Free, Jefferson County, Miss., September 1865, M826 (Miss.), Reel 30, BRFAL; "in long festoons": Charles Nordhoff, *The Cotton States in the Spring and Summer of 1875* (New York: D. Appleton and Co., 1876), pp. 69–70; "humble": J. R. Stone to James A. Bates, Suffolk, Va., 28 February 1866, M1048 (Va.), Reel 44, BRFAL; Berlin et al., eds., *Destruction of Slavery*, pp. 190–91; Edmund L. Drago, "The Black Household in Dougherty County, Georgia, 1870–1900," *Journal of Southwest Georgia History* 1 (Fall 1983): 48.

42. "because": report of A. S. Dyer, Jacksonport, Ark., 31 August 1866, M979 (Ark.), Reel 24, BRFAL; Loring and Atkinson, *Cotton Culture*, p. 6.

43. "masters": J. W. Sharp to O. Brown, Lexington, Va., 31 January 1867, M1948 (Va.), Reel 46, BRFAL; "with such": A. W. Brobst to T. S. Free, Jefferson County, Miss., September 1865, M826 (Miss.), Reel 30, BRFAL; "a negro": Loring and Atkinson, *Cotton Culture*, p. 17. On the decline of abuse in December, see, for example, G. R. Chandler to J. M. Schofield, Winchester, Va., 31 January 1867, M1048 (Va.), Reel 46, BRFAL.

44. Wright, *Old South, New South*, p. 94.

45. "in idleness": Loring and Atkinson, *Cotton Culture*, p. 137. See, for example, Jonathan Wiener, *Social Origins of the New South: Alabama, 1860–1885* (Baton Rouge: Louisiana State University Press, 1978), p. 69; Robert Preston Brooks, *The Agrarian Revolution in Georgia, 1865–1912* (Madison: University of Wisconsin Press, 1914), pp. 46–47; Gerald Jaynes, *Branches Without Roots: Genesis of the Black Working Class in the American South, 1862–1882* (New York: Oxford University Press, 1986), p. 187; Davis, *Good and Faithful Labor*, pp. 99, 175; George Campbell, *White and Black: The Outcome of a Visit to the United States* (London: Chatto and Windus, 1879), p. 150.

46. On the so-called isolated sharecropping family, see Jaynes, *Branches Without Roots*, p. 222; Davis, *Good and Faithful Labor*, p. 178. See also Cohen, *At Freedom's Edge*, chaps. 2, 4.

47. "almost": John T. Trowbridge, *The South: A Tour of Its Battlefields and Ruined Cities* (New York: Arno Press, 1969; orig. pub. 1866), p. 544; Verney, "Trespassers in the Land of Their Birth."(n.47)

48. "the irregular": DeForest, *A Union Officer*, pp. 95–96; "They are unruly": Loring and Atkinson, *Cotton Culture*, p. 14; Hannibal D. Norton to Jacob F. Chur, Morganton, N.C., 27 November 1868, M843 (N.C.), Reel 23, BRFAL; A. Evans to William Sinclair, Sherman, Tex., 15 January 1867, M821 (Tex.), Reel 20, BRFAL; Armstead L. Robinson, "Worser Dan Jeff Davis: The Coming of Free Labor During the Civil War, 1861–1865," in Thavolia Glymph, Harold D. Woodman, Barbara Jeanne Fields, and Armstead L. Robinson, eds., *Essays on the Postbellum Southern Economy* (College Station: Texas A & M University Press, 1985), pp. 11–47.

49. "his": *U.S. Commissioner of Agriculture Report for 1867* (Washington, D.C.: GPO, 1868), p. 421; Mary Anne Gibson, FWP *Slave Narrs.*, SS2, vol.

5 (Tex. Narrs.), 1979, pt. 4, pp. 1469–70; "a right . . . corn-bread . . . tied": Dennett, *South As It Is*, p. 36.

50. Aaron Nunn, FWP *Slave Narrs.*, SS2, vol. 8 (Tex. Narrs.), 1979, pt. 7, pp. 2955–56; E. A. Rozlay to W. W. Smith, Orangeburg, S.C., December 1865, M869 (S.C.), Reel 34, BRFAL; Louis W. Stevenson to O. Brown, Lynchburg, Va., 31 January 1867, M1048 (Va.), Reel 46, BRFAL.

51. Alrutheus Ambush Taylor, *The Negro in the Reconstruction of Virginia* (Washington, D.C.: Association for the Study of Negro Life and History, 1926), p. 102; "lounging": James Haugh to W. H. Sterling, Amilie City, La., 20 March 1867, M1027 (La.), Reel 27, BRFAL; King, *Great South*, p. 69.

52. "We want": S. F. Willard to W. H. Smith, Georgetown, S.C., 13 November 1865, M869 (S.C.), Reel 34, BRFAL; "a few . . . clean": W. H. H. Peck to C. D. Kinsman, Tuscaloosa, Ala., 9 July 1866, M809 (Ala.), Reel 18, BRFAL; "go abroad": Watson R. Wentworth to T. F. P. Crandon, Tappahannock, Essex County, Va., 24 February 1866, M1048 (Va.), Reel 44, BRFAL. See also Shofner, *Nor Is It Over Yet*, p. 72; Taylor, *Negro in the Reconstruction of Virginia*, p. 110; Engs, *Freedom's First Generation*, pp. 168–70.

53. John Belcher, FWP *Slave Narrs.*, SS1, vol. 6 (Miss. Narrs.), 1977, pt. 1, pp. 107–10.

54. "have an ambition": A. E. Niles to H. W. Smith, Greenville, S.C., 13 July 1866, M869 (S.C.), Reel 34, BRFAL; "their little": report of C. C. Sibley, Atlanta, Ga., 1 February 1868, M798 (Ga.), Reel 32, BRFAL; Alabama planter quoted in Loring and Atkinson, *Cotton Culture*, p. 13.

55. "clannishness": Joel Williamson, *After Slavery: The Negro in South Carolina During Reconstruction, 1861–1877* (Chapel Hill: University of North Carolina Press, 1965), p. 312; Herbert G. Gutman, *The Black Family in Slavery and Freedom, 1750–1925* (New York: Pantheon, 1976), pp. 212–13.

56. "reasons": Dennett, *South As It Is*, p. 342; "plantation schools": see, for example, report of R. A. Wilson, Demopolis, Ala., 31 August 1868, M809 (Ala.), Reel 18, BRFAL; "found that the freedmen": J. A. Mower to O. O. Howard, New Orleans, La., October 1866, M1027 (La.), Reel 27, BRFAL; report of E. G. Barber, Monticello, Ark., 30 September 1865, M979 (Ark.), Reel 23, BRFAL; "who are learning": J. H. Archer to J. B. Kidder, Acompato, Tex., 10 January 1867, M821 (Tex.), Reel 20, BRFAL; report of E. M. Wheelock, Galveston, Tex., 31 January 1866, M821 (Tex.), Reel 29, BRFAL; report of Clarence Mauch, Austin, Tex., 30 November 1868, M821 (Tex.), Reel 29, BRFAL; James D. Anderson, *The Education of Blacks in the South, 1860–1935* (Chapel Hill: University of North Carolina Press, 1988).

57. "Employers . . . willing": report of Thomas L. Bevill, Forest Home, Ala., 27 April 1866, M809 (Ala.), Reel 18, BRFAL; "to encourage . . . everything": Martin Havens to William P. Austin, Princess Anne County, Va., 31 January 1867, M1048 (Va.), Reel 46, BRFAL.

58. "Localized labor": planter's letter to *Hinds County* [Mississippi] *Gazette*, 6 December 1867, in LaWanda Cox and John Cox, eds., *Reconstruction, the Negro, and the New South* (Columbia: University of South Carolina Press, 1973), p. 354; "partly" quoted in Davis, *Good and Faithful Labor*, p. 170; Sylvia H. Krebs, "Will the Freedmen Work? White Alabamians Adjust to Free Black Labor," *Alabama Historical Quarterly* 36 (Summer 1974): 157; Currie, *Enclave: Vicksburg and Her Plantations*, p. 172. See also Leon F. Litwack, *Been in the Storm So Long: The Aftermath of Slavery* (New York: Knopf, 1979), p. 416.

59. "elevation": Schurz, *Report on the Condition of the South*, p. 25. On the erosion of independence among other groups of American workers during this period, see, for example, Alan Dawley, *Class and Community: The Industrial Revolution in Lynn* (Cambridge: Harvard University Press, 1976); Mary H. Blewett, *Men, Women, and Work: Class, Gender, and Protest in the New England Shoe Industry, 1780–1910* (Urbana: University of Illinois Press, 1988); Daniel T. Rodgers, *The Work Ethic in Industrializing America, 1850–1920* (Chicago: University of Chicago Press, 1978); David Montgomery, *Beyond Equality: Labor and the Radical Republicans, 1862–1872* (New York: Knopf, 1967); Steven Hahn, *The Roots of Southern Populism: Yeoman Farmers and the Transformation of the Georgia Upcountry, 1850–1890* (New York: Oxford University Press, 1983); Lacy K. Ford, *Origins of Southern Radicalism: The South Carolina Upcountry, 1800–1860* (New York: Oxford University Press, 1988).

Chapter 2
The Pride of Race and Its Limits: White Field Workers

1. Rosser H. Taylor, ed., "Postbellum Southern Rental Contracts," *Agricultural History* 17 (April 1943): 122–23.

2. Laurence Shore, *Southern Capitalists: The Ideological Leadership of An Elite, 1832–1885* (Chapel Hill: University of North Carolina Press, 1986), p. 160.

3. Eric Foner, *Reconstruction: America's Unfinished Revolution, 1863–1877* (New York: Harper & Row, 1988), pp. 426–28; Richard Nelson Current, *Those Terrible Carpetbaggers* (New York: Oxford University Press, 1988), pp. 355–57.

4. Colonel John D. Williams is listed in the 1860 Slave Population schedule for Laurens County as the owner of 250 slaves: U.S. Census, *Eighth Census of the United States* (1870), Population Schedule of the *Eighth Census*, Slave Schedule, vol. 3, Laurens Co., S.C., p. 31 (microfilm reel no. 653, roll no. 1233). See also Lacy K. Ford, *Origins of Southern Radicalism: The South Carolina Upcountry, 1800–1860* (New York: Oxford University Press, 1988), p. 234.

5. "White Labor in Cotton Growing," *Report of the Commissioner of Agriculture for 1876* (Washington, D.C., GPO, 1877:), p. 136.

6. Edwin Q. Bell, "In Lieu of Labor," *DeBow's Review* 4, After War Series (July/August 1867): 69.

7. Hill quoted in Shore, *Southern Capitalists*, p. 116; Jonathan M. Wiener, *Social Origins of the New South: Alabama, 1860–1885* (Baton Rouge: Louisiana State University Press, 1978), pp. 192–93.

8. John William DeForest, *A Union Officer in the Reconstruction* (New Haven, CT: Yale University Press, 1948), pp. 140, 53, 52. Cf. Grady McWhiney, *Cracker Culture: Celtic Ways in the Old South* (Tuscaloosa: University of Alabama Press, 1988).

9. "With": report of C. C. Sibley, Atlanta, Ga., 1 February 1868, M798 (Ga.), Roll 32, Bureau of Refugees, Freedmen, and Abandoned Lands (hereafter BRFAL), Record Group 105, National Archives, Washington, D.C.; "loved": Everett Dick, *The Dixie Frontier: A Social History of the Southern Frontier From the First Transmontane Beginnings to the Civil War* (New York: Knopf, 1948), p. 23; "the dull": DeForest, *Union Officer*, p. 52; "lounge": John R. Dennett, *The South As It Is: 1865–1866* (New York: Viking, 1965), p. 42; Alice B. Keith, "White Relief in North Carolina, 1865–1867," *Journal of Social Forces* 17 (March 1939): 337–55.

10. "Destitute": report of George O'Reilly, Gainestown, Ala., 17 October 1866, M809 (Ala.), Reel 18, S1040, BRFAL; pipes/snuff: Edward King, *The Great South: A Record of Journeys . . .* (Hartford, CT: American Publishing Company, 1875), p. 340 (for a description of a poor white woman in northern Alabama who "pulls from her pocket a pine stick, with an old rag saturated in snuff wrapped around it, and inserts it between her dainty lips" see p. 774); Charles Nordhoff, *The Cotton States in the Spring and Summer of 1875* (New York: D. Appleton and Co., 1876), p. 39.

11. Railroad director to the Confederate Secretary of War, February 1864, in Ira Berlin et al., eds., *Freedom: A Documentary History of Emancipation, 1861–1867*, series 1, vol. 1, *The Destruction of Slavery* (Cambridge: Cambridge University Press, 1985), pp. 735–36.

12. "they were not slaves" quoted in Foner, *Reconstruction: America's Unfinished Revolution*, p. 213; "not willing": Francis Butler Simkins and Robert Hilliard Woody, *South Carolina During Reconstruction* (Chapel Hill: University of North Carolina Press, 1932), p. 247; John Scott Strickland, "'No More Mud Work': The Struggle for the Control of Labor and Production in Low Country South Carolina, 1863–1880," in Winfred B. Moore, Jr. and Walter J. Fraser, Jr., eds., *The Southern Enigma: Essays on Race, Class, and Folk Culture* (Westport, CT: Greenwood Press, 1983), pp. 43–62; Robert Preston Brooks, *The Agrarian Revolution in Georgia, 1865–1912* (Madison: University of Wisconsin Press, 1914), p. 31; "Hoe hands" quoted in Ulrich Bonnell Phillips, "Plantations with Slave Labor and Free," *American Historical Review* 30 (July 1925): 751.

See also Winston Lee Kinsey, "The Immigrant in Texas Agriculture During Reconstruction," *Agricultural History* 53 (1979): 125–41; Ronald L. F. Davis, *Good and Faithful Labor: From Slavery to Sharecropping in the Natchez District, 1860–1890* (Westport, CT: Greenwood Press, 1982), p. 126; Walter L. Fleming, "Immigration to the Southern States," *Political Science Quarterly* 20 (June 1905): 276–97; Sylvia H. Krebs, "Will the Freedmen Work? White Alabamians Adjust to Free Black Labor," *Alabama Historical Quarterly* 36 (Summer 1974): 151–63; Victor B. Howard, *Black Liberation in Kentucky: Emancipation and Freedom, 1862–1884* (Louisville: University Press of Kentucky, 1983), p. 95.

13. Lucy M. Cohen, "Entry of Chinese to the Lower South from 1865 to 1870: Policy Dilemmas," *Southern Studies* 17 (1978): 5–37.

14. C. W. Howard [of Kingston, Ga.], "Condition of Agriculture in the Cotton States," *Report of the Commissioner of Agriculture for 1874* (Washington, D.C.: GPO, 1875), p. 223.

15. "indeed": impressment agent for Randolph County, Ala., to the chief impressment agent, 1 June 1864, in Berlin et al., eds., *Destruction of Slavery*, p. 759; Francis W. Loring and C. F. Atkinson, *Cotton Culture and the South Considered With Reference to Emigration* (Boston: A. Williams, 1869), p. 93.

16. Frederick Law Olmsted, *A Journey in the Back Country, 1853–1854* (New York: Schocken, 1970; orig. pub. 1860), pp. 218–19.

17. On antebellum white social structure, see James Oakes, *The Ruling Race: A History of American Slaveholders* (New York: Knopf, 1982); J. William Harris, *Plain Folk and Gentry in a Slave Society: White Liberty and Black Slavery in Augusta's Hinterlands* (Middletown, CT: Wesleyan University Press, 1985); J. Mills Thornton, *Politics and Power in a Slave Society: Alabama, 1800–1860* (Baton Rouge: Louisiana State University Press, 1978); Guion Griffis Johnson, *Antebellum North Carolina: A Social History* (Chapel Hill: University of North Carolina Press, 1937); Herbert Weaver, *Mississippi Farmers, 1850–1860* (Nashville, TN: Vanderbilt University Press, 1945); Randolph B. Campbell, "Planters and Plain Folks: The Social Structure of the Antebellum South," in John Boles and Evelyn Thomas Nolen, eds., *Interpreting Southern History: Historiographical Essays in Honor of Sanford W. Higginbotham* (Baton Rouge: Louisiana State University Press, 1987), pp. 48–77. On popular terminology for poor whites, see Christopher S. Johnson, "Identifying the Antebellum Southern Poor White: A Preliminary Study of Sources and Methods," *Southern Historian* 8 (Spring 1987): 54–63; A. N. J. Den Hollander, "The Tradition of 'Poor Whites,'" in W. T. Couch, ed., *Culture in the South* (Chapel Hill: University of North Carolina Press, 1934), pp. 403–31; Theodore Saloutos, "Southern Agriculture and the Problems of Readjustment, 1865–1877," *Agricultural History* 30 (April 1956): 58–76; Edward Magdol and Jon L. Wakelyn, eds., *The Southern Common People: Studies in Nineteenth-*

NOTES TO PAGES 54–56

Century Social History (Westport, CT: Greenwood Press, 1980).

18. Steven Hahn, *The Roots of Southern Populism: Yeoman Farmers and the Transformation of the Georgia Upcountry, 1850–1890* (New York: Oxford University Press, 1983); Ted Ownby, "The Defeated Generation at Work: White Farmers in the Deep South, 1865–1890," *Southern Studies* 13 (Winter 1984): 325–47; John Solomon Otto, "Southern 'Plain Folk' Agriculture: A Reconsideration," *Plantation Society in the Americas* 2 (April 1983): 29–36; Morton Rothstein, "The Antebellum South as a Dual Economy: A Tentative Hypothesis," *Agricultural History* 41 (October 1967): 373–82; Lacy K. Ford, "Yeoman Farmers in the South Carolina Upcountry: Changing Production Patterns in the Late Antebellum Period," *Agricultural History* 60 (Fall 1986): 17–37; Keith L. Bryant, Jr., "The Role and Status of the Female Yeomanry in the Antebellum South: The Literary View," *Southern Quarterly* 48 (Winter 1980): 73–88; Lacy K. Ford, "Self-Sufficiency, Cotton, and Economic Development in the South Carolina Upcountry, 1800–1860," *Journal of Economic History* 45 (June 1985): 261–67; Arthur C. Menius, "James Bennitt: Portrait of an Antebellum Yeoman," *North Carolina Historical Review* 58 (October 1981): 305–26.

19. Frederick A. Bode and Donald A. Ginter, *Farm Tenancy and the Census in Antebellum Georgia* (Athens: University of Georgia Press, 1986), pp. 4, 183; Hahn, *Roots of Southern Populism*, p. 66; Donald L. Winters, "Plain Folk of the Old South Reexamined: Economic Democracy in Tennessee," *Journal of Southern History* 53 (November 1987): 565–86; Donald L. Winters, "The Agricultural Ladder in Southern Agriculture: Tennessee, 1850–1870," *Agricultural History* 61 (Summer 1987): 36–52; Marjorie Stratford Mendenhall, "The Rise of Southern Tenancy," *Yale Review* 27 (September 1937): 110–29; Wayne Flynt, *Poor But Proud: Alabama's Poor Whites* (Tuscaloosa: University of Alabama Press, 1989), p. 61.

20. Ann Patton Malone, "Piney Woods Farmers of South Georgia, 1850–1900: Jeffersonian Yeomen in an Age of Expanding Commercialism," *Agricultural History* 60 (Fall 1986): 51–84; Grady McWhiney, "The Revolution in Nineteenth-Century Alabama Agriculture," *Alabama Review* (January 1978): 3–32; Roland M. Harper, "Development of Agriculture in Georgia from 1850 to 1920," *Georgia Historical Quarterly* 6 (May 1922, July 1922, October 1922, January 1923): 3–27, 97–121, 211–32, 323–54.

21. William L. Barney, "The Ambivalence of Change: From Old South to New in the Alabama Black Belt, 1850–1870," in Walter J. Fraser, Jr. and Winfred B. Moore, Jr., eds., *From the Old South to the New: Essays on the Transitional South* (Westport, CT: Greenwood Press, 1981), pp. 33–41; Edward L. Ayers, *Vengeance and Justice: Crime and Punishment in the Nineteenth-Century American South* (New York: Oxford University Press, 1984), pp. 104–11.

22. John Inscoe, "Mountain Masters: Slaveholding in Western North Carolina," *North Carolina Historical Review* 61 (April 1984): 143–73; "honest": Daniel

R. Hundley, *Social Relations in Our Southern States* (New York: H. B. Price, 1860), pp. 195–97; Avery Craven, "Poor Whites and Negroes in the Antebellum South," *Journal of Negro History* 15 (January 1930): 19–20; "chicken thieves": Frederick Law Olmsted, *A Journey in the Seaboard Slave States* (New York: Dix and Edward, 1856), p. 117; Flynt, *Poor But Proud*, pp. 4–10, 32–34.

23. Bertram Wyatt-Brown, *Southern Honor: Ethics and Behavior in the Old South* (New York: Oxford University Press, 1982), pp. 46, 160, 299; "half agricultural" quoted in Flynt, *Poor But Proud*, p. 32; "palm-reading": Hundley, *Social Relations*, pp. 266–67; Victoria Bynum, "On the Lowest Rung: Court Control Over Poor White and Free Black Women," *Southern Exposure* 12 (November–December 1984): 40–44. On the similar material condition of slaves and their poor-white overseers, see John Solomon Otto and Augustus Marion Burns III, "Black Folks and Poor Buckras: Archaeological Evidence of Slave and Overseer Living Conditions on an Antebellum Plantation," *Journal of Black Studies* 14 (December 1983): 185–200.

24. "The poor" quoted in Stephen V. Ash, *Middle Tennessee Society Transformed, 1860–1870: War and Peace in the Upper South* (Baton Rouge: Louisiana State University Press, 1988), p. 48; "ligaments": Harris, *Plain Folk and Gentry*, p. 94; Robert C. Kenzer, *Kinship and Neighborhood in a Southern Community: Orange County, North Carolina, 1849–1881* (Knoxville: University of Tennessee Press, 1987); Eugene Genovese, "Yeoman Farmers in a Slaveholders' Democracy," *Agricultural History* 49 (April 1975): 331–42; Ayers, *Vengeance and Justice*.

25. Barbara Jeanne Fields, "The Nineteenth Century American South: History and Theory," *Plantation Society in the Americas* 2 (April 1983): 7–28; Harry L. Watson, *Jacksonian Politics and Community Conflict: The Emergence of the Second American Party System in Cumberland County, North Carolina* (Baton Rouge: Louisiana State University Press, 1981); Orville Vernon Burton and Robert C. McMath, Jr., eds., *Class, Conflict, and Consensus: Antebellum Southern Community Studies* (Westport, CT: Greenwood Press, 1982); Ford, *Origins of Southern Radicalism*; Gail Williams O'Brien, *The Legal Fraternity and the Making of a New South Community, 1848–1882* (Athens: University of Georgia Press, 1986). See also the following review essays: Paul Goodman, "White Over White: Planters, Yeomen, and the Coming of the Civil War: A Review Essay," *Agricultural History* 54 (July 1980): 446–52; James Oakes, "The Politics of Economic Development in the Antebellum South," *Journal of Interdisciplinary History* 15 (Autumn 1984): 305–36.

26. "When the lands": Hundley, *Social Relations*, pp. 271–72; Oakes, *Ruling Race*; James D. Foust, "The Yeoman Farmer and Westward Expansion of U.S. Cotton Production" (Ph.D. diss., University of North Carolina, Chapel Hill, 1968); Joan E. Cashin, *A Family Venture: Men and Women in the*

Southern Frontier (New York: Oxford University Press, 1991).

27. For an overview, see James M. McPherson, *Battle Cry of Freedom: The Civil War Era* (New York: Oxford University Press, 1988).

28. See, for example, Michael W. Fitzgerald, "Radical Republicanism and the White Yeomanry During Alabama Reconstruction, 1865–1868," *Journal of Southern History* 54 (November 1988): 565–96; William T. Auman, "Neighbor Against Neighbor: The Inner Civil War in the Randolph County Area of Confederate North Carolina," *North Carolina Historical Review* 61 (January 1984): 59–92; Paul Escott, *Many Excellent People: Power and Privilege in North Carolina, 1850–1900* (Chapel Hill: University of North Carolina Press, 1985).

29. "deprecated": former governor of Virginia to the Confederate Secretary of War, 7 March 1863, in Berlin et al., eds., *Destruction of Slavery*, pp. 748–49; "teamsters": commander of the Confederate Department to the chairman of a South Carolina Legislative Committee, 10 December 1863, ibid., p. 715; "one fourth": Alabama slaveholder to the Confederate Secretary of War, ibid., p. 704.

30. Commander of a Confederate Alabama Regiment to the commander of the Confederate Post of Yorktown, Virginia; and the latter's reply, 19 June 1861, in Berlin et al., eds., *Destruction of Slavery*, pp. 684–85.

31. Berlin et al., eds., *Destruction of Slavery*, p. 675; W. E. B. DuBois, *Black Reconstruction in America* (New York: Atheneum, 1975; orig. pub. 1935), p. 72; "there is": Dennett, *South As It Is*, p. 191; "the overseers": chief engineer of the Confederate Department of the Gulf to a Confederate senator from Alabama, 29 December 1863, in Berlin et al., eds., *Destruction of Slavery*, p. 718.

32. "So common": Assistant Secretary of War John A. Campbell quoted in Ella Lonn, *Desertion During the Civil War* (New York: The Century Co., 1928), p. 29. See also Statement of a Tennessee Fugitive Slave, 23 December1862, in Berlin et al., eds., *Destruction of Slavery*, p. 299; Virginia farmer to the Confederate Secretary of War, 17 December 1864, ibid., p. 729.

33. "They soon" quoted in Flynt, *Poor But Proud*, p. 41; letter from Mary Cooper quoted in Lonn, *Desertion During the Civil War*, p. 13.

34. William L. Barney, "Patterns of Crisis: Alabama White Families and Social Change, 1850–1870," *Sociology and Social Research* 63 (April 1979): 524–43; Hahn, *Roots of Southern Populism*, p. 158; Robert A. Gilmour, "The Other Emancipation: Studies in the Society and Economy of Alabama Whites During Reconstruction" (Ph.D. diss., Johns Hopkins University, 1972); Ash, *Middle Tennessee Society Transformed*, pp. 233–37; Flynt, *Poor But Proud*, pp. 44–55; Peter Temin, "Patterns of Cotton Agriculture in Post-Bellum Georgia," *Journal of Economic History* 43 (September 1983): 661–74; David Weiman, "The Economic Emancipation of the Non-Slaveholding Class: Upcountry Farmers in the Georgia Cotton Economy," *Journal of Economic History* 45 (March 1985): 71–94; Forrest McDonald

and Grady McWhiney, "The South from Self-Sufficiency to Peonage: An Interpretation," *American Historical Review* 85 (December 1980): 1095–118. This process of increased agricultural commercialization was not limited to the rural South during this period. See, for example, Christopher Clark, *The Roots of Rural Capitalism: Western Massachusetts, 1780–1860* (Ithaca, NY: Cornell University Press, 1990).

35. "I see": report of Thomas J. Abel, Fort Smith, Ark., 31 March 1866, M979 (Ark.), Reel 23, BRFAL; "satisfied": Loring and Atkinson, *Cotton Culture*, p. 4. See also Robert Preston Brooks, *The Agrarian Revolution in Georgia, 1865–1912* (Madison: University of Wisconsin Press, 1914), p. 32; Gavin Wright, *Old South, New South: Revolutions in the Southern Economy Since the Civil War* (New York: Basic Books, 1986), p. 103.

36. "the introduction": Thomas Jackson to A. S. Flagg, Princess Anne, [Md.?], 8 February 1866, M1048 (Va.), Reel 44, BRFAL; "Some": J. W. Sharp to O. Brown, Lexington, Va., 31 January 1867, M1048 (Va.), Reel 46, BRFAL; Ownby, "Defeated Generation at Work," p. 336; Gavin Wright, "Postbellum Southern Labor Markets," in Peter Kilby, ed., *Quantity and Quiddity: Essays in U.S. Economic History* (Middletown, CT: Wesleyan University Press, 1987), p. 104. See also Nordhoff, *Cotton States*, p. 100.

37. "because . . . he would rather": Nordhoff, *Cotton States*, pp. 39, 70. See also King, *Great South*, p. 274.

38. Quoted in Fitzgerald, "Radical Republicanism and the White Yeomanry," p. 578.

39. "living": accounts of Freedmen's Bureau officials in Alabama, Senate Executive Doc. no. 27, 39 Cong., 1st sess., pp. 68, 73, 77 (reprinted in Walter L. Fleming, ed., *Documentary History of Reconstruction*, vol. 1 [New York: McGraw Hill, 1966; orig. pub. 1906–7], p. 20); "lone wimmen": DeForest, *Union Officer*, p. 50; report of C. W. Pierce, Demopolis, Ala., 24 October 1866, M809 (Ala.), Reel 18, BRFAL; "improvident": William K. White to T. W. Sunderland, Columbus, Miss., 30 September 1867, M826 (Miss.), Reel 30, BRFAL. See also J. W. Sprague to O. O. Howard, St. Louis, Mo., 7 September 1865, M979 (Ark.), Reel 23, BRFAL; report of Robert T. Smith, Opelika, Ala., 29 June 1867, M809 (Ala.), Reel 18, BRFAL; Foner, *Reconstruction*, p. 327; Dudley L. Poston, Jr. and Robert H. Weller, eds., *The Population of the South: Structure and Change in Social Demographic Context* (Austin: University of Texas Press, 1981), p. 7; Bynum, "Lowest Rung"; V. M. Peryham to J. Callis, Florence, Ala., 7 September 1866, M809 (Ala.), Reel 18, BRFAL; John A. Hynes to Capt. A. A. Preston, Sunflower Co., Miss., 15 July 1867, M826 (Miss.), Reel 30, BRFAL.

40. Klan quoted in Escott, *Many Excellent People*, p. 152.

41. Testimony of a Georgia freedwoman before the Southern Claims Commission, 22 March 1873, in Berlin et al., eds., *Destruction of Slavery*, pp. 150–51.

42. "home colony": report of L. J. Whiting, Montgomery, Ala., 25 October 1866, M809 (Ala.), Reel 18, BRFAL; "low down": DeForest, *Union Officer*, pp. 144–45.

43. Loring and Atkinson, *Cotton Culture*, p. 96; Dennett, *South As It Is*, p. 259; Gilmour, "Other Emancipation," pp. 57, 136.

44. "not disposed . . . bands . . . determined": E. O. C. Orde to O. O. Howard, Little Rock, Ark., 22 February 1867, M979 (Ark.), Reel 23, BRFAL; E. A. Rozlay to H. W. Smith, Orangeburg, S.C., 29 January 1866, M869 (S.C.), Reel 34, BRFAL; "lower orders . . . who show": George A. Williamson to H. W. Smith, Charleston, S.C., September 1866, M869 (S.C.), Reel 34, BRFAL; "whose hatred": Edward Murphy to O. Brown, Drummondtown, Va., 30 November 1866, M1048 (Va.), Reel 46, BRFAL. See also Berlin et al., eds., *Destruction of Slavery*, p. 677; Peter Kolchin, *First Freedom: The Responses of Alabama's Blacks to Emancipation and Reconstruction* (Westport, CT: Greenwood Press, 1972), p. 18.

45. "in as much": report of Frederick Schilplin, Pocohantas, Ark., 28 February 1868, M979 (Ark.), Reel 23, BRFAL; "seem to be": Albert A. Metzner to Acting Assistant Adjutant General, Clinton, Tex., 9 January 1867, M821 (Tex.), Reel 20, BRFAL; Jacqueline Jones, *Soldiers of Light and Love: Northern Teachers and Georgia Blacks, 1865–1873* (Chapel Hill: University of North Carolina Press, 1980), p. 81.

46. Ownby, "Defeated Generation at Work"; Hahn, *Roots of Southern Populism;* Otto, "Southern 'Plain Folk' Agriculture: A Reconsideration," pp. 29–36.

Chapter 3
The Family Economy of Rural Southerners, 1870 to 1930

1. William H. Holtzclaw, *The Black Man's Burden* (New York: Neale Publishing Company, 1915), pp. 17, 18, 27, 20, 25, 21, 31.

2. Ibid., pp. 32–36.

3. Gavin Wright, *The Political Economy of the Cotton South: Households, Markets, and Wealth in the Nineteenth Century* (New York: Norton, 1978), pp. 167–68; Gavin Wright, *Old South, New South: Revolutions in the Southern Economy Since the Civil War* (New York: Basic Books, 1986); David L. Carlton, "The Revolution from Above: The National Market and the Beginnings of Industrialization in North Carolina," *Journal of American History* 77 (September 1990): 445–75.

4. See, for example, Marjorie Mendenhall Applewhite, "Sharecropper and Tenant in the Courts of North Carolina," *North Carolina Historical Review* 31 (April 1954): 134–49; Charles L. Flynn, Jr., *White Land, Black Labor: Caste and Class in Late Nineteenth-Century Georgia* (Baton Rouge: Louisiana State University Press, 1983), p. 87; Alexander Keyssar, *Out of Work: The First Century of Unemployment in Massachusetts* (New York:

Cambridge University Press, 1986); Charles Stephenson, " 'There's Plenty Waitin' at the Gates': Mobility, Opportunity, and the American Worker," in Charles Stephenson and Robert Asher, eds., *Life and Labor: Dimensions of American Working-Class History* (Albany: State University of New York Press, 1986), pp. 72–91.

5. Wright, *Political Economy of the Cotton South*.

6. Jack Temple Kirby, "The Transformation of Southern Plantations, c. 1920–1960," *Agricultural History* 57 (July 1983): 257–76; "industrial": Ulrich B. Phillips, "The Decadence of the Plantation System," *Annals of the Academy of Political and Social Science* 35 (January–June 1910): 37–41; Pete Daniel, "The Metamorphosis of Slavery," *Journal of American History* 66 (June 1979): 88–99; John Dittmer, *Black Georgia in the Progressive Era, 1900–1920* (Urbana: University of Illinois Press, 1977).

7. "We want" quoted in Neil R. McMillen, *Dark Journey: Black Mississippians in the Age of Jim Crow* (Urbana: University of Illinois Press, 1989), p. 55; Jack Temple Kirby, *Rural Worlds Lost: The American South, 1920–1960* (Baton Rouge: Louisiana State University Press, 1987); James D. Anderson, *The Education of Blacks in the South, 1860–1930* (Chapel Hill: University of North Carolina Press, 1988); William Cohen, *At Freedom's Edge: Black Mobility and the Southern White Quest for Racial Control, 1861–1915* (Baton Rouge: Louisiana State University Press, 1991).

8. I. A. Newby, *Plain Folk in the New South: Social Change and Cultural Persistence, 1880–1915* (Baton Rouge: Louisiana State University Press, 1989); U.S. Bureau of the Census, *Historical Statistics of the United States, Colonial Times to the Present*, vol. 1 (Washington, D.C.: GPO, 1975), p. 465; Morgan J. Kousser, *The Shaping of Southern Politics: Suffrage Restriction and the Establishment of the One-Party South, 1880–1910* (New Haven, CT: Yale University Press, 1974), pp. 33, 241, 253. See also, for example, Flynn, *White Land, Black Labor*, pp. 54–55, 115–49, 151, 157; Harold Woodman, "Post-Civil War Southern Agriculture and the Law," *Agricultural History* 53 (January 1979): 319–37; Steven Hahn, "Hunting, Fishing, and Foraging: Common Rights and Class Relations in the Postbellum South," *Radical History Review* 26 (October 1982): 37–64.

9. Jane Maguire, *On Shares: Ed Brown's Story* (New York: Norton, 1975), pp. 48, 63.

10. Ibid., pp. 48, 9, 10, 19, 34, 14, 17.

11. Ibid., pp. 39, 40, 44, 45.

12. Ibid., pp. 48, 63, 54, 60–61, 65, 72.

13. Ibid., pp. 73, 76, 77.

14. Ibid., pp. 48–99, 37–98.

15. Lewis C. Gray et al., "Farm Ownership and Tenancy," U.S. Department of Agriculture (hereafter USDA), *Agricultural Yearbook for 1923* (Washington, D.C.: GPO, 1924), p. 548; "This" quoted in Wayne Flynt, *Poor But Proud: Alabama's Poor Whites* (Tuscaloosa: University of Alabama Press, 1989), p.

83. On the indices of material and educational well-being correlated with tenure status, see, for example, Eva Joffe, "Rural School Attendance in Alabama," U.S. Department of Labor, Children's Bureau, *Child Labor Bulletin* 7, no. 2 (1918): 107; Robin M. Williams and Olaf Wakefield, "Farm Tenancy in North Carolina, 1880–1935," North Carolina Agricultural Experiment Station with the Department of Agricultural Economics and Rural Sociology, AE-RS Information Series no. 1 (September 1937); J. A. Dickey and E. C. Branson, "How Farm Tenants Live," University of North Carolina Extension, *Bulletin* 2, no. 6 (16 November 1922).

16. Gavin Wright, "American Agriculture and the Labor Market: What Happened to Proletarianization?" *Agricultural History* 62 (Summer 1988): 182–209; W. J. Spillman and E. A. Goldenweiser, "Farm Tenantry in the United States," USDA *Agricultural Yearbook for 1916* (Washington, D.C.: GPO, 1917), p. 325; Gray et al., "Farm Ownership and Tenancy," p. 273; "Farm Family Living Among White Owner and Tenant Operators in Wake County," Agricultural Experiment Station of the North Carolina State College of Agriculture and Engineering and the North Carolina Department of Agriculture, *Bulletin* 269 (September 1929) (Raleigh): 13, 21; Williams and Wakefield, "Farm Tenancy in North Carolina," p. 30.

17. "the various": Gray et al., "Farm Ownership and Tenancy," p. 548; "That was": interview with Dorothy Slater Hawkins conducted by Melani McAlister, April 1990, p. 5 (interview in author's possession).

18. Maguire, *On Shares*, p. 121; Adrienne Lash Jones, "Jane Edna Hunter: A Case Study of Black Leadership, 1910–1950" (Ph.D. diss., Case Western Reserve University, 1982), p. 64.

19. Gray et al., "Farm Ownership and Tenancy," p. 555; Robert Tracy McKenzie, "Postbellum Tenancy in Fayette County, Tennessee: Its Implications for Economic Development and Persistent Black Poverty," *Agricultural History* 61 (Spring 1987): 28; A. G. Smith, "Farm Loan Bank and Tenancy," 1916, Entry 133, File no. 0095, Bureau of Agricultural Economics (hereafter BAE), Record Group 83, National Archives, Washington, D.C.; "Farm Ownership and Tenancy in the Black Prairie of Texas," USDA *Bulletin*, no. 1068 (1922): 4; W. S. Scarborough, "Tenancy and Ownership Among Negro Farmers in Southampton County, Virginia," USDA *Bulletin*, no. 1404 (1926): 16; Flynt, *Poor But Proud*, p. 85; Rupert B. Vance, *Human Factors in Cotton Culture: A Study in the Human Geography of the American South* (Chapel Hill: University of North Carolina Press, 1929); Margaret J. Hagood, *Mothers of the South: Portraiture of the White Tenant Farm Woman* (New York: Norton, 1977; orig. pub. 1939).

20. Gray et al., "Farm Ownership and Tenancy," p. 551; T. J. Woofter, Jr., "Landlord and Tenant on the Cotton Plantation," Works Progress Administration Research Monograph 5 (Washington, D.C.: GPO, 1936), p. 116; "black sharecroppers": Charles Orser, *Material Basis of the Postbellum*

Tenant Plantation: Historical Archaeology in the South Carolina Piedmont (Athens: University of Georgia Press, 1988), p. 110.

21. "In the": Nate Shaw (pseud. for Ned Cobb) quoted in Theodore Rosengarten, *All God's Dangers: The Life of Nate Shaw* (New York: Knopf, 1972), p. 112. On the strategies of households in response to the needs of dependents in the community, see, for example, Crandall A. Shifflett, *Patronage and Poverty in the Tobacco South: Louisa County, Virginia, 1860–1900* (Knoxville: University of Tennessee Press, 1982).

22. "The most": Arthur F. Raper, *Preface to Peasantry: A Tale of Two Black Belt Counties* (Chapel Hill: University of North Carolina Press, 1936), p. 153; "Laborers . . . provided": Department of the Interior, Census Office, *Report on Cotton Production in the United States*, pt. 2 (Washington, D.C.: GPO, 1884), pp. 77, 69; H. W. Hawthorne et al., "Farm Management and Farm Organization in Sumter County, Georgia," *USDA Bulletin*, no. 1034 (1922); U.S. Department of Commerce, Bureau of the Census, *Plantation Farming in the United States* (Washington, D.C.: GPO, 1916), p. 18. See also E. A. Boeger and E. A. Goldenweiser, "A Study of the Tenant Systems of Farming in the Yazoo-Mississippi Delta," *USDA Bulletin*, no. 337 (1916); C. O. Brannen, "Relation of Land Tenure to Plantation Organization," *USDA Bulletin*, no. 1269 (18 October 1924).

23. "as producers": planter quoted in *Report on Cotton Production*, pt. 1, p. 173; testimony of R. J. Redding, director of the Georgia Agriculture Experiment Station, of I. B. Nall, Agriculture Commissioner of Kentucky, and of Harry Hammond, *Report of the Industrial Commission on Agriculture and Agricultural Labor*, vol. 10 of the Commission's Reports, (Washington, D.C.: GPO, 1901), pp. 445, 804, 819; Flynn, *White Land, Black Labor*. See also H. M. Dixon, "An Economic Study of Farming in Sumter County, Georgia," *USDA Bulletin*, no. 492 (1917); Delores E. Janiewski, *Sisterhood Denied: Race, Gender, and Class in a New South Community* (Philadelphia: Temple University Press, 1985), p. 53; Orser, *Material Basis*, p. 147; testimony of J. Pope Brown, *Report of the Industrial Commission*, vol. 10, p. 71.

24. "the class": testimony of J. R. Godwin, Memphis planter, *Report of the Industrial Commission*, vol. 10, p. 477; "equal wage": Robert Higgs, "Racial Wage Differentials in Agriculture: Evidence from North Carolina in 1887," *Agricultural History* 52 (April 1978): 310.

25. Warren C. Whatley, "Southern Agrarian Labor Contracts as Impediments to Cotton Mechanization," *Journal of Economic History* 47 (March 1987): 45–70; H. A. Turner, "Labor Management in the Yazoo-Mississippi Delta," 1916, Entry 133, File no. 0174, BAE; M. A. Crosby, "Present Status of Farm Management Work in Alabama and Mississippi," 1915, Entry 133, File no. 1047, BAE; Rex E. Willard, "A Farm Management Study of Cotton Farms of Ellis County, Texas," *USDA Bulletin*, no. 659 (1918). See also Robert Higgs, "Race, Tenure, and Resource Allocation in Southern

Agriculture, 1910," *Journal of Economic History* 33 (March 1973): 149–69.

26. "the negro": Georgia planter quoted in Robert Preston Brooks, *The Agrarian Revolution in Georgia, 1865–1912* (Madison: University of Wisconsin Press, 1914), p. 64; LaWanda Fenlason Cox, "Tenancy in the United States, 1865–1900: A Consideration of the Validity of the Agricultural Ladder Hypothesis," *Agricultural History* 18 (July 1944): 97–105; John William Fanning, "Negro Migration: A Study of the Exodus of the Negroes Between 1920 and 1925 from Middle Georgia Counties" (M. S. thesis, University of Georgia, 1928); letter to the author from Gavin Wright, 3 January 1989, on effects of economic change on blacks and whites.

27. Lacy K. Ford, "Rednecks and Merchants: Economic Development and Social Tensions in the South Carolina Upcountry, 1865–1900," *Journal of American History* 71 (September 1984): 294–318; "I told": landlord quoted in Brooks, *Agrarian Revolution*, p. 490.

28. Frank J. Welch, "The Plantation Land Tenure System in Mississippi," Mississippi Agricultural Experiment Station, *Bulletin*, no. 385, State College, Mississippi (June 1943), p. 32; McMillen, *Dark Journey*, p. 130.

29. Wright, "American Agriculture and the Labor Market."

30. James R. Barrett, *Work and Community in the Jungle: Chicago's Packinghouse Workers, 1894–1922* (Urbana: University of Illinois Press, 1987), pp. 156–57; Keyssar, *Out of Work*, p. 124; Stephenson, "'There's Plenty Waitin' at the Gates'"; Virginia Yans-McLaughlin, *Family and Community: Italian Immigrants in Buffalo, 1880–1930* (Ithaca, NY: Cornell University Press, 1977); Jonathan Prude, *The Coming of Industrial Order: Town and Factory Life in Rural Massachusetts, 1800–1860* (Cambridge: Cambridge University Press, 1983); Thomas Dublin, "Women and Outwork in a Nineteenth-Century New England Town: Fitzwilliam, New Hampshire, 1830–1850," in Steven Hahn and Jonathan Prude, eds., *The Countryside in the Age of Capitalist Transformation: Essays in the Social History of Rural America* (Chapel Hill: University of North Carolina Press, 1985), pp. 51–70.

31. Harry Hodgson, "A Great Farmer at Work," *World's Work* 9 (January 1905): 5723–33; William F. Holmes, "Labor Agents and the Georgia Exodus, 1899–1900," *South Atlantic Quarterly* 79 (Autumn 1980): 444.

32. Orser, *Material Basis*, p. 154; testimony of William A. Gage, Memphis Cotton Commission merchant, *Report of the Industrial Commission*, vol. 10, p. 494; "factory": Brannen, "Relation of Land Tenure to Plantation Organization," p. 49.

33. Peek testimony in *Report of the Industrial Commission*, vol. 10, p. 459; "Population Movements (Negroes from South to North, April 1923)," Entry 90, File no. 0959, BAE; Fanning, "Negro Migration," pp. 33–34.

34. Alfred H. Stone, *Studies in the American Race Problem* (New York: Doubleday and Page, 1908), p. 112; D. A. McCandliss, Agricultural statisti-

cian, on Movement of Farm Labor, 20 April 1923, Entry 90, File no.. 0959, BAE; Brannen, "Relation of Land Tenure to Plantation Organization," p. 29; Carl Kelsey, *The Negro Farmer* (Chicago: Jennings and Pye, 1903), p. 50; Jacquelyn Dowd Hall et al., *Like a Family: The Making of a Southern Cotton Mill World* (Chapel Hill: University of North Carolina Press, 1987), p. 14.

35. Marjorie Felice Irwin, "The Negro in Charlottesville and Albermarle County," University of Virginia Phelps-Stokes Fellowship Paper no. 9 (1929), p. 9; Clyde Vernon Kiser, *Sea Island to City: A Study of St. Helena Islanders in Harlem and Other Urban Centers* (New York: Columbia University Press, 1932), p. 39; "had to keep": Kelsey, *Negro Farmer*, p. 39; "always": testimony of Robert Ransom Poole, Agricultural commissioner of Alabama, *Report of the Industrial Commission*, vol. 10, p. 919; Peter Gottlieb, *Making Their Own Way: Southern Blacks' Migration to Pittsburgh, 1916–1930* (Urbana: University of Illinois Press, 1987).

36. "situated": n 36 "Studies in the South," *Atlantic Monthly* 49 (June 1882): 749; "takes": testimony of George Henry White, representative from North Carolina, *Report of the Industrial Commission*, vol. 10, p. 430.

37. "while": Harriet A. Byrne, "Child Labor in Representative Tobacco-Growing Areas," U.S. Department of Labor, Children's Bureau Publication no. 155 (Washington, D.C.: GPO, 1926), p. 21; "hill . . . Labor": H. A. Turner, "Bledsoe Plantation, Leflore County, Mississippi, 1915," pp. 12–13, Entry 133, File no. 0221, BAE; Flynt, *Poor But Proud*, p. 79. See also A. G. Smith, "A Farm Management Study in Anderson County, South Carolina," *USDA Bulletin*, no. 651 (1918); Ruth Alice Allen, *The Labor of Women in the Production of Cotton* (New York: Arno Press, 1975; orig. pub. 1931).

38. "women": testimony of Harry Hammond, *Report of the Industrial Commission*, vol. 10, p. 819; "went . . . would": Mamie Garvin Fields with Karen Fields, *Lemon Swamp and Other Places: A Carolina Memoir* (New York: Free Press, 1983), p. 106; Maguire, *On Shares*, p. 22 ("it seem like I would sleep some walkin' home"); John Belcher interview in the Federal Writers Project Slaves Narratives, collected in George P. Rawick, ed., *The American Slave: A Composite Autobiography*, Supple-mentary Series (SS) 1, vol. 6 (Miss. Narrs.), pt. 1 (Westport, CT: Greenwood Press, 1978), pp. 110–11 (hereafter with the name of the interviewee, FWP *Slave Narrs.*, the volume, publication date, and page number).

39. Rosengarten, *All God's Dangers*, pp. 21, 78, 108, 131, 128, 115.

40. See, for example, Elizabeth Rauh Bethel, *Promiseland: A Century of Life in a Negro Community* (Philadelphia: Temple University Press, 1981); Sydney Nathans, "Gotta Mind to Move, A Mind to Settle Down: Afro-Americans and the Plantation-Frontier," in *A Master's Due: Essays in Honor of David Herbert Donald*, ed. William J. Cooper et al. (Baton Rouge: Louisiana State Universty Press, 1985), pp. 204–22; Manning Marable, "The Politics of Black Land Tenure, 1877–1915," *Agricultural History* 53 (January 1979):

142, 147–48; Marsha J. Darling, "The Growth and Decline of the Afro-American Family Farm in Warren County, North Carolina, 1910–1960" (Ph.D. diss., Duke University, 1982).

41. "areas": Gray et al., "Farm Ownership and Tenancy," p. 518; *Historical Statistics of the United States*, pt. 1, p. 465; Loren Schweninger, *Black Property Owners in the South, 1790–1915* (Urbana: University of Illinois Press, 1990), pp. 143–84.

42. M. A. Crosby, "Sam McCall, Successful Negro Farmer, 1912," Entry 133, File no. 1023, BAE; Donald Dewey Scarborough, "An Economic Study of Negro Farmers as Owners, Tenants, and Croppers" (M.A. thesis, University of Georgia, 1923), p. 12.

43. "a little": W. L. Bost interview, FWP *Slave Narrs.*, vol. 14 (N.C. Narrs.), 1972, pt. 1, p. 146; Thordis Simonsen, ed., *You May Plow Here: The Narrative of Sara Brooks* (New York: Norton, 1986), pp. 69, 106–7, 89. On the diets of rural Southerners, see W. O. Atwater and Charles D. Woods, "Dietary Studies with Reference to the Food of the Negro in Alabama in 1895 and 1896," USDA Office of Experiment Stations *Bulletin*, no. 38 (Washington, D.C.: GPO, 1897). On the inverse relationship between tenancy and household foodstuff self-sufficiency, see Louis Ferleger, "Self-Sufficiency and Rural Life on Southern Farms," *Agricultural History* 58 (July 1984): 314–29.

44. "never . . . set": Fields, *Lemon Swamp*, p. 73; "purgatory . . . if": Dickey and Branson, "How Farm Tenants Live," p. 12; "unless": George Dyer quoted in Hall et al., *Like a Family*, pp. 11–12. See also Harold D. Woodman, "Postbellum Social Change and Its Effects on Marketing the South's Cotton Crop," *Agricultural History* 56 (January 1982): 215–30; L. C. Gray, "Helping Landless Farmers to Own Farms," USDA, *Agricultural Yearbook for 1920* (Washington, D.C.: GPO, 1921), p. 277.

45. "lay up": testimony of R. J. Redding, *Report of the Industrial Commission*, vol. 10, p. 448; Joffe, "Rural School Attendance in Alabama," p. 106.

46. "much . . . to": George Campbell, *White and Black: The Outcome of a Visit to the United States* (London: Chatto and Windus, 1879), pp. 155, 335; Shifflett, *Patronage and Poverty*, p. 53; "Farm Family Living Among White Owners and Tenant Operators in Wake County," p. 33; "at . . . now . . . went . . . when": Simonsen, ed., *You May Plow Here*, pp. 58, 144. See also Lorenzo J. Greene and Carter G. Woodson, *The Negro Wage Earner* (Washington, D.C.: Association for the Study of Negro Life and History, 1930), p. 30; T. J. Woofter, *Black Yeomanry: Life on St. Helena Island* (New York: Octagon Books, 1978; orig. pub. 1930).

47. "ride out": Simonsen, ed., *You May Plow Here*, p. 105; "ever'": Charles S. Johnson, *Shadow of the Plantation* (Chicago: University of Chicago Press, 1934), p. 105; Yoder quoted in Hall et al., *Like a Family*, p. 7.

48. "big eyes . . . at home": Rosengarten, *All God's Dangers*, pp. 119, 61; W. E. B. DuBois, "The Negro American Family," Atlanta University Study no. 13

(Atlanta, GA: Atlanta University Press, 1908), p. 129; "the more": Johnson, *Shadow of the Plantation*, p. 143.

49. Laura Montgomery interview, FWP *Slave Narrs.*, SS 1, vol. 9 (Miss. Narrs.), 1972, pt. 4, pp. 1556–57; Mary Anne Gibson interview, FWP *Slave Narrs.*, SS 2, vol. 5 (Tex. Narrs.), 1979, pt. 4, pp. 1469–71.

50. Hickum quoted in Hall et al., *Like a Family*, pp. 38–39. See also Newby, *Plain Folk in the New South*.

51. "So": Georgia landowner quoted in Flynn, *White Land, Black Labor*, p. 135; Lawrence Goodwyn, *Democratic Promise: The Populist Moment in America* (New York: Oxford University Press, 1976).

52. "Now": Georgia man quoted in Barton C. Shaw, *The Wool-Hat Boys: Georgia's Populist Party* (Baton Rouge: Louisiana State University Press, 1984), p. 84; C. Vann Woodward, *Tom Watson: Agrarian Rebel* (New York: Oxford University Press, 1975); Gregg Cantrell and D. Scott Barton, "Texas Populists and the Failure of Biracial Politics," *Journal of Southern History* 55 (November 1989): 659–92; Gerald H. Gaither, *Blacks and the Populist Revolt: Ballots and Bigotry in the "New South"* (University: University of Alabama Press, 1977); Bruce Palmer, *"Man Over Money": The Southern Populist Critique of American Capitalism* (Chapel Hill: University of North Carolina Press, 1980).

53. "My . . . If": Maguire, *On Shares*, pp. 28, 27; "They avoided": Onnie Lee Logan with Katherine Clark, *Motherwit: An Alabama Midwife's Story* (New York: E. P. Dutton, 1989), p. 58; interview with Ollie Smith conducted by her granddaughter Colette Blount, Toledo, Ohio, in December 1987, p. 36 (typescript in author's possession). See also Rosengarten, *All God's Dangers*: "My daddy stood back off of white folks considerably," p. 50.

Chapter 4
Shifting and "Shiftlessness": Annual Plantation Turnover, 1870 to 1930

1. Harry Crews, *A Childhood: The Biography of a Place* (New York: Harper & Row, 1978), pp. 13–14.

2. "flitting": Joan Jensen, *Loosening the Bonds: Mid-Atlantic Farm Women, 1750–1850* (New Haven: Yale University Press, 1986), pp. 42–43; "moral obligation . . . leave": housewife quoted in David Katzman, *Seven Days a Week: Women and Domestic Service in Industrializing America* (New York: Oxford University Press, 1978), pp. 193–94; Daniel T. Rodgers, "Tradition, Modernity, and the American Industrial Worker: Reflections and Critique," *Journal of Interdisciplinary History* 7 (Spring 1977): 655–81.

3. "Shifted": John Lee Coulter, "The Rural Life Problem of the South," *South Atlantic Quarterly* 12 (1913): 64; "hit . . . lit": Neil R. McMillen, *Dark Journey: Black Mississippians in the Age of Jim Crow* (Urbana: University of Illinois, 1989), p. 150; "their one . . . planters": Charles S. Johnson,

Shadow of the Plantation (Chicago: University of Chicago Press, 1934), p. 25; Jonathan B. Pritchett, "The Term of Occupancy of Southern Farmers in the First Decades of the Twentieth Century," *Historical Methods* 20 (Summer 1987): 107–12.

4. "there is": testimony of Harry Hammond, *Report of the Industrial Commission on Agriculture and Agricultural Labor*, vol. 10 of the Commission's Reports (Washington, D.C.: GPO, 1901), p. 831; "all social": Coulter, "Rural Life Problem of the South," pp. 64–65. See, for example, Gavin Wright, "Postbellum Southern Labor Markets," in *Quantity and Quiddity: Essays in United States Economic History*, ed. Peter Kilby (Middletown, CT: Wesleyan University Press, 1987), p. 109; Rex E. Willard, "A Farm Management Study of Cotton Farms of Ellis County, Texas," *U.S. Department of Agriculture* (hereafter *USDA*) *Bulletin*, no. 659 (1918): 19; testimony of Pitt Dillingham, *Report of the Industrial Commission*, vol. 10, pp. 164–5.

5. "I": interview with Ollie Smith conducted by her granddaughter Colette Blount, Toledo, Ohio, December 1987 (typescript in author's possession); "Children": E. C. Branson, "Social Occasions and Contacts in a Rural County," *Journal of Social Forces* 1 (January 1923): 163. See also Margaret J. Hagood, *Mothers of the South: Portraiture of the White Tenant Farm Woman* (New York: Norton, 1977; orig. pub. 1939); Thomas J. Edwards, "Negro Farmers of Alabama II: Sharecroppers," *Southern Workman* 8 (September 1911): 533–36; J. A. Dickey and E. C. Branson, "How Farm Tenants Live," University of North Carolina Extension *Bulletin* 2, no. 6 (16 November 1922): 22; W. E. B. DuBois, "Of the Quest for the Golden Fleece," in *The Souls of Black Folk: Essays and Sketches* (Chicago: A. C. McClurg Co., 1904), pp. 135–63.

6. William Cohen, *At Freedom's Edge: Black Mobility and the Southern White Quest for Racial Control, 1861–1915* (Baton Rouge: Louisiana State University Press, 1991), chap. 8.

7. "tenant stealers": Ray Stannard Baker, *Following the Color Line: An Account of Negro Citizenship in the American Democracy* (New York: Doubleday and Page, 1908), p. 79; "local": C. O. Brannen, "Relation of Land Tenure to Plantation Organization," *USDA Bulletin*, no. 1269 (Washington, D.C.: GPO, 1924), p. 44; "expend": William Alexander Percy, *Lanterns on the Levee: Recollections of a Planter's Son* (Baton Rouge: Louisiana State University Press, 1973; orig. pub. 1941), p. 299; McMillen, *Dark Journey*, p. 142; Leon Dash, *When Children Want Children: The Urban Crisis of Teenage Childbearing* (New York: William Morrow, 1989), p. 244 (interview with elderly North Carolina sharecropper).

8. See, for example, Ralph Shlomowitz, "'Bound' or 'Free'? Black Labor in Cotton and Sugar Farming, 1865–1880," *Journal of Southern History* 50 (November 1984): 574.

9. "restless and roving . . . made": Edwin DeLeon, "Ruin and Reconstruction

of the Southern States. A Record of Two Tours in 1863 and 1873,"
Southern Magazine 14 (January/March, 1874): 23, 301; "The negro": A
South Carolinian [Belton O'Neall Townsend], "South Carolina Society,"
Atlantic Monthly 39 (June 1877): 677; "restless . . . natural": testimony of
William C. Stubbs, director of the Louisiana Experiment Station, *Report of
the Industrial Commission*, pp. 770, 109; "evil": Lewis C. Gray et al., "Farm
Ownership and Tenancy," *USDA Agricultural Yearbook for 1923* (Wash-
ington, D.C.: GPO, 1924), p. 596. See also U. S. Department of Com-
merce, Bureau of the Census, *Historical Statistics of the United States,
Colonial Times to 1970*, pt. 1 (Washington, D.C.: GPO, 1975), p. 465.

10. W. J. Spillman and E. A. Goldenweiser, "Farm Tenantry in the United
States," *USDA Agricultural Yearbook for 1916* (Washington, D.C.: GPO,
1917), p. 344; Brannen, "Relation of Land Tenure," p. 74; Gray et al.,
"Farm Ownership and Tenancy," p. 590; Charles Orser, *The Material Basis
of the Postbellum Tenant Plantation: Historical Archaeology in the South
Carolina Piedmont* (Athens: University of Georgia Press, 1988), pp. 116–17
(figures compiled from the 1935 Census of Agriculture); Robin M.
Williams and Olaf Wakefield, "Farm Tenancy in North Carolina,
1880–1935," North Carolina Agricultural Experiment Station with the
Department of Agricultural Economics and Rural Sociology, AE-RS
Information Series no. 1 (September 1937), p. 48. See also Gavin Wright,
*Old South, New South: Revolutions in the Southern Economy Since the
Civil War* (New York: Basic Books, 1986), p. 93. A 1935 study of South
Carolina Piedmont counties showed that only 7.6 percent of owners had
moved in the past year, compared with 39 percent of tenants. These ratios
were also comparable for the two different kinds of North Carolina farmers
for 1910, 1925, 1930, and 1935. In 1922 USDA investigators reported that
seven of the former Confederate states showed an annual turnover rate
among tenants to be 30 to 40 percent, with the other four states showing
rates of 20 to 30 percent. See Thomas J. Woofter, *Landlord and Tenant on
the Cotton Plantation*, Works Progress Administration, Division of Social
Research, Monograph 5 (Washington, D.C.: GPO, 1936).

11. "tenantry": Spillman and Goldenweiser, "Farm Tenantry," p. 343; "A lot":
Mack Duncan quoted in Jacquelyn D. Hall et al., *Like a Family: The
Making of a Southern Cotton Mill World* (Chapel Hill: University of North
Carolina Press, 1988), p. 40. See also Jay Mandle, *The Roots of Black
Poverty: The Southern Plantation Economy After the Civil War* (Durham,
NC: Duke University Press, 1978), p. 16. Contrast the relationship between
age of household head and tenure status, according to race, as revealed by
the data in Gray et al., "Farm Ownership and Tenancy," p. 551. On the
increase in white tenants, see Delores E. Janiewski, *Sisterhood Denied:
Race, Gender and Class in a New South Community* (Philadelphia: Temple
University Press, 1985); and Steven Hahn, *The Roots of Southern Populism:
Yeoman Farmers and the Transformation of the Georgia Upcountry*,

1850–1890 (New York: Oxford University Press, 1983). On the small number of black tenants working kin's land, see H. A. Turner, "The Ownership of Tenant Farms in the United States," *USDA Bulletin*, no. 1432 (1926): 47.

12. "free, white": letter of Thomas B. Davis to the author, Bridgeport, Conn., 15 November 1987, p. 3; "confined": testimony of James Barrett, farmer, Augusta, Georgia, *Report of the Industrial Commission*, vol. 10, p. 46; W. C. Scroggs, "Inter-State Migration of Negro Population," *Journal of Political Economy* 25 (December 1917): 1034–43. On 1923 population movements in general, and the Florida and Louisiana cases in particular, see "Population Movements (Negroes from South to North, April 1923)," Entry 90, File no. 0959, Bureau of Agricultural Economics (hereafter BAE), Record Group 83, National Archives, Washington, D.C. Cf. Richard Vedder et al., "Demonstrating Their Freedom: The Post-Emancipation Migration of Black Americans," *Research in Economic History* 10 (1986): 213–39. The authors describe the so-called "sunshine variable" as a factor affecting blacks' migration patterns. See also Baker, *Following the Color Line*, p. 101; Cohen, *At Freedom's Edge*, chap. 9.

13. Alfred Holt Stone, *Studies in the American Race Problem* (New York: Doubleday and Page, 1908), pp. 127, 109, 125, 128–30.

14. Ibid., pp. 130, 131, 132.

15. Ibid., pp. 145–47.

16. Letter from Thomas B. Davis to the author, Bridgeport, Conn., 15 November 1987, p. 5; "Sometimes": testimony of O. B. Stevens, *Report of the Industrial Commission*, vol. 10, pp. 908–9.

17. "oily": testimony of George Henry White, U.S. Representative from North Carolina, *Report of the Industrial Commission*, vol. 10, p. 428; Ruthe Winegarten, "I Am Annie Mae: The Personal Story of a Black Texas Woman," *Chrysalis* 4 (Spring 1980): 16–17; Jennifer Roback, "Southern Labor Law in the Jim Crow Era: Exploitative or Competitive?" *University of Chicago Law Review* 51 (Fall 1984): 1161–92; William Cohen, "Negro Involuntary Servitude in the South, 1865–1940: A Preliminary Analysis," *Labor History* 42 (February 1976): 31–60.

    On the fining of a labor solicitor (hired by Delta planters) in Arkansas, see the report of Charles S. Bouton, Little Rock, Ark.,14 April 1923, Entry 90, File no. 0959, BAE.

18. In describing life on the expansive George Yerger Plantation, in Mounds, Louisiana, around the time of World War I, Daniel D. Ewing tells of his own father, an accountant who always wore a pistol, and of a gunfight that erupted in the middle of the night when a family tried to move to a nearby plantation. "You don't": interview with Daniel D. Ewing conducted by the author August 1986, in Wellesley, Mass. (typescript in author's possession). "oppressive tactics": testimony of Charles W. Holman, *Industrial Relations: Final Report and Testimony Submitted to Congress*, 64 Cong., 1st sess., Senate Doc. no. 415 (Washington, D.C.: GPO, 1916), p. 8954; "the present . . . so": Lewis Cecil Gray, "Southern Agriculture, Plantation System, and the Negro

Problem," *Annals of the American Academy of Political and Social Science* 40 (March 1912): 97; "note": Rosengarten, *All God's Dangers*, p. 162; Harold D. Woodman, "Post Civil-War Agriculture and the Law," *Agricultural History* 53 (January 1979): 317–39; "he did": William H. Holtzclaw, *The Black Man's Burden* (New York: Neale Publishing Co., 1915), p. 138. See also George K. Holmes, "The Peons of the South," *Annals of the American Academy of Political and Social Science* 4 (1894): 265–74; Pete Daniel, "The Metamorphosis of Slavery, 1865–1900," *Journal of American History* 66 (June 1979): 88–99.

19. "as the . . . Emergencies": Helen M. Dart, "Maternity and Child Care in Selected Rural Areas of Mississippi," Rural Child Welfare Series no. 5, Children's Bureau Pub. no. 88 (Washington, D.C.: GPO, 1921) p. 14; "Ain't . . . The stability": Dickey and Branson, "How Farm Tenants Live," pp. 15–16, 22. See also Crandall A. Shifflett, *Patronage and Poverty in the Tobacco South: Louisa County, Virginia, 1860–1900* (Knoxville: University of Tennessee Press, 1982), p. 41; Merle Prunty, Jr., "The Renaissance of the Southern Plantation," *Geographical Review* 45 (October 1955): 471; Wayne Flynt, *Poor But Proud: Alabama's Poor Whites* (Tuscaloosa: University of Alabama Press, 1989), p. 86.

20. Testimony of O. B. Stevens, *Report of the Industrial Commission*, vol. 10, p. 908; "paper loss": Johnson, *Shadow of the Plantation*, p. 111; "if you": Blount interview with Ollie Smith, p. 34; "The owner": Johnson, *Shadow of the Plantation*, p. 121.

21. Wright, "Postbellum Southern Labor Markets," p. 120. Cf. Mandle, *Roots of Black Poverty*, pp. 21–22.

22. "the very . . . naturally . . . For similar": Spillman and Goldenweiser, "Farm Tenantry in the United States," p. 345; "stable . . . selection . . . Reliable . . . undesirable . . . as quickly": Brannen, "Relation of Land Tenure to Plantation Organization," p. 50; "If you": testimony of J. R. Godwin, Memphis, Tenn., *Report of the Industrial Commission*, vol. 10, p. 479.

23. "the uncertainties": Howard A. Turner, "An Account of Runnymeade Plantation," Leflore County, Miss., January 1916, Entry 133, file no. 0179, BAE. See also the contract quoted in Carl Kelsey, *The Negro Farmer* (Chicago: Jennings and Pye, 1903), p. 56. On concessions made to potential tenants in January, see Rosengarten, *All God's Dangers*, pp. 162–63.

24. "never . . . I worked": Richards quoted in Johnson, *Shadow of the Plantation*, p. 127; "bolt": H. A. Turner, "Bledsoe Plantation, Leflore County, Mississippi, 1915," Entry 133, File no. 0221, BAE.

25. "There": testimony of White, *Report of the Industrial Commission*, vol. 10, p. 419; Barney Alford interview in the Federal Writers Project Slave Narrs., collected in George P. Rawick, ed. *The American Slave: A Composite Autobiography*, Supplementary Series 1, vol. 6 (Miss. Narrs.), pt. 1 (Westport, CT: Greenwood Press, 1978), pp. 43–44 (hereafter with the name of the interviewee, FWP *Slave Narrs.*, the volume, publication date, and page number); "cajolery": Alfred Holt

Stone, "The Negro and Agricultural Development," *Annals of the American Academy of Political and Social Science* 35 (January 1910): 13. H. H. Wooten found that "as a rule," contracts between owners and croppers were oral: "The Credit Problems of North Carolina Farmers," Agricultural Experiment Station of the North Carolina State College of Agriculture and Engineering and the North Carolina Department of Agriculture *Bulletin*, no. 271 (May 1930): 8. See also the Tyrell County, North Carolina, landlord quoted in Frenise A. Logan, "Factors Influencing the Efficiency of Negro Farm Laborers in Post-Reconstruction North Carolina," *Agricultural History* 33 (October 1959): 185–89.

26. Stone, *Studies in the American Race Problem*, pp. 119–20; manager quoted in Sydney Nathans, "Gotta Mind to Move, A Mind to Settle Down: Afro-Americans and the Plantation Frontier," in *A Master's Due: Essays in Honor of David Herbert Donald*, ed. William J. Cooper et al. (Baton Rouge: Louisiana State University Press, 1985), p. 211; James R. Green, "Tenant Farmer Discontent and Socialist Protest in Texas, 1901–1917," *Southwestern Historical Quarterly* 81 (1977): 133–54. Mississippi Delta planters interviewed in the early 1940s reported that, out of a sample of sixty-four black families, some were considered "troublemakers." Frank T. Welch, "The Plantation Land Tenure System in Mississippi," Mississippi State College Experiment Station, State College, Mississippi, 1943, pp. 28–29. See also Charles L. Flynn, Jr., *White Land, Black Labor: Caste and Class in Late Nineteenth-Century Georgia* (Baton Rouge: Louisiana State University Press, 1983), p. 77, for evidence of blacklisting of cropper families.

27. "energy": "Farm Family Living Among White Owner and Tenant Operators in Wake County," Agricultural Experiment Station of the North Carolina State College of Agriculture and Engineering and the North Carolina Department of Agriculture, *Bulletin*, no. 269 (September 1929): 13. Tenancy encouraged early marriage. See Stuart E. Tolnay, "Black Family Formation and Tenancy in the Farm South, 1900," *American Journal of Sociology* 90 (September 1984): 305–25.

28. David C. Barrow, Jr., "A Georgia Plantation," *Scribner's Monthly* 21 (April 1881): 834; Department of the Interior, Census Office, *Report on Cotton Production in the United States*, pt. 2 (Washington, D.C.: GPO, 1884), p. 519; "some": Turner, "An Account of Runnymeade Plantation," p. 5; "When": Rosengarten, *All God's Dangers*, p. 135. See also testimony of P. H. Lovejoy, merchant planter, Hawkinsville, Ga., *Report of the Industrial Commission*, vol. 10, p. 75.

29. Carter G. Woodson, *A Century of Negro Migration* (New York: AMS Press, 1970; orig. pub. 1918), pp. 147–92; Marjorie Felice Irwin, "The Negro in Charlottesville and Albermarle County," Publications of the University of Virginia, Phelps-Stokes Fellowship Paper, no. 9 (1929): 27.

30. "nobody": Johnson, *Shadow of the Plantation*, p. 117; "largely": M. A.

Crosby, "Report on the Delta Farms Company, Bolivar County, Mississippi, 1914," Entry 133, File no. 1013, BAE; "I've": Rosengarten, *All God's Dangers*, p. 116. See also Janiewski, *Sisterhood Denied*, p. 50.

31. H. A. Turner, "Notes on the Plantation of J. E. Wannamaker," October 1913, Entry 133, File no. 0260, BAE; letter of Thomas B. Davis to the author, Bridgeport, Conn., 15 November 1987, pp. 4–5.

32. Wright, "Postbellum Southern Labor Markets," p. 133. On labor contracts in the tobacco region, for example, see Rick Gregory, "Robertson County and the Black Patch War, 1904–1909," *Tennessee Historical Quarterly* 39 (Fall 1980): 341–58.

33. "refuse": testimony of William Carter Stubbs, *Report of the Industrial Commission*, vol. 10, p. 771; "old [planter's] joke": letter of Thomas B. Davis to the author, Bridgeport, Conn., 15 November 1987; "'Scuse me": Johnson, *Shadow of the Plantation*, p. 98; "succeed[ed]": testimony of O. B. Stevens, *Report of the Industrial Commission*, vol. 10, p. 911. See also D. D. Wallace, "Southern Agriculture: Its Conditions and Needs," *Popular Science Monthly* 64 (January 1904): 252.

34. W. E. B. DuBois, "The Negro American Family," Atlanta University Study no. 13 (Atlanta: Atlanta University Press, 1908), p. 129.

35. Interview with Eli Davison, FWP *Slave Narrs.*, vol. 4 (Tex. Narrs.), 1972, pt. 1, p. 297; "a policy": Turner, "An Account of Runnymeade Plantation," p. 3.

36. "down there": Rosengarten, *All God's Dangers*, p. 117; "corporate": Shepard Krech III, "Black Family Organization in the Nineteenth Century: An Ethnographic Perspective," *Journal of Interdisciplinary History* 12 (Winter 1982): 429–52; "living . . . pilgrims": Dickey and Branson, "How Farm Tenants Live," pp. 20–21. See also E. C. Branson, "Farm Tenancy in the South. Part II: The Social Estate of White Farm Tenants," *Journal of Social Forces* 1 (May 1923): 450–57.

37. Blount interview with Ollie Smith, p. 21; Coulter, "Rural Life Problem of the South," pp. 64–65; Rex E. Willard, "Farm Management Study of Cotton Farms of Ellis County," p. 19; "established:" Gray et al., "Farm Ownership and Tenancy," pp. 596–97; W. S. Scarborough, "Tenancy and Ownership Among Negro Farmers in Southampton County, Virginia," *USDA Bulletin*, no. 1404 (1926): 24; Woofter, *Landlord*, p. 114; "little interest": Dart, "Maternity and Child Care in Selected Rural Areas of Mississippi," p. 14. See also testimony of Pitt Dillingham, *Report of the Industrial Commission*, vol. 10, pp. 164–65; Ronald L. F. Davis, *Good and Faithful Labor: From Slavery to Sharecropping in the Natchez District, 1860–90* (Westport, CT: Greenwood Press, 1982), p. 179.

38. "Anyone . . . insisted": Arthur F. Raper, *Preface to Peasantry: A Tale of Two Black Belt Counties* (Chapel Hill: University of North Carolina Press, 1936), pp. 218–19; "responsiveness": Wright, "Postbellum Southern Labor

Markets," p. 109; "jus": interview with Teshah Young, FWP *Slave Narrs.*, vol. 5 (Texas Narrs.), 1972, pt. 4, p. 237.

39. Hodgson, "A Great Farmer at Work," p. 5727; interviews with Daphne L. E. Curtis, FWP *Slave Narrs.*, vol. 6 (Ala. Narrs.), 1972, p. 252; Levi Ashley, FWP *Slave Narrs.*, SS 1, vol. 6 (Miss. Narrs.), 1977, pt. 1, p. 44; planter on ten years' residency quoted in *Report on Cotton Production in the U.S.*, pt. 2, p. 519.

40. "Papa": Johnson, *Shadow of the Plantation*, p. 85; Blount interview with Ollie Smith, pp. 15–16.

Chapter 5
Bound and Free Black and White Laborers Between Field and Factory: The South's Rural Nonagricultural Sector, 1875 to 1930

1. Employees v. Pebble Phosphate Company, Pierce, Florida, Docket no. 691a, 1918, pp. 32–33, Entry 4, File no. 0197, Record Group 2, National War Labor Board, National Archives, Washington, D.C. (hereafter RG 2, NA).

2. Employees v. Palmetto Phosphate Company, Tampa, Florida, Docket no. 687, 1918, p. 69, Entry 4, File no. 0001, RG 2, NA.

3. Employees v. Armour Fertilizer Works, Bartow, Florida, Docket no. 689, 1918, Entry 4, File no. 0112, RG 2, NA.

4. Ibid., p. 53.

5. Employees vs. Pebble Phosphate Company, p. 22, RG 2, NA.

6. "crackers . . . indolent . . . most": quoted in Arch Fredric Blakey, *The Florida Phosphate Industry: A History of the Development and Use of a Vital Mineral* (Cambridge, MA: Harvard University Press, 1973), p. 51; for statistics on phosphate output, see U.S. Department of Commerce, Bureau of the Census, *Fourteenth Census of the United States* (1920), vol. 11, *Mines and Quarries* (Washington, D.C.: GPO, 1922), p. 24. See also Tom W. Shick and Don H. Doyle, "The South Carolina Phosphate Boom and the Stillbirth of the New South, 1867–1920," *South Carolina Historical Magazine* 86 (January 1985): 1–31; Joseph Struthers, "Phosphate Rock," U.S. Department of Commerce, Bureau of the Census, Special Reports of the Census Office, *Mines and Quarries* (Washington, D.C.: GPO, 1902), pp. 919–30; Carroll D. Wright, *The Phosphate Industry of the United States*, Sixth Special Report of the Commissioner of Labor (Washington, D.C.: GPO, 1893), pp. 21–69, 71–86; U.S. Department of Commerce, Bureau of the Census, *Fifteenth Census of the United States* (1930), vol. 4, *Population*, (Washington, D.C.: GPO, 1932), p. 353.

7. "colored . . . laborers": Employees v. Palmetto Phosphate Company, pp. 43–44; "low grade": ibid., pp. 87, 58, 54; regarding schools, see Employees v. Armour Fertilizer Works, p. 26. See also McClung Callender to William

P. Harvey, Tampa, Fla., 17 October 1918, in Employees v. International Agricultural Corporation, Mulberry, Fla., Docket no. 690, 1918, Entry 4, File no. 0197, RG 2, NA.

8. "immunity": Employees v. Armour Fertilizer Works, RG 2, NA. See Blakey, *Florida Phosphate Industry*, pp. 61–75, for a detailed account of the 1919 strike.

9. "constantly . . . a fertile . . . not": Ray Stannard Baker, *Following the Color Line: An Account of Negro Citizenship in the American Democracy* (New York: Doubleday and Page, 1908), pp. 31, 83. For discussions of biracial union organizing in the South during this period, see, for example, Robin D. G. Kelley, *Hammer and Hoe: Alabama Communists During the Great Depression* (Chapel Hill: University of North Carolina Press, 1990); Gary M. Fink and Merl E. Reed, eds., *Essays in Southern Labor History: Selected Papers, Southern Labor History Conference, 1976* (Westport, CT: Greenwood Press, 1977).

10. "simple . . . Heretofore": Arthur H. Codington to Attorney General, Macon, Ga., 17 April 1911, Box 10802, File no. 50–222, U.S. Department of Justice Classified Subject Files Correspondence, RG 60, National Archives, Washington, D.C. (hereafter Justice Department Peonage Files).

11. "Hinesville, Georgia (Camp Stewart Area)," *Hearings Before the Select Committee Investigating National Defense Migration*, House of Representatives, 77th Cong., 2nd sess., pt. 32, Huntsville, Ala., Hearings (May 1942), p. 12071 (hereafter *National Defense Migration Hearings*).

12. "cotton mills": Edwin DeLeon, "Ruin and Reconstruction of the Southern States," *Southern Magazine* 14 (June 1874): 587; "old": Walter L. Fleming, "Immigration of the Southern States," *Political Science Quarterly* 20 (June 1905): 276; Gavin Wright, *Old South, New South: Revolutions in the Southern Economy Since the Civil War* (New York: Basic Books, 1986), p. 49.

13. R. P. Brooks, "A Local Study of the Race Problem: Race Relations in the Eastern Piedmont Region of Georgia," *Political Science Quarterly* 26 (June 1911): 219; Howard W. Odum, *Southern Regions of the United States* (Chapel Hill: University of North Carolina Press, 1936), p. 58; C. Vann Woodward, *Origins of the New South, 1877–1913* (Baton Rouge: Louisiana State University Press, 1951), p. 311; James C. Cobb, *Industrialization and Southern Society, 1877–1984* (Lexington: University Press of Kentucky, 1984); James C. Cobb, "Beyond Planters and Industrialists: A New Perspective on the New South," *Journal of Southern History* 54 (February 1988): 45–68; Don D. Lescohier, "Sources of Supply and Conditions of Employment of Harvest Labor in the Wheat Belt," *U.S. Department of Agriculture* (hereafter *USDA*) *Bulletin*, no. 1211 (1924); David R. Goldfield, *Cotton Fields and Skyscrapers: Southern City and Region, 1607–1980* (Baton Rouge: Louisiana State University Press, 1982), pp. 109–24; Peter J. Rachleff, *Black Labor in the South: Richmond, Virginia, 1865–1890* (Philadelphia: Temple University

Press, 1984); T. J. Woofter, "The Negroes of Athens, Georgia," Phelps-Stokes Fellowship Studies, no. 1, *Bulletin* of the University of Georgia 15 (December 1913): 41.

14. Manuscript Manufacturing Census for 1880, National Archives, Washington, D.C.; data based on information from 10-86-6, Microfilm reel 17 (S.C.); 10-87-8, T1134, reel 48 (Tex.); 10-87-6, T1132, reel 31 (Va.); 10-87-7, T1136, reel 15 (La.), 10-87-5, T1135, reel 30 (Tenn.), Microfilm Room of the National Archives. See also Wright, *Old South, New South*, p. 205; Vernon H. Jensen, *Lumber and Labor* (New York: Farrar and Rinehart, 1945), p. 77.

15. A. Berglund et al., *Labor in the Industrial South: A Survey of Wages and Living Conditions in Three Major Industries of the New Industrial South* (Charlottesville, VA.: Institute for Research in the Social Sciences, 1930), p. 62; Keith Dix, *Work Relations in the Coal Industry: The Hand-Loading Era, 1880–1930* (Morgantown: West Virginia University, Division of Social and Economic Development, Center for Extension and Continuing Education, 1977), pp. 80–93; "Laborers": Thomas D. Clark, *The Greening of the South: The Recovery of Land and Forest* (Lexington: University Press of Kentucky, 1984), p. 18; "the environment . . . All that": Archer H. Mayor, *Southern Timberman: The Legacy of William Buchanan* (Athens: Univer-sity of Georgia Press, 1988), p. 42; "wet work . . . soaked . . . accumulation": M. Loretta Sullivan and Ethel Ericson, "Women's Employment in Vegetable Canneries in Delaware," *Women's Bureau Bulletin*, no. 62 (1927): 22, 25.

16. John R. Wennersten, "The Almighty Oyster: A Saga of Old Somerset and the Eastern Shore, 1850–1920," *Maryland Historical Magazine* 74 (March 1978): 85–90; William N. Pentazes, "The Greeks of Tarpon Springs: An American Odyssey," *Tampa Bay History* 1 (Spring / Summer 1979): 28; James Buck, "Biscayne Sketches at the Far South," *Tequesta* 39 (1979): 70–85; Thomas D. Clark, "Kentucky Logmen," *Journal of Forest History* 25 (July 1981): 152–53.

17. Nollie Hickman, *Mississippi Harvest: Lumbering in the Longleaf Pine Belt, 1840–1915* (University: University of Mississippi Press, 1962), pp. 120–38; A. J. Nichol, "The Oyster Packing Industry of Baltimore: Its History and Current Problems," University of Maryland, 1937; "a time": USDA, *Agricultural Yearbook for 1923* (Washington, D.C.: GPO, 1924), p. 161; *Fourteenth Census of the United States* (1920), vol. 11, *Mines and Quarries*, p. 94; "Some days": Nick Lindsay, "An Oral History of Edisto Island: Sam Gadsden Tells the Story" (Goshen, IN: Pinchpenny Press, 1975), p. 61. Information on the sensitivity of small rural enterprises to climate and other natural conditions was gleaned from volumes pertaining to Southern businesses in the R. G. Dun and Co. Collection, Baker Library, Harvard University Graduate School of Business Administration, Cambridge, Mass.

18. Clark, *Greening of the South*, pp. 14–33; Jeffrey R. Dobson and Roy Doyon, "Expansion of the Pine Oleoresin Industry in Georgia, 1842 to ca. 1900,"

Studies in the Social Sciences 18 (1979): 43–57; Wennersten, "Almighty Oyster," pp. 80–93; Jack Temple Kirby, *Rural Worlds Lost: The American South, 1920–1960* (Baton Rouge: Louisiana State University Press, 1987), pp. 275–333; Thomas D. Clark, "The Impact of the Timber Industry on the South," *Mississippi Quarterly* 25 (Spring 1972): 141–64.

19. "clacker": Wayne Flynt, *Poor But Proud: Alabama's Poor Whites* (Tuscaloosa: University of Alabama Press, 1989), p. 119; "token": testimony of William Carter Stubbs, *Report of the Industrial Commission on Agriculture and Agricultural Labor*, vol. 10 of the Commission's Reports (Washington, D.C.: GPO, 1901), p. 777; "aluminum": letter of McClung Callender to William P. Harvey, Chief of Investigation, Tampa, Fla., 17 October 1918, in Employees v. International Agricultural Corporation, Mulberry, Fla., Docket no. 690, 1918, Entry 4, File no. 0197, RG 2, NA; "paper and brass": Bill Haywood, *Bill Haywood's Book: The Autobiography of William D. Haywood* (New York: International Publishers, 1929), p. 242; "Grown men": Reginald Millner, "Conversations with the 'Ole Man': The Life and Times of a Black Appalachian Coal Miner [James E. Millner]," in William H. Turner and Edward J. Cabbell, eds., *Blacks in Appalachia* (Lexington: University Press of Kentucky, 1985), p. 219.

20. "back breaking . . . was . . . it was": Samuel T. Sewell, "I Remember . . . Oyster Dredging in the 1890s," *Baltimore Sun Magazine* (6 March 1966): 2; Blakey, *Florida Phosphate Industry*, pp. 79–80; J. B. Hoeing, *Report on the Phosphate Rocks of Central Kentucky* (Frankfort: Kentucky Geological Survey, 1915); Hickman, *Mississippi Harvest*, pp. 121–25; Clark, *Greening of the South*, p. 23; James Battle Averit, "Turpentining with Slaves in the 30s and 40s," and Albert Pridgen, "Turpentining in the South Atlantic Country," both in Thomas Gamble, ed., *Naval Stores: History, Production, Distribution, and Consumption* (Savannah: Review Publishing and Printing Co., 1921), pp. 27, 101–4.

21. Carter Goodrich, *The Miner's Freedom: A Study of the Working Life in a Changing Industry* (Boston: Marshall Jones, 1925), pp. 13, 16, 34, 23–24, 41–43, 6, 56.

22. Miner quoted in William Spier, "A Social History of Manganese Mining in the Batesville District of Independence County," *Arkansas Historical Quarterly* 36 (Summer 1977): 134–35, 137, 139, 140; "You worked": William Spier, "We Was All Poor Then: The Subeconomy of a Farming Community, 1900–1925" (interview with Albert Wilson), *Southern Exposure* 2 (Fall 1974): 86.

23. Shick and Doyle, "South Carolina Phosphate Boom and the Stillbirth of the New South," pp. 11–12.

24. "or however": Viola D. Paradise, "Child Labor and the Work of Mothers in Oyster and Shrimp Canning Communities on the Gulf Coast," Children's Bureau Publication, no. 98 (1922): 32; Helen C. Dwight, "In Mississippi Canneries—A Continued Story," *Child Labor Bulletin* 5 (August 1916):

103–6; Edward F. Brown, "The Neglected Human Resources of the Gulf Coast States," *Child Labor Bulletin* 2 (May 1913): 112–16; Mrs. Alice E. Taylor to Mr. Parker, Avery Island, La., 22 March 1908, Box 10788, File no. 50–273, Justice Department Peonage Files; "The Bohemians . . . only . . . Most": Monroe N. Work, "The Negroes of Warsaw, Georgia," *Southern Workman* 37 (January 1908): 34.

25. Henry C. Goodnow, "In the Tie Woods of Texas," *Southern Industrial and Lumber Review* 12 (August 1904): 24.

26. "We have": testimony of O. B. Stevens, *Report of the Industrial Commission*, vol. 10, p. 913; Lorenzo J. Greene and Carter G. Woodson, *The Negro Wage Earner* (Washington, D.C.: Association for the Study of Negro Life and History, 1930), pp. 154, 288–89 ("The disagreeable aspect of this occupation has always made such work repugnant to whites except in supervisory capacities"); "Some men": Goodnow, "In the Tie Woods of Texas," p. 24.

27. Mark Schmitz, "The Transformation of the Southern Cane Sugar Sector, 1860–1930," *Agricultural History* 53 (January 1979): 279–80; Stanley Engerman, "Contract Labor, Sugar, and Technology in the Nineteenth Century," *Journal of Economic History* 43 (September 1983): 635–60; Lucy M. Cohen, *Chinese in the Post–Civil War South: A People Without a History* (Baton Rouge: Louisiana State University Press, 1984), pp. 52–58, 107–8, 114, 116, 142–47; J. Vincenza Scarpaci, "Labor for Louisiana's Sugar Cane Fields: An Experiment in Immigrant Recruitment," *Italian Americana* 7 (Fall-Winter 1981): 19–41. See also George T. Surface, "The Sugar Cane Industry," *Annals of the American Academy of Political and Social Science* 35 (January 1910): 25–36; J. Carlyle Sitterson, *Sugar Country: The Cane Sugar Industry in the South, 1753–1950* (Lexington: University Press of Kentucky, 1953); Louis Ferleger, "Farm Mechanization in the Southern Sugar Sector after the Civil War," *Louisiana History* 23 (Winter 1982): 21–34.

28. "in the woods": Charlotte Todes, *Labor and Lumber* (New York: International Publishers, 1931), p. 83; Mayor, *Southern Timberman*, p. 41; Jensen, *Lumber and Labor*, p. 76; Ruth A. Allen, *East Texas Lumber Workers: An Economic and Social Picture, 1870–1950* (Austin: University of Texas Press, 1961), p. 53; "Orange on the Sabine," *Southern Industrial and Lumber Review* 14 (May 1907): 42.

29. Mayor, *Southern Timberman*, pp. 25–30, 69–70, 71, 74–75. See also George Creel, "The Feudal Towns of Texas," *Harper's Weekly* 60 (23 January 1915): 76–78.

30. "It is": Alfred T. Brainerd, "Colored Mining Labor," *Transactions of the American Institute of Mining Engineers* 14 (1885–86): 79; Ronald L. Lewis, *Black Coal Miners in America: Race, Class, and Community Conflict, 1780–1980* (Lexington: University Press of Kentucky, 1987), pp. 191–93; Donald T. Barnum, "The Negro in Bituminous Coal Mining," Report no.

14, "Racial Policies of American Industry," Wharton School of Finance and Commerce (Philadelphia: University of Pennsylvania, 1970); Joe William Trotter, Jr., *Coal, Class, and Color: Blacks in Southern West Virginia, 1915–1932* (Urbana: University of Illinois Press, 1990).

31. Lewis, *Black Coal Miners*, pp. 58–78, 121–42.

32. Crandall A. Shifflett, *Coal Towns: Life, Work and Culture in Company Towns of Southern Appalachia, 1800–1960* (Knoxville: University of Tennessee Press, 1991); Price Fishback, "Segregation in Job Hierarchies: West Virginia Coal Mining, 1906–1932," *Journal of Economic History* 44 (September 1984): 755–74; Sterling D. Spero and Abram L. Harris, *The Black Worker: A Study of the Negro and the Labor Movement* (New York: Columbia University Press, 1931), p. 226; Lewis, *Black Coal Miners*, pp. 192–93; "felt . . . Blacks felt": Millner, "Conversations with the 'Ole Man,'" p. 220.

33. Kenneth R. Bailey, "A Judicious Mixture: Negroes and Immigrants in the West Virginia Mines, 1880–1917," *West Virginia History* 34 (January 1973): 141–61; Fishback, "Segregation in Job Hierarchies," p. 764; Shifflett, *Coal Towns*. Eastern Europeans also seemed more amenable to long, regular work hours compared to whites native to the area. In 1905 the superintendent of the Louisville Coal and Coke Company in West Virginia informed the company's vice president that he would hire Hungarians because "the miners we have . . . will not work but three or four hours a day, and we cannot make any showing with such men." Quoted in Dix, *Work Relations in the Coal Industry*, pp. 54–55.

34. Shick and Doyle, "Phosphate Boom," p. 15; Blakey, *Florida Phosphate Industry*, p. 53; "Hit": Lindsay, "An Oral History of Edisto Island," p. 23. See also George Campbell, *White and Black: The Outcome of a Visit to the United States* (London: Chatto and Windus, 1879), pp. 351–52.

35. "Those": Jean Ann Scarpaci, "Immigrants in the New South: Italians in Louisiana's Sugar Parishes, 1880–1910," in Milton Cantor, ed., *American Workingclass Culture: Explorations in American Labor and Social History* (Westport, CT: Greenwood Press, 1979), p. 379; Alfred Holt Stone, "Italian Cotton-Growers in Arkansas," *American Monthly Review of Reviews* 35 (February 1907): 212–13; testimony of William Carter Stubbs, *Report of the Industrial Commission*, vol. 10, p. 777.

36. Hickman, *Mississippi Harvest*, p. 125; T. Bradford Laws, "The Negroes of Cinclare Central Factory and Calumet Plantation," *U.S. Department of Labor Bulletin*, no. 38 (January 1902): 95–120; U.S. Manufacturing Census for 1880, 10-87-7, T1136 (La.), n.p., NA; Sullivan and Ericson, "Women's Employment in Vegetable Canneries"; Nichol, "Oyster-Packing Industry of Baltimore"; Paradise, "Child Labor and the Work of Mothers in Oyster and Shrimp Canning Communities."

37. Dwight Pitcaithley, "Zinc and Lead Mining Along the Buffalo River," *Arkansas Historical Quarterly* 37 (Winter 1978): 239–305; Spier, "Social

History of Manganese Mining," p. 244; Blakey, *Florida Phosphate Industry*.
38. All quotations from Edw. N. Munns, "Women in Southern Lumbering Operations," *Journal of Forestry* 17 (1919): 144. George B. Tindall, *The Emergence of the New South, 1913–1945* (Baton Rouge: Louisiana State University Press, 1967), pp. 55–56; James E. Fickle, "Management Looks at the 'Labor Problem': The Southern Pine Industry During World War I and the Postwar Era," *Journal of Southern History* 40 (February 1974): 61–76.
39. Matthew J. Mancini, "Race, Economics, and the Abandonment of Convict Leasing," *Journal of Negro History* 63 (Fall 1978): 339–52; John Dittmer, *Black Georgia in the Progressive Era, 1900–1920* (Urbana: University of Illinois Press, 1977), p. 83; Mary Grace Quackenbos to William R. Harr, Washington, D.C., 11 February 1910, Box 10805, File no. 50-359, Justice Department Peonage Files; Hamilton Holt, ed., *Life Stories of Undistinguished Americans as Told by Themselves* (New York: James Pott and Co., 1906), p. 183–98.
40. *U.S. Department of Labor Bulletin*, no. 5 (July 1896): 443–78; Edward Ayers, *Vengeance and Justice: Crime and Punishment in the Nineteenth-Century American South* (New York: Oxford University Press, 1984), chap. 6; Blake McKelvey, "A Half Century of Southern Penal Exploitation," *Journal of Social Forces* 13 (October 1934): 113; Blake McKelvey, "Penal Slavery and Southern Reconstruction," *Journal of Negro History* 20 (April 1935): 153–59. Frank Tannenbaum lists various forms of punishment, evidence culled from state investigating committees, in *Darker Phases of the South* (New York: Putnams, 1924). See also George Washington Cable, *The Silent South, Together with the Freedman's Case in Equity and, The Convict Lease System* (New York: Scribner's Sons, 1889).
41. "men": Hugh Penn Brinton, "Negroes Who Run Afoul the Law," *Journal of Social Forces* 11 (October 1932): 96–101; Jesse F. Steiner and Roy M. Brown, *The North Carolina Chain Gang: A Study of County Convict Road Work* (Chapel Hill: University of North Carolina Press, 1927), pp. 155, 164–72; Ayers, *Vengeance and Justice*, pp. 197–200.
42. "We have": committee quoted in Tannenbaum, *Darker Phases of the South*, p. 102; "big": J. C. Powell, *The American Siberia Or Fourteen Years' Experience in a Southern Convict Camp* (Chicago: Donohue, Henneberry, and Co., 1891), p. 186. See also, for example, "The Prison Labor Problem in Georgia: A Survey by the Prison Industries Reorganization Administration" (n.p., 1937).
43. Pridgen, "Turpentining in the South Atlantic Country," p. 104; J. B. Thomas to Governor Park Trammel, Jacksonville, Fla., 15 April 1914; "and I . . . I pray": W. L. Bobbitt to Governor Park Trammel, Palatka, Fla., n.d., Box 10801, File no. 50-177, Justice Department Peonage Files; "thinking": Powell, *American Siberia*, p. 335.
  Regardless of how they entered the camps, the few women in them

often experienced a kind of degradation rivaled only by life on a slave plantation. Although women (most of them black) represented 7 percent of the total Southern prison population in the late nineteenth century, they probably constituted no more than 2 or 3 percent of all convicts at work in privately owned or state maintained work camps. In the 1890s Virginia, Georgia, and Texas employed the highest number of female prisoners in productive labor (82, 67, and 62 respectively). Some of these worked as cooks and laundresses for the men or were forced into prostitution in the camps, while others toiled as part of work crews in turpentine orchards and railroad camps. See, for example, "Convict Labor"; "Peonage in Georgia," *Independent* 55 (24 December 1903): 3079–81; N. Gordon Carper, "Slavery Revisited: Peonage in the South," *Phylon* 37 (March 1976): 94; Jerrell H. Shofner, "Postscript to the Martin Tabert Case: Peonage as Usual in the Florida Turpentine Camps," *Florida Historical Quarterly* 60 (October 1981): 164–65; Nicolas Fischer Hahn, "Female State Prisoners in Tennessee: 1831–1979," *Tennessee Historical Quarterly* 39 (Winter 1980): 485–97.

44. J. E. Pennypacker, "Convict Labor for Road Work," *USDA Bulletin*, no. 414 (Washington, D.C.: GPO, 1916), p. 108; "one open side": McKelvey, "A Half Century of Southern Penal Exploitation," pp. 113–19; "Tied": testimony of George Henry White, *Report of the Industrial Commission*, vol. 10, p. 431; "were better": W. O. Saunders, "Cleaning Out North Carolina's Convict Camps," *Survey* (15 May 1915): 152; "house boats . . . 'match box' shacks": Todes, *Labor and Lumber*, pp. 83–84; "Report on Experimental Convict Road Camp, Fulton Co., Ga.," *USDA Bulletin*, no. 583 (1918). See also the harrowing, surrealistic description of a road camp in Toni Morrison's novel *Beloved* (New York: Knopf, 1987), pp. 106–13.

45. Fran Ansley and Brenda Bell, eds., "East Tennessee Coal Mining Battles: Miners' Insurrections/Convict Labor," *Southern Exposure* 1 (Winter 1974): 152; "the means . . . If there . . . unproarious . . . constant": Marc N. Goodnow, "Turpentine: Impressions of the Convict Camps of Florida," *The Survey* 34 (1 May 1915): 103–7.

46. "When": Mr. Thompson and "brought": Mrs. S. O. Sanders, in Ansley and Bell, eds., "East Tennessee Coal Mining Battles," pp. 152, 154. See also Bruce Reynolds, "Convict Labor, the Montserrat Experience," *Missouri Historical Review* 57 (October 1982): 47–63.

47. "The work": Powell, *American Siberia*, p. 27; "palmetto scrubs": Goodnow, "Turpentine: Impressions of the Convict Camps of Florida," p. 103; "content": Richard Barry, "Slavery in the South To-Day," *Cosmopolitan Magazine* 42 (March 1907): 488; "needed labor . . . These conditions": "Statement by S. A. Robert, Jr., and Lee Coleman, Division of Land Economics, Bureau of Agricultural Economics, Atlanta, Georgia," *Hearings Before the Select Committee Investigating National Defense Migration*,

House of Representatives, 77th Cong., 2nd sess., pt. 32, Huntsville, Ala., Hearings (May 1942), p. 12177 (hereafter *National Defense Migration Hearings*).

Actual descriptions of this work process thus contrast mightily with the romantic pronouncements of naval stores operators, who declared that the "servants of the turpentine orchards" benefited from particularly healthful "balsamic properties which the pine trees are constantly distilling in the air" (Averit, "Turpentining with Slaves in the '30s and '40s," p. 27).

48. "the conditions": Arthur H. Codington to attorney general, Macon, Ga., 21 August 1912, Box 10802, File no. 50-236; "a long": Fred C. Cubberly to attorney general, Pensacola, Fla., 29 September 1911, Box 10801, File no. 50-168; "wild": Ernest F. Cochran to attorney general, Anderson, S.C., 15 February 1910, Box 10805, File no. 50–359; "but simply": Charlton R. Beattie to attorney general, New Orleans, La., 31 August 1911, Box 10788, File no. 50-277, Justice Department Peonage Files.

49. Report of A. W. Davis, Pensacola, Fla., 1 November 1916, Box 10801, File no. 50-178, Justice Department Peonage Files; "long-distance": Wright, *Old South, New South*, p. 91.

50. "this . . . Here . . . The monumental": Barry, "Slavery in the South To-Day," pp. 481, 490–91; Pete Daniel, *The Shadow of Slavery: Peonage in the South, 1901–1969* (New York: Oxford University Press, 1972). See also Jerrell H. Shofner, "Mary Grace Quackenbos, A Visitor Florida Did Not Want," *Florida Historical Quarterly* 58 (January 1980): 273–90.

51. "they were": Powell, *American Siberia*, p. 243; Robert David Ward and William Warren Rogers, *Convicts, Coal, and the Banner Mine Tragedy* (Tuscaloosa: University of Alabama Press, 1987); Merle E. Reed, "Lumberjacks and Longshoremen: The IWW in Louisiana," *Labor History* 13 (Winter 1972): 49; "one of": Daniel Nelson, "Mudsills and Bottom Rails in the Twentieth Century," *Reviews in American History* 17 (September 1989): 430.

52. "little": W. O. Saunders, "Cleaning Out North Carolina's Convict Camps," *The Survey* (15 May 1915): 152; "Families": Harry Crews, *A Childhood: The Biography of a Place* (New York: Harper & Row, 1978), p. 13.

53. *Report of the Industrial Commission on Agriculture and on Taxation in Various States*, vol. 11 of the Commission's Reports (Washington, D.C.: GPO, 1901), pp. 95–96; "notoriously": A. Berglund et al., *Labor in the Industrial South*, pp. 53, 60; "about the country": Goodnow, "In the Tie Woods of Texas," p. 24; "Orange on the Sabine," p. 42; "I worked": Nick Lindsay, "An Oral History of Edisto Island: The Life and Times of Bubberson Brown," (Goshen, IN: Pinchpenny Press, 1977), p. 59; "who . . . ten-inch": Crews, *A Childhood*, pp. 5–7. One of Sam Gadsden's contemporaries, Bubberson Brown, recalls his father's description of life at the Bartow (phosphate) mines camp near Charleston, where "They had a killing over there *every* Saturday

night": Nick Lindsay, "An Oral History of Edisto Island ," p. 25.

54. "restricted . . . nomads . . . batcher . . . sort of": Goodnow, "In the Tie Woods of Texas," p. 24; interview with Nanny Suttles in Warren Moore, *Mountain Voices: A Legacy of the Blue Ridge and Great Smokies* (Chester, CT: Globe Pequot Press, 1988), p. 115; Spier, "A Social History of Manganese Mining," pp. 143, 146.

55. Interview with Melvin Profitt in Laurel Shackelford and Bill Weinberg, eds., *Our Appalachia: An Oral History* (New York: Hill and Wang, 1977), pp. 200, 201, 207.

56. "There is": Work, "The Negroes of Warsaw, Georgia," p. 37.

57. Ibid., p. 38; Laws, "The Negroes of Cinclare Central Factory and Calumet Plantation," pp. 95–120.

58. "she kin . . . There is": Lewis W. Hine, "The Child's Burden in Oyster and Shrimp Canneries," *Child Labor Bulletin* 2 (May 1913): 108, 111. See also Pauline Goldmark, "Child Labor in Canneries," *Annals of the American Academy of Political and Social Science* 35, supplement (March 1910): 152–54.

59. Laws, "Negroes of Cinclare Central Factory"; George W. Henderson, "Life in the Louisiana Sugar Belt," *Southern Workman* 35 (April 1906): 207–15; Jean Scarpaci, "A Tale of Selective Accommodation: Sicilians and Native Whites in Louisiana," *Journal of Ethnic Studies* 5 (1977): 37–50; Alice Channing, "Child Labor on Maryland Truck Farms," Children's Bureau Publication no. 123 (1923); W. T. B. Williams, "Local Conditions Among Negroes. I. Gloucester County, Virginia," *Southern Workman* 35 (February 1906): 103–6; William Taylor Thom, "The Negroes of Litwalton, Virginia: A Social Study of the 'Oyster Negro,'" *Department of Labor Bulletin* 37 (November 1901): 1115–70.

60. Hine, "The Child's Burden in Oyster and Shrimp Canneries," p. 106; Paradise, "Child Labor and the Work of Mothers in Oyster and Shrimp Canning Communities on the Gulf Coast," pp. 76–77; "fooled . . . this . . . and there": Alice E. Taylor to Mr. Parker, Avery Island, La., 22 March 1911, Box 10788, File no. 50-273, Justice Department Peonage Files. See also Sitterson, *Sugar Country*, pp. 308–23.

61. Berglund et al., *Labor in the Industrial South*, p. 53.

62. Interview with Marvin Gullett in Shackelford and Weinberg, eds., *Our Appalachia*, p. 218. On textile mills, see Jacquelyn Dowd Hall et al., *Like a Family: The Making of a Southern Cotton Mill World* (Chapel Hill: University of North Carolina Press, 1987); Cathy McHugh, *Mill Family: The Labor Systems in the Southern Cotton Textile Industry, 1880–1915* (New York: Oxford University Press, 1988).

63. "John": interview with Marvin Gullet in Shackelford and Weinberg, eds., *Our Appalachia*, pp. 218, 223; Ward and Rogers, *Convicts, Coal, and the Banner Mine Tragedy*, p. 15.

64. Lumber worker quoted in Mayor, *Southern Timberman*, p. 59.

65. Interview with Nancy Suttles in Moore, *Mountain Voices*, pp. 195–96; "It was": interview with Talmadge Allen and "where": interview with Marvin Gullett, in Shackelford and Weinberg, eds., *Our Appalachia*, pp. 238, 221; Allen, *East Texas Lumber Workers*, p. 102; Mayor, *Southern Timberman*, p. 79.

66. "silk stocking": interview with Frances Turner in Shackelford and Weinberg, eds., *Our Appalachia*, pp. 211–12; Shifflett, *Coal Towns*; Lewis, *Black Coal Miners*, pp. 121–42; William P. Tams, Jr., *The Smokeless Coal Fields of West Virginia: A Brief History* (Morgantown: West Virginia University Library, 1963), pp. 60–63.

67. Bailey, "A Judicious Mixture," p. 158; "many legal": Mayor, *Southern Timberman*, p. 73. Cf. "A Camp Physician. The Alabama Mining Camp," *Independent* 63 (3 October 1907): 790–91.

68. "generational": Ronald L. Lewis, "From Peasant to Proletarian: The Migration of Southern Blacks to Central Appalachian Coalfields," *Journal of Southern History* 55 (February 1989): 77–102; Kirby, *Rural Worlds Lost*, pp. 275–333; *Report of the United States Coal Commission*, U.S. Congress, Sen. Doc. 195, 68th Cong., 2d sess. (Washington, D.C.: GPO, 1925), pp. 1412–20; "abandoned": Jensen, *Lumber and Labor*, p. 85; Clark, *Greening of the South*, p. 24.

69. Malcolm Ross, *Machine Age in the Hills* (New York: Macmillan, 1933), pp. 3, 128.

Chapter 6
"A Golden Florida Made Ready for Them Too":
East Coast Migratory Laborers, 1890 to 1990

1. Zora Neale Hurston, *Their Eyes Were Watching God* (London: J. M. Dent & Sons, 1937), p. 193.

2. Joan Pascal and Harold G. Tipton, "Vegetable Production in South Florida," in *Hearings Before the Select Committee Investigating National Defense Migration*, House of Representatives, 77th Cong., 2nd sess., pt. 33, Washington Hearings (with Florida and New Jersey Supplement), 22 May, 11 and 19 June 1942, p. 12936 (hereafter *National Defense Migration Hearings*, with part no.).

3. Phil Decker, "Cleselia," *Migration Today* 13 (1985): 26.

4. Kenneth G. Castro et al., "Transmission of HIV in Belle Glade, Florida: Lessons for Other Communities in the United States," *Science* 239 (8 January 1988): 193–97; Jon Nordheimer, "Poverty-Scarred Town Now Stricken by AIDS," *New York Times*, 2 May 1985, p. 16; Lydia Martin and Richard Wallace, "Migrant Farm Workers Feeling the Freeze," *Miami Herald*, 7 January 1990, p. 18A; "Godforsaken": Sara Rimer, "Spotlight Fades on

AIDS in Town, But the Disease and Stigma Remain," *New York Times,* 14 November 1990, p. A16. See also "Women in Florida Industries," U.S. Department of Labor, Women's Bureau *Bulletin,* no. 80 (1930).

Nordheimer quotes K. Stuart Goldberg, local director of the Florida Rural Legal Services Office in Belle Glade: "Just blocks from City Hall are places that rival the godawful slums of any third world capital."

5. Statement of Clarence R. Bitting, President, United States Sugar Corp., Clewiston, Fla., *Hearings Before the Select Committee to Investigate the Interstate Migration of Destitute Citizens,* House of Representatives, 77th Cong., 3d sess., pt. 2, Montgomery Hearings, 14, 15, 16 August 1940, p. 507 (hereafter *Interstate Migration Hearings,* with part no.); Earl Lomon Koos, "They Follow the Sun" (Jacksonville: Bureau of Maternal and Child Health, Florida State Board of Health, 1957), p. 40.

6. "I might": worker quoted in Monica Lucille Heppel, "Harvesting the Crops of Others: Migrant Farm Labor on the Eastern Shore of Virginia" (Ph.D. diss., American University, 1982), p. 166; "a nice": testimony of Luther Jones, Belle Glade, and testimony of William Yearby (Negro), Belle Glade, *National Defense Migration Hearings,* pt. 33, pp. 12672–73, 12656. Black witnesses at these hearings were consistently identified by their race; whites never were.

7. "through": Bureau of Agricultural Economics and the Farm Security Administration, U.S. Department of Agriculture (hereafter USDA), "Backgrounds of the War Farm Labor Problem," *National Defense Migration Hearings,* Huntsville Hearings, 7 and 8 May 1942, pt. 32, p. 12347; "Because": Harald A. Pedersen, "Mechanized Agriculture and the Farm Laborer," *Rural Sociology* 19 (June 1954):149.

8. "no one's": Diana Zimmerman, "America's Nomads," *Migration Today* 9 (1981): 26; "at best": Arthur T. Sutherland, "The Migratory Labor Problem in Delaware," U.S. Department of Labor, Women's Bureau *Bulletin,* no. 185 (Washington, D.C.: GPO, 1941), p. 2. Journalistic exposés include Dale Wright, *They Harvest Despair* (Boston: Beacon Press, 1965); Nels Anderson, *Men on the Move* (Chicago: University of Chicago Press, 1940); Truman Moore, *The Slaves We Rent* (New York: Random House, 1965). The number and diversity of racial and ethnic groups on the eastern seaboard helps to account for the lack of labor organization among migrants in that part of the country; on the other hand, with its large Hispanic contingent, the West Coast migratory work force responded positively to the union leadership of Cesar Chavez, in both political and cultural terms, during the 1960s.

9. "Farm Labor and the Labor Supply Situation on the Eastern Shore of Maryland, 1941," *National Defense Migration Hearings,* Baltimore Hearings, 1 and 2 July 1941, pt. 15, p. 6215; Carey McWilliams, *Ill Fares the Land: Migrants and Migratory Labor in the United States* (Boston: Little, Brown, 1942), p. 164; "We depend": *Migratory Labor in American*

Agriculture: Report of the President's Commission on Migratory Labor, 1951 (Washington, D.C.: GPO, 1951), p. 3. For an overview, see Jack Temple Kirby, *Rural Worlds Lost: The American South, 1920–1960* (Baton Rouge: Louisiana State University Press, 1987), pp. 275–308. See also "Truck Farming in Tidewater Virginia," *Southern Workman* 34 (January 1905): 79–86; L. C. Corbett, "Truck Farming in the Atlantic Coast States," *U.S. Department of Agriculture Yearbook for 1907* (Washington, D.C.: GPO, 1908), pp. 425–34.

10. C. Horace Hamilton, "The Social Effects of Recent Trends in the Mechanization of Agriculture," *Rural Sociology* 4 (March 1939): 3–19; Fred C. Frey and T. Lynn Smith, "The Influence of the AAA Cotton Program Upon the Tenant, Cropper, and Laborer," *Rural Sociology* 1 (December 1936): 483–505; "floating": *Interstate Migration Hearings,* Washington Hearings, 3, 6, 9 and 10 December 1940, pt. 9, pp. 3775–77; statement by Howard Stovall, director, Delta Council, Stoneville, Mississippi, *Interstate Migration Hearings,* pt. 2, p. 608; Joseph Interrante, "You Can't Go to Town in a Bathtub: Automobile Movement and the Reorganization of Rural American Space, 1900–1930," *Radical History Review* 21 (Fall 1979): 151–68. See also Alvin T. Bertrand, "The Social Processes and the Mechanization of Southern Agricultural Systems," *Rural Sociology* 13 (March 1948): 31–39; Arthur Raper, "The Role of Agricultural Technology in Southern Social Change," *Rural Sociology* 25 (October 1946): 21–30; Herbert R. Padgett, "Florida's Migratory Worker," *Rural Sociology* 18 (October 1953): 267–72. For a firsthand (and somehat romantic) account of hobo fruit pickers in the Lake Erie region, see Charles Sampson, "Peach Harvest," *American Mercury* 15 (October 1928): 223–28.

11. Statement of Roberta C. Williams, staff associate, National Travelers' Aid Association, *Interstate Migration Hearings,* pt. 9, p. 3614; statement of M. Clifford Townsend, Director, Office of Defense Relations, USDA, *National Defense Migration Hearings,* Washington, D.C. Hearings, 15, 16, and 17 July 1941, pt. 16, p. 6561; C. W. E. Pittman, "Atlantic Coast Migratory Movement of Agricultural Workers: War Years," USDA Publication, Washington, D.C., 1946.

12. Donald Hughes Grubb, "A History of the Atlantic Coast Stream of Agricultural Migrants" (M.A. thesis, University of Florida, 1959); G. Thomas-Lycklama a Nijeholt, *On the Road for Work: Migratory Workers on the East Coast of the United States* (Boston: Martinus Nijhoff Publishing, 1980), p. 74; Tux Turkel, "Migrant Blues: Hispanics Increase the Flow of Farm Workers," *Maine Sunday Telegram,* 26 August 1990, pp. 1B, 14B. The Immigration Reform and Control Act of 1986 only gradually stemmed the flow of illegal aliens. Under its provisions, workers who had entered the country before 1982 were granted amnesty. At the same time, new penalties leveled against employers who hired undocumented workers

had the effect of heightening racial and ethnic discrimination against foreign-born American citizens.

13. William H. Metzler, "Migratory Farm Workers in the Atlantic Coast Stream: A Study in the Belle Glade Area of Florida," USDA Circular no. 966 (January 1955): 2, 28; Nijeholt, *On the Road for Work,* pp. 79–82; Pittman, "Atlantic Coast Migratory Movement," pp. 27–37. See also Jay A. Bonsteel, "Truck Soils of the Atlantic Coast," *U.S. Department of Agriculture Yearbook for 1912* (Washington, D.C.: GPO, 1913), pp. 417–32.

14. Testimony of William Yearby, *National Defense Migration Hearings,* pt. 33, p. 12652; "a fluctuating": Pittman, "Atlantic Coast Migratory Movement," p. 25; "Statement by Dr. Harold Hoffsommer . . . Interstate Migration of Louisiana Strawberry Pickers [and] Cotton Pickers in the Mississippi River Delta," *Interstate Migration Hearings,* pt. 2, pp. 450–61.

15. "Truck farming": A. Oemler, "Truck Farming," *Report of the Commissioner of Agriculture for 1885* (Washington, D.C.: GPO, 1885), p. 585; "Living": Ruth Alice Allen, *The Labor of Women in the Production of Cotton* (Chicago: University of Chicago Libraries, 1931), p. 113; "these people": manager quoted in Edward A. Gargan, "New York's Harvest Draws a Stream of Migrant Labor," *New York Times,* 6 November 1984, p. B5.

16. "combined": testimony of William Harrell, *National Defense Migration Hearings,* pt. 33, p. 6151; "Well": testimony of Frank Collins, Migratory Camp, Belle Glade, *Interstate Migration Hearings,* pt. 2, pp. 497–501; Jerry Woods Weeks, "Florida Gold: The Emergence of the Florida Citrus Industry, 1865–1895" (Ph.D. diss., University of North Carolina, Chapel Hill, 1977), p. 70. On the South as a low-wage economy, see Gavin Wright, *Old South, New South: Revolutions in the Southern Economy Since the Civil War* (New York: Basic Books, 1986). On the Midwest berry stream, see Melvin S. Brooks, "The Social Problems of Migrant Farm Laborers," Department of Sociology, Southern Illinois University, Carbondale, 1960; Wells A. Sherman et al., "Strawberry Supply and Distribution in 1914," *USDA Bulletin,* no. 237 (1915); O. W. Sleussner and J. C. Gilbert, "Marketing and Distribution of Strawberries in 1915," *USDA Bulletin,* no. 477 (1917): 16. See also testimony of Robert Patton, Camp Osceola, Fla., FSA Migratory Labor Camp, Belle Glade, *National Defense Migration Hearings,* pt. 33, pp. 12739–44; Paul S. Taylor, "Migratory Farm Labor in the United States," *Monthly Labor Review* 44 (March 1937): 537–49. On white "fruit tramps" see Herman LeRoy Emmet, *Fruit Tramps: A Family of Migrant Farmworkers* (Albuquerque: University of New Mexico Press, 1990).

17. "there were": T. J. Woofter, Jr., "Southern Population and Social Planning," *Journal of Social Forces* 14 (October 1935): 18; "the labor": Harold Hoffsommer, "Social Aspects of Farm Labor in the South," *Rural Sociology*

3 (December 1938): 440; "the [living] conditions": testimony of Eleanor Roosevelt, *Interstate Migration Hearings*, pt. 9, p. 3745; tables 1 and 2, *Interstate Migration Hearings*, pt. 2, pp. 566–67; testimony of John Beecher, ibid., p. 563; "You can't": *National Defense Migration Hearings*, pt. 33, p. 12932; "They want": testimony of Elijah Boone, *Hearings Before the Subcommittee on Migratory Labor of the Committee on Labor and Public Welfare*, U.S. Senate, 91st Cong., 1st and 2d sess. (1969–70): pt. 1, *Who Are the Migrants?*, p. 183. See also Labor Division, Farm Security Administration, "Farm Labor and the Labor Supply Situation on the Eastern Shore of Maryland," *National Defense Migration Hearings*, pt. 15, p. 6220.

18. "always": Charles L. Chute, "The Cost of the Cranberry Sauce," *The Survey* 27 (2 December 1911): 1283; interview with Albert J. Abramson, Philadelphia, Pa., 8 April 1990 (his grandmother took her children into the fields surrounding Philadelphia, c. 1900–20, until her husband, formerly a ragpicker, opened up his own store in the city). See also McWilliams, *Ill Fares the Land*, pp. 155, 271–72; Ruth McIntire, "Children in Agriculture," National Child Labor Committee Pamphlet 284 (February 1918); Nijeholt, *On the Road for Work*, p. 23.

19. "to prefer": Josiah C. Folsom, "Truck-Farm Labor in New Jersey, 1922," *USDA Bulletin*, no. 1285 (April 1925): 15; "lower . . . paying": testimony of Luther I. Chandler, president of Goulds Growers, *National Defense Migration Hearings*, pt. 33, p. 12825; "in the midst": testimony of Elijah Boone, *Who Are the Migrants? Hearings*, p. 185; Weeks, "Florida Gold: The Emergence of the Florida Citrus Industry," p. 70; M. Loretta Sullivan and Ethel Erickson, "Women's Employment in Vegetable Canneries in Delaware," Women's Bureau *Bulletin*, no. 62, (1927): 10, 29; "Cranbury, NJ," August 1939, report in Labor Division, FSA files, quoted in *National Defense Migration Hearings*, pt. 32, p. 12365.

20. "when": testimony of Kenneth Roberts, *National Defense Migration Hearings*, pt. 33, p. 13004; "came": Harry Schwartz, *Seasonal Farm Laborers in the United States* (New York: Columbia University Press, 1945), p. 41; "husbands": testimony of J. M. Seabrook, manager, Seabrook Farms, Bridgeton, N.J., *National Defense Migration Hearings*, pt. 33, p. 13020; "When the head": "Effect of the National Defense Program on the Program of the FSA in Region IV, States of Virginia, West Virginia, Tennessee, North Carolina, and Kentucky," *National Defense Migration Hearings*, 18, 19, and 21 July 1941, pt. 17, p. 6867; "Employment and Housing Problems of Migratory Workers in New York and New Jersey Canning Industries, 1943," Women's Bureau *Bulletin*, no. 198 (1944).

21. George Otis Coalson, "The Development of the Migratory Farm Labor System in Texas, 1900–1954" (Ph.D. diss., University of Oklahoma, 1955), p. 153; *Migratory Labor in American Agriculture*, pp. 17–39, 48, 134; Heppel, "Harvesting the Crops of Others," p. 59; "If I had": quoted in Alec

Wilkinson, "A Reporter at Large (Sugarcane): Big Sugar, Pt. II," *The New Yorker*, 24 July 1989, p. 64.

22. "most readily . . . family . . . together . . . keeping": Heppel, "Harvesting the Crops of Others," pp. 180, 183–84, 196, 199–200; Coalson, "Development of the Migratory Farm Labor System in Texas," p. 43; McWilliams, *Ill Fares the Land,* pp. 208–81.

23. "a godsend . . . want": "Puerto Rican Farm Workers in Florida: Highlights of A Study," U.S. Department of Labor, Bureau of Employment Security, 1955, pp. 2, 3, 5; M. Daniel Suwyn, "For Migrants, A Way to Escape: Breaking the Cycle with School," *Wilmington* [Del.] *News Journal,* 12 August 1984, pp. A1, A8; Tony Dunbar and Linda Kravitz, *Hard Traveling: Migrant Farm Workers in America* (Cambridge, MA: Ballinger, 1976).

24. Letter from L. L. Chandler to Lemuel B. Schofield, 23 October 1941, *National Defense Migration Hearings,* pt. 33, p. 12811; *Migratory Labor in American Agriculture,* p. 55; "The White": Wilkinson, "Big Sugar, Pt. II," p. 55; "the boss . . . back . . . cars . . . Ou": Tito Craige, "Boat People Tough It Out: Haitian Immigrants Struggle to Survive in North Carolina," *Migration Today* 13 (1985): 32–34. On foreign competition in the truck-farm business, see James L. McCorkle, Jr., "Problems of a Southern Agrarian Industry: Cooperation and Self-Interest," *Southern Studies* 15 (Fall 1978): 241–54.

25. "who": quoted in Jon Nordheimer, "Older Migrants' Years of Toil in Sun End in Cold Twilight," *New York Times,* 29 May 1988, pp. A1, A26; "traveled": "Eastern Region," *Interstate Migration Hearings,* pt. 10, p. 4138; "When . . . why . . . had . . . We": testimony of Johnnie Belle Taylor, *National Defense Migration Hearings,* pt. 33, pp. 12627–28. See also Molly Murray, "A Dry Year for Watermelons," *Wilmington* [Del.] *News Journal,* 18 August 1985, p. C8.

26. "There does . . . partially": FBI report and worker quoted in Wilkinson, "Big Sugar, Pt. II," pp. 46, 52; "The earnings": Folsom, "Truck-Farm Labor in New Jersey, 1922," p. 26. See also testimony of James Sotille, president, South Dade Farms, Inc., *National Defense Migration Hearings,* pt. 33, p. 12833; Grubbs, "A History of the Atlantic Coast Stream," p. 95. In addition to the *Interstate Migration Hearings* (1940) and the *National Defense Migration Hearings* (1941–1943), the other multivolume series, *Hearings Before the Subcommittee on Migratory Labor of the Committee on Labor and Public Welfare,* U.S. Senate, 91st Cong., 1st and 2d sess. (1969–70), includes the following parts: pt. 1: *Who Are the Migrants?;* pt. 2: *Migrant Subculture;* pts. 3A, 3B: *Efforts to Organize;* pt. 6C: *Pesticides and the Farmworker;* pts. 4A, 4B: *Farmworker Legal Problems;* pt. 7B: *Manpower and Economic Problems;* pt. 8B: *Who Is Responsible?* (hereafter quoted as title of part).

27. "How much . . . just . . . It": field investigator quoted in Koos, "They Follow the Sun," p. 47; Budd N. Shenkin, *Health Care for Migrant Workers: Policies and Politics* (Cambridge, MA: Ballinger, 1974). See

also a report by the Housing Assistance Council for the American Association of Retired Persons, "After the Harvest: The Plight of Older Farmworkers" (c. 1989).

28. "like cattle . . . like hogs . . . live . . . Do": quoted in Harry M. Bremer, "People Who Go to Tomatoes: A Study of Four Hundred Families," National Child Labor Committee Pamphlet no. 215 (March 1914): 2, 6; "wild Florida": testimony of P. L. Hinson, Deerfield Beach, Fla., *National Defense Migration Hearings*, pt. 33, p. 12786; "no closed": Lewis W. Hine and Edward F. Brown, "The Child's Burden in Oyster and Shrimp Canneries," National Child Labor Committee, May 1913, p. 28; testimony of Jerry Wells, *National Defense Migration Hearings*, pt. 33, p. 12680; "We just": testimony of Mrs. Johnnie Belle Taylor (Negro), Camp Okeechobee, Fla., FSA Migratory Labor Camp, Belle Glade, *National Defense Migration Hearings*, pt. 33, p. 12628. See also excerpt from *Miami News*, 10 April 1970, "Hunger, Lack of Jobs Stalk Florida's Migrant Pickers," *Who Is Responsible? Hearings*, p. 5475.

29. "its water": statement by William H. Weems, MD., county physician for Palm Beach County, Fla., *Interstate Migration Hearings*, pt. 2, p. 599; "didn't": testimony of James Roberts, Pocomoke City, Md., *National Defense Migration Hearings*, pt. 15, p. 6161; Herbert Hill, *No Harvest for the Reaper: The Story of the Migratory Agricultural Worker in the United States* (New York: NAACP, c. 1958), p. 21; "and if": testimony of Newlon Lloyd, *Who Are the Migrants? Hearings*, p. 195.

30. "In this": testimony of Bryan McLendon, Belle Glade, Fla., *National Defense Migration Hearings*, pt. 33, p. 12645; testimony of James Roberts, Pocomoke City, Md., *National Defense Migration Hearings*, pt. 15, p. 6156; testimony of John Beecher, supervisor, Florida Migratory Labor Camps, FSA, *Interstate Migration Hearings*, pt. 2, p. 535; "a crew . . . You": testimony of Newlon Lloyd, *Who Are the Migrants? Hearings*, p. 197.

31. "His labor": testimony of John Beecher, *Interstate Migration Hearings*, pt. 2, p. 536; Koos, "They Follow the Sun," pp. 34–35; testimony of Francis A. Raymaley, county agricultural agent, Bridgeton, N.J., *National Defense Migration Hearings*, pt. 33, p. 12986; "lay in": testimony of Elijah Boone, *Who Are the Migrants? Hearings*, p. 174.

32. "historic economy": *National Defense Migration Hearings*, pt. 32, p. 12047; Mach quoted in *National Defense Migration Hearings*, pt. 33, p. 12969; Grubbs, "A History of the Atlantic Coast Stream," pp. 76–77; Diane Zimmerman, "America's Nomads, Pt. II" *Migration Today* 9 (1981): 34–38; *Migratory Labor in American Agriculture*, pp. 59–61. See also Louis J. Ducoff, "Migratory Farm Workers in 1949," Agricultural Information Bulletin no. 25, Bureau of Agricultural Economics, USDA, 1950.

East Coast truck farms were smaller operations than West Coast agribusinesses. In 1959, for example, one thousand migrant labor camps were located in New York State alone. In 1966 the average number of workers per camp was thirty-seven. See Olaf F. Larson, "Migratory Agricultural Workers in the Eastern Seaboard States," in *Rural Poverty in the United States: A Report by the President's National Advisory Commission on Rural Poverty* (Washington, D.C.: GPO, 1968), p. 452.

33. "During": Arthur S. Evans, Jr., and David Lee, *Pearl City, Florida: A Black Community Remembers* (Boca Raton: Florida Atlantic University Press, 1990), p. 17; Schwartz, *Seasonal Farm Labor in the United States; The Everglades News*, Canal Point, Fla., 23 January 1942, excerpt quoted in *National Defense Migration Hearings*, pt. 33, p. 12930; "just sit . . . they might": testimony of Bryan McLendon, ibid., p. 12649; "You go": eight-year-old boy quoted in Hill, *No Harvest for the Reaper*, p. 20.

34. "dat muck": Hurston, *Their Eyes Were Watching God*, p. 193; "applied": testimony of Elijah Boone, *Who Are the Migrants? Hearings*, p. 191; "The worst": mother quoted in Robert Coles, *Children of Crisis*, vol. 2: *Migrants, Sharecroppers, Mountaineers* (Boston: Little, Brown, 1967), p. 52. See also *Pesticides and the Farmworker Hearings*.

35. "I need": statement of Rudolfo Juarez, migrant farmworker, Florida, *Who Is Responsible? Hearings*, p. 5489; "closed out": testimony of Mrs. Dorothea Brower, West Palm Beach, Fla., *National Defense Migration Hearings*, pt. 33, pp. 12791–92; "in cooperation . . . a summer": excerpt from the Belle Glade *Herald*: "Belle Glade Colored School Has Summer Term," *National Defense Migration Hearings*, pt. 33, p. 12863; "local police": testimony of L. L. Chandler, ibid., p. 12824.

On the role of the U.S. Employment Service and Farm Placement Service in placing migrants, see, for example, C. W. E. Pittman, "Migratory Agricultural Workers of the Atlantic Seaboard," *Employment Security Review* 7 (June 1948): 3–6; Preston R. Riley, "Guiding Migratory Workers on the Eastern Seaboard," *Employment Security Review* 20 (March 1953): 7–11.

36. On subsisting on sweet potatoes, see R. Sharpe, "Hunger Haunts Migrant Workers Caught in Drought," *Wilmington* [Del.] *News Journal*, 1 August 1986, p. A4; Martin and Wallace, "Migrant Farm Workers Feeling the Freeze," p. 18A; "Some live": Steven Fromm, "State Fears Huge Influx of Migrants," *Delaware State News*, 2 June 1985, pp. 1, 2.

37. Ed Domaingue, "Migrants: An Invisible Army of 25,000 Languishes in Poverty in Polk," excerpt from *Lakeland* [Fla.] *Leader*, 13 July 1970, in *Who Is Responsible? Hearings*, p. 5568.

38. "not . . . landless . . . the beans . . . big": John Beecher, testimony before *Senate Committee on Education and Labor, Supp. Hearings*, pt. 2, 15 May 1940, p. 337, quoted in *National Defense Migration Hearings*, pt. 33, p. 12927; "Big Lake": Hurston, *Their Eyes Were Watching God*, p. 193.

39. Frey and Smith, "The Influence of the AAA Cotton Program," pp. 485, 503; "odd jobs": Sutherland, "Migratory Labor Problem in Delaware," p. 18; "Interstate Migration of Louisiana Strawberry Pickers," *Interstate Migration*

Hearings, pt. 2, pp. 459–60; "residue": testimony of C. W. E. Pittman, *National Defense Migration Hearings,* pt. 28, p. 10763; C. W. E. Pittman, "Atlantic Coast Migratory Movement of Agricultural Workers," p. 25.

40. "frosted out": testimony of M. M. Carter, Camp Osceola, Fla., FSA Migratory Labor Camp, Belle Glade, *National Defense Migration Hearings,* pt. 33, p. 12776; "I got": testimony of William Bryant (Negro), Camp Okeechobee, Fla., FSA Migratory Labor Camp, Belle Glade, ibid., p. 12609; "It wouldn't": testimony of Richard Mitchell (Negro), FSA Migratory Labor Camp, Swedesboro, N.J., *National Defense Migration Hearings,* pt. 33, pp. 13029–30; Arthur Raper and F. Howard Forsyth, "Cultural Factors Which Result in Artificial Farm Labor Shortages," *Rural Sociology* 8 (March 1943): 6–7.

41. Quoted in Ronald B. Taylor, *Sweatshops in the Sun: Child Labor on the Farm* (Boston: Beacon Press, 1973), pp. 48–50.

42. *Migratory Labor in American Agriculture,* p. 148; Metzler, "Migratory Farm Workers in the Atlantic Coast Stream," p. 11; "the camp's" quoted in Gargan, "New York's Harvest Draws a Stream of Migrant Labor," p. B5; Louis J. Ducoff, "Migratory Farm Workers: A Problem in Migration Analysis," *Rural Sociology* 16 (September 1951): 217–24; Refugio I. Rochin, "Farm Worker Service and Employment Programs," in Robert D. Emerson, ed., *Seasonal Agricultural Labor Markets in the United States* (Ames: Iowa State University Press, 1984), pp. 437–46.

43. "powerful . . . they": testimony of Allison T. French, manager, West Palm Beach Office, U.S. Employment Service, *National Defense Migration Hearings,* pt. 33, p. 12715; Wilkinson, "Big Sugar, Pt. I," p. 41.

44. "some": testimony of Allison T. French, *National Defense Migration Hearings,* pt. 33, p. 12715; "busted": testimony of Bryan McLendon, ibid., p. 12647. See also testimony of William Bryant and Daniel DeBruyne, ibid., pp. 12611, 12704–5; Evans and Lee, *Pearl City, Florida,* p. 22.

　　In contrast to experienced white packinghouse workers who might follow a single crop from Florida to the Eastern Shore of Maryland, or to Mississippi or Kentucky, most black migrants eschewed specializing in one crop or another, a move that would have severely limited their choices in following leads for work up and down the coast. Only potatoes, less fragile and perishable than other food crops, seemed to attract the most down and out workers, those who had no choice but to withstand hard work and heat while grubbing in the dirt all day.

45. Dorothy Nelkin, *On the Season: Aspects of the Migrant Labor System* (ILR Paperback no. 8, November 1970, New York State School of Industrial and Labor Relations, Cornell University, Ithaca, NY, 1970), pp. 17–19; "begins": "Police Powers to Stop Labor Slow-Down Requested—Draft Board Resolution Urges Stoppage of Labor Walk Outs," *Belle Glade Herald,* 15 May 1942, excerpt quoted in *National Defense Migration Hearings,* pt. 33, p. 12680.

46. Testimony of James E. Beardsley, *National Defense Migration Hearings*, pt. 33, p. 12566; "cane cutter's": *Interstate Migration Hearings*, pt. 2, p. 507; "cane . . . Enjoy . . . Cash": Wilkinson, "Big Sugar, Pt. II," p. 41; "clinging . . . I guess": Neil Henry, "A Harvest of Hunger for Migrants: On the Eastern Shore, Drought Ravages Lives of Farm Workers," *Washington Post*, 27 August 1986, pp. A1, A12; "six rooms": testimony of William Yearby, *National Defense Migration Hearings*, pt. 33, p. 12545; W. L. Wheatley, Clayton, Del., to Jerry Wells, in ibid., p. 12678.

47. Taylor, *Sweatshops in the Sun*, p. 63; Mary Heaton Vorse, "America's Submerged Class: The Migrants," *Harper's* 106 (February 1953): 89; "scrambling . . . scrimping": quoted in Taylor, *Sweatshops in the Sun*, p. 64; "they can": testimony of Luther Jones, *National Defense Migration Hearings*, pt. 33, p. 12668.

48. Testimony of Johnnie Belle Taylor, *National Defense Migration Hearings*, pt. 33, pp. 12627–28; "if he": testimony of Luther Jones, ibid., p. 12667.

49. Heppel, "Harvesting the Crops of Others;" testimony of Rudolfo Juarez, *Who Is Responsible? Hearings*, p. 5483; Nijeholt, *On the Road for Work*, p. 125; "quality": Nelkin, *On the Season*, p. 25; "black men": Wilkinson, "Big Sugar, Pt. I," p. 55.

50. "More than": Metzler, "Migratory Farm Workers in the Atlantic Coast Stream," pp. 56–57; Brooks, "The Social Problems of Migrant Farm Laborers," p. 160; "travelling . . . we": testimony of Mrs. Albert Thomas, *Interstate Migration Hearings*, pt. 9, p. 3736; Allen, *Labor of Women in the Production of Cotton*, p. 114.

51. Dunbar and Kravitz, *Hard Traveling*, p. 113; Nijeholt, *On the Road for Work*, pp. 139–41; "Education": "Lack of Educational Facilities," *Interstate Migration Hearings*, pt. 2, p. 540.

52. "feared": "Social Situation of Florida Migrants," *Interstate Migration Hearings*, pt. 2, p. 536; E. John Kleinert, "The Florida Migrant," *Migrant Subculture Hearings*, pp. 545–47; "I ain't": J. K. deGroot, "A Migrant Life—Like They Told Him: 'Your Lot's Hard and You Got to Bear the Load,'" from *Miami Herald*, 21 August 1970, in *Who Is Responsible? Hearings*, p. 5556. See also Dunbar and Kravitz, *Hard Traveling*, p. 123; Coles, *Migrants, Sharecroppers, Mountaineers*, p. 112.

53. See, for example, Heppel, "Harvesting the Crops of Others," pp. 197–211.

54. "quacks . . . hospitals": testimony of John Beecher, *Interstate Migration Hearings*, pt. 2, p. 542; "with": Koos, "They Follow the Sun," p. 8; "a thread . . . through": Nelkin, *On the Season*, p. 48.

55. "all them": Vorse, "America's Submerged Class," p. 89; "rural": McWilliams, *Ill Fares the Land*, p. 226; "factories": Bremer, "Strawberry Pickers of Maryland," p. 70; "job stress": McWilliams, *Ill Fares the Land*, p. 180; "for . . . worked": *Migratory Labor in American Agriculture*, p. 89.

56. Koos, "They Follow the Sun," p. 38; "migrants": Nelkin, *On the Season*, p.

47; "playing . . . the aim": William Friedland, "Labor Waste in New York: Rural Exploitation and Migrant Workers," *Trans-Action* 6 (February 1969): 50; "All day": Hurston, *Their Eyes Were Watching God,* p. 194.

57. *Migratory Labor in American Agriculture,* p. 130.

58. Peter T. Kilborn, "Tomato Pickers' Hope for Better Life Becomes Victim as Industry Steps In," *New York Times,* 9 May 1991, p. A18. The word "pin-hooker" reportedly derives from the Spanish *pintar,* "to paint or to ripen."

59. Maurice E. Volands, "Human Relations on Michigan Fruit and Vegetable Farms," *Manpower and Economic Problems Hearings,* p. 4586; "in the . . . not . . . they": testimony of Mrs. Elnore Jackson (Negro), Belle Glade, Fla., *National Defense Migration Hearings,* pt. 33, p. 12630. See also Ralph Moss, "Complexity of Florida's Agricultural Labor Supply," *Employment Security Review* 22 (March 1955): 10–12; statement of P. O. Davis, director of Agricultural Extension Service, *Interstate Migration Hearings,* pt. 2, p. 427; *Migratory Labor in American Agriculture,* p. 130; Larson, "Migratory Agricultural Workers in the Eastern Seaboard States," p. 442.

60. All quotes from Jane Mayer, "Seaford, Del., Shows How Crack Can Savage Small-Town America," *Wall Street Journal,* 4 May 1989, pp. A1, A8.

Chapter 7
Separate Ways: Deep South Black and Appalachian White Migrants to the Midwest

1. "the irresponsible": memorandum on exodus of Negroes from the South, p. 3, Records of Secretary William B. Wilson, File 13/65, Race Riot East St. Louis, Illinois—1917 (Box 205), General Records of the Department of Labor, Record Group (RG) 174, National Archives (NA), Washington, D.C.; "Before" quoted in James R. Grossman, *Land of Hope: Chicago, Black Southerners, and the Great Migration* (Chicago: University of Chicago Press, 1989), p. 18; "like plants": Mary Mebane, *Mary* (New York: Viking Press, 1981), p. 168. See also "The Master Called Me to Preach the Bible," in Audrey Olsen Faulkner et al., eds., *When I Was Comin' Up: An Oral History of Aged Blacks* (Hamden, CT: Archon Books, 1982), p. 84; Emmett J. Scott, *Negro Migration During the War* (New York: Arno Press and the *New York Times,* 1969; orig. pub. 1920), p. 6; Florette Henri, *Black Migration: Movement North, 1900–1920; The Road from Myth to Man* (New York: Anchor Books, 1976).

2. Burniece Avery, *Walk Quietly Through the Night and Cry Softly* (Detroit, MI: Balamp Press, 1977), pp. 6, 9, and passim. See also Burniece Avery, "Coal Mine Disaster Sparked Move to Detroit," *Detroit Free Press,* 30 November 1987, p. 6A. I would like to acknowledge Thomas Sugrue for bringing these sources to my attention.

3. "families": Carl T. Schmidt, "Changes in American Agriculture and Some of the Results," *Hearings before the Select Committee to Investigate the*

Interstate Migration of Destitute Citizens, 77th Cong., 3d sess., Washington Hearings, 3, 6, 9, and 10 December 1940, pt. 9, p. 3771 (hereafter *Interstate Migration Hearings,* with part no.); Clay Hathorn, "Down and Out in the Delta: Poverty Along the Mississippi," *The Nation,* 9 July 1990, pp. 50–53; "The concentration": John F. Kain and Joseph J. Persky, "The North's Stake in Rural Poverty," in *Rural Poverty in the United States: A Report by the President's National Advisory Commission on Rural Poverty* (Washington, D.C.: GPO, 1968), p. 290. See also Carter Goodrich et al., *Migration and Economic Opportunity: The Report of the Study of Population Redistribution* (Philadelphia: University of Pennsylvania Press, 1936), p. 131.

4. "our own": Harriet L. Arnow, *The Dollmaker* (New York: Macmillan, 1954), pp. 116–17; "the mostly": interview with Charlotte Gibson in Todd Gitlin and Nanci Hollander, *Uptown: Poor Whites in Chicago* (New York: Harper & Row, 1970), p. 254; See for example the song by Hazel Dickens, "West Virginia, Oh My Home," quoted in Douglas Imbrogno, "Songs of Home," *Southern Exposure* 18 (Winter 1990): 43.

5. "scuff": "Nine Luzianne Coffee Boxes," in Faulkner et al., eds., *When I Was Comin' Up,* p. 60; "rural . . . urban": Bernice Milburn Moore, "Present Status and Future Trends in the Southern White Family," *Journal of Social Forces* 16 (March 1938): 410; "leave off": William Attaway, *Blood on the Forge* (New York: Monthly Review Press, 1987; orig. pub. 1941), p. 64; Marjorie Felice Irwin, "The Negro in Charlottesville and Albermarle County," University of Virginia Phelps-Stokes Fellowship Paper, 1929, pp. 24–29.

6. "born": George Hyland and Richard Peet, "Appalachian Migrants in Northern Cities," *Antipode* 5 (March 1973): 35; Jack Temple Kirby, *Rural Worlds Lost: The American South, 1920–1960* (Baton Rouge: Louisiana State University Press, 1987), pp. 276, 309, 320.

7. On rural migrants who gave to interviewers the name of a town as their home, see, for example, Gitlin and Hollander, *Uptown,* p. 153 ("Actually, I'm from thirteen miles out from Hazard [Kentucky], but you have to say you're from somewhere"); John Friedl, "Health Care: The City Versus the Migrant," in Allen Batteau, ed., *Appalachia and America: Autonomy and Regional Dependence* (Lexington: University Press of Kentucky, 1983), p. 180.

In *Farewell—We're Good and Gone: The Great Black Migration* (Bloomington: Indiana University Press, 1989), Carole Marks seems to equate "skilled" black laborers with industrial workers of all kinds. See also Frank T. Cherry, "Southern In-Migrant Negroes in North Lawndale, Chicago, 1949–50: A Study of Internal Migration and Adjustment" (Ph.D. diss., University of Chicago, 1965), pp. 112–14.

On the role of the rural nonagricultural sector in pointing the way north for rural blacks, see Peter Gottlieb, *Making Their Own Way:*

Southern Blacks' Migration to Pittsburgh, 1916–1930 (Urbana: University of Illinois Press, 1987), pp. 12–62.

8. James P. Comer, *Maggie's American Dream: The Life and Times of a Black Family* (New York: New American Library, 1988), pp. 57, 3, 15, 75, 16; "go to . . . couldn't": "They're Hypocritic" and "Work Made Me a Lady," in Faulkner et al., *When I Was Comin' Up*, pp. 103, 45.

9. The issues of "training" and "preparation" for Northern industrial life are explored in more detail in chapter 8.

10. "just . . . He . . . Why . . . But": Thordis Simonsen, ed., *You May Plow Here: The Narrative of Sara Brooks* (New York: Norton, 1986), pp. 165, 195, 212, 217; "I daydreamed": "They're Hypocritic," in Faulkner et al., *When I Was Comin' Up*, p. 107. Darlene Clark Hine explores black women's vulnerability to sexual abuse by white men in "Rape and the Inner Lives of Black Women in the Middle West: Preliminary Thoughts on the Culture of Dissemblance," *Signs* 14 (Summer 1989): 912–20. See also Bob Blauner, *Black Lives, White Lives: Three Decades of Race Relations in America* (Berkeley: University of California Press, 1989), pp. 21–22; Comer, *Maggie's American Dream.*

11. "a star": interview with a Polly Turner Cancer in the Federal Writers Project Slave Narrs., collected in George P. Rawick, ed., *The American Slave: A Composite Autobiography* Supplementary Series (SS) 1, (Miss. Narrs)., pt. 2, (Westport, CT: Greenwood Press, 1977), p. 336; Statement of John P. Ferris, director, Commerce Department of T.V.A., Knoxville, Tenn., *Interstate Migration Hearings*, pt. 9, p. 3800; "She" quoted in Rhoda Halperin, *The Livelihood of Kin: Making Ends Meet 'The Kentucky Way'* (Austin: University of Texas Press, 1990), p. 35. See also John D. Photiadis and Harry K. Schwarzweller, *Change in Rural Appalachia: Implications for Action Programs* (Philadelphia: University of Pennsylvania Press, 1970); testimony of Macon Lewis, Wilson, N.C., *Interstate Migration Hearings*, pt. 8, p. 3435; Elizabeth Rauh Bethel, *Promiseland: A Century of Life in a Negro Community* (Philadelphia: Temple University Press, 1981), p. 116; Olaf F. Larson, "Wartime Migration and the Manpower Reserve on Farms in Eastern Kentucky," *Rural Sociology* 8 (June 1943): 148–61; Howard W. Beers, *Farm Population Changes in Eastern Kentucky, 1941–42* (Lexington: University of Kentucky Press, 1943).

12. Jerrell H. Shofner, "Florida and the Black Migration," *Florida Historical Quarterly* 57 (January 1979): 267–88; Marks, *Farewell—We're Good and Gone*, pp. 19–48; Grossman, *Land of Hope*, pp. 13–122; Scott, *Negro Migration During the War*; R. H. Leavell et al., *Negro Migration in 1916–1917* (Washington, D.C.: GPO, 1919).

13. Neil Fligstein, *Going North: Migration of Blacks and Whites from the South, 1900–1950* (New York: Academic Press, 1981); Robert C. Weaver, "Economic Factors in Negro Migration—Past and Present," *Journal of Social Forces* 18 (October 1939): 90–101; Clyde B. McCoy and James S.

Brown, "Appalachian Migration to Midwestern Cities," in William W. Philliber and Clyde B. McCoy, eds., *The Invisible Minority: Urban Appalachians* (Lexington: University Press of Kentucky, 1981), pp. 35–78.

14. Shofner, "Florida and the Black Migration," p. 276; "left": John William Fanning, *Negro Migration: A Study of the Exodus of Negroes Between 1920 and 1925 from Middle Georgia Counties . . .* , Phelps-Stokes Fellowship Fund Study, 1928, p. 32.

15. "Nothing" quoted in Clyde V. Kiser, *Sea Island to City: A Study of St. Helena Islanders in Harlem and Other Urban Centers* (New York: Atheneum, 1969; orig. pub. in 1932), p. 132.

16. "Scared of Everything When I Grew Up," in Faulkner et al., *When I Was Comin' Up*, pp. 29, 42.

17. Jacquelyn Dowd Hall et al., *Like A Family: The Making of a Cotton Mill World* (Chapel Hill: University of North Carolina Press, 1987); "to oil": Lionel L. Jones, Louisiana agricultural statistician, 16 April 1923, and "more": H. H. Schutz, agricultural statistician, Tex., 23 April 1923, Entry 90, File no. 0959, Population Movements, Bureau of Agricultural Economics, RG 83, NA, Washington, D.C., Microfilm reel 21, *Black Workers in the Era of the Great Migration* (hereafter BAE); statement of E. S. Morgan, regional director, Farm Security Administration, *Interstate Migration Hearings*, pt. 2, Montgomery Hearings, 14, 15, and 16 August 1940, p. 703.

18. "the black": Mebane, *Mary*, p. 207; "loved": Harry Crews, *A Childhood: The Biography of a Place* (New York: Harper & Row, 1978), p. 128; interview with Will Pennington in Laurel Shackelford and Bill Weinberg, eds., *Our Appalachia: An Oral History* (Lexington: University Press of Kentucky, 1977), p. 323; E. S. Morgan, "Displacement of Farm Families Caused by National Defense Activities in Alabama, Georgia, South Carolina and Florida," *Hearings Before the Select Committee Investigating National Defense Migration*, House of Representatives, 77th Cong., 2d sess., Huntsville Hearings, 7 and 8 May 1942, pt. 32, pp. 12047–48 (hereafter *National Defense Migration Hearings*, with pt. no.); "a battery . . . They'll": ibid., p. 12079; "a white": Charles Denby, *Indignant Heart: Testimony of a Black American Worker* (London: Pluto Press, 1979), p. 46; "You know": Comer, *Maggie's American Dream*, p. 19.

19. Goodrich et al., *Migration and Economic Opportunity*, pp. 54–123; "stranded": statement of William H. Stauffer, Commissioner of Public Welfare for the State of Virginia, *Interstate Migration Hearings*, Washington, D.C., 29 November, 2 and 3 December 1940, pt. 8, p. 3134; Ronald D. Eller, *Miners, Millhands and Mountaineers: Industrialization in the Appalachian South, 1880–1930* (Knoxville: University of Tennessee Press, 1982), p. 157; "cooped": Barbara Zigli, "For One Early Migrant, Memories of a Hard Life," in Cincinnati *Enquirer* Staff, *Urban Appalachians* (Cincinnati: Cincinnati *Enquirer*, 1981), pp. 4–5.

20. Pete Daniel, *Breaking the Land: The Transformation of Cotton, Tobacco, and Rice Cultures Since 1880* (Urbana: University of Illinois Press, 1985), pp. 63–152; Gavin Wright, *Old South, New South: Revolutions in the Southern Economy Since the Civil War* (New York: Basic Books, 1986), pp. 164, 223, 235; "God's gift": Schmidt, "Changes in American Agriculture," *Interstate Migration Hearings,* pt. 9, p. 3776; Michael J. McDonald and John Muldowny, *TVA and the Dispossessed: The Resettlement of Population in the Norris Dam Area* (Knoxville: University of Tennessee Press, 1982); "for the . . . enforced": Morgan, "Displacement of Farm Families," *National Defense Migration Hearings,* pt. 32, p. 12075; Paul S. Taylor, "Farming and Labor Displacement in the Cotton Belt, 1937. Part 1. Northwest Texas," *Monthly Labor Review* 46 (March 1938): 595–607; and Paul S. Taylor, "Power Farming and Labor Displacement. Part 2. Southwestern Oklahoma and Mississippi Delta," *Monthly Labor Review* 46 (April 1938): 852–67.

21. "the size": Harold C. Hoffsommer, "Landlord-Tenant Relations and Relief in Alabama," Federal Emergency Relief Administration (hereafter FERA) Confidential Research *Bulletin* 2738 (10 July 1934), p. 2, vol. 4, Works Progress Administration Collection, RG 69, NA, Washington, D.C. (hereafter WPA); "open": A. R. Mangus, "The Rural Negro on Relief, February, 1935," FERA Research *Bulletin* 6950 (17 October 1935), pp. 4–5, WPA.

22. "didn't": Mebane, *Mary,* p. 53; Guy B. Johnson, "The Negro and the Depression in North Carolina," *Journal of Social Forces* 12 (October 1933): 108.

23. "relative": statement by Dr. Harold Hoffsommer, *Interstate Migration Hearings,* pt. 2, p. 452; testimony of Loula Dunn, commissioner of public welfare, State of Alabama, ibid., pp. 640–50; testimony of David A. Griffin, ibid., pp. 778–81; Kirby, *Rural Worlds Lost,* p. 320. See also Harold Hoffsommer, "The Disadvantaged Farm Family in Alabama," *Rural Sociology* 2 (December 1937): 382–92.

24. Louis Cantor, *A Prologue to the Protest Movement: The Missouri Sharecropper Demonstration of 1939* (Durham, NC: Duke University Press, 1969), pp. 93–94; Ralph Ellison, "Camp Lost Colony," *New Masses* (6 February 1940): 18–19; "found . . . over": Virginia Cocalis, "They Came From Missouri," *Land Policy Review* 4 (February 1941): 16–17.

25. "the usual": Morgan, "Displacement of Farm Families," *National Defense Migration Hearings,* pt. 32, p. 12068. The story of the Crews family is in Crews, *A Childhood,* pp. 36, 125, 127, 132, 136, 138. See also Roger Biles, "The Urban South in the Great Depression," *Journal of Southern History* 56 (February 1990): 71–100.

26. "submarginal": Goodrich et al., *Migration and Economic Opportunity,* p. 73; "well-established": James S. Brown and George A. Hillery, Jr., "The Great Migration, 1940–1960," in Thomas R. Ford, ed. *The Southern Appalachian Region* (Lexington: University of Kentucky Press, 1962), p. 63. See also Robin M. Williams and Olaf Wakefield, "Farm Tenancy in North

Carolina, 1880–1935," North Carolina Agricultural Experiment Station, AE-RS Information Series no. 1 (September 1937), p. 29; T. J. Woofter, "Rural Relief and the Back-to-the-Farm Movement," *Journal of Social Forces* 14 (March 1936): 382–88; Kirby, *Rural Worlds Lost,* pp. 51–114, 275–308; Erdmann Doane Beynon, "The Southern White Laborer Migrates to Michigan," *American Sociological Review* 3 (June 1938): 333–43.

27. Mary Breckinridge, "The Corn-Bread Line," *Survey* 64 (15 August 1930): 422–23.

28. "relief": Richard Sterner, *The Negro's Share: A Study of Income, Consumption, Housing, and Public Assistance* (New York: Harper & Brothers, 1943), pp. 235, 416–18; "fearful": Hoffsommer, "Landlord-Tenant Relations and Relief in Alabama," "summary," n.p. See also Jill Quadagno, "From Old Age Assistance to Supplemental Security Income: The Political Economy of Relief in the South," in Margaret Weir et al., *The Politics of Social Policy in the United States* (Princeton, NJ: Princeton University Press, 1988); Raymond Wolters, *Negroes and the Great Depression: The Problem of Economic Recovery* (Westport, CT: Greenwood Press, 1970); Jacqueline Jones, *Labor of Love, Labor of Sorrow: Black Women, Work and the Family From Slavery to the Present* (New York: Basic Books, 1985), pp. 216–21.

29. "conventional . . . is": Hoffsommer: "Landlord-Tenant Relations and Relief in Alabama," "summary," n.p.; "households": A. D. Edwards, "Female Heads of Rural Relief and Non-Relief Households, Oct., 1933," FERA Research *Bulletin* 5439 (7 June 1935), p. 1, WPA; "split": Mangus, "The Rural Negro on Relief, Feb. 1935," WPA. See also Frank J. Welch, "The Plantation Land Tenure System in Mississippi," Mississippi State College Agricultural Experiment Station *Bulletin,* no. 385, State College, Mississippi (June 1943); E. L. Langsford and B. H. Thibodeaux, "Plantation Organization and Operation in the Yazoo-Mississippi Delta Area," Technical Bulletin no. 682, May 1939, U.S. Department of Agriculture, Washington, D.C.; Richard Couto, "A Place to Call Our Own," *Southern Exposure* 9 (Fall 1981): 16–22; "Rural Problem Area Survey Report No. 11: The Cotton Growing Area of the Old South: Monroe County, Mississippi," FERA Research *Bulletin* 3838 (26 October 1934), p. 6, WPA.

    On p. 10 of his report, Hoffsommer notes, "It is probably not too much to say that the cropper system can only be maintained by the subordination of the tenant group. . . . Something more than pure economics is involved. There are also the questions of social and political domination. . ."

30. "emptying . . . landlords": C. W. E. Pittman, "Some Aspects of Agricultural Employment in North Carolina," *National Defense Migration Hearings,* Washington, D.C., 18, 19, and 21 July 1941, pt. 17, pp. 6864, 6857.

31. "to try": John N. Webb and Malcolm Brown, "Migrant Families," Works Progress Administration Research Monograph 18 (Washington, D.C.: GPO, 1938), pp. 23–24. See also Larry H. Long, "Poverty Status and

Receipt of Welfare Among Migrants and Nonmigrants in Large Cities," *American Sociological Review* 39 (February 1974): 46–56.

32. See, for example, Nicholas Lemann, *The Promised Land: The Great Black Migration and How It Changed America* (New York: Knopf, 1991). Lemann provides a useful account of the impact of the mechanical cotton picker on Deep South sharecropping families, but he errs in suggesting that "white" tenant-based farming was "quite different" from "black" sharecropping and that migration during this period was an exclusively black phenomenon (p. 28).

33. Daniel M. Johnson and Rex R. Campbell, *Black Migration in America: A Social Demographic History* (Durham, NC: Duke University Press, 1981), pp. 101–23; Quintard Taylor, "The Great Migration: The Afro-American Communities of Seattle and Portland during the 1940s," *Arizona and the West* 23 (Summer 1981): 109–26. See also Conrad Taueber, "Migration and Rural Population Adjustment," *Rural Sociology* 5 (1940): 399–410.

34. Morgan, "Displacement of Farm Families," *National Defense Migration Hearings,* pt. 32, p. 12061.

35. "Most . . . 'If'": ibid, pp. 12076, 12083; James G. Maddox, "The Role of Low-Income Farm Families in the War Effort," *National Defense Migration Hearings,* Washington, D.C., 12 and 13 February 1942, pt. 28, p. 10786.

36. "If I": Morgan, "Displacement of Farm Families," *National Defense Migration Hearings,* pt. 32, p. 12082; "If the man . . . All my family": Morgan, "Displacement of Farm Families," *National Defense Migration Hearings* pt. 32, pp. 12049–50, 12080; testimony of Roberta C. Williams, Florida Travellers' Aid, *Interstate Migration Hearings,* pt. 9, p. 3619; Frank S. Horne, "War Homes in Hampton Roads," *Opportunity* 20 (July 1942): 200–2; Howard B. Myers, "Defense Migration and Labor Supply," *Journal of the American Statistical Association* 37 (1942): 69–76.

37. "it wasn't": Arthur S. Evans, Jr. and David Lee, *Pearl City, Florida: A Black Community Remembers* (Boca Raton: Florida Atlantic University Press, 1990), p. 70; "upon . . . available . . . a considerable": Nineteenth Meeting, Seventh Regional Labor Supply Committee (Birmingham, 18 March 1942), pp. 2, 3, region 7 Folder, L. A. Oxley Files, U.S. Employment Service, RG 183, NA, Washington, D.C.; "Recent Migration Into Atlanta, Georgia, Jan. 14, 1942," *National Defense Migration Hearings,* pt. 27, p. 10457. See also Pete Daniel, "Going Among Strangers: Southern Reactions to World War II," *Journal of American History* 77 (December 1990): 886–911.

38. Brown and Hillery, "The Great Migration, 1940–1960," pp. 54–78; McCoy and Brown, "Appalachian Migration to Midwestern Cities," pp. 35–78; "Thus": Bill Montgomery, "The Uptown Story," *Mountain Life and Work* 44 (1968): 10.

39. "I . . . that": Barbara Zigli, "Back Home in Turner's Creek," in Cincinnati *Enquirer* Staff, *Urban Appalachians,* pp. 40–41; interview with Will Pennington in Shackelford and Weinberg, eds., *Our Appalachia,* p. 325;

Larson, "Wartime Migration and the Manpower Reserve on Farms in Eastern Kentucky," pp. 148–61.

40. "seem": J. Lewis Henderson, "In the Cotton Delta," *Survey Graphic* 36 (January 1947): 109; "I was": Bethel, *Promiseland,* p. 226; "And the": interview with Jim Ryan in Warren Moore, *Mountain Voices: A Legacy of the Blue Ridge and Great Smokies* (Chester, CT: Globe Pequot Press, 1988), p. 232. See also John Modell et al., "World War II in the Lives of Black Americans: Some Findings and an Interpretation," *Journal of American History* 76 (December 1989): 838–48.

41. Mynatt quoted in Barbara Zigli, "The Migration: Up from the Country," in Cincinnati *Enquirer* Staff, *Urban Appalachians,* p. 6.

42. Arnow, *Dollmaker.*

43. Davies and Bones quoted in T. E. Murphy, "The Orphans of Willow Run," *Saturday Evening Post,* 4 August 1945, p. 20.

44. Johnson and Campbell, *Black Migration in America,* pp. 114–51; Daniel, *Breaking the Land,* pp. 155–83; John D. Photiadis, "West Virginians in Their Own State and in Cleveland, Ohio," Appalachian Center Information Report 3, West Virginia University, 1970; William L. Hamilton et al., *The Causes of Rural to Urban Migration Among the Poor* (Cambridge, MA: Abt Associates, 1970), p. 303; interview with Barbara Mosely Caudill in Shackelford and Weinberg, eds., *Our Appalachia,* p. 309. See also Ernest E. Neal and Lewis W. Jones, "The Place of the Negro Farmer in the Changing Economy of the Cotton South," *Rural Sociology* 15 (March 1950): 30–41.

45. "of this": Moore, *Mountain Voices,* p. 241; "in the": Robert Coles, *Children of Crisis,* vol. 3, *The South Goes North* (Boston: Little, Brown, 1967), p. 313. Larry H. Long and Kristin A. Hansen, "Trends in Return Migration to the South," *Demography* 12 (November 1975): 601–14; Rex R. Campbell, Daniel M. Johnson, and Gary J. Stangler, "Return Migration of Black People to the South," *Rural Sociology* 39 (Winter 1974): 514–28; Kenneth R. Weiss, "Migration by Blacks from the South Turns Around," *New York Times,* 11 June 1989, p. 36; Eric Bates, "Southern Refugees," *Southern Exposure* 17 (Summer 1989): 52–56.

46. Interview with Richard Jackson in Shackelford and Weinberg, eds., *Our Appalachia,* pp. 373–76.

Chapter 8
Ghettos and the Lack of Them: Southern Migrants in the Midwest

1. Charles Denby, *Indignant Heart: Testimony of a Black American Worker* (London: Pluto Press, 1979), pp. 87–89.

2. Ibid., pp. 142–44.

3. Frank R. Crosswaith to Lester Granger (Industrial Secretary, National

Urban League), 4 August 1936, series 4, Box 5, Negro Labor Committee, 1935–36 Folder; Papers of the National Urban League, Library of Congress Manuscripts Division, Washington, D.C. The NUL papers reveal the organization's desperate struggle to find jobs—any jobs—for black migrants to the nation's largest Northern cities.

4. "from": Mary-Jane Grunsfeld, "Negroes in Chicago: Mayor's Committee on Race Relations," October 1944, n.p.; "being": James P. Comer, *Maggie's American Dream: The Life and Times of a Black Family* (New York: New American Library, 1988), p. 114; "racial . . . of course": interview with Howard Sampson in Bob Blauner, *Black Lives, White Lives: Three Decades of Race Relations in America* (Berkeley: University of California Press, 1989), p. 120.

5. "culture": Lizabeth Cohen, *Making a New Deal: Industrial Workers in Chicago, 1919–1939* (New York: Cambridge University Press, 1990), pp. 324, 333–49, 365; "I learned": Sylvia Woods, "If I Had Known Then What I Know Now," in Darlene Clark Hine et al., *The Black Woman in the Middle West Project: A Comprehensive Guide: Illinois and Indiana* (Indianapolis: Indiana Historical Bureau, 1986), p. 23; "We threw": interview with Sylvia Woods in Alice Lynd and Staughton Lynd, eds., *Rank and File: Personal Histories by Working-Class Organizers* (Princeton, NJ: Princeton University Press, 1981), pp. 127–28.

6. See, for example, Stanley Lieberson, *A Piece of the Pie: Blacks and White Immigrants Since 1880* (Berkeley: University of California Press, 1980); Dorothy K. Newman, "The Negro's Journey to the City—Part II," *Monthly Labor Review* 88 (June 1965): 644–49.

7. Denby, *Indignant Heart*, p. 120.

8. See, for example, Dorothy K. Newman et al., *Protest, Politics, and Prosperity: Black Americans and White Institutions, 1940–1975* (New York: Pantheon Books, 1978); J. F. Cogan, "The Decline in Black Teenage Employment, 1950–1970," *American Economic Review* 72 (September 1982): 621–39.

9. "he moves": Elmer Akers, "Southern Whites in Detroit" (typescript, Ann Arbor, MI, 1936), p. 6, University Microfilms OP 70,108 (I would like to acknowledge Thomas Sugrue for drawing this essay to my attention); "immune": E. Russell Porter, "When Cultures Meet—Mountain and Urban," *Nursing Outlook* 2 (June 1963): 418.

10. "It depends": Michael Maloney quoted in Barbara Zigli, "Prejudice, Stereotypes are Painful Obstacles," in Cincinnati *Enquirer* Staff, *The Urban Appalachians* (Cincinnati: Cincinnati *Enquirer,* 1981), p. 9; "We'd": Lewis M. Killian, "Southern White Laborers in Chicago's West Side" (Ph.D. diss., University of Chicago, 1949), p. 133; "nigger-rich" quoted in Edwin S. Harwood, "Work and Community Among Urban Newcomers: A Study of the Social and Economic Adaptation of Southern Migrants to Chicago" (Ph.D. diss., University of Chicago, 1966), p. 86.

11. Paul Frederick Cressey, "Social Disorganization and Reorganization in Harlan County, Kentucky," *American Sociological Review* 14 (June 1949): 389–94; "changeless . . . culture": Thomas E. Wagner, "The Silent Minority," *Horizons: The Magazine of the University of Cincinnati* 1 (June 1972): 6; "shallow": Rhoda Halperin, *The Livelihood of Kin: Making Ends Meet 'The Kentucky Way'* (Austin: University of Texas Press, 1990), p. 4.

12. Halperin, *Livelihood of Kin;* Allen Batteau, "Rituals of Dependence in Appalachian Kentucky," in Allen Batteau, ed., *Appalachia and America: Autonomy and Regional Dependence* (Lexington: University Press of Kentucky, 1983), pp. 142–67; D. K. Wilgus, "Country-Western Music and the Urban Hillbilly," *Journal of American Folklore* 83 (April-June 1970): 157–79; "I": interview with Florence Grier in Blauner, *Black Lives, White Lives,* p. 69; "They think": T. E. Murphy, "The Orphans of Willow Run," *Saturday Evening Post,* 4 August 1945, p. 110.

13. "Appalachia on Cleveland's East Side," *Appalachia: A Journal of the Appalachian Regional Commission* 5 (July–August 1972): 50; Harwood, "Work and Community Among Newcomers," p. 118.

14. Warren Whatley and Gavin Wright, "Getting Started in the Auto Industry: Black Workers and the Ford Motor Company, 1918–1947," paper presented at University of Massachusetts-Amherst, Fall 1990.

15. "coming": quoted in Warren C. Whatley, "Getting a Foot in the Door: 'Learning,' State Dependence, and the Racial Integration of Firms," *Journal of Economic History* 50 (March 1990): 61; "Cincinnati": Ernie Mynatt quoted in Zigli, "Founding Father of a Group's Struggle," in Cincinnati *Enquirer* Staff, *Urban Appalachians,* p. 36; "You can't": Danny Ray quoted in Hal Bruno, "Chicago's Hillbilly Ghetto," *The Reporter* 30 (4 June 1964): 30; James S. Brown and George A. Hillery, Jr., "The Great Migration, 1940–1960," in Thomas R. Ford, ed., *The Southern Appalachian Region: A Survey* (Lexington: University Press of Kentucky, 1962), p. 70.

16. John Leslie Thompson, "Industrialization in the Miami Valley: A Case Study of Interregional Labor Migration" (Ph.D. diss., University of Wisconsin, 1955); "Migration History," *Mountain Life and Work* 8 (August 1976): 4.

17. Thompson, "Industrialization in the Miami Valley," p. 132; "no trouble . . . there weren't": quoted in Martin J. Crowe, "The Occupational Adaptation of a Selected Group of Eastern Kentuckians in Southern Ohio" (Ph.D. diss., University of Kentucky, 1964), p. 134; "We started": George Shultz quoted in Barbara Zigli, "Dream of Moving Up Becomes True for Many," Cincinnati *Enquirer* Staff, *Urban Appalachians,* p. 17; "they were": Barbara Zigli, "The Migration: Up from the Country," in ibid., p. 6. See also Melvin Lurie and Elton Rayack, "Racial Differences in Migration and Job Search: A Case Study," *Southern Economic Journal* 33 (July 1966): 81–95.

18. "in what": "South Amherst, Oh.: Sandstone Miners Strike," and "This is": Ron Kidwell, "Urban Rank and File," both articles in *Mountain Life and*

Work 8 (August 1976): 32, 35; Crowe, "Occupational Adaptation," p. 114; Thompson, "Industrialization in the Miami Valley," p. 144. On job turnover, see, for example, Cohen, *Making a New Deal,* p. 197; Whatley and Wright, "Getting Started in the Auto Industry," p. 8.

19. William W. Philliber, *Appalachian Migrants in Urban America: Cultural Conflict or Ethnic Group Formation?* (New York: Praeger, 1981), pp. 27–37; "are . . . plants . . . ease": Raymond Paul Hutchens, "Kentuckians in Hamilton: A Study of Southborn Migrants in an Industrial City" (M.A. thesis, Miami University, 1942), pp. 96–97. See also Harry K. Schwarzweller, "Career Placement and Economic Life Chances of Young Men from Eastern Kentucky," University of Kentucky Agricultural Experiment Station *Bulletin* 686, Lexington, 1964.

20. "at least": Stanley B. Greenberg, *Politics and Poverty: Modernization and Response in Five Poor Neighborhoods* (New York: John Wiley, 1974), p. 53; Grace G. Leybourne, "Urban Adjustments of Migrants from the Southern Appalachian Plateaus," *Journal of Social Forces* 16 (December 1937): 238–46; Gary Fowler, "The Residential Distribution of Urban Appalachians," in William W. Philliber and Clyde B. McCoy, eds., *The Invisible Minority: Urban Appalachians* (Lexington: University Press of Kentucky, 1981), pp. 81–94; Roscoe Giffin, "Appalachian Newcomers in Cincinnati," in Ford, ed., *Southern Appalachian Region,* pp. 79–84.

21. "The folks": Hutchens, "Kentuckians in Hamilton," p. 72; "an enclaved": Kathryn Borman with Elaine Mueninghoff, "Lower Price Hill's Children: Family, School, and Neighborhood," in Batteau, ed., *Appalachia and America,* p. 221; Lee Rainwater, "Social and Cultural Problems of Migrants to Cities," in *Rural Poverty in the United States: A Report by the President's National Advisory Commission on Rural Poverty* (Washington, D.C.: GPO, 1960), pp. 251–52.

22. "capital city" [Detroit]: "Mountain Dreams," in Robert Coles and Jane Hallowell Coles, *Women of Crisis: Lives of Struggle and Hope* (New York: Delacorte Press/S. Lawrence, 1978), p. 80.

23. Clyde B. McCoy and James S. Brown, "Appalachian Migration to Midwestern Cities," in Philliber and McCoy, eds., *Invisible Minority,* pp. 35–78.

24. See, for example, Arnold R. Hirsch, *Making the Second Ghetto: Race and Housing in Chicago, 1940–1960* (Cambridge: Cambridge University Press, 1983); Allan H. Spear, *Black Chicago: The Making of a Negro Ghetto, 1890–1920* (Chicago: University of Chicago Press, 1967); Joe T. Darden et al., *Detroit: Race and Uneven Development* (Philadelphia: Temple University Press, 1987); Peter K. Eisinger, *The Politics of Displacement: Racial and Ethnic Transition in Three American Cities* (New York: Academic Press, 1980); Thomas F. Campbell, "Cleveland: The Struggle for Stability," in Richard Bernard, ed., *Snowbelt Cities: Metropolitan Politics in*

the Northeast and Midwest Since World War II (Bloomington: Indiana University Press, 1990), pp. 109–36, table A.4; Kenneth L. Kusmer, *A Ghetto Takes Shape: Black Cleveland, 1870–1930* (Urbana: University of Illinois Press, 1976).

25. "The displaced": Walker Percy, in Introduction, William Alexander Percy, *Lanterns on the Levee: Recollections of a Planter's Son* (Baton Rouge: Louisiana State University Press, 1973), p. xvi.

26. "just . . . All": Clarus Bakes, "Uptown: The Promised Land," *Chicago Tribune Magazine*, 22 September 1968, p. 33; "real": Dorothy Kunkin and Michael Byrne, "Appalachians in Cleveland" (Cleveland State University: Institute of Urban Studies, 1973), p. 12; Robert Elgie, "Rural Inmigration, Urban Ghettoization, and Their Consequences," *Antipode* 2 (1971): 38.

27. Erdmann Doane Beynon, "The Southern White Laborer Migrates to Michigan," *American Sociological Review* 3 (June 1938): 333–43; Akers, "Southern Whites in Detroit"; Dominic J. Capeci, *Race Relations in Wartime Detroit: The Sojourner Truth Housing Controversy of 1942* (Philadelphia: Temple University Press, 1984); "people": Robert Coles, "In the Places Where the Mountains Are Gone," *Children of Crisis*, vol. 3, *The South Goes North* (Boston: Little, Brown, 1967), p. 330; "the foothold": Killian, "Southern White Laborers in Chicago's West Side," p. 208, p. 12. See also B. J. Widick, *Detroit: City of Race and Class Violence* (Detroit: Wayne State University Press, 1989; orig. pub. 1972).

28. "The Negroes'": Harvey M. Choldin, "First Year in the Metropolis: A Study of Migration and Adjustment" (Ph.D. diss., University of Chicago, 1965), p. 95; Gene B. Peterson and Laure M. Sharp, "Southern Migrants to Cleveland: Work and Social Adjustment of Recent In-Migrants Living in Low-Income Neighborhoods," Bureau of Social Science Research, U.S. Department of Labor, Manpower Administration (July 1966), p. 66; Gene B. Peterson, Laure M. Sharp, and Thomas F. Drury, *Southern Newcomers to Northern Cities: Work and Social Adjustment to Cleveland* (New York: Praeger, 1977); Cohen, *Making a New Deal*, pp. 159–212. See also Ronald Freedman, *Recent Migration to Chicago* (Chicago: University of Chicago Press, 1950), p. 6.

29. "ambassadors": John C. Dancy, *Sand Against the Wind: The Memoirs of John C. Dancy* (Detroit: Wayne State University Press, 1966), p. 136. For the stories of Midwestern black families that struggled their way into the middle class, see Comer, *Maggie's American Dream*, and Burniece Avery, *Walk Quietly Through the Night and Cry Softly* (Detroit, MI: Balamp Press, 1977).

30. Harwood, "Work and Community among Urban Newcomers," pp. 98, 107–9; interviews with Bill and Amanda Carter and Popeye Adkins in Todd Gitlin and Nanci Hollander, *Uptown: Poor Whites in Chicago* (New York: Harper & Row, 1970), pp. 276, 298, 292, 224; "hearts": Coles, "In the

Places Where the Mountains Are Gone," *South Goes North,* p. 330.

31. "four . . . in common": Hutchens, "Kentuckians in Hamilton," pp. 57, 59; Michael E. Maloney, "The Social Areas of Cincinnati: An Analysis of Social Needs" (Cincinnati: Cincinnati Human Relations Commission, 1985), pp. 58, 23; "lives": "Problems in the Community," *Mountain Life and Work* 8 (August 1976): 6. See, for example, Kunkin, "Appalachians in Cleveland," p. 18; Casey Banas, "Uptown: Mecca for Migrants," *Southern Education Report* (March 1969): 10–13; John D. Photiadis, "West Virginians in Their Own State and in Cleveland, Ohio," Appalachian Center Information Report 3 (West Virginia University, 1970); Ronald Mincy, "Is There a White Underclass?" (Washington, D.C.: Urban Institute Discussion Paper, 1988). For a more detailed examination of these themes as revealed in a Washington, D.C., neighborhood of poor-white Southern migrants, see Joseph T. Howell, *Hard Living on Clay Street: Portraits of Blue Collar Families* (Garden City, NY: Anchor Books, 1973). See also James A. Maxwell, "Down from the Hills and Into the Slums," *The Reporter* 15 (13 December 1956): 27–29; Harry K. Schwarzweller et al., *Mountain Families in Transition: A Case Study of Appalachian Migration* (University Park: Pennsylvania State University Press, 1971), pp. 123–25; John Friedl, "Health Care: The City versus the Migrant," in Batteau, ed., *Appalachia and America,* pp. 189–209.

32. "My people": the Reverend Terry McAllen quoted in Coles, *South Goes North,* p. 397; "demanding": Hutchens, "Kentuckians in Hamilton," p. 91; "highly . . . social": Barbara Zigli, "Services Seemed Aimed for Others," in Cincinnati *Enquirer* Staff, *Urban Appalachians,* pp. 40–41; "either": Philliber, *Appalachian Migrants in Urban America,* p. 40. See also Shane Davies and Gary F. Fowler, "The Disadvantaged Urban Migrant in Indianapolis," *Economic Geography* 48 (April 1972): 153–67.

33. "Don't": Barbara Zigli, "A Distinctive Culture, But an Identity Crisis," in Cincinnati *Enquirer* Staff, *Urban Appalachians,* p. 13; Philliber, *Appalachian Migrants in Urban America,* pp. 39, 54, 66; Maloney, "Social Areas of Cincinnati," pp. 40–2; Borman with Mueninghoff, "Lower Price Hill's Children," pp. 210–26; Dan M. McKee and Phillip J. Obermiller, "From Mountain to the Metropolis: Urban Appalachians in Ohio" (Cincinnati: Ohio Urban Appalachian Awareness Project, 1978).

34. Ben R. Huelsman, "Urban Anthropolgy and the Southern Mountaineer," *Proceedings of the Indiana Academy of Science for 1968–1978* (1969): 97–103; "I thought": "Mountain Dreams," in Coles and Coles, *Women of Crisis,* p. 103. See also Halperin, *Livelihood of Kin,* p. 33; Patricia D. Beaver, *Rural Community in the Appalachian South* (Lexington: University Press of Kentucky, 1986), pp. 79–114; Roscoe Giffin, "From Cinder Hollow to Cincinnati," *Mountain Life and Work* 32 (1956): 19.

35. "alcoholic . . . good" quoted in Kunkin and Byrne, "Appalachians in Cleveland," p. 23; "all": Casey Hayden in "Chicago: JOIN Project," *Studies on the Left* 5 (Summer 1965): 117; Carol Stack, *All Our Kin: Strategies for*

Survival in a Black Community (New York: Harper & Row, 1974); "He's": Killian, "Southern White Laborers," p. 319; Choldin, "First Year in the Metropolis," p. 114.

36. James S. Brown, "The Family Behind the Migrant," *Mountain Life and Work* 44 (1968): 4–7; "biresidential": Halperin, *Livelihood of Kin,* pp. 95, 135; "stumble around . . . treadmill": Montgomery, "Uptown Story," p. 9; "back": Gerard A. Hyland, "Social Interaction and Urban Opportunity: The Appalachian In-Migrant in the Cincinnati Central City," *Antipode* 2 (December 1970): 75. See also Schwarzweller et al., *Mountain Families in Transition,* pp. 178–81; James Branscome, "Paradise Lost," *Southern Exposure* 1, no. 2 (1973): 29–41.

37. Gitlin and Hollander, *Uptown,* pp. 239–54 (the quote is on p. 253). These few tantalizing details about the life of Charlotte Gibson afford some intriguing parallels with that of her contemporary Ruby Daniels Haynes, a black migrant woman from Mississippi, who, together with her family, is profiled in Nicholas Lemann, *The Promised Land: The Great Black Migration and How It Changed America* (New York: Knopf, 1991).

38. "farm freedom": Ernie Mynatt quoted in Barbara Zigli, "The Founding Father of a Group's Struggle," in Cincinnati *Enquirer* Staff, *Urban Appalachians,* p. 36. See also Beaver, *Rural Community in the Appalachian South,* pp. 56–78.

39. Bruno, "Chicago's Hillbilly Ghetto": p. 28; "big . . . 'Guest' . . . the people": Cleo Y. Boyd, "Detroit's Southern Whites and the Store-Front Churches," Department of Research and Planning, Detroit Council of Churches, Detroit, 1958, p. 15, Box 44, Folder A8–25, Detroit Urban League Papers, Michigan Historical Collections, Bentley Library, University of Michigan, Ann Arbor; "retained": Ellen J. Stekert, "Focus for Conflict: Southern Mountain Medical Beliefs in Detroit," *Journal of American Folklore* 83 (April–June 1970): 117.

40. "cultural . . . social": Barbara Zigli, "Appalachian Groups Active, But Often Divided," pp. 32–34; "Dream of Moving Up Comes True for Many," pp. 16–17; and "Despite Numbers, Appalachians Lack Political Clout," pp. 18–19, in Cincinnati *Enquirer* Staff, *Urban Appalachians;* Ercel S. Eaton, *Appalachian Yesterdays* (Fairfield, OH: Appalachian Yesterdays Co., 1982). See also Giffin, "Appalachian Newcomers in Cincinnati," pp. 82–83.

41. Greenberg, *Politics and Poverty,* pp. 49, 198; "if . . . We": quoted in Jim Roher, "South Lebanon, Ohio: Down Home Up Here," in Cincinnati *Enquirer* Staff, *Urban Appalachians,* p. 48.

42. "the salvation . . . Guest": Brewster Campbell and James Pooler, "Hallelujah in Boom Town," *Colliers* 113 (1 April 1944): 18–19, 52–53; Alan Clive, *State of War: Michigan in World War II* (Ann Arbor: University of Michigan Press, 1979), pp. 170–84. For the view that "The old subdued, muted, murderous Southern race war was transplanted into a high-speed industrial background" in Detroit, see Thomas Sancton, "The Race Riots," *New Republic* 109 (5 July 1943): 9. See also Nathan L. Gerrard, "Churches

of the Stationary Poor in Southern Appalachia," in John D. Photiadis and Harry K. Schwarzweller, eds., *Change in Rural Appalachia: Implications for Action Programs* (Philadelphia: University of Pennsylvania Press, 1970), p. 110; Thomas R. Ford, "Status, Residence, and Fundamentalist Religious Beliefs in Southern Appalachia," *Social Forces* 34 (October 1960): 41–49.

43. "take": John Ashley quoted in Coles, "In the Places Where the Mountains Are Gone," in *South Goes North*, p. 382; Harwood, "Work and Community Among Urban Newcomers," pp. 89, 109, 144, 160–62; "Southern": Richie Rothstein, and "with . . . potential . . . drink . . . virtually": Rennie Davis, "Chicago: JOIN Project," pp. 123–24.

44. "We . . . most . . . They": Boyd, "Detroit's Southern Whites," pp. 11, 6; "was . . . blacks . . . They": Joseph S. Stern, Jr., "Findlay Market and Over-the-Rhine Revisited," *Cincinnati Historical Society Bulletin* 34 (Spring 1976): 25–26; "Advertisement in Daily Requests 'No Southerners,'" *Michigan Chronicle*, 1 May 1943, p. 4. See also George Henderson, "Southern Whites: A Neglected Urban Problem," *Journal of Secondary Education* 41 (March 1966): 111–14.

45. For a case study of the Chicago Urban League as a mediator of class and race relations, see Preston H. Smith II, "The Limitations of Racial Democracy: The Politics of the Chicago Urban League, 1916–1940" (Ph.D. diss., University of Massachusetts, 1989).

46. "slave": interview with Jesse Reese, in Lynd and Lynd, eds., *Rank and File: Personal Histories by Working Class Organizers*, (Princeton. NJ: Princeton University Press, 1981) p. 99; "People": Martha Strong quoted in Nancy Gabin, *Feminism in the Labor Movement: Women and the United Auto Workers, 1935–1975* (Ithaca, NY: Cornell University Press, 1990), p. 79.

47. William H. Harris, *The Harder We Run: Black Workers Since the Civil War* (New York: Oxford University Press, 1982), p. 120. See also the multivolume series, Philip S. Foner and Ronald L. Lewis, eds., *The Black Worker: A Documentary History from Colonial Times to the Present* (Philadelphia: Temple University Press, 1978–1983); Ruth Milkman, *Gender at Work: The Dynamics of Job Segregation by Sex During World War II* (Urbana: University of Illinois Press, 1987), pp. 54, 126.

48. "Not": Rosina C. Tucker quoted in Jack Santino, *Miles of Smiles, Years of Struggle: Stories of Black Pullman Porters* (Urbana: University of Illinois Press, 1989), p. 57; "saw": Reese interview in Lynd and Lynd, eds., *Rank and File*, p. 103; "done": worker quoted in Cohen, *Making a New Deal*, p. 367; August Meier and Elliott Rudwick, *Black Detroit and the Rise of the UAW* (New York: Oxford University Press, 1979); Robert Korstad and Nelson Lichtenstein, "Opportunities Found and Lost: Labor Radicals and the Early Civil Rights Movement," *Journal of American History* 75 (December 1988): 786–811.

49. Herbert Hill, "The AFL-CIO and the Black Worker: Twenty-Five Years After the Merger," *Journal of Intergroup Relations* 10 (Spring 1982): 14;

Richard B. Freeman and James L. Medoff, *What Do Unions Do?* (New York: Basic Books, 1984), p. 29; Norman Hill, "Blacks and the Unions: Progress Made, Problems Ahead," *Dissent* (Fall 1989): 496–500.

50. "evangelical . . . the": Peter Friedlander, *The Emergence of a UAW Local, 1936–1939: A Study in Class and Culture* (Pittsburgh: University of Pittsburgh Press, 1975), pp. 146, 67. See also William D. Jenkins, *Steel Valley Klan: The Ku Klux Klan in Ohio's Mahoning Valley* (Kent, OH: Kent State University Press, 1990); Dan Georgakas and Marvin Surkin, *Detroit, I Do Mind Dying: A Study in Urban Revolution* (New York: St. Martin's Press, 1975); Sam Stark, "Destination Detroit," *Southern Exposure* 17 (Summer 1989): 57–60. For examples of UAW stalwarts whose fathers were Appalachian coal miners and UMW members, see Richard Feldman and Michael Betzold, eds., *End of the Line: Autoworkers and the American Dream* (Urbana: University of Illinois Press, 1988), pp. 40, 104, 169.

51. "had acquired . . . niggermation": Georgakas and Surkin, *Detroit, I Do Mind Dying:* pp. 36, 101–27; "tight-knit, . . . plantation": Greenberg, *Politics and Poverty*, p. 187; "a war": "Blind-Pig Raid Was Spark," *Detroit Free Press*, 24 July 1967, p. 2A (for evidence of white looters, see "An Orgy of Pillage Erupts Behind Fire and Violence," *Detroit Free Press*, 25 July 1967, p. 8A); See also Sidney Fine, *Violence in the Model City: The Cavanaugh Administration, Race Relations, and the Detroit Riot of 1967* (Ann Arbor: University of Michigan Press, 1989).

52. Meier and Rudwick, *Black Detroit and the Rise of the UAW;* James A. Geschwender, *Class, Race, and Worker Insurgency* (Cambridge: Cambridge University Press, 1977). On the attitudes of older black women toward the LRBW, see Georgakas and Surkin, *Detroit, I Do Mind Dying,* pp. 116, 122.

53. Spence quoted in Blauner, *Black Lives, White Lives,* pp. 32–33. See also Ronald Smothers, "South's New Blacks Find Comfort Laced with Strain," *New York Times,* 23 September 1991, p. A1.

54. Gregory Pappas, *The Magic City: Unemployment in a Working-Class Community* (Ithaca, NY: Cornell University Press, 1989), pp. 3, 12, 13, 15, 98, 115.

55. Ibid., pp. 123, 124, 170.

56. Ibid., pp. 128–36.

Chapter 9
American "Underclasses" in the Late Twentieth Century

1. U.S. Department of Commerce, Bureau of the Census, "Money Income and Poverty Status in the United States, 1989," Current Population Reports, Consumer Income, Series P-60, no. 168, 1990, pp. 65–69, 102; "worst . . . large": Physician Task Force on Hunger in America, "Hunger Counties 1986:

The Distribution of America's High-Risk Areas," Harvard University School of Public Health, January 1986, p. 16; Gerald David Jaynes and Robin Williams, Jr., eds., *A Common Destiny: Blacks and American Society* (Washington, D.C.: National Academy Press, 1989), pp. 286–88; "Five Million Children: A Statistical Profile of Our Poorest Citizens," National Center for Children in Poverty, School of Public Health, Columbia University, New York, 1990, pp. 19–22; Mark C. Berger and Glenn C. Blomquist, "Income Opportunities and the Quality of Life of Urban Residents," in Michael G. H. McGeary and Laurence E. Lynn, Jr., eds., *Urban Change and Poverty* (Washington, D.C.: National Academy Press, 1988), pp. 74–77; U.S. Equal Employment Opportunity Commission (EEOC), "Indicators of Equal Employment Opportunity—Status and Trends," Washington, D.C., 1990. See also Reynolds Farley, *Blacks and Whites: Narrowing the Gap?* (Cambridge, MA: Harvard University Press, 1984).

2. Erol R. Ricketts and Isabel V. Sawhill, "Defining and Measuring the Underclass," *Journal of Policy Analysis and Management* 7 (Winter 1988): 316–25. In her article "The Underclass: An Overview," (*Public Interest* 96 [Summer 1989]), Sawhill states, "Underclass neighborhoods are often thought of as 'inner-city areas,' or 'ghettos.' Our data indicate that they are, indeed, distinctly urban places; we find almost none in rural America" (p. 6).

3. But see, for example, U.S. Congress, Office of Technology Assessment, *Health Care in Rural America*, OTA-H-434 (Washington, D.C.: GPO, September 1990), and a summary of a study by the Center on Budget and Policy Priorities, Washington, D.C., showing that the rural poor lack health insurance, medical coverage, and access to physicians in greater proportions than urban residents ("Study Finds Medical Care Wanting in Rural U.S.," *New York Times*, 13 March 1991, p. A20).

4. Stephen J. Gould, "Taxonomy as Politics: The Harm of False Classification," *Dissent* 37 (Winter 1990): 73–78.

5. "emblematic": Jim Sleeper, "New York Stories," *New Republic*, 10 and 17 September 1990, p. 20; Joan Didion, "New York: Sentimental Journeys," *New York Review of Books*, 17 January 1991, pp. 45–56; "tangle": Lillian Smith, *Killers of the Dream* (New York: Norton, 1961), p. 27. See also Jim Sleeper, *The Closest of Strangers: Liberalism and the Politics of Race in New York* (New York: Norton, 1990).

6. Edmund S. Morgan, *American Slavery, American Freedom: The Ordeal of Colonial Virginia* (New York: Norton, 1975), p. 387. See also Jack P. Greene, *Pursuits of Happiness: The Social Development of Early Modern British Colonies and the Formation of American Culture* (Chapel Hill: University of North Carolina Press, 1988).

7. Theodore R. Marmon et al., *America's Misunderstood Welfare State: Persistent Myths, Enduring Realities* (New York: Basic Books, 1990), pp. 128–74.

8. Sar A. Levitan, *Programs in Aid of the Poor* (Baltimore: Johns Hopkins University Press, 1990), pp. 49, 198.

9. Robert B. Reich, *The Work of Nations: Preparing Ourselves for 21st Century Capitalism* (New York: Knopf, 1991), pp. 196–224.

10. Lisabeth B. Schorr with Daniel Schorr, *Within Our Reach: Breaking the Cycle of Disadvantage* (New York: Anchor Books, Doubleday, 1989); Jo Sanders, *Staying Poor: How the Job Partnership Act Fails Women* (Metuchen, NJ: Scarecrow Press, 1988); "Punishing the Poor," Cover Section, *Southern Exposure* 19 (Summer 1991): 14–30.

11. "quasi-military . . . act": Elijah Anderson, *Streetwise: Race, Class, and Change in an Urban Community* (Chicago: University of Chicago Press, 1990), p. 178; Mercer L. Sullivan, *"Getting Paid": Youth Crime and Work in the Inner-City* (Ithaca, NY: Cornell University Press, 1989).

12. "nostalgia": William Finnegan, "A Reporter at Large: A Street Kid in the Drug Trade—Part I," *The New Yorker,* 10 September 1990, p. 77, and "the idea . . . washing": "A Reporter at Large: A Street Kid in the Drug Trade—Part II," *The New Yorker,* 17 September 1990, p. 66; "When": Philadelphia woman quoted in "Children of the Underclass," *Newsweek,* 11 September 1989, p. 24.

13. "I'm": "3 Arrested in Killing of Infant in Bronx," *New York Times,* 1 August 1990, p. B3; Herbert Gans, "Deconstructing the Underclass: The Term's Dangers as a Planning Concept," *Journal of the American Planning Association* 56 (Summer 1990): 271–77; Paul A. Jargowsky and Mary Jo Bane, "Ghetto Poverty: Basic Questions," in Laurence E. Lynn, Jr. and Michael G. H. McGeary, eds., *Inner-City Poverty in the United States* (Washington, D.C.: National Academy Press, 1990), pp. 16–67; Patricia Ruggles, *Drawing the Line: Alternative Poverty Measures and Their Implications for Public Policy* (Washington, D.C.: Urban Institute Press, 1990); William Julius Wilson, *The Truly Disadvantaged: The Inner City, the Underclass, and Public Policy* (Chicago: University of Chicago Press, 1987); Barbara Omalade, "It's a Family Affair: The Real Lives of Black Single Mothers" (Latham, NY: Kitchen Table Women of Color Press, 1986).

14. Joseph B. Treaster, "A Dealer in Crack: Feeding a Family, and Fewer Addicts," *New York Times,* 16 May 1991, p. 1; "freak . . . around": John Tierney, "Newark's Spiral of Drugs and AIDS," *New York Times,* 16 December 1990, p. 46; Finnegan, "A Reporter at Large: A Street Kid in the Drug Trade, part II," p. 80. See also Alex Kotlowitz, *There Are No Children Here: The Story of Two Boys Growing Up in the Other America* (New York: Doubleday, 1991).

15. Christopher Jencks and Kathryn Edin, "The Real Welfare Problem," *The American Prospect* 1 (Spring 1990): 31–50; Jagna Wojcicka Sharff, "The Underground Economy of a Poor Neighborhood," in Leith Mullings, ed., *Cities of the United States: Studies in Urban Anthropology* (New York:

Columbia University Press, 1987), pp. 19–50; Marta Tienda and Haya Stier, "Joblessness and Shiftlessness: Labor Force Activity in Chicago's Inner City," in Christopher Jencks and Paul E. Peterson, eds., *The Urban Underclass* (Washington, D.C.: Brookings Institution, 1991), pp. 135–54.

16. "with . . . Lee": William M. Adler, "Nothing to Lose," *Southern Exposure* 18 (Winter 1990): 25.

17. Ida Susser and John Kreniski, "The Welfare Trap: A Public Policy for Deprivation," in Mullings, ed., *Cities of the United States,* pp. 51–70; "slaves": Joseph W. Scott and Albert Black, "Deep Structures of African-American Family Life: Female and Male Kin Networks," *Western Journal of Black Studies* 13 (Spring 1989): 21; Lawrence M. Meade, "The Logic of Workfare: The Underclass and Work Policy," *Annals of the American Academy of Political and Social Science* 501 (January 1989): 156–69; U.S. EEOC, "Indicators of Equal Employment Opportunity," p. 52; James A. Geschwender and Rita Carroll-Seguin, "Exploding the Myth of African-American Progress," *Signs* 15 (Winter 1990): 285–99.

18. Grant Pick, "The Life of Johnny Washington: Notes from the Underclass," *Utne Reader* (November/December 1988): 40–48; "your": Isabel Wilkerson, "Middle-Class Blacks Try to Grip a Ladder While Lending a Hand," *New York Times,* 26 November 1990, p. 1.

19. Edwina U. Andrews and Scott Geron, "Surviving the '80s: How Public Aid Recipients Cope with Benefit Cutbacks" (Chicago: Taylor Institute, June 1984), p. 71; "So . . . Many": quoted in Richard Louv, "Hope in Hell's Classroom," *New York Times Magazine,* 25 November 1990, p. 63.

20. Douglas S. Massey and Nancy A. Denton, "Hypersegregation in U.S. Metropolitan Areas," *Demography* 26 (August 1989): 391; Philip Kaufman and Mary J. Frase, "Dropout Rates in the United States: 1989," U.S. Department of Education, Office of Educational Research and Improvement, NCES 90–659 (1990), p. 15; John Kasarda, "Urban Industrial Transition and the Underclass," *Annals of the American Academy of Political and Social Science* 501 (January 1989): 26–47; Mercer Sullivan, "Absent Fathers in the Inner City," ibid., pp. 48–58; John D. Kasarda, "Opportunity Foreclosure Zones," *New Perspectives Quarterly* 6 (Summer 1989): 16–21; "If": Finnegan, "A Reporter At Large: A Street Kid in the Drug Trade"—part II," p. 76; "made": quoted in Theodore Rosengarten, *All God's Dangers: The Life of Nate Shaw* (New York: Knopf, 1974), p. 21; Ze'ev Chafets, *Devil's Night: and Other True Tales of Detroit* (New York: Random House, 1990), pp. 30–39.

21. "heavenly": Sullivan, "Absent Fathers," p. 77; E. Franklin Frazier, *The Negro Family in the United States* (Chicago: University of Chicago Press, 1939; rev. ed., 1966), pp. 114–26.

22. "It's": Veda Usilton quoted in Leon Dash, *When Children Want Children: The Urban Crisis of Teenage Childbearing* (New York: William Morrow,

1989), pp. 208–9; "down . . . that": Finnegan, "A Reporter at Large," pt. I, p. 63, pt. II, p. 84; Elijah Anderson, "Sex Codes and Family Life Among Poor Inner-City Youths," *Annals of the American Academy of Political and Social Science* 501 (January 1989): 59–78.

23. "not": Jane Gross, "Grandmothers Bear A Burden Sired by Drugs," *New York Times,* 9 April 1989, p. 1; Daniel Lazare, "Crack and AIDS: The Next Wave?" *Village Voice,* 8 May 1990, p. 30; "There" quoted in Gina Kolata, "In Cities, Poor Families are Dying of Crack," *New York Times,* 11 August 1989, p. 13.

24. "We'll" quoted in Michael Massing, "D.C.'s War on Drugs: Why Bennett Is Losing," *New York Times Magazine,* 23 September 1990, p. 91.

25. Terry Williams, *The Cocaine Kids: The Inside Story of a Teenage Drug Ring* (Reading, MA: Addison-Wesley, 1989); Jonathan Rieder, "Adventure Capitalism," *New Republic,* 19 November 1990, pp. 36–40; Philippe Bourgois, "Just Another Night on Crack Street," *New York Times Magazine,* 12 November 1989, p. 64; Jack Katz, *Seductions of Crime: Moral and Sensual Attractions in Doing Evil* (New York: Basic Books, 1988).

26. "There's": Craig Wolff, "Guns Offer New York Teenagers a Commonplace, Deadly Allure," *New York Times,* 5 November 1990, p. 1; "truly deviant": John J. DiIulio, Jr., "The Impact of Inner-City Crime," *Public Interest* 96 (Summer 1989): 32; "Nobody": Mike Barnicle, "Reclaiming a Stolen Treasure," *Boston Globe,* 22 March 1990, p. 31. For a summary of a study released in March 1991 by the National Center for Health Statistics, see "Guns Take Ever-Higher Toll Among Young Blacks," *New York Times,* 17 March 1991, p. 31.

27. "fed up": Don Terry, "Death and a Leather Coat: Family Mourns Slain Man," *New York Times,* 27 November 1990, p. B2; "All": Don Terry, "In Harlem, Death Is an Old and Busy Neighbor," *New York Times,* 6 May 1990, p. 36; Sara McClanahan and Irwin Garfinkel, "Single Mothers, the Underclass, and Social Policy," *Annals of the American Academy of Political and Social Science* 501 (January 1989): 93.

28. John Paul Jones III and Janet E. Kodras, "Restructured Regions and Families: The Feminization of Poverty in the United States," *Annals of the Association of American Geographers* 80 (June 1990): 163–83; Hoyt Gimlin, "The Continuing Decline of Rural America," *Editorial Research Reports* 1 (20 July 1990): 414–19; Green quoted in Henry Maurer, *Not Working: An Oral History of the Unemployed* (New York: Holt, Rinehart and Winston, 1979), p. 185.

29. Marta Tienda, "Puerto Ricans and the Underclass Debate," *Annals of the American Academy of Political and Social Science* 501 (January 1989): 105–19; Constance L. Hays, "Hispanic Population Suffering Along with Massachusetts Economy," *New York Times,* 25 December 1989, p. 18.

30. Quoted in Sandy Tolan, "The Border Boom: Hope and Heartbreak," *New*

York Times Magazine, 1 July 1990, p. 21; Robert B. South, "Transnational 'Maquiladora' Location," *Annals of the Association of American Geographers* 80 (December 1990): 549–70; Lou DuBose and Ellen Hosmer, "Borderline Jobs," *Southern Exposure* 18 (Fall 1990): 30–33; Reich, *The Work of Nations.*

31. "the oldest . . . the corporations": Howell Raines, "Alabama Bound," *New York Times Magazine,* 3 June 1990, p. 48; Emily Bentley et al., "Bottom of the Class," *Southern Exposure* 17 (Winter 1989): 14–19; Jonathan Maslow, "Mississippi: Literate at Last," *Atlantic,* August 1990, 28; Peter T. Kilborn, "Charges of Exploitation Roil a Catfish Plant," *New York Times,* 10 December 1990, p. 1.

32. William L. Hamilton et al., *The Causes of Rural to Urban Migration Among the Poor* (Cambridge, MA: Abt Associates, 1970), p. 305; "Women of the Rural South: Economic Status and Prospects" (Lexington, KY: Southeast Women's Employment Coalition, 1986), pp. 51–56. See also Bruce Ergood and Bruce E. Kuhre, eds., *Appalachia: Social Context Past and Present* (Dubuque, IA: Kendall/Hunt, 1976). On the "shallow rural," see Rhoda Halperin, *The Livelihood of Kin: Making Ends Meet "The Kentucky Way"* (Austin: University of Texas Press, 1990).

33. "chronic": U.S. Department of Agriculture, Economic Research Service, "White Americans in Rural Poverty," Agricultural Economic Report no. 124, November 1967, p. 5; "Men": Linda Flowers, *Throwed Away: Failures of Progress in Eastern North Carolina* (Knoxville: University of Tennessee Press, 1990), p. 58; Charles S. Aikin, "A New Type of Black Ghetto in the Plantation South," *Annals of the Association of American Geographers* 80 (June 1990): 223–46; Tekie Fessehatzion and Bichaka Fayissa, "Public Assistance and Job Search Behavior of the Rural Poor—Evidence from the Mississippi Delta," *Review of Black Political Economy* 18 (Winter 1990): 79–91; "Sad Song of the Delta," *Newsweek,* 24 June 1991, pp. 14–18.

34. Diana Sugg et al., "The Face of Poverty," *Southern Exposure* 17 (Winter 1989): 37–41; "Women of the Rural South," p. 18; Smith interview in Eric Bates, "The Home Front," *Southern Exposure* 18 (Winter 1990): 20.

35. "hidden . . . a man:" Peter Anderson, "The Rural Poor: Misery on the Back Roads of New England," *Boston Globe Magazine,* 16 September 1990, p. 21; Kathryn H. Porter, "Poverty in Rural America: A National Overview," Center on Budget and Policy Priorities (Washington D.C.: GPO, 1989). For a fictional account see Carolyn Chute, *The Beans of Egypt, Maine* (New York: Ticknor and Fields, 1985).

36. See, for example, the chapters entitled "The Minnesota Iron Range Dislocated Worker Project," and "The GM-UAW Metropolitan Pontiac Retraining and Employment Program (PREP)" in Robert F. Cook, ed., *Worker Dislocation: Case Studies of Causes and Cures* (Kalamazoo, MI: W. E. Upjohn Institute for Employment Research, 1987), pp. 31–54; "catastrophic" quoted in Vince Rause, "Pittsburgh Cleans Up Its Act,"

New York Times Magazine, 26 November 1989, p. 58; Department of Labor, "Trade Adjustment Assistance for Workers," Fact Sheet No. 86-12; Kent Jones, "Structural Adjustment in the United States Steel Industry: A North-South Perspective," International Employment Policies Working Paper no. 14, International Labour Office, Geneva, Switzerland, 27 October 1987, p. 125. See also Thomas G. Fuechtmann, *Steeples and Stacks: Religion and Steel Crisis in Youngstown* (Cambridge: Cambridge University Press, 1989); Barry Bluestone and Bennett Harrison, *The Deindustrialization of America: Plant Closings, Community Abandonment, and the Dismantling of Basic Industry* (New York: Basic Books, 1982); Katherine S. Newman, *Falling from Grace: The Experience of Downward Mobility in the American Middle Class* (New York: Free Press, 1988); Keith Bradsher, "Hanging on in Textile Country," *New York Times,* 7 June 1991, pp. D1, D3.

37. "We": William E. Schmidt, "Hard Work Can't Stop Hard Times," *New York Times,* 25 November 1990, pp. 1, 30. See also Osha Gray Davidson, *Broken Heartland: The Rise of America's Rural Ghetto* (New York: Free Press, 1990).

38. Greene, *Pursuits of Happiness.*

39. Tony Hiss, *The Experience of Place* (New York: Knopf, 1990).

Selected Bibliography

MANUSCRIPT COLLECTIONS

National Archives of the United States. Washington, D.C.
Manuscript Manufacturing Census for 1880.
Record Groups 2, National War Labor Board; 16, Department of Agriculture; 60, Department of Justice Peonage Files; 69, Records of the Work Projects Administration; 83, Bureau of Agricultural Economics; 105, Bureau of Refugees, Freedmen, and Abandoned Lands (portions avaliable on microfilm); 174, Department of Labor; and 183, U.S. Employment Service.

Note: Portions of Record Groups 2, 16, 83, 174, and 183 are available on microfilm. See James R. Grossman, ed., *Black Workers in the Era of the Great Migration, 1916–1929*. Frederick, MD: University Publications of America, 1986. The Department of Justice Peonage Files (Record Group 60) are available on microfilm in their entirety. See Pete Daniel, ed., *The Peonage Files of the United States Department of Justice, 1901–1945.* Frederick, MD: University Publications of America, 1989.
National Urban League papers. Library of Congress Manuscripts Division, Washington, D.C.

SELECTED BIBLIOGRAPHY

R. G. Dun and Co. Collection, Baker Library, Harvard University Graduate School of Business Administration, Cambridge, MA.

PUBLISHED GOVERNMENT DOCUMENTS

Atwater, W. O., and Charles D. Woods. "Dietary Studies with Reference to the Food of the Negro in Alabama." *U.S. Department of Agriculture Bulletin*, no. 38 (1897).

Boeger, E.A., and E. A. Goldenweiser. "A Study of the Tenant Systems of Farming in the Yazoo-Mississippi Delta." *U.S. Department of Agriculture Bulletin*, no. 337 (1916).

Brannen, C. O. "Relation of Land Tenure to Plantation Organization." *U.S. Department of Agriculture Bulletin*, no. 1269 (1924).

Brown, Edward F. "The Neglected Human Resources of the Gulf Coast States." *Child Labor Bulletin* 2 (May 1913): 112–16.

Byrne, Harriet A. "Child Labor in Representative Tobacco-Growing Areas." Children's Bureau Publication, no. 155 (1926).

Channing, Alice. "Child Labor on Maryland Truck Farms." Children's Bureau Publication, no. 123 (1923).

Cocalis, Virginia. "They Came From Missouri." *Land Policy Review* 4 (February 1941): 15–19.

Dart, Helen M. "Maternity and Child Care in Selected Rural Areas of Mississippi." Rural Child Welfare Series no. 5, Children's Bureau Publication, no. 88 (1921).

Ducoff, Louis J. "Migratory Farm Workers in 1949." Agriculture Information Bulletin no. 25, Bureau of Agricultural Economics (1950).

Folsom, Josiah C. "Truck-Farm Labor in New Jersey, 1922." U.S. Department of Agriculture *Bulletin*, no. 1285 (1925).

Free, Benjamin J. "Seasonal Employment in Agriculture." Works Progress Administration (September 1938).

Haskell, E. S. "A Farm Management Survey in Brooks County, Georgia." *U.S. Department of Agriculture Bulletin*, no. 648 (1918).

Klein, Bruce W., and Philip L. Rones. "A Profile of the Working Poor." *Monthly Labor Review* 112 (October 1989): 3–13.

Langsford, E. L., and B. H. Thibodeaux. "Plantation Organization and Operation in the Yazoo-Mississippi Delta Area." Technical Bulletin, no. 882 (May 1939).

Leavell, R. H. et al. *Negro Migration in 1916–17*. U.S. Department of Labor, Division of Negro Economics (1919).

Metzler, William H. "Migratory Farm Workers in the Atlantic Coast Stream." U.S. Department of Agriculture Circular no. 966 (January 1955).

Moss, Ralph. "Complexity of Florida's Agricultural Labor Supply." *Employment Security Review* 22 (March 1955): 10–11.

Oemler, A. "'Truck Farming." *Report of the Commissioner of Agriculture* (1885): 583–627.

Paradise, Viola I. "Child Labor and the Work of Mothers in Oyster and Shrimp Canning Communities on the Gulf Coast." Children's Bureau Publication, no. 98 (1922).

Pennypacker, J. E. "Convict Labor for Road Work." *U.S. Department of Agriculture Bulletin,* no. 414 (1916).

Pittman, C. W. E. "Atlantic Coast Migratory Movement of Agricultural Workers: War Years." Extension Farm Labor Program (c. 1946).

———. "Migratory Agricultural Workers of the Atlantic Seaboard." *Employment Security Review* 7 (June 1948): 3–6.

Scarborough, W. S. "Tenancy and Ownership Among Negro Farmers in Southampton County, Virginia." *U.S. Department of Agriculture Bulletin,* no. 1404 (1926).

Smith, A. G. "A Farm Management Study in Anderson County, South Carolina." *U.S. Department of Agriculture Bulletin,* no. 651 (1918).

Struthers, Joseph. "Phosphate Rock." U.S. Department of Commerce, Bureau of the Census, Special Reports of the Census Office, *Mines and Quarries* (1902).

Sullivan, M. Loretta, and Ethel Erickson. "Women's Employment in Vegetable Canneries in Delaware." Women's Bureau *Bulletin,* no. 62 (1927).

Sutherland, Arthur T. "The Migratory Labor Problem in Delaware." Women's Bureau *Bulletin,* no. 185 (1941).

Taylor, Paul S. "Migratory Farm Labor in the United States." *Monthly Labor Review* (Bureau of Labor Statistics) 44 (March 1937): 537–50.

Thom, William Taylor. "The Negroes of Litwalton, Virginia: A Social Study of the 'Oyster Negro.'" Department of Labor *Bulletin* 37 (1901): 1115–70.

U.S. Bureau of the Census. *Money Income and Poverty Status in the United States: 1989.* Current Population Reports, Series P-60, no. 168, 1990.

———. *Transitions in Income and Poverty Status: 1985–86.* Current Population Reports, Series P-70, no. 18, 1990.

U.S. Congress. House. Select Committee Investigating National Defense Migration. House of Representatives. *Hearings Before the Select Committee Investigating National Defense Migration.* 77th Cong., 1st and 2d sess., 1941–1943. Parts 11–33.

———. Select Committee to Investigate the Interstate Migration of Destitute Citizens. *Hearings Before the Select Committee to Investigate the Interstate Migration of Destitute Citizens.* House of Representatives, 76th Cong., 3d sess., 1940–1941. Parts 1–10.

———. Senate. Subcommittee on Migratory Labor of the Committee on Labor and Public Welfare. *Hearings Before the Subcommittee on Migratory Labor of the Committee on Labor and Public Welfare.* United States Senate, 90th Cong., 1st and 2d sess.; 91st Cong., 1st and 2d sess., 1969–1970. 8 parts.

U.S. Department of Agriculture. *Agricultural Yearbooks.* 1907, 1912, 1916, 1920, 1923.

————. *White Americans in Rural Poverty.* Economic Research Service, Agricultural Economic Report no. 124 (November 1967).

U.S. Department of Commerce. *Plantation Farming in the United States.* Washington, D.C.: GPO, 1916.

U.S. Department of Education. Office of Educational Research and Improvement. *Dropout Rates in the United States: 1989.* NCES 90–659 (September 1990).

U.S. Department of the Interior. Census Office. *Report on Cotton Production in the United States,* pts. 1 and 2. Washington, D.C.: GPO, 1884.

U.S. Industrial Commission. *Reports.* vol. 10: *Report of the Industrial Commission on Agriculture and Agricultural Labor* (Washington, D.C.: GPO, 1901); vol. 11: *Report of the Industrial Commission on Agriculture and on Taxation of Various States* (Washington, D.C.: GPO, 1901).

U.S. National Advisory Commission on Rural Poverty. *Rural Poverty in the United States: A Report by the President's National Advisory Commission on Rural Poverty.* Washington, D.C.: GPO, 1968.

U.S. President's Commission on Migratory Labor. *Migratory Labor in American Agriculture: Report of the President's Commission on Migratory Labor.* Washington, D.C.: GPO, 1951.

Webb, John N. *The Migratory-Casual Worker.* Works Progress Administration, Division of Social Research, Monograph 7, 1937.

Willard, Rex E. "A Farm Management Study of Cotton Farms of Ellis County, Texas." *U.S. Department of Agriculture Bulletin,* no. 659 (1918).

Woofter, Thomas J. *Landlord and Tenant on the Cotton Plantation.* Works Progress Administration, Division of Social Research, Monograph 5. Washington, D.C.: GPO, 1936.

Primary Sources

BOOKS

Allen, Ruth Alice. *The Labor of Women in the Production of Cotton.* New York: Arno Press, 1975; orig. pub. 1931.

Anderson, Elijah. *Streetwise: Race, Class, and Change in an Urban Community.* Chicago: University of Chicago Press, 1990.

Arnow, Harriet. *The Dollmaker.* New York: Macmillan, 1954.

Attaway, William. *Blood on the Forge.* New York: Monthly Review Press, 1987; orig. pub. 1941.

Avery, Burniece. *Walk Quietly Through the Night and Cry Softly.* Detroit, MI: Balamp Press, 1977.

Baker, Ray Stannard. *Following the Color Line: An Account of Negro Citizenship in the American Democracy.* New York: Doubleda and Page, 1908.

Beaver, Patricia D. *Rural Community in the Appalachian South.* Lexington: University Press of Kentucky, 1986.

Berlin, Ira, et al., eds. *Freedom: A Documentary History of Emancipation, 1861–1867.* Series 1, vol. 1: *The Destruction of Slavery;* vol. 3: *The Wartime Genesis of Free Labor: The Lower South.* Cambridge: Cambridge University Press, 1985, 1990.

Blauner, Bob. *Black Lives, White Lives: Three Decades of Race Relations in America.* Berkeley: University of California Press, 1989.

Cable, George Washington. *The Silent South, Together with the Freedman's Case in Equity, and the Convict Lease System.* New York: Scribner's Sons, 1889.

Chafets, Ze'ev. *Devil's Night: And Other True Tales of Detroit.* New York: Random House, 1990.

Cincinnati *Enquirer* Staff. *The Urban Appalachians.* Cincinnati: Cincinnati *Enquirer,* 1981.

Coles, Robert. *Children of Crisis.* Vol. 2, *Migrants, Sharecroppers, Mountaineers;* vol. 3, *The South Goes North.* Boston: Little, Brown, 1971.

Comer, James P. *Maggie's American Dream: The Life and Times of a Black Family.* New York: New American Library, 1988.

Crews, Harry. *A Childhood: The Biography of a Place.* New York: Harper & Row, 1978.

Dancy, John C. *Sand Against the Wind: The Memoirs of John C. Dancy.* Detroit: Wayne State University Press, 1966.

Dash, Leon. *When Children Want Children: The Urban Crisis of Teenage Childbearing.* New York: William Morrow, 1989.

Davidson, Osha Gray. *Broken Heartland: The Rise of America's Rural Ghetto.* New York: Free Press, 1990.

DeForest, John William. *A Union Officer in the Reconstruction.* New Haven, CT: Yale University Press, 1948.

Denby, Charles. *Indignant Heart: Testimony of a Black American Worker.* London: Pluto Press, 1979.

Drake, St. Clair, and Horace R. Cayton. *Black Metropolis: A Study of Negro Life in a Northern City.* New York: Harper & Row, 1962; orig. pub. 1945.

Dunbar, Tony, and Linda Kravitz. *Hard Traveling: Migrant Farm Workers in America.* Cambridge, MA: Ballinger Publishing Co., 1976.

Evans, Arthur S., Jr., and David Lee. *Pearl City, Florida: A Black Community Remembers.* Boca Raton: Florida Atlantic University Press, 1990.

Faulkner, Audrey Olsen, et al., eds. *When I Was Comin' Up: An Oral History of Aged Blacks.* Hamden, CT: Archon Books, 1982.

Fields, Mamie Garvin with Karen Fields. *Lemon Swamp and Other Places: A Carolina Memoir.* New York: Free Press, 1983.

Flowers, Linda. *Throwed Away: Failures of Progress in Eastern North Carolina.* Knoxville: University of Tennessee Press, 1990.

Friedlander, Peter. *The Emergence of a UAW Local, 1936–1939: A Study in Class and Culture.* Pittsburgh: University of Pittsburgh Press, 1975.

Gamble, Thomas, ed. *Naval Stores: History, Production, Distribution, and Consumption.* Savannah, GA: Review Publishing and Printing Co., 1921.

Gitlin, Todd, and Nanci Hollander. *Uptown: Poor Whites in Chicago.* New York: Harper & Row, 1970.

Goodrich, Carter. *The Miner's Freedom: A Study of the Working Life in a Changing Industry.* Boston: Marshall Jones, 1925.

Goodrich, Carter, et al. *Migration and Economic Opportunity: The Report of the Study of Population Redistribution.* Philadelphia: University of Pennsylvania Press, 1936.

Gwaltney, John Langston. *Drylongso: A Self-Portrait of Black America.* New York: Vintage Books, 1980.

Hagood, Margaret J. *Mothers of the South: Portraiture of the White Tenant Farm Woman.* New York: Norton, 1977; orig. pub. 1939.

Halperin, Rhoda. *The Livelihood of Kin: Making Ends Meet "The Kentucky Way."* Austin: University of Texas Press, 1990.

Hill, Herbert. *No Harvest for the Reaper: The Story of the Migratory Agricultural Worker in the United States.* New York: NAACP, 1958.

Hine, Darlene Clark, Patrick Kay Bidelman, and Shirley M. Herd. *The Black Women in the Middle West Project: A Comprehensive Resource Guide: Illinois and Indiana.* Indianapolis: Indiana Historical Bureau, 1986.

Holt, Hamilton, ed. *Life Stories of Undistinguished Americans As Told By Themselves.* New York: James Pott and Co., 1906.

Holtzclaw, William H. *The Black Man's Burden.* New York: Neale Publishing Co., 1915.

Hundley, Daniel R. *Social Relations in Our Southern States.* New York: H. B. Price, 1860.

Jaynes, Gerald David, and Robin Williams, Jr. *A Common Destiny: Blacks and American Society.* Washington, D.C.: National Academy Press, 1989.

Jensen, Vernon H. *Lumber and Labor.* New York: Farrar and Rinehart, 1945.

Johnson, Charles S. *Shadow of the Plantation.* Chicago: University of Chicago Press, 1934.

Kiser, Clyde Vernon. *Sea Island to City: A Study of St. Helena Islanders in Harlem and Other Urban Centers.* New York: Columbia University Press, 1932.

Kotlowitz, Alex. *There Are No Children Here: The Story of Two Boys Growing Up in the Other America.* New York: Doubleday, 1991.

Logan, Onnie Lee with Katherine Clark. *Motherwit: An Alabama Midwife's Story.* New York: E. P. Dutton, 1989.

Loring, Francis W., and C. F. Atkinson. *Cotton Culture and the South*

Considered with Reference to Emigration. Boston: A. Williams, 1869.

Lynd, Alice, and Staughton Lynd, eds. *Rank and File: Personal Histories by Working-Class Organizers.* Princeton, NJ: Princeton University Press, 1981.

Maguire, Jane. *On Shares: Ed Brown's Story.* New York: Norton, 1975.

Mebane, Mary. *Mary.* New York: Viking Press, 1981.

Moore, Warren. *Mountain Voices: A Legacy of the Blue Ridge and Great Smokies.* Chester, CT: Globe Pequot Press, 1988.

Nelkin, Dorothy. *On the Season: Aspects of the Migrant Labor System.* Ithaca, NY: New York State School of Industrial and Labor Relations, Cornell University, 1970.

Newman, Katherine S. *Falling from Grace: The Experience of Downward Mobility in the American Middle Class.* New York: Free Press, 1988.

Odum, Howard W. *Southern Regions of the United States.* Chapel Hill: University of North Carolina Press, 1936.

Olmsted, Frederick Law. *A Journey in the Back Country, 1853–1854.* New York: Schocken, 1970; orig. pub. 1860.

Pappas, Gregory. *The Magic City: Unemployment in a Working-Class Community.* Ithaca, NY: Cornell University Press, 1989.

Percy, William Alexander. *Lanterns on the Levee: Recollections of a Planter's Son.* Baton Rouge: Louisiana State University Press, 1973; orig. pub. 1941.

Peterson, Gene B., et al. *Southern Newcomers to Northern Cities: Work and Social Adjustment in Cleveland.* New York: Praeger, 1977.

Petry, Ann. *The Street.* Boston: Houghton Mifflin, 1946.

Powell, J. C. *The American Siberia, Or Fourteen Years' Experience in a Southern Convict Camp.* Chicago: Donohue, Henneberry, and Co., 1891.

Raper, Arthur F. *Preface to Peasantry: A Tale of Two Black Belt Counties.* Chapel Hill: University of North Carolina Press, 1936.

Rawick, George P. *The American Slave: A Composite Autobiography.* Westport, CT: Greenwood Press, vols. 1–19, 1972; vols. 1–12, Supplementary Series 1, 1977; vols. 1–9, Supplementary Series 2, 1979.

Rosengarten, Theodore. *All God's Dangers: The Life of Nate Shaw.* New York: Knopf, 1972.

Shackelford, Laurel, and Bill Weinberg, eds. *Our Appalachia: An Oral History.* New York: Hill and Wang, 1977.

Simonsen, Thordis, ed. *You May Plow Here: The Narrative of Sara Brooks.* New York: Norton, 1986.

Steiner, Jesse F., and Roy M. Brown. *The North Carolina Chain Gang: A Study of County Convict Road Work.* Chapel Hill: University of North Carolina Press, 1927.

Stone, Alfred H. *Studies in the American Race Problem.* New York: Doubleday and Page, 1908.

Sullivan, Mercer L. *"Getting Paid": Youth Crime and Work in the Inner-City.* Ithaca, NY: Cornell University Press, 1989.

Taylor, Ronald B. *Sweatshops in the Sun: Child Labor on the Farm.* Boston: Beacon Press, 1973.

Todes, Charlotte. *Labor and Lumber*. New York: International Publishers, 1931.

Vance, Rupert B. *Human Factors in Cotton Culture: A Study in the Social Geography of the American South*. Chapel Hill: University of North Carolina Press, 1929.

Williams, Terry. *The Cocaine Kids: The Inside Story of a Teenage Drug Ring*. Reading, MA: Addison-Welsey, 1989.

Wilson, William Julius. *The Truly Disadvantaged: The Inner City, the Underclass, and Public Policy*. Chicago: University of Chicago Press, 1987.

ARTICLES AND PAMPHLETS

Adler, William M. "Nothing to Lose." *Southern Exposure* 18 (Winter 1990): 22–27.

Aikin, Charles S. "A New Type of Black Ghetto in the Plantation South." *Annals of the Association of American Geographers* 80 (June 1990): 223–46.

Andrews, Edwina Uehara, and Scott Geron. "Surviving the 80s: How Public Aid Recipients Cope With Benefit Cutbacks." Chicago: Taylor Institute, 1984.

Barrow, David C., Jr. "A Georgia Plantation." *Scribner's Monthly* 21 (April 1881): 830–36.

Barry, Richard. "Slavery in the South To-Day." *Cosmopolitan Magazine* 42 (March 1907): 481–91.

Bentley, Emily, et al. "Bottom of the Class." *Southern Exposure* (Winter 1989): 14–19.

Berlin, Ira, et al., eds. "The Terrain of Freedom: The Struggle Over the Meaning of Free Labor in the U.S. South." *History Workshop* 22 (Autumn 1986): 108–30.

Beynon, Erdmann Doane. "The Southern White Laborer Migrates to Michigan." *American Sociological Review* 3 (June 1938): 333–43.

Brainerd, Alfred T. "Colored Mining Labor." *Transactions of the American Institute of Mining Engineers* 14 (1885–86): 79.

Branson, E.C. "Social Occasions and Contacts in a Rural County." *Journal of Social Forces* 1 (January 1923): 162–63.

Breckinridge, Mary. "The Corn-Bread Line." *The Survey* 64 (15 August 1930): 422–23.

Bremer, Harry M. "People Who Go to Tomatoes: A Study of Four Hundred Families." National Child Labor Committee pamphlet, no. 215 (March 1914).

Brooks, Robert P. "A Local Study of the Race Problem: Race Relations in the Eastern Piedmont Region of Georgia." *Political Science Quarterly* 26 (June 1911): 193–221.

Brown, Edward F. "The Neglected Human Resources of the Gulf Coast States." *Child Labor Bulletin* 2 (May 1913).

Brown, James S. "The Family Behind the Migrant." *Mountain Life and Work* 44 (1968): 4–7.

Castro, Kenneth G., et al. "Transmission of HIV in Belle Glade, Florida: Lessons for Other Communities in the United States." *Science* 239 (8 January 1988): 193–97.

Chute, Charles L. "The Cost of the Cranberry Sauce." *The Survey* 27 (2 December 1911): 1281–84.

Coulter, John Lee. "The Rural Life Problem of the South." *South Atlantic Quarterly* 12 (1913): 60–71.

Creel, George. "The Feudal Towns of Texas." *Harper's Weekly* 60 (23 January 1915): 76–78.

Cressey, Paul Frederick. "Social Disorganization and Reorganization in Harlan County, Kentucky." *American Sociological Review* 14 (June 1949): 389–94.

DeLeon, Edwin. "Ruin and Reconstruction of the Southern States." *Southern Magazine* 14 (June 1874): 17–44; (March 1874): 287–309; (May 1874): 453–82; (June 1874): 561–90.

Dickey, J. A., and E. C. Branson. "How Farm Tenants Live." University of North Carolina Extension *Bulletin* 2, no. 6 (16 November 1922).

DiIulio, John J. "The Impact of Inner-City Crime." *Public Interest* 96 (Summer 1989): 28–46.

DuBois, W. E. B. "The Negro American Family." Atlanta University Study no. 13. Atlanta: Atlanta University Press, 1908.

Fessehatzion, Tekie, and Bichaka Fayissa. "Public Assistance and Job Search Behavior of the Rural Poor—Evidence from the Mississippi Delta." *Review of Black Political Economy* 18 (Winter 1990): 79–91.

Fleming, Walter L. "Immigration to the Southern States." *Political Science Quarterly* 20 (June 1905): 276–97.

Frey, Fred C., and T. Lynn Smith. "The Influence of the AAA Cotton Program Upon the Tenant, Cropper, and Laborer." *Rural Sociology* 1 (December 1936): 483–505.

Goodnow, Henry C. "In the Tie Woods of Texas." *Southern Industrial and Lumber Review* 12 (July 1904): 14–15; (August 1904): 25–26.

Goodnow, Marc N. "Turpentine: Impressions of the Convict Camps of Florida." *The Survey* 34 (1 May 1915): 103–7.

Henderson, George W. "Life in the Louisiana Sugar Belt." *Southern Workman* 35 (April 1906): 207–15.

Hill, Herbert. "The AFL-CIO and the Black Worker: Twenty-Five Years After the Merger." *Journal of Intergroup Relations* 10 (Spring 1982): 5–78.

Hine, Lewis W. "Baltimore to Biloxi and Back: The Child's Burden in Oyster and Shrimp Canneries." *The Survey* 30 (3 May 1913): 167–72.

———. "The Child's Burden in Oyster and Shrimp Canneries." *Child Labor Bulletin* 2 (1913): 105–11.

Hodgson, Harry. "A Great Farmer at Work." *World's Work* 9 (January 1905): 5723–33.

Jencks, Christopher, and Kathryn Edin. "The Real Welfare Problem." *The American Prospect* 1 (Spring 1990): 31–50.

Joffe, Eva. "Rural School Attendance in Alabama." *Child Labor Bulletin* 7 (1918): 101–25.

Jones, John Paul III, and Janet E. Kodras. "Restructured Regions and Families: The Feminization of Poverty in the United States." *Annals of the Association of American Geographers* 80 (June 1990): 163–83.

Kasarda, John D. "Opportunity Foreclosure Zones." *New Perspectives Quarterly* 6 (Summer 1989): 16–21.

Koos, Earl Lomon. "They Follow the Sun." Bureau of Maternal and Child Health, Florida State Board of Health, Jacksonville, FL, 1957.

Laing, James T. "The Negro Miner in West Virginia." *Journal of Social Forces* 14 (March 1936): 416–22.

Leybourne, Grace G. "Urban Adjustments of Migrants from the Southern Appalachian Plateaus." *Journal of Social Forces* 16 (December 1937): 238–46.

Lindsay, Nick. "An Oral History of Edisto Island: The Life and Times of Bubberson Brown." Goshen, IN: Pinchpenny Press, 1977.

———. "An Oral History of Edisto Island: Sam Gadsden Tells the Story." Goshen, IN: Pinchpenny Press, 1975.

Louv, Richard. "Hope in Hell's Classroom." *New York Times Magazine* (25 November 1990), p. 30.

Maloney, Michael E. "The Social Areas of Cincinnati: An Analysis of Social Needs." Cincinnati: Cincinnati Human Relations Commission, 1985.

Montgomery, Bill. "The Uptown Story." *Mountain Life and Work* 44 (September 1968): 8–18.

Munns, Edw. N. "Women in Southern Lumbering Operations." *Journal of Forestry* 17 (February 1919): 144–49.

Nichol, A. J. "The Oyster-Packing Industry of Baltimore: Its History and Current Problems." University of Maryland (August 1937).

Omalade, Barbara. "It's a Family Affair: The Real Lives of Black Single Mothers." Latham, NY: Kitchen Table: Women of Color Press, 1986.

Pedersen, Harald A. "Mechanized Agriculture and the Farm Laborer." *Rural Sociology* 19 (June 1954): 143–51.

Phillips, Ulrich B. "The Decadence of the Plantation System." *Annals of the American Academy of Political and Social Science* 35 (January-June 1910): 37–41.

Raper, Arthur. "The Role of Agricultural Technology in Southern Social Change." *Rural Sociology* 25 (October 1946): 221–30.

Rickets, Erol R., and Isabel V. Sawhill. "Defining and Measuring the Underclass." *Journal of Policy Analysis and Management* 7 (Winter 1988): 316–25.

Stone, Alfred Holt. "Italian Cotton-Growers in Arkansas." *American Monthly Review of Reviews* 35 (February 1907): 209–13.

Taylor, Rosser H., ed. "Post-Bellum Southern Rental Contracts." *Agricultural History* 17 (April 1943): 121–28.

Vorse, Mary Heaton. "America's Submerged Class: The Migrants." *Harper's* 106 (February 1953): 86–93.

Welch, Frank J. "The Plantation Land Tenure System in Mississippi." Mississippi Agricultural Experiment Station *Bulletin,* no. 385, State College, Mississippi (June 1943).

Wilgus, D. K. "Country-Western Music and the Urban Hillbilly." *Journal of American Folklore* 83 (April-June 1970): 157–79.

Wilkinson, Alec. "A Reporter at Large (Sugarcane): Big Sugar, Pts. I and II," *The New Yorker,* 17 July 1989, pp. 41–69; 24 July 1989, pp. 42–65.

Williams, Robin M., and Olaf Wakefield. "Farm Tenancy in North Carolina, 1880–1935." North Carolina Agricultural Experiment Station with the Department of Agricultural Economics and Rural Sociology, AE-RS Information Series No. 1 (September 1937).

Winegarten, Ruthe. "I Am Annie Mae: The Personal Story of a Black Texas Woman." *Chrysalis* 4 (Spring 1980): 15–23.

Woofter, T. J. "The Negroes of Athens, Georgia." Phelps-Stokes Fellowship Studies no. 1, *Bulletin of the University of Georgia* 14 (December 1913).

Wooten, H. H. "Credit Problems of North Carolina Cropper Families." Agricultural Experiment Station of the North Carolina State College of Agriculture and Engineering and the North Carolina Department of Agriculture *Bulletin,* no. 271 (May 1930).

Work, Monroe H. "The Negroes of Warsaw, Georgia." *Southern Workman* 37 (January 1908): 29–40.

Secondary Sources

BOOKS

Allen, Ruth A. *East Texas Lumber Workers: An Economic and Social Picture, 1870–1950.* Austin: University of Texas Press, 1961.

Anderson, James D. *The Education of Blacks in the South, 1860–1935.* Chapel Hill: University of North Carolina Press, 1988.

Ash, Stephen V. *Middle Tennessee Society Transformed, 1860–1870: War and Peace in the Upper South.* Baton Rouge: Louisiana State University Press, 1988.

Ayers, Edward L. *Vengeance and Justice: Crime and Punishment in the Nineteenth Century American South.* New York: Oxford University Press, 1984.

Batteau, Allen, ed. *Appalachia and America: Autonomy and Regional Dependence.* Lexington: University Press of Kentucky, 1983.

Bethel, Elizabeth Rauh. *Promiseland: A Century of Life in a Negro Community.* Philadelphia: Temple University Press, 1981.

Blakey, Arch Fredric. *The Florida Phosphate Industry: A History of the Development and Use of a Vital Mineral.* Cambridge, MA: Harvard University Press, 1973.

Bode, Frederick A., and Donald A. Ginter. *Farm Tenancy and the Census in Antebellum Georgia.* Athens: University of Georgia Press, 1986.

Clark, Thomas D. *The Greening of the South: The Recovery of Land and Forest.* Lexington: University Press of Kentucky, 1984.

Clive, Alan. *State of War: Michigan in World War II.* Ann Arbor: University of Michigan Press, 1979.

Cohen, Lizabeth. *Making a New Deal: Industrial Workers in Chicago, 1919–1939.* New York: Cambridge University Press, 1990.

Cohen, Lucy M. *Chinese in the Post–Civil War South: A People Without a History.* Baton Rouge: Louisiana State University Press, 1984.

Cohen, William. *At Freedom's Edge: Black Mobility and the Southern White Quest for Racial Control, 1861–1915.* Baton Rouge: Louisiana State University Press, 1991.

Daniel, Pete. *Breaking the Land: The Transformation of Cotton, Tobacco, and Rice Cultures Since 1880.* Urbana: University of Illinois Press, 1985.

———. *The Shadow of Slavery: Peonage in the South, 1901–1969.* Urbana: University of Illinois Press, 1972.

Davis, Ronald L. F. *Good and Faithful Labor: From Slavery to Sharecropping in the Natchez District, 1860–1890.* Westport, CT: Greenwood Press, 1982.

Eller, Ronald D. *Miners, Millhands and Mountaineers: Industrialization of the Appalachian South, 1880–1930.* Knoxville: University of Tennessee Press, 1982.

Ergood, Bruce, and Bruce E. Kuhre, eds. *Appalachia: Social Context Past and Present.* Dubuque, IA: Kendall/Hunt, 1976.

Escott, Paul D. *Many Excellent People: Power and Privilege in North Carolina, 1850–1900.* Chapel Hill: University of North Carolina Press, 1985.

Fite, Gilbert C. *Cotton Fields No More: Southern Agriculture, 1865–1980.* Lexington: University Press of Kentucky, 1984.

Fligstein, Neil. *Going North: Migration of Blacks and Whites from the South, 1900–1950.* New York: Academic Press, 1981.

Flynn, Charles L., Jr. *White Land, Black Labor: Caste and Class in Late Nineteenth Century Georgia.* Baton Rouge: Louisiana State University Press, 1983.

Flynt, Wayne. *Poor But Proud: Alabama's Poor Whites.* Tuscaloosa: University of Alabama Press, 1989.

Foner, Eric. *Reconstruction: America's Unfinished Revolution, 1863–1867.* New York: Harper & Row, 1988.

Ford, Lacy K. *Origins of Southern Radicalism: The South Carolina Upcountry, 1800–1860.* New York: Oxford University Press, 1988.

Ford, Thomas R. *The Southern Appalachian Region: A Survey.* Lexington: University Press of Kentucky, 1962.

Georgakas, Dan, and Marvin Surkin. *Detroit, I Do Mind Dying: A Study in Urban Revolution.* New York: St. Martin's Press, 1975.

Glymph, Thavolia, et al. *Essays on the Postbellum Southern Economy.* College Station: Texas A & M University Press, 1985.

Gottlieb, Peter. *Making Their Own Way: Southern Blacks' Migration to Pittsburgh, 1916–1930.* Urbana: University of Illinois Press, 1987.

Grossman, James R. *Land of Hope: Chicago, Black Southerners, and the Great Migration.* Chicago: University of Chicago Press, 1989.

Hahn, Steven. *The Roots of Southern Populism: Yeoman Farmers and the Transformation of the Georgia Upcountry, 1850–1890.* New York: Oxford University Press, 1983.

Hahn, Steven, and Jonathan Prude, eds. *The Countryside in the Age of Capitalist Transformation: Essays in the Social History of Rural America.* Chapel Hill: University of North Carolina Press, 1983.

Hall, Jacquelyn Dowd, et al. *Like a Family: The Making of a Southern Cotton Mill World.* Chapel Hill: University of North Carolina Press, 1987.

Harris, J. William. *Plain Folk and Gentry in a Slave Society: White Liberty and Black Slavery in Augusta's Hinterlands.* Middletown, CT: Wesleyan University Press, 1985.

Hickman, Nollie. *Mississippi Harvest: Lumbering in the Longleaf Pine Belt, 1840–1915.* University: University of Mississippi Press, 1962.

Janiewski, Delores E. *Sisterhood Denied: Race, Gender, and Class in a New South Community.* Philadelphia: Temple University Press, 1985.

Jaynes, Gerald. *Branches Without Roots: Genesis of the Black Working Class in the American South, 1862–1882.* New York: Oxford University Press, 1986.

Jencks, Christopher, and Paul E. Peterson, eds. *The Urban Underclass.* Washington, D.C.: Brookings Institution, 1991.

Johnson, Daniel M., and Rex R. Campbell. *Black Migration in America: A Social Demographic History.* Durham, NC: Duke University Press, 1981.

Katz, Jack. *Seductions of Crime: Moral and Sensual Attractions in Doing Evil.* New York: Basic Books, 1988.

Katz, Michael. *In the Shadow of the Poorhouse: A Social History of Welfare in America.* New York: Basic Books, 1986.

Keyssar, Alexander. *Out of Work: The First Century of Unemployment in Massachusetts.* New York: Cambridge University Press, 1986.

Kirby, Jack Temple. *Rural Worlds Lost: The American South, 1920–1960.* Baton Rouge: Louisiana State University Press, 1987.

Kunkin, Dorothy, and Michael Byrne. *Appalachians in Cleveland.* Cleveland: Institute of Urban Studies of the Cleveland State University, 1972.

Lemann, Nicholas. *The Promised Land: The Great Black Migration and How It Changed America.* New York: Knopf, 1991.

Lewis, Ronald L. *Black Coal Miners in America: Race, Class, and Community Conflict, 1780–1980.* Lexington: University Press of Kentucky, 1987.

Litwack, Leon F. *Been in the Storm So Long: The Aftermath of Slavery.* New York: Knopf, 1979.

McMillen, Neil R. *Dark Journey: Black Mississippians in the Age of Jim Crow.* Urbana: University of Illinois Press, 1989.

McWilliams, Carey. *Ill Fares the Land: Migrants and Migratory Labor in the United States.* Boston: Little, Brown, 1942.

Marks, Carole. *Farewell—We're Good and Gone: The Great Black Migration.* Bloomington: Indiana University Press, 1989.

Marmon, Theodore, et al. *America's Misunderstood Welfare State: Persistent Myths, Enduring Realities.* New York: Basic Books, 1990.

Mayor, Archer H. *Southern Timberman: The Legacy of William Buchanan.* Athens: University of Georgia Press, 1988.

Mohr, Clarence L. *On the Threshold of Freedom: Masters and Slaves in Civil War Georgia.* Athens: University of Georgia Press, 1986.

Newman, Dorothy, et al. *Protest, Politics, and Prosperity: Black Americans and White Institutions, 1940–1975.* New York: Pantheon Books, 1978.

a Nijeholt, G. Thomas-Lycklama. *On the Road for Work: Migratory Workers on the East Coast of the United States.* Boston: Martinus Nijhoff Publishing, 1980.

Orser, Charles. *The Material Basis of the Postbellum Tenant Plantation: Historical Archaeology in the South Carolina Piedmont.* Athens: University of Georgia Press, 1988.

Philliber, William W. *Appalachian Migrants in Urban America: Cultural Conflict or Ethnic Group Formation?* New York: Praeger, 1981.

Philliber, William W., and Clyde B. McCoy, eds., *The Invisible Minority: Urban Appalachians.* Lexington: University Press of Kentucky, 1981.

Ransom, Roger, and Richard Sutch. *One Kind of Freedom: The Economic Consequences of Emancipation.* New York: Cambridge University Press, 1977.

Reich, Robert B. *The Work of Nations: Preparing Ourselves for 21st Century Capitalism.* New York: Knopf, 1991.

Schwarzweller, Harry K., et al. *Mountain Families in Transition: A Case Study of Appalachian Migration.* University Park: Pennsylvania State University Press, 1971.

Shaw, Barton C. *The Wool-Hat Boys: Georgia's Populist Party.* Baton Rouge: Louisiana State University Press, 1984.

Shifflett, Crandall A. *Coal Towns: Life, Work, and Culture in Company Towns of Southern Appalachia, 1880–1960.* Knoxville: University of Tennessee Press, 1991.

———. *Patronage and Poverty in the Tobacco South: Louisa County, Virginia, 1860–1900.* Knoxville: University of Tennessee Press, 1982.

Shofner, Jerrell H. *Nor Is It Over Yet: Florida in the Era of Reconstruction, 1863–1867.* Gainesville: University Press of Florida, 1974.

Sitterson, J. Carlyle. *Sugar Country: The Cane Sugar Industry in the South, 1753–1950.* Lexington: University Press of Kentucky, 1953.

Tindall, George B. *The Emergence of the New South, 1913–1945.* Baton Rouge: Louisiana State University Press, 1967.

Trotter, Joe William. *Black Milwaukee: The Making of an Industrial Proletariat, 1915–1945.* Urbana: University of Illinois Press, 1985.

———. *Coal, Class, and Color: Blacks in Southern West Virginia, 1915–1932.* Urbana: University of Illinois Press, 1990.

Turner, William H., and Edward J. Cabbell, eds. *Blacks in Appalachia.* Lexington: University Press of Kentucky, 1985.

Woodman, Harold D. *King Cotton and His Retainers: Financing and Marketing the Cotton Crop of the South, 1800–1925.* Lexington: University Press of Kentucky, 1968.

Woodson, Carter G. *A Century of Negro Migration.* New York: AMS Press, 1970; orig. pub. 1918.

Woodward, C. Vann. *Origins of the New South, 1877–1913.* Baton Rouge: Louisiana State University Press, 1951.

Wright, Gavin. *Old South, New South: Revolutions in the Southern Economy Since the Civil War.* New York: Basic Books, 1986.

———. *The Political Economy of the Cotton South: Households, Markets, and Wealth in the Nineteenth Century.* New York: Norton, 1978.

ARTICLES AND PAMPHLETS

American Association of Retired Persons. "After the Harvest: The Plight of Older Farmworkers." c. 1989.

Armstrong, Thomas F. "Georgia Lumber Workers, 1880–1917: The Social Implications of Work." *Georgia Historical Quarterly* 67 (Winter 1983): 436–50.

"Appalachia on Cleveland's East Side." *Appalachia: A Journal of the Appalachian Regional Commission* (July–August 1972): 52.

Bailey, Kenneth R. "A Judicious Mixture: Negroes and Immigrants in the West Virginia Mines, 1880–1917." *West Virginia History* 34 (January 1973): 141–61.

Bardhan, Prana K. "Labor-Tying in a Poor Agrarian Economy: A Theoretical and Empirical Analysis." *Quarterly Journal of Economics* 98 (August 1983): 501–14.

Biles, Roger. "The Urban South in the Great Depression." *Journal of Southern History* 56 (February 1990): 71–100.

Billings, Dwight, et al. "Culture, Family, and Community in Preindustrial Appalachia." *Appalachian Journal* 13 (Winter 1986): 154–70.

Bynum, Victoria. "On the Lowest Rung: Court Control Over Poor White and Free Black Women." *Southern Exposure* 12 (November–December 1984): 40–44.

Carlton, David L. "The Revolution from Above: The National Market and the Beginnings of Industrialization in North Carolina." *Journal of American History* 77 (September 1990): 445–75.

SELECTED BIBLIOGRAPHY

Cimbala, Paul. "The Freedmen's Bureau, the Freedmen, and Sherman's Grant in Reconstruction Georgia, 1865–1867." *Journal of Southern History* 55 (November 1989): 597–632.

Clark, Thomas D. "The Impact of the Timber Industry on the South." *Mississippi Quarterly* 25 (1972): 141–64.

———. "Kentucky Logmen." *Journal of Forest History* 25 (July 1981): 144–58.

Cobb, James C. "Beyond Planters and Industrialists: A New Perspective on the New South." *Journal of Southern History* 54 (February 1988): 45–68.

Cox, LaWanda Fenlason. "Tenancy in the United States, 1865–1900: A Consideration of the Validity of the Agricultural Ladder Hypothesis." *Agricultural History* 18 (July 1944): 97–105.

Daniel, Pete. "The Metamorphosis of Slavery, 1865–1900." *Journal of American History* 66 (June 1979): 88–99.

Engerman, Stanley. "Contract Labor, Sugar, and Technology in the Nineteenth Century." *Journal of Economic History* 43 (September 1983): 635–60.

Ferleger, Louis. "Farm Mechanization in the Southern Sugar Sector After the Civil War." *Louisiana History* 23 (Winter 1982): 21–34.

Fickle, James E. "Management Looks at the 'Labor Problem': The Southern Pine Industry During World War I and the Postwar Era." *Journal of Southern History* 40 (February 1974): 61–76.

Fields, Barbara Jeanne. "The Nineteenth-Century American South: History and Theory." *Plantation Society in the Americas* 2 (April 1983): 7–28.

———. "Slavery, Race, and Ideology in the United States of America." *New Left Review* 181 (May/June 1990): 95–118.

Fishback, Price. "Segregation in Job Hierarchies: West Virginia Coal Mining, 1906–1932." *Journal of Economic History* 44 (September 1984): 755–74.

Fitzgerald, Michael W. "Radical Republicanism and the White Yeomanry During Alabama Reconstruction, 1865–1868." *Journal of Southern History* 54 (November 1988): 565–96.

Geschwender, James A., and Rita Carroll-Seguin. "Exploding the Myth of African-American Progress." *Signs* 15 (Winter 1990): 285–99.

Hahn, Steven. "Hunting, Fishing, and Foraging: Common Rights and Class Relations in the Postbellum South." *Radical History Review* 26 (October 1982): 37–64.

Hine, Darlene Clark. "Rape and the Inner Lives of Black Women in the Middle West: Preliminary Thoughts on the Culture of Dissemblance." *Signs* 14 (Summer 1989): 912–20.

Holmes, William F. "Labor Agents and the Georgia Exodus, 1899–1900." *South Atlantic Quarterly* 79 (Autumn 1980): 436–48.

Inscoe, John C. "Mountain Masters: Slaveholding in Western North Carolina." *North Carolina Historical Review* 61 (April 1984): 143–73.

Irwin, Marjorie Felice. "The Negro in Charlottesville and Albermarle County." University of Virginia, Phelps-Stokes Fellowship Paper, 1929.

Kirby, Jack Temple. "Black and White in the Rural South." *Agricultural History* 58 (July 1984): 411–22.

Lewis, Ronald L. "From Peasant to Proletarian: The Migration of Southern Blacks to the Central Appalachian Coalfields." *Journal of Southern History* 55 (February 1989): 77–102.

McDonald, Forrest, and Grady McWhiney. "The South From Self-Sufficiency to Peonage: An Interpretation." *American Historical Review* 85 (December 1980): 1095–118.

McKee, Dan M., and Phillip J. Obermiller. "From Mountain to Metropolis: Urban Appalachians in Ohio." Cincinnati: Ohio Urban Appalachian Awareness Project, 1978.

McKelvey, Blake. "A Half Century of Southern Penal Exploitation." *Journal of Social Forces* 13 (October 1934): 112–23.

Malone, Ann Patton. "Piney Woods Farmers of South Georgia, 1850–1900: Jeffersonian Yeomen in an Age of Expanding Commercialism." *Agricultural History* 60 (Fall 1986): 51–84.

Mancini, Matthew J. "Race, Economics, and the Abandonment of Convict Leasing." *Journal of Negro History* 63 (Fall 1978): 339–52.

Marable, Manning. "The Politics of Black Land Tenure, 1877–1915." *Agricultural History* 53 (January 1979): 142–52.

Menius, Arthur C. "James Bennitt: Portrait of an Antebellum Yeoman." *North Carolina Historical Review* 58 (October 1981): 305–26.

Nieman, Donald G. "Black Political Power and Criminal Justice: Washington County, Texas, 1868–1884." *Journal of Southern History* 55 (August 1989): 391–420.

Ownby, Ted. "The Defeated Generation at Work: White Farmers in the Deep South, 1865–1890." *Southern Studies* 13 (Winter 1984): 325–47.

Photiadis, John D. "West Virginians in Their Own State and in Cleveland, Ohio." Appalachian Center Information Report 3, West Virginia University, 1970.

Pritchett, Jonathan B. "The Term of Occupancy of Southern Farmers in the First Decades of the Twentieth Century." *Historical Methods* 20 (Summer 1987): 107–12.

Scarpaci, J. Vincenza. "Labor for Louisiana's Sugar Cane Fields: An Experiment in Immigrant Recruitment." *Italian Americana* 7 (Fall/Winter 1981): 19–41.

Shick, Tom W., and Don H. Doyle. "The South Carolina Phosphate Boom and the Stillbirth of the New South, 1867–1920." *South Carolina Historical Magazine* 86 (January 1985): 1–31.

Shlomowitz, Ralph. "'Bound' or 'Free'? Black Labor in Cotton and Sugarcane Farming, 1865–1880." *Journal of Southern History* 50 (November 1984): 569–96.

Shofner, Jerrell H. "Florida and the Black Migration." *Florida Historical Quarterly* 57 (January 1979): 267–88.

———. "Forced Labor in the Florida Forests, 1880–1950." *Journal of Forest History* 25 (January 1981): 14–25.

———. "Mary Grace Quackenbos, A Visitor Florida Did Not Want." *Florida Historical Quarterly* 58 (January 1980): 273–90.

———. "Postscript to the Martin Tabert Case: Peonage as Usual in the Florida Turpentine Camps." *Florida Historical Quarterly* 60 (October 1981): 161–73.

Spier, William. "A Social History of Manganese Mining in the Batesville District of Independence County." *Arkansas Historical Quarterly* 36 (Summer 1977): 130–57.

———. "We Was All Poor Then: The Subeconomy of a Farming Community, 1900–1925." *Southern Exposure* 2 (Fall 1974): 80–90.

Stern, Joseph S., Jr. "Findlay Market and Over-the-Rhine Revisited." *Cincinnati Historical Society Bulletin* 34 (Spring 1976): 25–44.

Walker, Juliet E. K. "The Legal Status of Free Blacks in Early Kentucky." *Filson Club Historical Quarterly* (October 1983): 382–95.

Weiman, David. "The Economic Emancipation of the Non-Slaveholding Class: Upcountry Farmers in the Georgia Cotton Economy." *Journal of Economic History* 45 (March 1985): 71–94.

Wennersten, John R. "The Almighty Oyster: A Saga of Old Somerset and the Eastern Shore, 1850–1920." *Maryland Historical Magazine* 74 (March 1978): 80–93.

Whatley, Warren C. "Southern Agrarian Labor Contracts as Impediments to Cotton Mechanization." *Journal of Economic History* 47 (March 1987): 45–70.

Winters, Donald L. "Plain Folk of the Old South Reexamined: Economic Democracy in Tennessee." *Journal of Southern History* 53 (November 1987): 565–86.

Woodman, Harold D. "Postbellum Social Change and Its Effects on Marketing the South's Cotton Crop." *Agricultural History* 56 (January 1982): 215–30.

———. "Post–Civil War Southern Agriculture and the Law." *Agricultural History* 53 (January 1979): 319–37.

Wright, Gavin. "American Agriculture and the Labor Market: What Happened to Proletarianization?" *Agricultural History* 62 (Summer 1988): 182–209.

Unpublished Dissertations, Working Papers, and Typescripts

Akers, Elmer. "Southern Whites in Detroit." C. 1940. Typescript.

Blount, Colette. "Oral History Interview with Ollie Smith." January 1988. Typescript in author's possession.

Cherry, Frank T. "Southern In-Migrant Negroes in North Lawndale, Chicago, 1949–50: A Study of Internal Migration and Adjustment." Ph.D. diss., University of Chicago, 1965.

Choldin, Harvey M. "First Year in the Metropolis: A Study of Migration and Adjustment." Ph.D. diss., University of Chicago, 1965.

Coalson, George Otis. "The Development of the Migratory Farm Labor System in Texas: 1900–1954." Ph.D. diss., University of Oklahoma, 1955.

Cox, LaWanda Fenlason. "Agricultural Labor in the United States, 1865–1900, With Special Reference to the South." Ph.D. diss., University of California, Berkeley, 1942.

Crowe, Martin J. "The Occupational Adaptation of a Selected Group of Eastern Kentuckians in Southern Ohio." Ph.D. diss., University of Kentucky, 1964.

Darling, Marsha Jean. "The Growth and Decline of the Afro-American Family Farm in Warren County, North Carolina, 1910–1960." Ph.D. diss., Duke University, 1982.

Fanning, John William. "Negro Migration." M.S. thesis, University of Georgia, 1928.

Foust, James D. "The Yeoman Farmer and Westward Expansion of U.S. Cotton Production." Ph.D. diss., University of North Carolina, Chapel Hill, 1968.

Gilmour, Robert A. "The Other Emancipation: Studies in the Society and Economy of Alabama Whites During Reconstruction." Ph.D. diss., Johns Hopkins University, 1972.

Grubbs, Donald Hughes. "A History of the Atlantic Coast Stream of Agricultural Migrants." M.A. thesis, University of Florida, 1959.

Harwood, Edwin S. "Work and Community Among Urban Newcomers: A Study of the Social and Economic Adaptation of Southern Migrants to Chicago." Ph.D. diss., University of Chicago, 1966.

Heppel, Monica Lucille. "Harvesting the Crops of Others: Migrant Farm Labor on the Eastern Shore of Virginia." Ph.D. diss., American University, 1982.

Hutchens, Raymond Paul. "Kentuckians in Hamilton: A Study of Southborn Migrants in an Industrial City." M.A. thesis, Miami University, 1942.

Jones, Adrienne Lash. "Jane Edna Hunter: A Case Study of Black Leadership, 1910–1950." Ph.D. diss., Case Western Reserve University, 1982.

Killian, Lewis M. "Southern White Laborers in Chicago's West Side." Ph.D. diss., University of Chicago, 1949.

McAlister, Melani. "Making Do: An Oral History with Daughters of a Share-Tenant Family in the Arkansas Hill Country [Katie Slater McAlister and Dorothy Slater Hawkins]." May 1990. Typescript in author's possession.

Mincy, Ronald. "Is There a White Underclass?" Washington D.C.: Urban Institute Discussion Paper, 1988.

Scarborough, Donald Dewey. "An Economic Study of Negro Farmers as Owners, Tenants, and Croppers." M.A. thesis, University of Georgia, 1923.

Smith, Preston H. II. "The Limitations of Racial Democracy: The Politics of the Chicago Urban League." Ph.D. diss., University of Massachusetts, 1989.

Thompson, John Leslie. "Industrialization in the Miami Valley: A Case Study of Interregional Labor Migration." Ph.D. diss., University of Wisconsin, 1955.

Weeks, Jerry Woods. "Florida Gold: The Emergence of the Florida Citrus Industry, 1865–1895." Ph.D. diss., University of North Carolina, 1977.

Index

Adams, Louisa, 24
Affirmative Action, 6
African-Americans, 292; culture of,
197–198, 240; labor mobility and,
postbellum, 15–16; as migrant work-
ers, 167–170, 173–181, 189–200;
prejudice toward, 5–8, 15–16, 86–87,
257; stereotypes regarding, 2; *See
also* Black field workers; Civil War;
East Coast migrant workers;
Freedmen; Ghettos; Industry, rural
nonagricultural; Midwest migration;
Plantation system; Sharecropping
system; Slavery
Agricultural Adjustment Act of 1933,
172
Agricultural Adjustment
Administration (AAA), 217, 222
AIDS epidemic, 8, 169, 275
Aid to Families with Dependent
Children (AFDC), 8, 188, 189, 258,
269, 272, 273, 278, 286, 287
Alabama: current poverty in, 286;
debt peonage in, 107; freedmen in,
25, 26, 32–34, 40–43, 206–207;
migrant workers in, 190, 206–207;
nonagricultural chain gangs in,
150; nonagricultural workers in,
92, 93, 133, 142–144, 150, 165;
out-migration from, 209, 212, 213;
public assistance in Great
Depression, 223; shifting of field
workers in, 117; slum dwellers of
Great Depression, 220; small farm-
owners in, 96, 98–99; vagrancy laws
in, 25; white field workers in,
50–51, 54–56, 58, 59, 61, 66, 67;
World War II defense industry in,
177–178, 225, 226
Alcoholism, 287
Alford, Barney, 118
Allen, Ruth, 174